ANCIENT NATURAL HISTORY

In this fascinating study, Roger French shows how ancient natural history was the gathering and presentation of *historiae*, items worthy of note by the philosopher, populariser or marvel-monger. This book examines the relationship between the physical world, the gods, Greek philosophy and the purposes of those who expressed such different notions about 'nature'. Roger French pays particular attention to Aristotle's animals, Theophrastus' plants and Strabo's geography. Pliny's *Natural History* is also examined in some detail. One of the major themes of the book is how natural history was treated differently by different societies; the Greeks, Romans, Jews and Christians.

The resulting picture is one of surprising diversity of belief and practice. Rather than a continuity of 'ideas', we see each new generation and each different group using extant writings simply as a resource for their own interpretative constructions. The same natural-historical material could serve the purposes of the Greek philosopher looking at nature as well as the purposes of the Christian allegorist. Roger French argues convincingly that none of these purposes were *scientific*; ancient natural history had much more to do with Macedonian and Roman military expansion than with early science'.

Roger French is Director of the Wellcome Unit for the History of Medicine, University of Cambridge. He has written widely on subjects in the history of science.

SCIENCES OF ANTIQUITY
Series Editor: Roger French
Director, Wellcome Unit for the History of Medicine,
University of Cambridge

Sciences of Antiquity is a series designed to cover the subject matter of what we call science. The volumes discuss how the ancients saw, interpreted and handled the natural world, from the elements to the most complex of living things. Their discussions on these matters formed a resource for those who later worked on the same topics, including scientists. The intention of this series is to show what it was in the aims, expectations, problems and circumstances of the ancient writers that formed the nature of what they wrote. A consequent purpose is to provide historians with an understanding of the materials out of which later writers, rather than passively receiving and transmitting ancient 'ideas', constructed their own world view.

ANCIENT ASTROLOGY
Tamsyn Barton

ANCIENT NATURAL HISTORY
Histories of nature
Roger French

ANCIENT NATURAL HISTORY

HISTORY

Histories of nature

Roger French

London and New York

First published 1994
by Routledge
11 New Fetter Lane, London EC4P 4EE

Simultaneously published in the USA and Canada
by Routledge
29 West 35th Street, New York, NY 10001

© 1994 Roger French

Typeset in Garamond by
Ponting–Green Publishing Services,
Chesham, Buckinghamshire
Printed and bound in Great Britain by
Biddles Ltd, Guildford and King's Lynn

British Library Cataloguing in Publication Data
A catalogue record for this book is available from
the British Library

Library of Congress Cataloging in Publication Data
French, R.K. (Roger Kenneth)
Ancient natural history: histories of nature/Roger French.
p. cm. – (Sciences of antiquity series)
Includes bibliographical references (p.) and index.
1. Natural history–History. 2. Science, Ancient.
I. Title. II. Series.
QH15.F74 1994
508'.09'01–dc20 94–5131

ISBN 0–415–08880–1 (hbk)
0–415–11545–0 (pbk)

CONTENTS

PLATES

vii

GENERAL SERIES INTRODUCTION

PURPOSE OF THE SERIES

The purpose of this series of volumes is to provide the reader who is not necessarily a classical scholar with a broad view of some areas of ancient interest to which the term 'science' has customarily been attached. Many readers with an interest in history are well aware of the importance of perceptions of Greek philosophy in the later cultural and intellectual history of the West, but will not have to hand an authoritative guide to the various philosophies of the Greeks and Romans. The ancient material used by philosophers and others in later periods is here described in its ancient context. But the needs of the modern reader, who may want information on one particular area of the sciences, has been kept in mind.

These two purposes, to give ancient 'science' in its context and to direct the reader's attention to fields of study that he recognises, coincides with a fresh look at ancient 'science'. First, as a practical matter, in a wide survey such as this it is clearly undesirable to proceed by means of modern categories such as 'physiology' or 'physics' when such terms meant something very different in the past. It is more appropriate to use subject areas that were recognised in antiquity, in order that some account can be given of them that reflects both ancient – rather than modern – categorisation and their cultural context.

Second, seeking 'the sciences' means going further afield than the liberal arts of classical and medieval education. Medicine, for example, (to mention briefly the subjects covered by the series) was a vocational rather than liberal discipline, as clearly defined in the ancient world as now, for there have always been people who have tried to cure disease and maintain health. Mathematics also in a sense defines its own subject areas (arithmetic and geometry) in a way that largely coincides in the modern and ancient periods (and which also partly coincided with the quadrivium).[1] Natural history too is a category recognisable equally to Romans, at least, as to moderns. Astronomy without its constant companion astrology is perhaps a modern category rather than ancient and its *separate* history is partly a construction of scientific historians.[2] Astrology is as recognisable as medicine, with a body of practitioners, clients and a technical subject matter, practised in a society of which the economic, intellectual, religious and political aspects all had a historical role to play. Natural philosophy in the sense of speculation about the ultimate principles and constituents of the natural world is, from evidence from the pre-Socratics and Aristotle, also an ancient category that is recognisable today. The series also looks at the practical way in which the Greeks handled the physical, natural world, which the theory of their sciences speculated about.

SCIENCE IN ANTIQUITY?

Third, in seeking the sciences in antiquity we have to think carefully about what we mean by 'science'. Can we find science in the ancient world? Why is the title of this series *Sciences of Antiquity* and not the more straightforward *Science in the Ancient World*? For many years seeing science in the ancient world was unproblematic. It went hand in hand with seeing science as 'exploration of nature' or something similar. But it is no longer enough to think that science is adequately characterised in this way nor that it is a simple unveiling of the truth of nature. Science is a human enterprise and so also a human construction. As historians we must consider what kind of undertaking science is and how far back we can take the term 'science' without losing its essential meaning and therefore seriously distorting the historical picture.[3]

'Science' is an old word in English and is derived from the Latin *scientia*, which, like the Greek *philosophia*, meant knowledge in general. In English for many centuries 'a science' could mean anything taught in the schools and the collective term 'sciences' of the present title of the series still retains an older and more general usage than our present meaning of 'science'; and this is why it has been used. It is only in this sense that science existed before scientists. The word 'scientist' came (from mixed parentage) into English not long before the middle of the nineteenth century, when the word 'science' began to take on a modern meaning. That is, when the science of natural philosophy came to predominate and to capture the name 'science', a new name was needed for the people who practised it.[4] Usage is everything: 'science' has now connotations of purpose and methods that are quite out of place when describing the entirely different enterprises of the ancient world. But so familiar are we with the apparently timeless validity of scientific truths that we give them in their timelessness, a past, a history for them to unfold themselves in. If we believe in the timelessness of their truths then it is tempting to make the timelessness and the truths the yardsticks against which is measured man's success in recognising them in the past. But man in the ancient world was doing something else, and did not have a duty to recognise our truths. What he *was* doing was some kind of philosophy, most often natural philosophy.

MODERN SCIENCE

If we are to agree or disagree about the existence of science in the distant past, we must first agree on what science is. A brief, ordinary characterisation of science would surely include most of the following: (i) It is objective. The scientist puts his passions aside and relies on reason. (ii) It is non-religious. No longer does an instinct veneration for a creator structure the search into nature. In being objective, passionless, creatorless, it alone produces tangible truth, which in modern society is given privileged status (and which science often consciously opposes to faith). (iii) It is experimental in its verification of its theories. (iv) Science and the research that continues to build it are in practice directed to the practical business of manipulating nature. Its self-confidence is increased by every successful manipulation of nature: it appears to be self-proving. (v) Its manipulative nature has strong links to technology. (vi) It has universal law-like statements, often mathematical and with Boyle's law as a paradigm.[5]

Little of this can be found in the ancient world. No one in antiquity strove through philosophy to manipulate nature except perhaps the Magi and the doctors (and it is very questionable whether they were using philosophy). Control of the human mind (achieving *ataraxia*, freedom from fear) was a much more common goal; and *ataraxia* was a subjective state, quite different from the objective goals of science. Nor does science seek to enforce a moral or religious code of behaviour in its practitioners, as much ancient philosophy did. Mathematics was an available resource when science was constructed, but its earlier connection with the natural world was at the metaphysical and religious level if at all. Natural philosophy had understanding nature as one of its goals, but since this aim did not include manipulation, it did not use technology. Often natural philosophy denied the power of the gods to intervene in human affairs, but that did not prevent philosophy being a manifestly religious affair. It was not experimental.

Even less satisfactory have been attempts to show that the 'science' of the Greeks *failed* to have certain features of modern science, and so was limited in its nature and progress.[6] Failure implies some shortfall in an enterprise with a known goal: what could such an enterprise have been in the ancient world? It is clear that ancient philosophers did not always expect their subject to progress and certain that none of them were aiming at modern science. Others have extended the argument and asserted that some activties of the Greeks were scientific in a limited way, and that for example doctors and root-cutters were gaining scientific knowledge of plants, while others were working on geometry or explaining how thunderstorms happen. Quite apart from the question of why these people were doing these things it surely is the case that the broad principles of science apply to all of its parts – this is the reason for calling anything 'scientific' – and that it is not a collection of localised explanations. That science is a unitary thing is recognised by all of its practitioners whatever their own branch of it may be. Certainly what the Greeks thought about plants, geometry and thunderstorms may have prompted later people to think about them too, or even to adopt Greek explanations; but even when such a process extended down to the age of science it does not mean that the Greeks were practising science. At most they were writing what came to be used as resources for people who did come to practise science. Perhaps you want to build a garage. It has to be a certain shape in order to house your car, which is its function, and the thing that identifies it as a garage. You may take the bricks from a derelict Victorian stable, which was another shape for a related reason. But your use of the bricks does not make the stable an early garage, in an age without cars.

Fragments of world-views (like bricks) may certainly look scientific when presented in isolation. Fragments presented collectively, as in source-books of ancient or medieval 'science' and put (silently) into modern categories, take on an authority which none of the fragments had in its own context.[7] More persuasive are examples of 'the scientific attitude' which are often used to show how the ancients, although getting the details wrong, were investigating nature in the right spirit. So much has been said about myth, magic, superstition and rationality,[8] objectivity and science, largely by scientific historians, that the terms are largely debased currency.[9]

Some historians have recently recognised that to see science in antiquity we have to have a definition of science so broad as to be meaningless.[10] Whether it is Aristotle's 'all men by nature desire to know' (he said it in the *Metaphysics* and by any account it is a broad definition) or a 'systematic knowledge of nature'[11] we are left with something so vague that it can scarcely have a history.[12] Why, after all, should we use a modern term to denote ancient usage, when the categories and terms of the past are better?

HISTORY AND PHILOSOPHY

The people whom scientific historians see as practising science in the more or less distant past often said, sometimes volubly, what they were doing. They called it philosophy and strove rather to stress the unity of knowledge than the separateness of its parts. Part of it was concerned with the natural world, but this part was not marked off from the others by any strict boundaries.[13] Philosophy too has its historians, and it is not difficult to gain from the historical literature the notion that philosophy is and was a free and intellectual enquiry into fundamentals.[14] The historian in contrast sees that ancient philosophers could be as interested in factual minutiae as much as fundamentals. They were often practical people, using their philosophy to bring about a certain state of mind and way of life (which are not goals of modern philosophy). Sometimes they are more visible as capitalists and engineers.[15] They also advised governments and often got into trouble. As educators they had to be careful what they taught if they wished to retain their schools or their lives: intellectual, certainly, but not always free.

BUILDING HISTORIES

(i) Whigs and genes

So if there was no such thing as science in the ancient world, why have people thought that there was? To answer this we shall need to look first at the historiographical tradition that made 'ancient science' a natural explanandum. Then we must offer an alternative.

If we pause for a moment and look at the history of history-of-science we see that it has two characteristics that help to solve the problem. First, history of science is often tied to philosophy of science, a circumstance that reflects the beliefs of the founders of the subject – that is, that science, being so important and successful, must have some special method. Second, it attracted the attention of specialists in various departments of science, who seemed by their speciality to be well equipped. Like the philosophers, whom we have just mentioned, the scientist-as-historian who looks at the past of his subject naturally sees it as developing to the maturity that represented it in his own time. This is close to the practice of the Whig historians who notoriously saw old political constitutions as stages in the development of the Whig constitution rather than answers to old political problems. The time has gone when it would be appropriate to criticise Whig history, but what we find in current treatments of histories of ancient 'science' is what we might call genetic history. In this, ideas or other contributions are represented as passing down through the ages like genes or seeds, becoming fertile or dying according to the ground on which they fell and on their innate viability. Here the identity resides within the gene, which may perhaps – in genetic history – be seen as genuinely scientific or having been recognised in a scientific spirit. But ideas are not genetic, do not happen on their own without some world-system, nor outside people. The historical dynamism is not with the transmission of ideas but with the efforts of successions of people trying make sense and order of their world. They may in doing this make use of what was thrown up by previous attempts, if such things are available, intelligible, interesting and relevant, but the continuity of 'ideas' so often seen by historians is the generation of notions afresh by every active mind that reads or sees paper or papyrus from the past and interprets and reconstructs according to his own problems, aims and methods.

The apparent naturalness of genetic history is summed up in an aphorism of Pascal, which expresses clearly how the West developed (and at a critical time) a tradition of looking at history which sought out and emphasised continuities: 'The entire succession of men through the whole course of ages must be regarded as one man, always living and incessantly learning.'[16] Quite so; Pascal's 'one man' kept an accumulating bank balance of ideas within his head, never died in one culture or was born in another, never suffered passion or fashion except Pascal's brand of intellectualism and represents a construct, mankind, taking actions that only the physical man can do.

(ii) Legitimation

One reason for writing a history of a subject has generally been to give legitimation to a new discipline. Phrenologists in the nineteenth century went back to Plato as confidently as psychologists in the twentieth to show that though the subject was new, yet its principles were known, unnamed, to the greatest of the ancients. If like the Frenchman Riolan in the seventeenth century, you thought you had worked out how the blood moved in the body, it strengthened your case by showing that Hippocrates had known it, but had not built it up into a system. When the great Dutch teacher Boerhaave had become convinced of Newtonian mechanism, he wanted to show that Hippocrates too had been a mechanist. We would not in these cases allow that there was any real history of phrenology, psychology or mechanism.

History can be used to legitimate one's own activity also in the converse way. Aristotle often set out to strengthen his own arguments by destroying those of people he chose to regard as his predecessors. He represented them as engaged in the same task as himself, whereby it became easier to show how they had failed and he had won. For example, there is almost no evidence save for that from Aristotle that Thales ever indulged in natural philosophy. He was well known for giving political advice and for his practical inventions, but it is Aristotle who put him at the origin of the 'history of science', which he did for his own purposes.[17] Much the same can be said of Anaximander and Anaximenes. The same kind of historical construction was made by the Alexandrian scholars who compiled an 'Ionian succession' of philosophers.[18] The Christians naturally showed that the arguments of the old philosophers, where not frankly wrong, were at least incomplete gropings towards the religious truth. With the aid of a higher order of knowing, revealed knowledge, they could both stand above the pagan philosophers and draw support from them, when viewed 'historically'.

Part of the power of history to legitimate a discipline[19] is derived from its frequent use in teaching the discipline. Law students are taught Roman Law and chemistry students Avagadro's hypothesis. The material chosen is selected for its ability to illustrate how the modern truths of the subject emerged at the pioneering hands of the subject's heroes and the result is at once a genetic 'history of ideas' and a Whig evolutionary history. So history of science has been pedagogic and legitimating. All are self-serving and the historian of history-of-science sees too many parallels in the past to accept such devices at face value. He sees that the professional job of the historian of science is to find science in the past, who often measures his success by how much he finds.

Because we see most clearly in the past what is of most interest to us as moderns, we are being selective. There is a strong sense in which we are *constructing* history in our own image; and doing so moreover partly from fragments of similar constructions of our predecessors. This of course appears to confirm our interpretation, in that some scholar in the past thought so too; and the scholar becomes more famous for agreeing with us.

INTELLECTUAL PATERNITIES

It is in this way that Western Europe *chose* its intellectual ancestry. Part and parcel of this is that far from natural philosophy and science being an effect of a classical cause, or a growth or a rebirth from a classical seed, or some more general self-executive bequest of the Greeks, it was the other way round. Just as Aristotle had chosen *his* opponents and thus made them into his ancestors, the men of the Middle Ages and then the Renaissance sought out and so reconstituted ancient philosophy. They did so for their own purposes and so were selective. The early church *chose* Plato when it needed intellectualism to defend itself and attack opponents. It chose Aristotle in the early thirteenth century for similar reasons.

The men of the Renaissance too chose to see their intellectual parentage in ancient Greece. Before – say – the Council of Florence the language of Greece was not widely known in the West. Greece was distant geographically and culturally. Indeed the Latins were traditionally hostile to the Greeks, having defeated them with a diverted crusade in the early thirteenth century and having set up a brief Latin Empire over Byzantium. The Greeks thought of the Latins as barbarians, and became even more Greek in reaction. After the collapse of Constantinople Greece ceased to exist. Greek refugees from the Turks brought with them new and exciting philosophies and political ambitions. From then on the desire to restore, recreate and relive the classical Greek cultural experience expanded hugely.

Similar forces have played a part in much more recent history, that is, in history of science. During and immediately after the Second World War historians of science like Schrödinger[20] and of medicine like Temkin[21] looked with fresh need at the ancient Greeks. They wanted to see some continuity between themselves and the Greeks. The ancientness of European thought, conceived in this way, offered some form of stability at a time of change as great as that of the collapse of Constantinople. That science (and technology) was a dominant force in people's lives had been demonstrated in a most potent way in the development and use of nuclear weapons. There was also, then, a new urgency to explain and understand science, which included its history. It seemed natural that scientists were best qualified to do this.[22] Two heroic claims illustrate the new perception of 'Greek science': 'Nearly our entire intellectual education originates from the Greeks',[23] and 'It is an adequate description of science to say that it is "thinking about the world in a Greek way". That is why science has never existed except among peoples who came under the influence of Greece.'[24]

But what can 'influence' be here? In ordinary language of course we know what such a phrase as 'coming under the influence of' means. But when 'influence' is used as an historical explanation it is generally misleading. It implies a power stretching over the ages, energised by some innate quality, perhaps intellectual virtuosity, truth or beauty. Or perhaps what is meant is that influence is influential because of transmitted ideas. The same arguments can be used against influence, as a sort of active miasma into which people wander, as against ballistic ideas. Influence starts with the person who is influenced. He sees it in what he reads or is taught if a number of other conditions are appropriate. The reader's circumstances may make him admire and find consolation in what he reads, like those of Schrödinger or Boethius, or not, like those of Gregory IX or the Caliph Omar (who respectively bowdlerised Aristotle and ordered the burning of the library in Alexandria). It is with the notion of 'influence' that much history of ancient 'science' was written, while the classical scholars looked the other way.[25]

SELECTIVE SURVIVAL OF TEXTS

In considering how people have looked at history and have constructed it in various ways, an important fact is that the bulk of our historiographical tradition was formed in the Christian centuries, and practised upon material taken from Islamic hands. This has had two effects. First, whether actively or passively, both religions filtered out texts that could not be accommodated to the prevailing religious system. Second, both systems needed self-justifying histories in which everything had to have a place in a scheme of things that led to an ultimate enlightenment. The church needed philosophy only to defend itself from or win over people to whom philosophy was important. The church legitimated its use of philosophy by giving it a history, accepting it as limited knowledge that had pointed in the right direction and which had given some understanding to people who had lived before Christ.[26] Monotheism seemed to be a stage of development preparatory to the Christian revelation. In short a history was constructed which emphasised continuity and development towards a final enlightenment. The texts that survived naturally seemed to reinforce this.

Nor should we allow this manipulation of history by the church to lead us into the trap of imagining a history of antagonism between religion and 'science'. Natural philosophy had religious purposes for most of its history, in the absence of science. Only when science *did* find itself in opposition to the doctrine of Creation after Darwin was there a conflict. Defenders of science began to strengthen their case by showing that the conflict *had a history*. Suddenly parts of the past were luminous with a new significance and the mantle of the scientist, at odds with religion, passed backwards to Galileo, Vesalius and beyond.[27]

RESOURCES FOR HISTORY

It may seem perverse to introduce a series of books on ancient topics partly by means of a history of more recent ways of looking at the past. But it does help us to decide what history means for a topic so difficult to define as science. It also contributes to the purpose of this series, in that readers with knowledge of later periods may be invited to think about the nature of Greek 'science' in those periods. Rather than of transmission, influence and so on, we can tell a story of how ancient writings came to be used as *resources* by later writers. Aristotle's descriptions of eternal and godless species of animals were a resource, a mine of information that could be quarried by the Arabs in arguing that God was distant from the world and by the Christians up to the nineteenth century in arguing that on the contrary God was very close to the world.

The history of resources is also consistent with the other purpose of the series. The contributors each examine their subject areas as ancient practices undertaken for ancient reasons: like later generations the ancients used what resources they knew about and could understand, if those resources were relevant and interesting. Necessarily they selected, out of context, the fragments of the resource that had these qualities, and put them to different uses in another context, that of their own philosophy, religion, politics and so on. It is in this way that the sciences of antiquity reflect the society out of which they grew.

This emphasis on the reinterpretation by each generation – indeed by each person – of the resources of the past should not obscure the fact that some of our subject areas were the concern of groups of people who had much in common. Indeed, it was argued above that the subject areas of this series were recognisable in the ancient world, which means that each was practised by more than a single man. The doctors could see medicine as a discipline that would grow on the basis of accumulated experience, and so to an extent were consciously laying the foundations for the development of an autonomous discipline. Aristotle too recognised that natural philosophy was an exercise that might by further observations in the future resolve problems obscure to him. But they were not laying the foundations of our disciplines. Just as both Aristotle and the doctors constructed histories to legitimate their own activity and to mark it off from others, so by the same token when they looked to the future they saw an extended Aristotelian natural philosophy and a future (let us say) Asclepiad medicine. Nothing else would count as the real thing.

We might also be tempted to argue that a number of people close in time and space might have beliefs enough in common to constitute an autonomous discipline that might have a history. Institutions have their social history, of course, and it can be said more realistically of them than of ideas that they preserve their integrity over successive generations of people who constitute them. But there is a parallel historical danger of giving institutions (like ideas) a chronological momentum of their own: for an institution to survive, it must offer some advantages to its members. Moreover, simple community of belief would be largely invisible in historical terms: it is only change that gets noticed historically, and change is initiated by people.

While science is an enterprise that becomes unrecognisable when dismembered as we go back in time, so the parts of it that some people see in the past are actually parts of other enterprises, in the context of which alone they can be understood. Where we only have fragments of early figures, like the pre-Socratics, it is impossible to know what their business was. What has survived has done so precisely because someone else picked things they were interested in out of the original; so that the process of selection and survival tells us something about the selectors but not enough about the original enterprise for us to reconstruct it. As Lloyd says, the earlier pre-Socratics were 'different [from each other] in their *interests*, in the *style* and *medium* they used in communicating their ideas, and in the *attitude toward* and *role in* society'.[28] They do not form an 'Ionian succession' or a succession of any similar kind. Even when we do know something of an enterprise, it is different from anything 'scientific'. To return to Thales, the traditional father of science, he is actually better known for his politics, for diverting a river and cornering the market in olive presses.[29] It is true that he predicted an eclipse and fell down a well while watching the stars, but these are slender qualifications for a scientist. The Pythagorean concern with mathematics was a religious and ethical enterprise rather than a philosophical. Cicero's admiration of animals is a link in a chain of argument about the existence of the gods.[30] Seneca's is part of a practical procedure aimed at *ataraxia*; both were Stoic enterprises. Using 'science' in the past *creates* problems because it looks different from philosophy; in doing so it also – because of a perceived opposition between science and religion – obscures the relationship between philosophy and religion.

NOTES

1 W. H. Stahl, *Roman Science. Origins, Development and Influence to the Later Middle Ages*, Madison, Wisc., 1962, p.9.
2 It is a construction in that many historians represent the ancient writers as contributing to an ideal intellectual enquiry. For many of the ancients astronomy was simply the mathematics needed to practise astrology. There are a number of still popular textbooks on early 'physics' and astronomy that do not mention the word 'astrology'. What is implied by such an exclusion is that astronomy became scientific precisely by throwing off what was unscientific.
3 This is not to deny that much first rate-work has been done by those who do see science in the Greek world. The scholarship of Geoffrey Lloyd in particular has been of immense value and the change of emphasis that I suggest here should not be taken as an attack on it. See Lloyd's collection of essays over a span of thirty years and his present assessment: G. E. R. Lloyd, *Methods and Problems in Greek Science*, Cambridge, 1991.

4 On the identity of science see Andrew Cunningham, 'Getting the game right: some plain words on the identity and invention of science', *Studies in History and Philosophy of Science, 19*, 3 (1988), 365–389.

5 See the useful discussion by David C. Lindberg, *The Beginnings of Western Science. The European Scientific Tradition in Philosophical, Religious and Institutional Context, 600 BC to AD 1450*, Chicago, 1992, ch. 1. Lindberg gives a list similar to the one given here, where each item is an *alternative* view of science, held by different groups. This allows him to find science in the past, based on one or more of these views, although he is surely correct to see the advantages of also using the term 'natural philosophy'.

6 Historians of the 'physical' or 'exact' sciences have been particularly prone to see breath-taking advances in Greek science that were nevertheless halted by things like their aversion to experiments and ignorance of statistics.

7 Characteristically source-books omit the contexts, often including even the chronological, of their ancient extracts, and group them into modern categories: statics, dynamics, optics, acoustics, chemistry and chemical technology, biology (including natural selection), botany (including classification), physiological psychology.

8 These words in particular vary in meaning depending on who says them, and it is best to preserve a historical relativity or neutrality. 'Superstition' after all is simply someone else's religion. It meant originally the prayers of Roman parents that their child should survive them, that is, be a *superstes*. The nature or manner of their prayer attracted the derision of others, whose pejorative views have prevailed. 'Rationality' has come to mean 'discovery of truth' but is best seen as 'use of argument'.

9 The prime orientation of all these terms is one of approval or disapproval from a locus within modern society (with its science); overwhelmingly in the last generation of historians of science the tendency was to give a *moral* reading, so that disapproval was reserved for *failure* to be modern science. 'Objectivity', 'rationality' and 'science' were, like 'democracy' – a paradigm example – all in contrast *virtues*, conceived as moral but presented as objective.

10 W. H. Stahl opens his *Roman Science* refreshingly with doubts about whether his subject is either Roman or science; but nevertheless he builds up a balanced and useful picture of the Roman sources of medieval knowledge.

11 This is a phrase still to be found in frequently used works on early 'physics' and astronomy. In such contexts, 'science' is also largely mathematical, and so begins in Egypt. Where the term 'systematic' is used it is as often as not applied to stone-age cave paintings; to accept the idea we should have to accept that of stone-age scientists.

12 The most important recent enquiry into the history of science that looks at the *nature* of science is Lindberg, *Beginnings of Western Science*. Lindberg allows that 'science' has changed in form, content, method and function, which does not seem to leave much by which we can recognise it in the past or identify it as an enterprise. His principle of not looking for fragments of modern science in the past is of course sound, but his

solution, to adopt the definition of science 'as broad as that of the actors of the past' essentially begs the question. But this is a valuable book, and the reader should also consult David C. Lindberg and Robert S. Westman, *Reappraisals of the Scientific Revolution*, Cambridge, 1990, especially for the historiographical reorientation discussed in both books.

13 In most cases 'natural philosophy' is a better term to use than 'science'. Strictly, natural philosophy in the West was part of school Aristotelianism from the thirteenth century to the Enlightenment, and can be readily extended to cover the expressly dissenting views of those who reacted against it.

14 Historians of 'the exact sciences' have likewise often characterised them as being purely intellectual exercises.

15 See Lloyd, *Methods and Problems*.

16 Quoted by L. Edelstein, *The Idea of Progress in Antiquity*, Baltimore, 1967, p.91.

17 See Lloyd, 'The social background of early Greek philosophy and science', in Lloyd, *Methods and Problems*, pp.121–40; p.130.

18 A. H. Armstrong, *An Introduction to Ancient Philosophy*, London, 1968, p.116.

19 Often histories are strategies to protect reformulations. See L. Graham, W. Lepenies and P. Weingart, *Functions and Uses of Disciplinary Histories*, Dordrecht, 1983.

20 See Erwin Schrödinger, (*Nature and the Greeks*, Cambridge, 1954) who reports on the 'wave' of people, mostly scientists, who began to think in this way.

21 O. Temkin, 'An essay on the usefulness of medical history for medicine', *Bulletin of the History of Medicine*, *19* (1946), 9–47, and see Sigerist's introduction to the volume.

22 Schrödinger, himself a theoretical physicist, was a model for many. Schrödinger also wanted to avoid, by returning to perceived Greek sources, the apparent warfare of science and religion, another divisive factor in post-war Europe.

23 Theodor Gomperz, quoted by Schrödinger, *Nature and the Greeks*.

24 John Burnet, quoted by Schrödinger, *Nature and the Greeks*.

25 In his inaugural lecture as professor of ancient philosophy and science Geoffrey Lloyd notes the traditional aversion of the classical scholar to examine authors other than the great literary masters. Lloyd, *Methods and Problems*, pp.352–371; p.354.

26 The view was widely held by the Greek Fathers in particular, and has remained a Christian conception down to the present.

27 See A. D. White, *A History of the Warfare of Science with Theology in Christendom* (1896), 2 vols, Toronto and London, 1960.

28 Lloyd, 'Social background', p.133. Down to Parmenides there is no evidence that the pre-Socratics recognised themselves as belonging to any group of philosophers or enquirers into nature.

29 Lloyd, 'Social background', p.130.

30 Cicero puts the argument into the mouth of Balbus, the Roman Stoic, in the *De Natura Deorum*.

INTRODUCTION

HISTORIAE AND NATURE

Many of the general points made above are illustrated by the subject matter of the present volume. We shall be looking at the enterprises that certain figures were engaged upon. We shall see what resulted from their work and the extent to which this was a resource for those who came later. This means that some figures whose enterprises we cannot now identify will receive less attention than is traditional. We shall see many examples of how, in making constructions from available resources, authors can look to the unwary as though they are receiving transmitted ideas or knowledge. We shall also see that, in constructing knowledge rather than passively receiving it, some authors worked hard to give it a Greek, others a Roman paternity. There are examples of authors constructing histories to legitimate their views, and examples of religious and political aspects of resources militating for or against their survival. There are abundant examples of philosophers seeking to be close to the sources of political power and often suffering as a result. We shall see that in the last analysis what counted as knowledge for our authors did not depend upon its truth-value in our terms, or on its being a dimly perceived contribution to our science, but on the identity and intentionality of their own enterprise.

In looking at natural history we are concerned with nature in a particular way. We are not, that is, concerned with questions of ontology or metaphysics, nor with questions about the fundamental structure of matter, or other things which the Greeks gave thought to and which are discussed in other volumes in this series. We are concerned with how the Greeks reported things worthy of note – *historiae* – in the natural world, mostly animals and plants. We shall

1

see that there was generally a chronological component of these 'histories', and that what 'nature' meant differed in significant ways from author to author.

For the Greeks, a *historia* was an enquiry into what was remarkable.[1] It was research, and the Greeks who travelled and interviewed people about *historiae* looked down their noses at those who confined themselves to libraries. Many remarkable things of course had been done by men, and 'history' in this sense could cover civil and political history. Many actions worthy of note had also been done in strange and exotic places, and 'history' in this sense also included physical descriptions of distant and exotic things.

The historical writers made use of a particular device to convince their readers: the appearance of impartiality. They were not writing stories with morals, pieces for the theatre to provoke and amuse, political rhetoric, epic poetry or anything else with its own declared purpose. Among recognised forms of literature in Greece, history was alone in its 'generic assumption of impartiality'.[2] No doubt as a form of presentation it gained credibility as direct reporting by appearing to avoid special pleading and personal opinion. Lists of magistrates and city annals looked objective. Chorography was a means of dating external events. Closer to natural history was ethnography, accounts of foreign lands and people. Voyage reports form a group here, for example that of Scylax of Caryanda, and of Hecataeus, who wrote two books *Periodos Ges*, a 'circuit of the earth', which had utilitarian accounts of distances between ports with theoretical discussions of land masses. The rules of the genre allowed discussion of local dynasties, reports of marvels and even tales of marvels, provided they were tales actually heard.[3] Collections of *historiae* could also have the same objective appearance. True, some *historiae* were selected for their strangeness, but for example the collaborative 'history of animals' put together in the Lyceum under Aristotle was systematic and impartial. Modern science gains credibility by the same device of presentation, and this is why Aristotle's *historiae* have been called scientific.[4] It could equally be argued that science has borrowed its style of presentation from history.[5]

History also had a role to play in the formation of national identity. The Greeks based their education on Homer, and Homer has accounts of happenings in the past which helped to shape the Greeks' feeling of Greekness. This in turn helped to identify what was strange and worthy of note, and how barbaric the barbarians were. Partly what came into natural history was determined by these attitudes. In Rome Cato's *Origines* in a similar way emphasised the Romanness of things. Cato saw history as a proper occupation of a public figure in his spare time, and related it to the training of future politicians. He used history in politics as polemic and apologia. Cato wanted to show that the Italian cities had worthy histories, that the Romans and Greeks were related, that the Romans had selected the good things from Greek culture and that the newly developing literary form of Latin was equivalent to Greek, and that above all the Romans need not feel culturally inferior to the Greeks. But his own style was borrowed from the Greeks and his countrymen kept on borrowing from the Greeks.[6]

HERODOTUS AND DISTANT PLACES

There would seem no reason for anyone in the ancient world to write a natural history of their own back garden. Wonderful, *historia*-things, were distant. Acquaintanceship with distant things implies travel, generally military or commercial. This in turn implies political and economic vigour. It is no accident that the first Greeks we know of to visit the distant East – India – were actually working for the Persians, the great ancient rivals of the Greeks. Herodotus records that the first Greek to visit India was Scylax of Caryanda, used by Darius I (fifth century BC) to explore the Indus river and the coast next to Arabia (with a view to military operations).[7] Scylax was away two and a half years and reported on the one-eyed men, those with ears big enough to sleep in and those with feet big enough to act as parasols (marvels probably addressed to a Greek audience).

Ctesias of Cnidus[8] was another Greek working for the Persian royal family (in the late fifth and early fourth centuries). Here then it is the Persians who are the economic and military power, to be followed in turn by the Macedonians, Parthians and Romans. From merchants and others Ctesias compiled the *Indika*, an account of men and animals in the Indian subcontinent. Like Scylax's work, this was probably written for the entertainment of a Greek audience, and we find here the first report of improbably strange facts of natural history. Among the animals is the fierce martichore, which we shall meet again; the rivers of honey, the quantity of gold and gems, the richness of the soil, the longevity of the inhabitants and the fertility of their livestock are reports guaranteed to make an impact on the curiosity of his readers.

But to a Greek like Herodotus marvellous things also came from

Persia. He was not, as Scylax and Ctesias had been, familiar with the country, and part of his wonder was at the strange things that Persian adventures in foreign parts had brought back. But Herodotus was familiar with the ancient country of Egypt[9] which he had visited in the manner of one looking for *historiae*. In one such quest he came to a vast pile of bones, where ibises killed winged serpents flying in from Arabia.[10] There was already considerable Ionian interest in Egypt and its history, and Herodotus looks like a Greek tourist, quizzing the priests and searching out the sights. The greatest of them was the annual emergence of the land from the floods of the Nile. Greek visitors even before Herodotus[11] had wondered how and why this happened. Was it to do with the Etesian winds? With Ocean? With the melting of distant snows? Herodotus, in discussing these things in a little detail, appears to be setting an agenda for later Greek natural history, but we shall see that there were special reasons why successive generations of Greeks returned to these questions. Herodotus' queries about the unknown source of the Nile, about the crocodile and fabled phoenix were undoubtedly used by later Greeks and no doubt prompted their interest.[12]

HISTORIA AND HISTORY

While people on the fringes of the world as the Greeks knew it were seen as odd, they were also often seen as primitive in both a good and a bad sense. Often the Greeks thought of Ocean as the original source of life and so those who lived near it were of old stock, never having been civilised. But this could give them virtues lost when civilisation gave rise to moral failings. This is similar to the way in which animals were often said to be superior to men because they did not have vices. As uncivilised the primitives were stronger and were often represented as overcoming wild animals in fights.[13] Later, a number of the authors whom we consider in this volume give chronological accounts of human development, in which the historically early is conflated with the distant and bizarre, so that *historia* is both 'strange' and 'old'. Whether men were primitively born from Ocean or at first lived on the rough hilltops, the story is the same one of progress to the fertile plains and ultimately to the civilisation and then degeneracy of cities.

'Natural' history was therefore an enquiry into the natural world. Often it had a chronological component which explained how things had come to be. It was an area recognised in the ancient world as a part of philosophy. Aristotle's collection of *historiae* about animals, the *Historia Animalium*, is sometimes called a natural history,[14] and the obvious name for Pliny's vast collection of detail was the *Historia Naturalis*. Histories of nature in the ancient world polarise around Aristotle and Pliny.

This volume covers *historiae* of nature over about a thousand years. In this period we are concerned too with 'nature', about which the histories were written. Our term for nature has to represent both what the Greeks meant by *physis* and the Romans by *natura*, with which they translated the Greek. *Physis* meant 'the nature of a thing' and was applied equally to Greek drama as to animals and plants. The Greeks enjoyed speculating about the theory of these things, which did not help the Romans when they wanted to express Greek doctrines in their own cultural terms. It was a difficult matter to translate accurately into Latin, as both Lucretius and Cicero[15] found, and scholarly Romans generally learned Greek instead. But *natura* and *physis* came to have a second meaning very different from 'the nature of a thing' for they were also used to mean 'the nature of the world'. This change is linked to the changes in philosophy and religion that occurred as the Romans took political control of Greece and the Greeks took cultural control of the Romans.

1

ARISTOTLE AND THE NATURES OF THINGS

THE GREEKS AND ANIMALS

Histories of science customarily begin with Greek philosophy, and Greek philosophy conventionally starts with Thales of Miletus. The Greeks themselves counted Thales as among the seven sages at the foundation of their culture, and among the philosophers of ancient Greece there were those who deliberately tried to explain how natural events occurred: they looked at nature, *physis*, and gave natural, *physical* explanations. A *physikos* was a recognised kind of person in ancient Greece.[1]

In offering such explanations these physical philosophers of the period before Socrates are generally credited with doing away with explanations based on the actions of the gods. This has been seen as a good thing, sometimes as the origin of science itself, sometimes as the triumph of rationality over superstition and myth, and often as part of the intellectual ferment of the 'Greek miracle' of the sixth century.

To a certain extent these historical views are based on the Greeks' own traditional view of their past. It was, naturally, a very special past for them, because it was Greek. It was also naturally an intellectual past because when the Greeks began to talk about their philosophy, uppermost in their minds was the superiority of thinking over action. It was also useful for the philosophers to have a history of their subject, not only to give it the dignity of age, reaching back to the roots of Greek society, but to show how the particular form of it practised by particular philosophers was an improvement of what had gone before. We shall see later in this chapter how Aristotle profited on both counts.

But when we look closer at how the Greeks wrote about the

productions of nature – the subject matter of natural history – we see a little how the conventional history of Greek philosophy was constructed for their own purposes by the Greeks themselves. Let us begin our closer – and alternative – look with a slave, Aesop. He had a fund of entertaining and instructive stories, about animals, which are still common currency. We all know about the fox who, failing to secure a bunch of grapes from the vine, tried to convince himself that they were anyway sour. The dog in the manger who kept out the cattle when he could not eat their food himself is equally familiar. Aesop's fables became well known and he was freed by his master. He even gave political advice to the Athenians, who were contriving to rid themselves of Peisistratus in exchange for another ruler, with a fable perhaps less well known: the frogs wanted a leader and called upon Zeus to send them one. Zeus sent a block of wood. The frogs were pleased; but in due course became dissatisfied and asked for another. Zeus sent a water snake. The moral of the parable is clear: do not change what you have, for fear of something worse. Generally the moral hangs on the nature of the animal, for foxes are sly to the point of deceiving themselves, dogs can be aggressive without deriving benefit, frogs are unwise. Such a view of animals remained part of Greek culture as much as that of other nations and races. It is present in Aristotle perhaps less than any other author we shall look at, but it nevertheless remained a common attitude. We shall see that right at the end of our period it returned strongly, in a new form.

Aesop, who died in about 560 BC, was a contemporary of Thales. As a slave he was naturally not included by the Greeks among the founders of their philosophy. But his fables became part of Greek literature and in later biographies he is given the dignity of dining with the seven wise men – another example of how history is constructed for later purposes. While the natural philosophers, the people whom Aristotle called his predecessors, were marking themselves off from others as men who were seeking to find godless explanations of natural things, other Greeks pursued a philosophy-less kind of wisdom, of which the wisdom of Aesop's fables is an example.[2] Aristotle's predecessors were the men we call the pre-Socratics because in our history of Greek philosophy a great turning point came when the young Socrates turned away from the study of nature and towards that of man and his life. The work of the pre-Socratics has survived only in fragments and we cannot really identify the kind of enterprise they were engaged in. Aristotle pictures them as (in removing the gods) being entirely materialist; but that is because he is trying to put some non-material causality into natural change. Later historians have seen the fragments as seminal, providing insights into what Greek philosophy was thought to be when it was apparently at the beginnings of Western culture.

But contemporary Greeks did not always see the natural philosophers as cultural heroes. A refreshing view of them from the non-philosophy side of Greek life is that of Aristophanes. He seized the essential Aesopian message that the behaviour of animals can carry a moral for man, and that conversely men can behave like animals. *The Wasps* parodies the stinging litigiousness of the Athenians. The birds in the comedy of that name construct a city in the sky which acts as a barrier between the gods and men. The men who persuade them to do so first flatter the birds by reminding them that according to Aesop the lark was born before other creatures, indeed, even before the earth itself. (When its father died, the lark therefore had nowhere to bury him and had to entomb him in his own head.) The birds hesitate over collaboration, bearing in mind Aesop's fable of the fox and the eagle; but finally convinced, the foundations of the city are laid by thirty thousand cranes flying from Libya with stones. The birds and the frogs form the chorus respectively here and in *The Frogs*. But it is in *The Clouds* that we see the non-philosophical wisdom of the Greeks looking sideways at the natural philosophers. The object of ridicule is Socrates. It is the young Socrates, still deep into a study of nature and representing natural philosophers as a kind. He also teaches rhetoric, and it is for his reputation of being able to prove that the false is true that he is sought out by a father troubled by debt on account of his son's extravagance. The father wishes to be able to prove that he has in fact made no pledges nor borrowed any money.

He accordingly goes to see Socrates. He is reproved by the servant for making so much noise beating on Socrates' door lest he cause a miscarriage in the birth of an idea. It sometimes happens, said the servant; an idea successfully born was the realisation that gnats buzz not through their probosces but through their trumpet-shaped backsides. But a sublime idea was lost when a lizard in the roof defecated on Socrates as he gazed open-mouthed at the revolutions of the moon. Passing animals whose lowered heads were studying what went on below ground and whose elevated rumps were studying astronomy, the father finds Socrates suspended from the roof in a basket the better to mingle with the rarefied air and learn about the heavens. He is, Aristophanes makes plain, a vulgar little fellow, not too careful about his personal hygiene, and making a great show of his atheism and natural reasons. In place of Zeus are the clouds of the title: they are the Chorus, and the source of all natural-philosophical ideas. They personally produce all the meteorological events that were to be of enduring interest in the 'natural-history' part of natural philosophy throughout the ancient period: lightning, thunder, rain, the rising of the Nile, snow and frost (the clouds also supply Socrates with his easy and false arguments and they support all idle poets who mention clouds). Socrates' *physikos* allows no other divine being except the clouds and has a natural explanation for the meteorological events that frightened people who throught they were the vengeance of the gods.

> *Strepsiades* (the father): But by the Earth! is our Father, Zeus, the Olympian, not a god?
> *Socrates*: Zeus! What Zeus? Are you mad? There is no Zeus.
> *Strepsiades*: What are you saying now? Who causes the rain to fall? Answer me that!
> *Socrates*: Why, 'tis these and I will prove it. Have you ever seen it raining without clouds? Let Zeus cause rain with a clear sky and without their presence!
> *Strepsiades*: By Apollo, that is powerfully argued! For my own part I always thought it was Zeus pissing into a sieve. But tell me, who is it makes the thunder, which I so much dread?

Socrates explains that it is not Zeus but the Celestial Whirlwind that makes the clouds bump into each other, making thunder; and that it is not Zeus who hurls lightning at perjurers (for it often strikes oak trees – unlikely perjurers – and temples dedicated to Zeus himself) but a dry wind that had accumulated in the clouds and which emerges explosively.

For Aristophanes these natural explanations were simply inadequate and shallow accounts of great mysteries, as he indicates in the play by having Strepsiades likening the thunder to his own rumbling indigestion after eating too much stew at the Panathenaea, and lightning to the explosion of a sow's belly he was cooking and had forgotten to prick.[3] Strepsiades, too old to learn from the brash young Socrates, sends his son instead. He proves an apt pupil and returns to thrash his father for a wholly rational and natural reason. Strepsiades ends the play by destroying Socrates' house with an axe and fire ('What am I up to? Why, I am entering upon a subtle argument with the beams of the house.'). Of course, in getting the most from his parody Aristophanes is hardly giving us a historical narrative, but for a satire to be effective there must be enough truth for the audience to recognise the people and their actions that are being satirised. No restraint was made from the outside on the Old Comedy, and Aristophanes could be as direct and as savage as he wished to the fashions of intellectualism, naturalism and atheism.[4] The play was performed in 423 BC, nearly a quarter of a century before the death of Socrates, and perhaps indeed he was better known at the time as a natural philosopher. The direction of Aristophanes' satire seems to be well aimed given that the charges on which Socrates was tried, abandonment of the gods and the corruption of youth, were the themes of *The Clouds*.[5]

ARISTOTLE AS NATURAL HISTORIAN

The natural philosophers in turn distanced themselves from the poets and tellers of fables. Aristotle, for example, trying to reach a physical explanation of the saltiness of the sea, dismisses the claim of his predecessor, Empedocles, that the seas were the sweat of the earth. Such might be satisfactory for a poet, says Aristotle, but it is not our method.[6] In a similar way he dismissed the argument of Democritus, who thought that the seas were diminishing, being sucked down by the whirlpool Charybdis. As an explanation Aristotle thought that this was no better than the fables of Aesop,[7] whom he clearly saw as belonging to another department of Greek life.

For later ages, Aristotle was far and away the greatest philosopher of antiquity as far as the natural world was concerned. Indeed, it was he who turned philosophical attention back to the natural world after Socrates had despaired of finding physical truth. For a long period he was a pupil of Plato in the Academy and for another long period he taught in his own school in Athens, the Lyceum. He was, then, wholly immersed in the business of philosophy. But it was not philosophy in our sense, which is much more limited in its subject area than that of Aristotle. For philosophising Greeks philosophy was 'love of knowledge', whether ethical, natural or any other kind. To love knowledge included ways of finding it, as well as having the knowledge itself, and Aristotle gave a lot of attention to this.

But to understand what kind of knowledge it was and how Aristotle set about finding it, we should know a little of his purposes and circumstances. He was a teacher. He taught the sons of Athenians who had a degree of wealth and a political share in the polis. Among the subjects he taught were ethics and rhetoric, which we might suppose to have been useful to those who were to argue about the best way of running the city. But it was quite typical of his teaching that he taught nothing that was directly useful, like a trade or a craft. Such things were done and taught by people who were obliged to do so for a living and did not therefore have the leisure to embrace all knowledge, the range of philosophy. Aristotle was providing, then, what we would call a liberal education. What came to be known in the later West as the seven liberal arts had indeed its origin in the Greek world,[8] but this was not what Aristotle was teaching. Three of the liberal arts were concerned with language and argument, and four of them with quantity, being aspects of mathematics; Aristotle did not think that mathematics described the realities of things.

But although Aristotle did not teach the liberal arts, there is a similarity between these and what Aristotle did teach. Language and argument, like Aristotle's dialectic and rhetoric, were useful to the free man (for whom the 'liberal' arts were appropriate) and indeed were almost the trade or craft knowledge of the class of citizens who helped to run the state. For the rest, it was politically important that this class of citizens should not be seen to be tied down to the technical knowledge of other classes of society: theirs had to be the broadest of concerns, and part of their status must have been derived from the nature of their education and knowledge. Plato taught moral philosophy and thought that the leaders of the state should be philosophers. In other words what Aristotle taught was determined not solely by its intrinsic interest to the enquiring mind, nor only by Aristotle's philosophical acumen, but by the nature of the city-state. Education was important for the state not only for the information it provided but for the social cohesion it imparted. Greek education was learning how to be Greek. Its first concern was with the language and it was based on Homer, the national poet. Greeks were Greeks not only by language, but by their political institutions, and Greeks were taught too about these. Historians of philosophy have commonly given most of their attention to the intellectual component of Greek philosophy and have produced as a result internal accounts of pure enquiry. But we shall find in this book that philosophy was a very practical business. Many people practised it to avoid fear and to bring order to life, both their own and other people's. Often this needed access to political power, and philosophers were rarely shy both of teaching about how society should be run and of taking part in running it. The Academy took an active interest in politics,[9] teaching legislators and politicians, and in 367, the year in which Aristotle arrived in Athens, Plato went to Syracuse to advise Dionysius II, its ruler. He was there again six years later; and when he died in 347 Aristotle went with Xenocrates to Assos, across the Aegean, to join other Platonists who had attracted the attention of Hermias, its ruler. They advised him to rule with less severity, in order to be able to rule longer. Aristotle was clearly interested in the exercise of political power. (He was also interested in Hermias' daughter, whom he married.) Aristotle's closest connection to political power was while he was tutor to Hermias' ally Alexander the Great during the latter's formative years, from age 13 to 19 (342–336).

So when Aristotle returned to Athens he, like Plato,[10] was concerned with politics and politicians. Aristotle was much involved with Antipater,[11] who was in charge of Athens on behalf of Alexander. There was a good deal of resentment in rich and up to now autonomous Athens over this Macedonian control (as Aristotle was to find at his cost) and in such a situation quite clearly what was taught by the philosophers to the potentially powerful had to be acceptable to the authorities. No political power allows subversion to be taught in its schools.

Bearing in mind the active interests of philosophers in the running of the state it might seem surprising that what Aristotle taught included the nature of plants, the insides of animals, the weather and the natural world at large. Of what use was knowledge of these things to the Athenian upper classes? The answer is partly the paradox that their very uselessness made them 'liberal' in the sense used above. They were also neutral in respect to the political claims of the Athenians and Macedonians. Aristotle taught that the natural world was ordered and purposeful, and arranged in a hierarchical fashion. He did not teach this *because* it was consistent with the ordered, purposeful and hierarchical political world; but it is easy to see that he would not have been suffered to teach radically different ideas for very long. He taught that Greeks were by nature leaders and that barbarians were by nature slaves. These were the same kind of 'natures' as animals and plants had, and natural explanations covered both fields. Aristotle also discussed how different political constitutions followed the natures of different peoples and the whole of his politics is concerned with the proper ordering of power from above for the greatest good.

The other part of the answer to the question of the apparent uselessness of Aristotle's natural works lies in the way Aristotle taught them. He held that the fact of having knowledge was Good for the philosopher, the educated man; and that to generate such knowledge by investigation or learning was to improve the soul. While for Plato there had been a strong religious component in philosophy, so that knowing was beautiful and divine, so for Aristotle there was a sort of intellectual morality in which the human soul achieved its purpose in knowing.

Since knowing was good, the more one knew the better. Of course, Aristotle did not mean detailed specialism, but what he called 'a kind of educational acquaintance'.[12] Knowledge had its purposes, whatever it related to; and the acquisition and expression of knowledge had likewise general canons independent of specialist information. This is why Aristotle's philosophical, or educational, programme is all-embracing, and why it is so internally consistent, its parts full of cross-references and the working out of general principles.[13]

We shall be looking at the parts of Aristotle's programme that relate to the natural world. It is here that he is a 'natural historian', for he is reporting on the *historiae* of things in nature. The general principles worked out in this programme are essentially few and simple. First, as a pupil of Plato-the-pupil-of-Socrates, Aristotle is conscious of the novelty of his undertaking. Socrates, we saw, had given up the study of nature when young and turned to human philosophy, and was followed by Plato. But all of them knew that earlier Greek philosophers, the men we call the pre-Socratics, had been concerned with nature. Aristotle called them his predecessors, and one of the general principles of his natural works is to show how they had been wrong in seeking purely material answers to questions about the nature and the origin of natural things.[14] For Aristotle this was an incomplete explanation, one that asserted that such-and-such a natural object owed all of its characteristics to being composed of this or that matter. This was profoundly unsatisfactory to Aristotle. It was plain to him that the natural world of animals, plants, minerals and elements was full of *purpose*. The identification of this purpose and the discovery of the means whereby it was achieved is another major principle of his natural history.[15]

The purpose that he saw in the world when correcting the accounts of the earlier philosophers, especially the atomists, was essentially the natural thing in its place in the world. That is to say, the material out of which it was made and the processes that gave rise to it were, according to Aristotle, *goal-directed,* the goal being the fully formed natural thing. This was the nature of the thing, that the thing developed in this way and had these attributes when fully formed. This was not a conscious or rational goal-directed programme (Aristotle after all had a sophisticated analysis of rationality) but was purely natural. The nature of the thing caused everything in the growth of the natural object to happen for its benefit. In the case of animals this meant that they had senses to perceive and follow what was good and to avoid what was bad. It meant that the individual animal could preserve itself by feeding. And when by the necessity of the matter that composed it the animal died, its nature had ensured that by means of the appropriate organs and behaviour the animal had generated more of its kind and so assured its kind a continued place in the eternal world. In this way the functioning of the organs of sense, of nutrition and of sexual generation became central themes of Aristotle's account of animals, stemming directly from the nature of the animal.

An important side of Aristotle as a natural historian is his view of history. But we must not let our view dictate the standard by which to measure Aristotle. For him *historia* was something worthy of report, not because extraordinary, but because significant in the philosophical acquisition of knowledge. In this respect the chronological sense of 'history' was important. There is a clear chronological component in Aristotle's use of the natures of things, discussed next. First it is by development and growth in the case of living things that their nature, their essence, is revealed. Second, it is characteristic of Aristotle's treatment that he gives a chronological account of how many of the parts of philosophy developed: by setting out the incomplete or erroneous views of 'our predecessors' Aristotle often strengthens his own argument and draws a picture of the growth if not the perfection of the subject to hand. This historical treatment was developed in the Lyceum also by Aristotle's colleagues. Meno had the task of writing a history of medicine, Eudemus that of mathematics and Theophrastus that of physics and metaphysics. The histories of the constitutions of different cities was a characteristic empirical and chronological enterprise, headed by Aristotle.[16] Such investigations, like those into the natural world, were 'empirical' because they concerned the particulars of perception, which in Aristotle's terms were 'best known to us'. His theory of knowledge allowed him to process these particulars of the natural world to arrive at philosophically more valuable knowledge, that relating to universals or natural principles, 'best known to nature'.[17]

Aristotle also used *historia* in a sense close to what we mean by 'history'. In pursuing natural philosophy and comparing what he was doing with what his predecessors had done, Aristotle was making philosophy self-reflexive. Its history became part of itself, both in illustrating its progress and in justifying itself by its links to recognised Greek cultural sources. Philosophy, and later science, have often been taught by means of historical examples of how their principles came to be established, and 'history of science' as a discipline sprang from material presented in this way. Aristotle was perhaps the first to make such material available in any quantity,[18] and his entire enterprise has been represented as an account of the history and development of human thought.[19]

In collecting together material that related to earlier natural philosophy, some of which was already old, Aristotle was essentially making an historical collection. The library that he gathered for the Lyceum was of supreme importance. It has been argued that this was the first European library,[20] and we shall on a number of occasions see its importance as a working and an accumulating collection. It grew from and in turn gave shape to the empirical side of the peripatetics' teaching and learning. It contained Aristotle's works, including those on animals, and the lost 158 political constitutions (said to be modelled on the animal books).[21] It had maps, dissection drawings and a diagram of the blood system. It had historical lists of winners at the games, accounts of religious festivals and collections of poetry. The work of the Lyceum centred on the library,[22] on the monthly meetings at the common table and on the lectures: esoteric in the morning, public and 'exoteric' in the afternoons or evenings.

ARISTOTLE'S 'NATURE'

Central to the issue of natural principles – what is best known to nature – is the question of what 'nature' itself meant to Aristotle. What nature meant to a succession of people is the central theme of this book, and it begins with Aristotle. To understand what he meant by 'nature', *physis,* we must first be aware of the two rather different meanings we attach to our word 'nature'. That we have two different meanings is the result of a cultural ancestry in which the Latin term *natura* was used in two ways, themselves derived from the Greeks: this too will become clear as this book continues. The first use of 'nature' today is as a general term covering the natural world and its natural principles. When we are feeling poetic we call it Mother Nature, and when we are in technological mode a thing can be Natural as opposed to Artificial. But we also use 'nature' to express the essential property of a thing, as in 'it is in the nature of cats to catch mice'. The uses are not exclusive of course, because if we should say 'it is natural for cats to catch mice' we seem to be referring both to the essential nature of a cat and to a general principle of nature. But when Aristotle talked about nature, he almost always meant the nature-of-a-thing. For him the natural world was a collection of natures-of-things, each a principle governing the development and behaviour of the individual thing. That is, there was no external set of principles by which natural things developed or interacted, no wisdom of a maternal Nature. Only in very rare instances is 'nature' a sort of generalisation from collective natures of things, and apart from this usage in the first book of the *Physics,* it is clear from Book 2 that 'Aristotle does not recognise any such thing as nature over and above the natures of particular things.'[23] In the words of another commentator, 'We will see that Aristotle's nature is *not* transcendent, but immanent as the species or soul of individuals.'[24] This is fundamentally important for the present book. It requires a mental effort to remember that Aristotle does *not* use anything comparable to our general term 'nature'; and one of the themes of this book is to show how such a meaning arose.

Using 'nature' in this sense not only enabled Aristotle to reject the pre-Socratic accounts of natural change, but also Plato's. Plato held that the material world had been put together by a divinity, the demiurge, whose actions were limited by the irreducible char-acteristics of matter. It has been argued[25] that this was seen by Aristotle as presenting a dualism between the conscious rationality and will of the demiurge and the mechanical necessity of matter. Aristotle's view of nature as immanent, local and not conscious avoided this.

Of course, Aristotle is treating the natural world 'philosophically' in not admitting the gods as causes of changes and to a certain extent this aligns him with the old philosophers. So in restoring *purpose* to the world Aristotle could not turn back to the gods and had to find a natural cause of change. Removing providential and interventionist gods also meant for Aristotle and the earlier philosophers that human history from the invention of the arts to the development of constitutions was dependent on human 'nature'. To believe that this history was human and natural was to believe that man could control it politically. There were even utopian planners in the fifth century BC,[26] and the philosophers, in the forefront of the move to see the natural and human side of history, were often close to the sources of power.

We need to dwell a little on these connections. In choosing to be a philosopher and in addition to study nature, Aristotle was taking an action that marked out his political and religious views in Athenian society. We have seen that philosophers could be unpopular in that society. Aristotle was joining a group characterised by their denial of the gods' actions in the physical world. This seems to be a more primary characteristic than 'searching into nature', because of the very different ways in which they interpreted 'nature'.[27] It is arguable in fact that the denial of the gods marked out the shape of natural philosophy: their absence defined what 'nature' was. The many different explanations by the philosophers of lightning had in common the principal feature that they did *not* attribute it to Zeus, as non-philosophical Greeks thought. We can even argue that explanations of lightning would not be part of natural philosophy unless lightning had once been attributed to a god. Philosophical explanations about earthquakes all agree that they are *not* caused by Poseidon (the 'earth-shaker'). Comets have natural explanations and are *not* portents from the gods. Rain is due to a variety of natural causes, and certainly not to Zeus answering what we should not describe here as a call of nature. For Homer, Zeus was 'the cloud-gatherer', which was the point at issue between Strepsiades and Socrates.[28] The rainbow was not the goddess Iris carrying a message from the gods but (perhaps) a coloured cloud.[29] Rainbows, rain, comets, lightning: not only do they share in having *some* kind of natural explanation and in not having a divine explanation, but they are brought into natural philosophy *because* they are not divine. But we can argue further. These are principal themes within 'meteorology': they *are* meteorology. The subject has not only had its boundaries fixed but its subject matter determined by the absence of the actions of the gods in things that frightened people.

It is sometimes necessary to exaggerate to make a point. Aristotle's natural philosophy looks as if it is shaped by natural categories of the physical world, like matter, motion, heavens and earth, meteorology. But if we look with Greek natural-philosophical categories in our minds we see that Aristotle's physics is concerned with showing that *all* motion, *all* physical change is natural, where 'natural' relates to Aristotle's own conception of 'nature' and agrees with that of the other philosophers only in excluding the gods. This gives Aristotle a god-free explanation that can be extended anywhere. He extends it first to the heavens and earth partly because these are the framework of the world and the simplest actual examples of motion in elementary matter; but also because the heavens were the traditional home of the gods and the earth the place where they affected the lives of man.[30] This is shown no longer to be the case by Aristotle's treating heaven and earth naturally. He extends it, second, into the very mechanisms by which the gods were thought to affect men: 'meteorology'. Certainly there are internal philosophical reasons for doing this, for the motions to be explained are of the next higher order and the matter is now mixed rather than elementary, but ultimately Aristotle is filling a space caused and shaped by the disappearance of the gods. Even when Aristotle's topic seems to have been outlined by his 'predecessors' it is because they too were working to fill previously godly spaces.

NATURAL PRINCIPLES: CAUSE, NECESSITY AND FORM

We have now glimpsed Aristotle as a natural historian and have seen that both his subject matter – nature – and his means of enquiring into it – history – centred on the internal nature-of-a-thing and the processes by which it gave rise to the natural object. These were not limited in Aristotle's philosophy to the world of living things but were directly related to his interpretation of physical things and the first principles that lay beneath it. So well are these first principles exhibited in Aristotle's studies of living things that no one is sure whether they are derived from here and applied more generally to the physical world or vice versa. But Aristotle presents the books on animals (that on plants is lost) and on the soul as applications of principles set out programmatically in the *Physics*, and all the later educators who used the whole of the nature books, the *libri naturales*, accepted this. Let us look briefly at some of these principles.

When Aristotle complained that his predecessors had given only material accounts of natural things, he did of course accept that matter was in some measure an explanation of things.[31] There was, he said, a material necessity by which the immovable characteristics of matter contributed to the characteristics of that mixture of matter that partly constituted the natural object. But in addition to this

Plate 1 A sacrificial calf. Some animals had a special relationship to the gods of the pantheon, and sacrifice was a means of propitiation. That auguries were taken from the abnormal appearance of the viscera meant that the priests had some notion of what was normal, that is, in accord with nature. From the Acropolis, Athens, *c.* 570 BC. (Museum of Classical Archaeology, Cambridge.)

Plate 2 The owl of Athena, symbolising wisdom. (Museum of Classical Archaeology, Cambridge.)

material necessity there was also, in Aristotle's view, what he called hypothetical necessity. This involved what was needed if some objective or goal were to be attained. A house may be built of brick, stone or wood, and these materials will give it certain characteristics. But if it is to be a house and not a pile of matter it will need to be of a certain shape and organisation. There will be stages to be gone through, planning, logistics, which are *necessary* for that end to be achieved. These necessities relate to the purpose of the whole in a way that matter on its own could not. Natural processes are analogous. Just as it is in the nature of a house to shelter people, so the nature of a thing provides the necessities for achieving the goal, the appearance and preservation of the natural thing.

Aristotle takes these two kinds of necessity as two *causes*.[32] The 'material cause' of a house is the bricks and mortar and wood. The material cause of living things is the irreducible matter of which they are composed, which Aristotle considered to be the simplest parts. These were the homogeneous parts, incapable of division into anything simpler; he is in part continuing the argument against the atomists. But in addition to such material causality, Aristotle is always looking for the *purpose* of things. This is what he calls the 'final cause' of a thing, the reason why it came into existence. It was a major determining principle of his natural works. In many ways the Aristotelian programme can be seen as an investigation into causes, and overwhelmingly the important one is the final cause. This was the enduring feature of Aristotelian natural philosophy. In addition to these two, Aristotle identified an efficient cause (the bricklayer in the case of the house) and a formal cause (the design the house must follow if it is to achieve its final cause).

We shall see how these principles were put into practice when looking in more detail at the natural books. Here we must note that these causes relate directly to another great Aristotelian principle, that of form and matter. To begin again with matter and to think again of Aristotle's opposition to his predecessors, we can see that the hypothetical necessities involved in achieving the final cause were partly concerned with the arrangement of matter. The nature of a thing disposes its matter to best advantage for that thing. The form of a house is the disposition of its parts to serve its purpose. Aristotle held in an abstract way that matter, without form, could potentially be anything (with stone one could build forts, cities, temples or ovens). Conversely, form without matter was, as it were, pure design to an end and Aristotle called it actuality. Between the extremes of potentiality and actuality all natural things and substances were in fact matter given perceptible qualities by form. They formed a range from the simplest objects, largely matter, to the most elaborate, where form was most notable. From the elements, mixtures and minerals, the scale rose to living things, animals and finally man.

Since the form related to a sort of design-for-purpose, it helped to identify what a thing essentially was. In living things, said Aristotle, the form is the soul, for the soul is the source of life. To be a living thing is to have soul. To live, feed, grow and generate one's kind is to have a vegetative soul, to live as a plant. To perceive and move in addition is the soul of an animal. To have a rational soul is to be a man. This is Aristotle's down-to-earth philosophical doctrine of soul. It is in contrast to that of Plato, who described a heavenly home for the soul and who saw philosophy as a sort of religious perfection of the soul in its earthbound workhouse. It is also in contrast to earlier Greek literature, which dealt in a number of ways with how the soul, or souls, represented some form of life after death. Aristotelian and Platonic teaching on the soul was fundamentally important in the later West, and forms another important thread through the centuries covered by this book.

NATURAL BOOKS: THE CURRICULUM AT THE LYCEUM

(i) Physical principles on earth and in heaven

Thus far we have glanced at Aristotle's intentions and first principles. We need now to make the acquaintance of the works in which these principles were put into practice. These works are what later scholars called the *libri naturales*, the 'natural books'. They were obviously intended by Aristotle and his colleagues as a group of works, directly related in their methods, designed to cover all aspects of the natural world, and proceeding from first principles to the most elaborate physical substrate in which those principles were seen in operation. Aristotle as a natural historian is Aristotle who is looking at the *historiae* of the natures of things.[33] The unity of this undertaking is emphasised also because Aristotle held that major intellectual fields remained discrete from each other, so that for example, geometry cannot provide truths for arithmetic or aesthetics.[34] Scholars cannot agree on the order in which Aristotle wrote his books, and so cannot arrive at a notion of how he might have announced and then carried out a programme of investigation into the natural world. There are many mutual cross-references between the natural books, and by and large it looks as though the books on the differences between animals and their causes were later than those dealing with physical principles. That few of them seem finished has probably more to do with Aristotle or his colleagues constantly adding to them in the Lyceum than with their being a logical conclusion of a research programme. They may have been lectures which Aristotle continuously brought up to date, yet which retained their interconnectedness and didactic functions for the benefit of beginners. The connections between the natural books is programmatic rather than chronological.

The beginning of the programme was the *Physics*. It does not set out with a programme of discussions that will follow, and possibly, if it was written early, Aristotle had not yet decided that a programme could or should follow. It must be the *Physics* that the 'later' *libri naturales* refer back to when they mention the beginning of the whole enterprise of interpreting nature.[35] So what was Aristotle's enterprise? In opening, the *Physics* tells the reader that systematic knowledge of disciplines is about its 'principles, causes or elements'. This is the discipline of *nature* and Aristotle comes as close as he ever does to 'nature' in an abstract sense. There are a number of things to note about this. 'Principle' is *arche,* with a main meaning of 'beginning'[36] and we can again see that Aristotle means that that out of which things grow is related to their essence: the nature of a thing.

Aristotle's term is *phusis* – or more traditionally *physis* – and the person who investigates it is *physikos.* Aristotle names only those of earlier generations, upon his disagreements with whom he builds his own version of the discipline. (Here it is Melissus and Parmenides.) It is clear that here the notion of chronological development, a form of *historia*, is important in revealing the essence of a thing. 'Beginning' as a meaning of *arche* (above) also implies the chronological component of Aristotle's treatment.

Aristotle's method of revealing the first principles is to begin with what is most obvious to the observer, the whole appearance of the natural world. His object is to find the common first principles which the natures of things have used in building up the complex whole. This appears to be analogous to the well known Aristotelian distinction between what is 'first in the senses' of man (a collection of particulars) and what is 'first in nature' (nature's first principles) and so is a version of the Aristotelian dialectic between empirical observation and demonstrable, rational knowledge.

Next in order seems to have been the work on the heavens and earth, *De Caelo et Mundo*,[37] which refers back in less than precise terms to 'our early (or first) discussions' or to the book on the principles of motion, or simply to the book on motion.[38] It seems then to have followed the *Physics* but not in a way that suggests any grand programme of teaching. Like many of the others *De Caelo* is not a finished work but a basis for teaching and research.[39] Its discussion is about how the principles of motion apply to the heavenly bodies and it therefore looks like an extension to the heavens of the principles of motion expressed in the *Physics*. It also makes forward references to the texts on generation and corruption and meteorology, where again the physical principles of motion are studied in particular cases. Thus we seem to see an Aristotelian programme of exposition from first principles to particular kinds of motion. Some broad schema of this kind must certainly have been in place in the Lyceum, or Aristotle's whole enterprise would have seemed fragmented. But *De Caelo* also refers back[40] to the text we now know as *De Incessu Animalium*. Probably Aristotle was working on the animal books in parallel with the physical ones, but had not yet developed the whole enterprise to a point where the programmatic theme – the development from first physical principles to their operation in complex circumstances – could be emphasised. It is only with the animal books that the quantity of cross-reference makes the nature of the programme clear.

In *De Caelo*, at all events, Aristotle deals with actual motion of the heavenly bodies and the earthly elements in accordance with his physical principles. It is again the question of the nature of the thing; and the natures of the heavenly bodies and earthly mixed bodies are simpler than those of animals. It is in the nature of stones that they fall, and in this sense the 'nature' of stones is an internal principle of motion. But Aristotle, perhaps in reaction to Plato[41] believed that nothing was moved of itself. This necessitated an external cause that called the internal principle of motion into action. It did so by being in the state in which the internal principle, and its object in which it inhered, potentially were. Thus the unmoved earth caused the stone to fall by its internal principle of motion, so that the stone comes to be at rest. Likewise, that which heats was, for Aristotle, hot. This causality is the actualisation of potential, and so falls into line with Aristotle's new methodology, with which he was seeking to overturn the materialism of his predecessors.

In addition to these causes of motion, Aristotle also listed another kind of motion – violent. If a man throws a stone, the stone acts against both its internal principle of motion and the unmoved mover, the earth, that realises the potential of the stone. But the internal principle of motion of the unnaturally moving stone overcomes the violence and returns the stone to rest on the earth. As for the motion of the heavenly bodies, it was an unquestioned principle for Aristotle that their circular motions, unlike that of terrestrial bodies, was perfect. It seems that Aristotle may have changed his mind about the naturalness of such motion, for the natural motion of the raised stone to the earth, in accordance with his physical principles, was straight. There are places where Aristotle says that circular motion, in this sense unnatural, must therefore be *voluntary* and proceed from the souls of the celestial bodies. At other places, and primarily in *De Caelo,* he rejects self-motion even for the heavenly bodies and says they are moved by an incorporeal unmoved mover, which calls their nature, *physis,* into action to achieve a perfection similar to its own. This is an action of love by the bodies, or rather the spheres that carry them, for the unmoved mover. It is analogous to the relationship between the 'nature' of the falling stone and the unmoved earth, and again we see how the achievement of purpose is the main plank of Aristotle's arguments against his predecessors.

Since Aristotle's attacks on the earlier natural philosophers is so characteristic a part of his exposition, we should briefly give our attention to it, since in *De Caelo* he is explicit about its purposes (and since this method gives such a strong chronological meaning to his reporting of *historiae*). As he says,[42] to expound one argument is to destroy another. Since Aristotle is still dealing with physical first principles his business is with words rather than things and his treatment is dialectical. We shall see that it is only later, in the animal books, that he is prepared to question even first principles if only the amount of empirical and observational knowledge was great enough. But Aristotle does not rely solely on demonstration in any strict sense to persuade his audience, and depends instead on the natural instinct to see an argument as a battle in which there will be a victor. It is a hollow triumph if the opponent does not turn up for the battle: a win by default, says Aristotle, acknowledging that his own argument will be stronger if others are heard and defeated. Aristotle saw the same process at work among the older natural philosophers and very characteristically decided to go one stage further. Where his predecessors pursued a topic only to the point where they concluded that they had defeated their opponents, Aristotle saw this as a practice dictated by argument rather than by the topic itself and the enquiry it called for. Even within himself, 'A man will even pursue a question in his own mind no farther than the point at which he finds nothing to say against his own arguments.'[43] But Aristotle's answer to this is not yet to return to the appearances involved in the topic and allow them to direct his further investigation, but to fabricate further potential objections and to proceed by means of overcoming them.

It is this mode of procedure that lends form to many of Aristotle's doctrines. The dialectical destruction of earlier opinions made possible the construction of a unified doctrine of nature. His unified doctrine was that of generation, or coming-to-be. He saw his predecessors as dealing only with prior causes, largely material, that as it were 'pushed' the natural object into being. Aristotle's general reply was that the natural object in its final form rather 'drew' the material and other components towards itself as a goal. All natural change was a *process*, with an end, a kind of generation. For Aristotle even the elements were generated. He saw that the earlier philosophers like Parmenides and Melissus had tried to find something unchanging in the flux of things by denying generation: they said it was an illusion and that in reality matter remained unchanged through a variety of combinations.[44] But Aristotle claimed superior knowledge in having made a special and indeed a higher study of Being (he means the *Metaphysics*) and argued that the eternity of the world and its component parts – the unchangeability sought by Parmenides and Melissus – lay in processes and not the matter itself, as Parmenides and Melissus had claimed.

Aristotle brings his general principle to bear on all kinds of natural change as he saw them, that is, locomotion, change of size and change of form.[45] Again, the earlier natural philosophers had discussed the causes of such motions, for example why fire rose and earth fell. Aristotle has some detailed criticism that need not delay us, such as asking how the geometrical principles that the Academics said underlay matter could have *weight* and make an object heavy,[46] but the thrust of his argument is once more that the nature of the thing is achieving an end in moving as it does. Even in so simple a motion as the falling of heavy things and the rise of light there is motion to the proper Form of the thing, where Form includes its natural place. Such motions are from one opposite to another within a category. Fire moving up is like a curable patient getting better, and not getting, for example, white: it is in his nature as curable. Where the nature of the thing includes the capacity for growth, it alters in size, not, for example, in health. Nature is an internal principle of motion, even of the elements. When air is generated from water, says Aristotle,[47] it naturally rises; having risen, it has stopped Becoming, and Is. It has moved from potentiality to actuality and has its final attributes, including place.

Because these processes are purposeful, they are orderly and natural. Aristotle accordingly attacks the atomists[48] on the grounds that the atoms are said to move randomly and that there can be no order in infinite space and with an infinite number of atoms. For Aristotle in an atomic universe there was nothing for nature to achieve. In contrast his own physical principles showed that the world was spherical, for all the elements moved to their proper place around the centre of the heaviest mass, as observation showed. The flux of natural things was replaced by the permanence of their kinds, the natures of which was the subject of Aristotle's natural history. In Aristotle's system, the perfection of the circular motion of the heavenly spheres encloses an eternal but finite world, outside which is voidless, bodyless infinity in which there is neither time nor place.[49]

Aristotle takes up this general principle of generation, or Becoming, in *On Generation and Corruption*. It is a theoretical work and must claim less of our attention when looking at Aristotle's natural history than those texts where he discusses how these first principles are manifested in the world of natures. But it shows how the Lyceum programme was developing. In *On Generation and Corruption*, there are more internal references, partly to a 'previous work' which can be identified as the *Physics*, partly again to earlier discussions of motion and partly – implicitly rather than explicitly – to *De Caelo* and to the *Metaphysics*.[50]

(ii) The meteorological part of natural history

By the time the teaching programme at the Lyceum reached the *Meteorologica* the enterprise of looking at the natures of things is clear. Aristotle was now prepared to refer to some larger plan in his educational scheme. He looked back much more clearly than before to the *Physics* and *De Caelo* and locates this study of meteorology in respect to them. He refers, too, to *On Generation and Corruption*.[51] He now also mentions an 'original undertaking'[52] which seems to have been a survey of the entire natural world, explicitly continuing up to plants and animals, including their description and analysis.[53]

After studying physics, the heavens and generation, says Aristotle, we are concerned with what our predecessors called meteorology. To a certain extent again Aristotle is following a group of studies undertaken by the pre-Socratics, and although he is very conscious of his own new approach, his words often imply that such discussions had been continued through the lifetimes of Socrates and Plato. Perhaps there were still atomists who stressed the natural causes of meteors in order to nullify people's fear of them. Likewise, discussing the milky way, Aristotle talks[54] of the 'schools' of the followers of Pythagoras, Anaxagoras and Democritus that endured for a time after their founders, perhaps to the recent past. Aristotle is able to refute many of their doctrines by means of the more recent discoveries of the astronomers, and he is again indulging in a sort of historical dialectic, where the chronological development of a topic is associated with the rejection of old arguments in the promulgation of new.

This chronological history of topics is strong in the *Meteorologica.* Aristotle has now done with the more or less abstract principles of motion in the works on physics and motion in heaven and earth. We are now in the actual world, from the stars down to earth, and Aristotle is dealing with things the ordinary Greeks knew about – the names of the winds, the source of the Nile, rainbows, lightning and comets. The elements of the earlier discussions are here presented in their mixtures, and mixtures as the basis of real, named things. This means that Aristotle can tell the *historiae* of things worthy of note: they are less perfect than the first elements and heavenly bodies[55] but as mixtures composing individuals, the natures-of-things are more complex and illustrate Aristotle's concern with purposeful generation, or change, more fully. A few examples will illustrate how Aristotle combines his first principles with the style of historical narrative of *historiae* that is seen in the collection of constitutions and the lists of winners at the games.

The background to these examples is straightforward. Aristotle is concerned with the physical world from the earth to where the sphere of fire impinges on that of the stars. All lower motions derive their order and power from the stars, mediated by what lay between. This was no more than matter. At root it was not elementary matter, for as we have seen, Aristotle held that the elements were interchangeable, or generated from each other.[56] This meant that there was no strict division between the concentric spheres of the elements, but a constant interchange as air for example turned into fire and moved upwards.[57] Aristotle thus maintained that there was some common substrate to the different elements, but he does not go into detail.[58] What is important for Aristotle is that it is all matter and so is potentially anything; and it manifests certain qualities as the result of rest or motion (ultimately derived from the circular motions of the heavenly bodies and transmitted through fire and air).[59] Contingent spheres of the 'elements' have similar motions[60] and these are the *material* causes of events in the lower world.

With this background Aristotle explains meteorological events in terms of qualitative change and the interchangeability of elements. A major principle for him is that the heat of the sun draws out from the earth two main kinds of exhalations, the moist and the dry. As these rise, so they may catch fire and produce shooting stars. Sometimes 'the cold' of the air forces out the heat from such exhalations, and this is seen as a sort of fire related to shooting stars.[61] All air according to Aristotle is potentially fire, and nowhere more so than at the top of its sphere, where it impinges on the lower surface of the sphere of fire. The heavenly bodies cause air to separate off as fire, causing the appearances that carried the name of comets.[62] Comets were a regular part of earlier natural-philosophical speculation, and Aristotle gives his usual historical treatment by dealing with the views of Anaxagoras, the Italian Pythgoreans, Hippocrates of Chios and his pupil Aeschylus.[63] Some of these, at least, believed that comets were conjunctions of planets, or planets that returned only after very long intervals. Apart from disagreeing on details (that they appear outside the narrow band of the zodiac, and that they have tails) Aristotle's claim for the superiority of his own explanation is largely that it rests on fewer assumptions (the two kinds of exhalation). The characteristically Aristotelian claim about all change being Becoming is distant.

A watery exhalation from the earth is also Aristotle's explanation of the formation, by condensation, of rain, hail and snow.[64] It is not condensation in our terms, but an elementary change: the peculiar nature of mountains *generates* rain from air that is potentially water.[65] This is the origin of rivers, and Aristotle thinks he has a better explanation of the formation of rivers than those who argued that they all flowed out of a huge underground reservoir that filled up in the winter.[66] Aristotle argues from itineraries that the biggest rivers flow from the biggest mountains. These were the travel-*historiae*, written, says Aristotle, by people with direct personal experience. Characteristically Aristotle adds a list of rivers and their mountains to make his point. The list ends (apart from Greek rivers) with the Nile as one of the two greatest rivers of all.

The Nile was a perpetual source of interest to the ancient world, both before and after Aristotle. Not only was it the lifeblood of Egypt, the only civilisation for the antiquity of which the Greeks had an admiration,[67] but unlike all other rivers it rose and flooded in the summer rather than the winter. Whether (as Jaeger maintains[68]) or not Aristotle actually wrote the tract attributed to him, *On the Inundation of the Nile,* he gave the topic some thought. He argued that its generative mountain was the Silver Mountain (which he does not locate). For Aristotle, the Nile fitted in well with his chronological treatment of *historiae.* From the old Greeks he knew that in the past Egypt had been different. He believed that in Homer's time Egypt was largely confined to Thebes and that Memphis did not exist. The continuing deposit of silt extended the delta at the mouth of the Nile, making new and habitable land, while (argued Aristotle) the land left now further from the sea continually dried out and became less habitable.[69] Aristotle knew of other cases in which for example the silting up of a lake by a river had badly damaged trade in the course of a single lifetime. He knew of long-term changes similar to that of Egypt at Argos and Mycenae. Generally, he says,[70] these changes are too slow to be noticed by the inhabitants; and generally too they come in cycles, so that silting is followed by flooding and earth emerging from the sea is swallowed again. The earth indeed is said to grow and decay like an animal, but in different places at different times (and caused by the heat of the sun).[71] Since for Aristotle the world is eternal, he has a lot of historical time in which to arrange these great and almost imperceptible cycles, greater than the lifetimes of nations, he says.[72] With this cyclical view of the chronological history of the *historiae* that he relates, Aristotle can readily refute the opinions of the old philosophers who had argued from the evidence of such terrestrial changes that the universe is in some process of decay or generation. It is the astronomers[73] again who have given Aristotle some idea of the immensity of the universe in comparison to the size of the earth, the changes of which look correspondingly less important than they did to the old natural philosophers. The Flood of Deucalion and the rivers that changed their courses where the old Graeci and Hellenes lived[74] were local changes in an eternally shifting and very small terrestrial globe. Even the fact that the great Nile itself once did not flow at all[75] must be kept in proportion.

As we have seen, it is apparent in the *Meteorologica* that Aristotle was covering the same ground as a number of his predecessors and even that there was a tradition of enquiry in which he felt himself to be. It was not only on broad questions like the nature of the first element (Anaxagoras thought it was fire; Aristotle says it is ether[76]) but also on specific issues, such as whether the sea is fed with springs, as rivers sometimes are,[77] or conversely that the sea is the source of all rivers.[78] Nor was it that such discussions were limited to the pre-Socratics, and when Aristotle discusses the names and the properties of the winds, their directions and their connection with the rising and the setting of the constellations,[79] we should recall the importance of the winds in maritime commerce and how they would have been discussed by sailors. Here Aristotle is engaged on a characteristic exercise. Since the time of the year was frequently denoted by the time of the rising and setting of constellations, the seasonal appearance of important winds could also be remembered by practical people on the same basis. It was Aristotle the natural philosopher who argued that the appearance of seasonal winds was *caused* by the motions of the heavenly bodies, as all lower and rectilinear motions were caused by the circular paths of the stars.[80] The rising and setting of the heavenly bodies was also important in medicine and in the agricultural calendar.[81]

Another part of non-philosophical Greek life to which Aristotle gave a natural-philosophical framework was the study of portents. We saw above that the supposed action of the gods had a role to play in the formation of natural philosophy. Here we should note that the gods' messages (like those supposedly carried by Iris) were also important. It was not only that Zeus traditionally discharged his lightning at men, but the Etruscans and Chaldeans for example had elaborate systems for giving portentous significance to the actual appearance of the lightning's path. Here Aristotle gives a natural-historical and natural-philosophical interpretation of things that seemed to the ordinary man significant for future events. These things often fell within the range of appearances noted by the soothsayers and used in making predictions. This multiplied the significance which the ordinary man gave to them. We shall see that the natural philosophy of the atomists had the aim of lessening the religious awe in which the ordinary man held such things, and although he disagreed with them on the nature of the physical world, Aristotle likewise argued away the mystery of such events. The ancient Greeks also gave attention to signs that foretold earthquakes.

From Aristotle we know that they were discussed by Anaxagoras, Anaximenes and Democritus.[82] From the amount of space he devotes to it we can imagine that signs of an impending earthquake were of enduring interest to Greeks and especially to their soothsayers. Perhaps it was a strange calm of natural things, said Aristotle, or an unexpected frost, or the appearance of strange clouds.[83] Aristotle links earthquakes and their signs to volcanic activity; if general, this must have added to their significance, especially in the auguries of the portent-mongers that he mentions.[84]

It has already been suggested why so much space was devoted to thunder and lightning in natural philosophy and here we should note that Aristotle gives the appearance of setting up a history of the topic by recalling[85] that Anaxagoras and Empedocles had written on these matters. Aristotle's explanation of earthquakes is that they are generated from air in motion – winds – generated by the exhalations called into existence from the earth by the sun, which we met above. He accordingly argues that earthquakes are seasonal (in following the sun) and even have their preferred time of day.[86] But his explanation is not essentially different in kind from those of Anaxagoras, who said that the earth is moved by the ether below it (as an explanation, too primitive for words, says Aristotle[87]), and of others, that water forces its way into the earth or that the earth breaks as it grows.

In other words Aristotle in these discussions of the behaviour of the elements as they appear in the world (as opposed to in theory) is not able to employ to the full his doctrine of natural change as an end-directed process governed ultimately by the nature-of-the-thing. He does his best in his discussion of thunder and lightning. He first prefers his own explanation to that of older ones because it had fewer fundamental principles. They are the two exhalations again.[88] The dry exhalation is squeezed out as the clouds cool on the top surface. Its collision with other clouds is thunder; it burns and this is lightning. Then he says[89] that the explanations of Anaxagoras and Empedocles – respectively that lightning is part of the upper ether and that it is intercepted sunlight – do not explain how lightning is *generated* when we see it, for on these explanations it would simply be the (unexplained) display of something that pre-existed. It would be like saying that snow and rain pre-exist and are simply sent to us from time to time. This seems to be part of Aristotle's general search for generation in his sense of end-directed process, but is severely limited by its subject matter, in comparison to the works on living things.

The same may be said for subterranean events. Below the earth is something similar to what he has described above the earth, and a smoky and a vaporous exhalation is said to produce minerals and metals respectively. Aristotle's preferred mode of theorising in all these cases seems to be to have a small number of principles – a double exhalation – to produce many phenomena, from rainbows to earthquakes and metals. The fourth book of the *Meteorologica* begins with some more theory on this level, in which of the four qualities hot and cold are active, dry and moist passive. This is similar to other active/passive pairs, like mover and moved, male and female, and gives Aristotle a modest opportunity to employ the principles of his wider theory of goal-directed change. Hot and cold perform operations, he says, moist and dry adopt forms. This is natural change and natural destruction.

What is at first sight surprising is that Aristotle now in the *Meteorologica* gives his attention to living things. Having announced that the work was to mark the boundary between the homogeneous 'similar' parts and the organic, he proceeds at once to the organic, where 'organ' is the manifestation of soul, and therefore of living beings. To us this looks wrong in a 'meteorology'. The *Meteorologia* even looks like an arbitrary section of the Lyceum curriculum that covers the transition between the non-living and the living; but let us listen to what Aristotle has to say.

When we do, we realise that Aristotle did not have our distinction between living and non-living. The former could arise from the latter and the principles of life lay in the heat of the sun as in the natural heat of living things that generated themselves. So after the elements and mixtures of the sublunar world came the particular class of mixtures, of the same elements, that were living. These contained a soul, to be sure, but a soul came into the category of Form, a thing possessed by any natural object with recognisable qualities and so was possessed also by non-living mixtures. Above all, the advantage of including a discussion of living things in a text on meteorology is that Aristotle can fully articulate his doctrine of change as end-directed.

That this is Aristotle's purpose becomes clear towards the end of the work. It is by making comparisons with living organisms and particularly animals that Aristotle can illustrate his fundamental physical principles better than he can in things where matter predominates over form. 'Matter is pure matter and the essence is pure definition', he says.[90] Here 'essence' as definition is equivalent to the nature of the thing, and Aristotle is pointing out that natural things exist in a scale determined by the greater involvement of form with matter. While the 'elements' are very close to matter (yet as perceptible are to a degree inFormed) and have a purpose (yet very often difficult to see), purpose is better seen in things where a function is plain. To explain what he means Aristotle uses images that came frequently to him, and which he used again in dealing with animals: the function of the eye is vision, and it is by this that we know it to be an eye. An eye of a statue is an eye in name only, having no function; a saw in a painting likewise has no function and cannot be properly be called a saw. While it may be difficult to explain the function of fire, it is easier to give that of flesh, and easier still to give that of the flesh of the tongue. Aristotle is essentially looking back from the clarity of his method in the work on animals to explain how simpler things, and especially the elements and simple mixtures – the homogeneous metals in the earth, for example, and the 'similar' parts of living bodies – act, suffer and achieve their function.

Let us complete our view of the natural history of the *Meteorologica* by seeing how Aristotle wished the 'similar' parts to be understood. These were the parts that he said were completely homogeneous, being in theory capable of indefinite division without ever producing something different – which would happen in the case of atomic matter, which would ultimately produce atom and void. This was another of Aristotle's arguments against the atomists and their detestable ignorance of purpose and order in the natures of things, and therefore was an important argument to him. The similar parts, in having recognisable qualities, were inFormed mixtures of the elements, and the metals formed by subterranean exhalations were in this same category as the flesh and bone of animals. The similar parts had their characteristic actions and passions, and Aristotle deals here with two of them, putrefaction and concoction, a pair of opposites. Both came about because some of the elementary qualities were active and others passive. The most active was the Hot. When the natural heat of a moist body is overcome by external heat, says Aristotle,[91] the result is putrefaction.

In contrast, when the natural heat of an object perfects the passive qualities, most often the Cold and the Moist, then true concoction occurs. This is the process by which a thing becomes itself, that is, by which its 'nature' is expressed. Aristotle is arguing in a characteristic way for a *process* between opposites. Corruption and generation are opposites. The action of the Hot on the Cold in concoction is an action of opposites and is akin to the action of the male on the female in generation and to the action of form on matter. All are ways in which the nature of the thing is perfected and Aristotle is seeking to make clear by reference to animals what happens in the similar parts. He accordingly gives some detail about the process of concoction, his principal example. Cooking and ripening are two examples, and like all concoctions, produce an object that is thicker and hotter. The ripening of fruits[92] is a process in which the natural heat of the plant gains mastery over the passive qualities and is complete when the seeds are capable of germinating: the process has a clear purpose. It should be noted that Aristotle sometimes equates the passive qualities (the Cold and the Dry) with the matter of the thing undergoing concoction. This is partly because he wants to establish a Form–Matter polarity so that the natural change can be seen as having both process and purpose, and partly that, strictly, 'matter' has no recognisable qualities and cannot be acted on without its potential being realised to some degree in a Quality.

In these ways Aristotle is making his major point that natural changes are end-directed and express the nature of the thing. He makes little distinction between processes that we would call natural and artificial. In a medical example, for instance, he says that the concoction of pus in a boil has a clear purpose (to ameliorate and expel a peccant humour). This is just the same as the fermentation of must into wine, or the boiling of substances to make food, drink or dyes,[93] purposes we might regard as artificial.

Having discussed the action of the Hot, Aristotle deals with the passive motions of the other qualities under its influence. Thus, he says,[94] the Moist is more easily moulded than the Dry. There is a strong sense too in which the Cold[95] is also passive, being part of water and earth. This would leave only heat as the active principle, in accordance with Aristotle's general preference for a single active cause – maleness, natural heat, the soul, air – shaping passive matter or its qualities. But the Cold also has a hand in changing things, for example by solidifying them, and in the books on animals Aristotle says that the nature of the animal uses heat and cold in this way in producing the diversity of the growing embryo from the homogeneous matter of the female. Here it is Aristotle's purpose to explain the forces that have shaped natural objects – the Cold that aggregated their parts, the Moist that did the opposite, for example. Since all objects were produced by the activity of the Hot, all retain some heat: like their retained Moist and Cold, this is not perceptible to the senses in a common-sense way. Aristotle says[96] that all actual bodies as elementary mixtures act on the senses in different ways, and their qualities are not singly perceived as such. But because their qualities, active and passive, remain within them, natural bodies can be investigated for both sorts; and Aristotle begins a long account of the *historiae* of different objects and substances. He wants to know how their passive qualities react to external active qualities. Do these objects burn or melt with heat? Do they break or submit to pressure? How do they react when soaked?[97] Are objects fissile, or do they shatter? Do they give off fumes when heated?[98] Aristotle is looking for correlations of differences, the technique he employed most powerfully in the works on animals. For example, he notes that some natural substances (like copper) do not change in water, but will melt with heat, while others (like wool or earth) will not melt but absorb water.[99] What he has in mind is that such changes reveal both the passive qualities (which abound in the 'similar' parts like metal and bone[100]) and the active qualities, cold and (more particularly) hot. Aristotle does not express entirely clearly how the techniques he describes in the *historiae* of 'tests' for the qualities indicate their presence, and much must rest on assumptions that seemed self-evident to him. For example, it was obvious that ash must contain a great deal of heat, because a great deal of heat had gone into the making of it. As we noted above there was a sense for Aristotle that matter was strongly qualitative; or the qualities were in a sense material. The Hot is *part* of ash, even though we cannot feel it by the senses.[101] Likewise watery bodies are cold, unless they retain an external heat, like wine.

The *Meteorologica* is presented as the last of a series of works dealing with homogeneous bodies: that is, the elements and the 'similar' parts, the discussion of which is preliminary to that of the compound and complex bodies which follow, principally those of plants and animals. 'Having explained all this we must describe the nature of flesh, bone, and the other homogeneous bodies severally', says Aristotle towards the end of the work.[102] This is where he makes the transition from qualities, elements and similar parts to function and final causality. He is now looking for 'an end' or function and uses another image that came naturally to him: a dead man is a man in name only, for while being composed of the same matter as a living man, he does not have those living actions by which we recognise a man. It is the same with statues of flautists: the stone flutes are not flutes because they cannot produce the sound that flutes are *for*. We meet both images again in the books on animals, and it seems to be at this point, towards the end of the *Meteorologica*, in the entire programme, that Aristotle wanted to distance himself from the physical and material causality of the pre-Socratics and fully articulate his new doctrine, the final cause. So now he ends up the work strongly, but very tersely, with a programmatic statement: the similar parts are basically characterised by action and passion, qualities both elementary and physical. But none of the things forming these, he says, would explain a box or a bowl. The box and bowl are artificial, but the same applies to nature. He is looking ahead to explaining the similar parts of plants and animals and, finally, the dissimilar parts and the organic bodies of animals and man.

(iii) The natural history of the soul

If we were to draw a diagram in which cross-references between the *libri naturales* were lines, from title to title, the result would be a little like a map of the London Underground. There are two main routes, the first beginning with the *Physics* and passing through the works on heaven and earth, generation and corruption to the *Meteorologica*, where we pass into the realm of the organic. Thereafter the main line passes through the works on the parts, causes, motion and generation of animals. As observed above, this does not represent a sequence of composition or the development of Aristotle's thought, but the order of teaching in a cycle in which the texts were continuously brought up to date.[103]

The second route begins with Aristotle's work on the soul, *De Anima*. There are few cross-references between this work and the early physical works and it is difficult to tell if this 'route' ran in parallel with the first or was somehow silently accommodated within it. *De Anima* leads directly to a text on the senses and things sensed, *De Sensu et Sensato*. This is a station with abundant connections to the later animal books and to the group of treatises that describe the special actions of the soul, like memory and sleep, and aspects of life, of which soul was the principle, like respiration, youth, old age and death. Aristotle seems to have taught about plants somewhere between the topic of youth and age and the last of the animal books, that on generation. The destination of both routes, by now perhaps combined, was a special study of man, and Aristotle sometimes says that the whole programme naturally led to a study of medicine.[104] It seems unlikely that such a task was undertaken at the Lyceum.

We cannot afford to spend too much space in a work on ancient natural history to Aristotle's work on the soul. It is certainly true that the soul was for him 'the principle of animal life', but this is much what we are looking at in studying the natures-of-animals in the later animal books (see below). Despite this the soul, very generally considered in Greek life as the cause of human understanding and even as the vehicle of immortality, was a central topic in Greek philosophy and as Aristotle said, knowledge of it was highly sought after on account of its nobility.[105] He both praised the nobility of the knowledge and warned against the difficulty of procuring it in a passage which is a direct counterweight to a famous passage (we shall also meet it below) in which he praises the *certainty* of knowledge derived from direct observation of animals, despite the apparent lack of charm of such knowledge.

This means that Aristotle in considering the soul cannot employ the favoured technique of listing empirical observations, as he did in the *historiae* of political constitutions, of animals or of the winners of the games. He is bound to give a great deal of largely dialectical examination to the views of his predecessors and also to take from them much of what seemed self-evident. He spends – even for Aristotle – an unusually large amount of space on refuting the opinions of earlier philosophers, but shares a great deal with them too. Thus the soul is the source of sensation and motion: Aristotle agrees that this is axiomatic,[106] although he disagrees with the atomists' account of the soul as consisting of atoms. In fact all of the first book of the work[107] is taken up with refuting (and in fact borrowing from) the old philosophers.[108]

This leaves Aristotle (he says) able to make a fresh start. It is no surprise to us now that the fresh start is another opportunity to display the sophistication of his method over the materialist explanations of his predecessors, or that his principles are form, matter, actuality, potentiality, substance, natural bodies, living bodies, and the soul as the form of a body having life potentially, 'the first grade of actuality of a natural body having life potentially in it'.[109] Apart from these sophistications of technique, Aristotle says[110] that his predecessors considered the human soul only, and thus (by implication) concentrated their attention on perception and reason. But Aristotle thought that all living things had a soul of one sort or another, and while plants simply grew, nourished and generated themselves, animals additionally perceived, remembered and moved, and man reasoned. It seemed then that reason was only one part of the soul and that in all of its other actions the soul required a material body. This, says Aristotle,[111] is why the study of the soul belongs to the study of *physis*, 'nature'. So Aristotle is drawing into his realm what his predecessors had thought belonged to some other field of study.

Aristotle further explains that a traditional natural philosopher would discuss, let us say, 'anger' in some such terms as the boiling of blood round the heart, while it would be the dialectician who would call anger some affection of the soul such as the need to return pain for pain received. So (Aristotle continues) traditional natural philosophy deals with the material conditions and dialectic with the 'formulable essence'. The formulable essence of, say, a house might be something like 'a protection against the weather' while its material conditions are its bricks and mortar. Aristotle, seeing himself as the new and genuine natural philosopher, wants to combine matter, form and particularly the formulable essence or purpose of the dialecticians in order to rise above the materialism of his predecessors, bring soul into the realm of physical studies and display the sophistication of his end-directed natural philosophy.[112]

We shall see in looking at his works on animals that Aristotle deals extensively with the physical attributes that he has in this work attributed to soul. These are primarily generation, by which the nature of the animal perpetuates the species, of which the individuals are perishable; nutrition, by which the individual maintains itself in order to do this; and locomotion, which makes nutrition possible. We shall look at these as aspects of the nature of the animal, and need here to report Aristotle's more abstract thinking on these topics.

We should first however give just a little more attention to Aristotle's reasons for making the study of soul a physical study. He makes a distinction between soul and mind, for the latter is an independent substance implanted within the soul and incapable of being destroyed. This corresponds to the traditional Greek *psyche* that was the personality of the individual and which in some manner preserved his identity in the afterlife. It was, for Aristotle as for his predecessors, a human thing and not part of the soul of animals. Indeed mind in this sense was distinctly not a physical thing: loss of its faculties in age or drunkenness was a failure of the body, not the mind. Emotions like loving and hating are not actions of the mind, but of that which has mind. For Aristotle it is the man, not the soul, that is angry: it is his blood that boils.[113] It is the same with reason, for like the emotions it may begin from or end in the soul, but is not an affection of it.

Arguing thus Aristotle is able to say that the soul does not move (except indirectly, as sailors are moved in their ship). But it may move other things, most notably the body: it is an Unmoved Mover,[114] one of the fundamental Aristotelian physical principles. Unmoved, the soul or mind is not spatially extended[115] and its unity is 'serial', its parts being thoughts. But its unity and continuity do not make it circular, despite the Platonists who found it appropriate that circles, and therefore the soul, are perfect and eternal. Very characteristically Aristotle wants the soul, or at least its parts, thoughts, to be *process*, not perfection. Thinking is *for* something, rather than being a constant action of a circular soul. Because it is for something, it has a conclusion when the process has finished, like speech. Speech expresses the results of thought and is a matter of making definitions or demonstrations, which are more like coming to an end than going on for ever in circles. So as ever with Aristotle all changes are processes directed towards an end or purpose. Even with thinking and speaking it is the end that determines the steps necessary for its completion. Likewise when the soul moves the body it does by intention or thought of the end.[116] What is important when an animal moves is the Good or Evil it can pursue or avoid, perceived by the senses and desired by the appetite as parts of the soul.[117] It followed for Aristotle that those who, like Democritus and Plato, give material accounts of how the soul moves the body are thinking about the process from the wrong end, beginning in a motion initiated by the soul and imparted to matter.[118]

ARISTOTLE'S *TREATISE ON ANATOMY*

Aristotle's well-known defence of direct observation of animals because it produced knowledge worthy of a philosopher in its certainty[119] was not the remark of an armchair philosopher. Dissection is often mentioned in the animal books. Sometimes it may be simply a report of dissections carried out elsewhere, and some of the references may be to dissections carried out by Aristotle's colleagues. But at other times it is clear that Aristotle had done the dissection himself. Indeed, he often refers to a treatise he had written 'on anatomy' (the English version of the Greek word for 'dissection').[120]

The work itself has been lost,[121] but there are several interesting points to be gathered from Aristotle's references to it. The first is that the picture we have of Aristotle as an empirical investigator – a natural historian – is added to by the report we have here of real procedures of dissection. The story of the stench from the opened corpse of a lion[122] is not a very philosophical anecdote (other than adding to the picture of the general smelliness of lions when alive) but it has the ring of reality. Once dissected, the internal organs of lions are seen to be like those of a dog (but Aristotle reports less than realistically that the lion's neck has a single bone).[123] Aristotle's advice on procedure also sounds realistic. To investigate the blood vessels, he advises, it is best to allow the animals to be investigated to starve until they are emaciated, and then strangle them suddenly.[124] This seems to be Aristotle's answer to the problem that normally in the dead animal, no doubt killed by cutting its throat, the vessels collapsed as the blood left them. In Aristotle's opinion this was why earlier investigators had given erroneous accounts of the vessels and the heart.[125] But his own technique seems to have been little better, for there follows at once Aristotle's notorious description of the three (rather than four) cavities of the heart and his very puzzling account of the great vessels, both of which have greatly exercised the commentators.[126] Evidence that Aristotle experienced the difficulties of dissection appears in his accounts of how the heart's position may shift during dissection, and of how to demonstrate the uterus of birds by inflation.[127] Apparently his only knowledge of human anatomy was of an aborted foetus of forty days, contained in its membrane.[128]

As an empirical observer, Aristotle was not content to dissect animals, and he also vivisected them. Discussing how during their development, animals, unlike plants, acquire the power to sleep, he observes that embryos still in the uterus can wake up during the procedures of vivisection.[129] He also remarks that chameleons continue to breathe and their hearts to beat while they are being cut up; and that it is a characteristic of insects as a group that they continue to live when cut into two.[130] It also amounted to vivisection when Aristotle opened a fertilised hen's egg to see the minute red spot of the heart pulsating. He also opened a series of developing eggs to watch the development of the parts (particularly the eyes, from which he peeled the membranes). When he cut open a ten-day chick and the foetus of the viviparous dogfish to see the disappearance of the yolk and membranes, it is perhaps unnecessary to suppose that he killed the animals first. [131]

The role of the senses in the empirical generation of knowledge for Aristotle is reflected in another feature of this lost work on dissection. It was illustrated. Aristotle often refers to his drawings when discussing the shape of a part. The reader of the *Historia*

Animalium – itself illustrated – is referred to the diagrams in the *Treatise on Dissections* for the shape of the uterus of the higher animals, fish and birds.[132] The same can be said of the diagrams of the genital organs of both sexes in fish and the viviparous animals, and of the egg and eyes of the sepia.[133] In his text Aristotle used capital letters to refer to capitals marked on the diagram,[134] and no doubt sought to express in drawings a complexity of shape that words could not adequately describe. More important, a visual comparison between the same organ in different animals could readily be made from drawings. This was very much part of Aristotle's enterprise. The *differentiae* of the gut in different animals, says Aristotle,[135] are to be found in the *Treatise on Dissections* and the *Historia Animalium*: both works were part of Aristotle's providing differences and correlations for which the causes were to be exposed in the *De Partibus Animalium*.

Although empirical in technique, Aristotle's dissections, vivisections and drawings were not undirected by reason. We can recall that his general interest in natural things was to enquire into the 'nature' of each. In animals it was nature as an internal principle of motion that provided for the stages of development towards the adult. The adult was the final cause of development and one of the Necessities of the adult in maintaining its life was nourishment. It was consideration of how the nature-of-the-animal achieved its ends that directed Aristotle's attention to the organs of nourishment and generation. This is why these two kinds of organs figure so largely in the *Treatise on Dissections*, where they could be compared so readily, especially in visual form. Because Aristotle has this theoretical reason for choosing what he looks for with empirical methods, what he finds is easily massaged into providing the correlations that will later be explained causally. Correlations between teeth (as part of the digestive system), horns (composed of the same matter) and the presence of cotyledons in the uterus were given in the text on anatomy as in the *Historia Animalium*.[136] Likewise significant *differentiae* of the sexual parts of lobsters were given in both texts.[137] Both texts also dealt with the absorption of food by the mesenteric vessels.[138]

So not only did reason direct what Aristotle looked for empirically, but his reasoning could be supported by apparently empirical observation. Aristotle believed that the heart was the functional centre of the body. It was, he said, midway between the incoming food and the outgoing waste. It was intimately associated with blood, the nourishment of the body. It was the first organ to be seen – by dissection[139] – in the developing embryo. It was the seat of all the faculties of the soul that could be located. All this could be backed up by empirical investigation. Aristotle dissected animals[140] and drew pictures of the heart and vessels[141] in the treatise on dissections to show that all blood vessels arise *from* the heart: to have the heart *supplied* by an incoming vessel[142] would have implied that it needed something that could only be made elsewhere in the body. What was in Aristotle's mind was functional direction – substances flowing from the heart to the bodily parts, particularly blood to nourish the growing embryo.[143] But direction cannot be shown in a static drawing of morphology – it belongs to interpretation: veins to not 'arise' or 'originate' or *go* anywhere unless one has function in mind.

THE HISTORY OF ANIMALS

(i) *Differentiae*

The text known for centuries in the later West as the *Historia Animalium* is presented, like the related text on dissections, as a collection of 'histories' drawn from animals. Animals for Aristotle were part of a hierarchy of existence within the world and existed in a scale of perfection with man at the top. The scale was not a continuum and Aristotle did not feel the need to argue that all possible animal types existed. As categories of things, animals were the expressions of their natures and Aristotle wanted to know how those natures were expressed. He presents the Lyceum's work on this problem as occurring in two stages – the apparently empirical collection of facts in the *Historia Animalium* and the subsequent causal analysis in the *De Partibus Animalium*. His principles of enquiry led on naturally to the two works on the generation and the motion of animals as investigations into the ways in which the nature-of-animals expressed itself.

But as in the case of the work on dissections, Aristotle's scheme of things meant in practice that what he was looking for, in the collection of observables that were *historiae,* was material to which he had already given some thought. It consists of selected topics that Aristotle knew were of importance for the arguments in the *Parts of Animals*. The *History of Animals* is not chronologically prior to the *Parts of Animals* and probably its compilation ran in parallel with that of the *Parts of Animals,* which continued to determine the selection of topics. Certainly the *History of Animals* is unfinished and in places badly edited. Aristotle and probably his colleagues as well continued to add to it without, in some cases, making sure they were not repeating themselves. We twice read that the voice of the cow is deeper than that of the bull[144] and the presence of the pinna guard in the crustacean pinna is noted in the same way twice.[145] There are two remarks to the effect that hair, when cut, grows up from the bottom, not from the point of cutting.[146] The whole work is a collection of fragments and Aristotle does not seem to have cast a final eye over it. D'Arcy Thompson calls it a Natural History, and detects the presence of at least one alien hand.[147] It does indeed seem like a collaborative effort, and no doubt what happened was that Aristotle set up the ground plan in terms of the topics mentioned above that were to illumine the natures of the animals. Perhaps he even drew up a list of questions to be asked by those going about to discover and record the *historiae.* The beginning of Book 5 looks like a rote of questions that could have been such a questionnaire. Aristotle and his colleagues got their information from sooth-sayers,[148] fishermen,[149] bee-keepers[150] and travellers who had seen exotic animals like the elephant and camel;[151] Aristotle often discusses these two animals together, either because they were thought of as the two largest animals or because information about them came from the same source (Plate 3).

Aristotle's technique was to look for *differentiae* between animals and their parts that would help him explain how their natures nourished, reproduced and moved. As we have seen, these were the principal activities by which the nature of the animal fulfilled itself and the reason why Aristotle gave so much attention to the organs of generation and nutrition,[152] but in the *Historia Animalium* Aristotle studiously refuses to draw inferences from the collection of observations. The natural method of procedure, he says,[153] is to arrive at the 'subjects and premises' of the argument later (that is, in the *De Partibus Animalium).* Thus the presence or absence of red blood is given prominence as a *differentia* between animals[154] without a discussion about blood as the nourishment of the body. Aristotle often makes generalisations among his observed particulars, but does not in this work draw inferences about causes. Thus he observes of animals with blood that all that fly have feathers or leathern wings.[155] Another is that non-winged quadrupeds all have blood; animals without blood, if they have feet, have many.

44

Plate 3 Red-figure perfume bottle showing a camel. The rider is in eastern dress: natural-history *historiae* came from the edge of the Greek world as known by the potter who made the bottle in Athens about 410–400 BC. (British Museum.)

(ii) Relationships between the natures

Since Aristotle's concern was with the natures of animals and how they expressed themselves, we are tempted to ask how those natures interacted. Since Aristotle did not believe in a transcendent 'nature' controlling the totality of an 'animal kingdom', what ensured, for example, that one species did not destroy another? Even to ask the question is to acknowledge that it is difficult to discard the world view of the nineteenth-century natural historian, for whom the balance between creatures was either a major plank of a natural theology in which God's providence allotted each creature its food; or was the result of the survival of the fittest, the very mechanism of evolution. To that extent it is rather an unhistorical question to ask, but there are places where Aristotle considered how the natures of animals interacted, and if he did not treat the question with the same urgency as later natural historians did, yet his treatment extends our knowledge of his view of the natures of animals.

The perfect adult form of the animal was the realised actuality of its nature, the definition on which discussion of the animal was based. It was the expression of its soul. Now, the adult animal not only had to feed itself (in order to reproduce its kind) but had a preference for this or that kind of food and for particular habits and habitats. These were preferences of its soul, and the material form of its body was what its nature had given it to satisfy these preferences. Some natures of animal preferred other animals as food and their bodies were accordingly fitted out with serrated teeth, claws and other equipment. The souls of such animals were aggressive, and their bodies correspondingly powerful. It was appropriate for Aristotle to believe that the souls of animals that served as prey were timorous. He does not say they were timorous *because* they were hunted, only that their bodies were capable of speed because their souls were timorous. So the souls of hunter and hunted interact through the actions of their bodies, but there is no external governing principle that is involved with this relationship.

In some cases, according to Aristotle, animals show specific likes and dislikes for each other and therefore interacted in a directed way. Such likes and dislikes became known from their Greek terms as sympathies and antipathies and were a much bigger part of later natural histories than they were of Aristotle's. In Aristotle these relationships were mostly concerned with food. That eagles and snakes antipathise because eagles feed on snakes[156] is a simple example. Likewise the ichneumon antipathises with its prey, the venom-spider. Owls are said to be antipathetic to wrens because the latter eats the former's eggs. Owls also are the enemy of crows, because the owl, able to see at night, steals the crows' eggs, but dim-sighted in daylight, cannot prevent the crow from stealing hers. Aristotle has a long list of antipathising creatures, almost all of whom are hunter and hunted or who compete for food. These things determine sympathies as well as antipathies, for example, the raven and the fox sympathise because they have a mutual enemy, the merlin.[157] Some sympathise simply because they have similar habits, as the snake and the fox, both of whom burrow underground. But overall Aristotle thinks that food is the main cause of sympathies and antipathies, and that if there were enough available, antipathies would disappear, so that wild animals would be tame to man and to each other.[158] Support for this argument is drawn from the tame crocodiles who take their abundant food from the hands of the Egyptian priests, and from the friendship between the crocodile and the trochilus, which feeds by cleaning the crocodile's teeth.[159]

In describing such sympathies and antipathies, Aristotle is clearly drawing on a range of sources. Such stories may have been part of folklore, and the crocodile and its trochilus no doubt came from Herodotus. Aesop had already made use of such things for his fables.[160] Soothsayers[161] watched the behaviour of animals, especially those that congregated or kept themselves apart, and had special names for them. It is likely that they had a formal list of observables for purposes of augury.[162] Aristotle's programme is then to give natural causes for the observed events, based on the important feature of the expressed nature of the animal, feeding. These antipathies also resulted in other kinds of behaviour that involved the interaction between the various natures. Aristotle noted the mobbing of the owl by small birds, which 'buffet him, and pull out his feathers', apparently from the same antipathy as shown by wrens. Sometimes it is the mode of life of the animal rather than food that makes animal enemies. An example is the antipathy between the ass and the lizard, which has a habit of getting into the ass's nostril.[163] Generation is also an important aspect of the behaviour of the animal's nature, and this too determines some form of interaction. Some fish school together at the spawning season, says Aristotle[164] and even hostile species will sometimes form a shoal. The need to generate young of course determines the interaction of male and female, even when the event is not pleasurable: Aristotle says the female heron cries tears of blood and screams during copulation and suffers pain in laying her eggs.[165]

An important aspect of the natures of animals is their basic character. Aristotle observes[166] that just as the physical organs of animals have their similarities and differences, so do their souls. Some are gentle, others fierce. Some are brave, cowardly, cunning, sagacious, or stupid. These are the same characteristics that man possesses, but animals have them to a lesser degree, and often only one of them. This is consistent with Aristotle's general position that apart from his ability to reason, man's soul is of the same kind as that of the animals. He is explaining in his own philosophical terms what must often have been in the society of his time a simple anthropomorphic projection of human features to animals. These predispositions of animal souls are another reason why the animals sometimes interact. Thus while sheep are said[167] to be stupid, wandering off aimlessly and getting lost, especially when the weather is bad, it is more general that animals of the same species help each other. Thus cattle generally move in herds to avoid the dangers of solitude.[168] Mares will adopt and nourish the colt of a dead mother, and in general herding animals protect their young in the inside of the herd. But again it is not some 'law' of an external nature that makes animals of a species co-operate for the good of the species. It is just that these individual animals are defined as those

Plate 4 The ichneumon. The ichneumon is generally identified with the modern mongoose, as in this model made in about 500 BC in Naucratis, Egypt (with Greek influence). (British Museum.) But in the natural-history literature of the ancient world the ichneumon is more often the traditional enemy of the crocodile, whose viscera it devours, rather than of the snake, the mongoose's enemy. Sometimes it was held to fight the *draco*, 'dragon', which could relate both to snakes and crocodiles. See also Chapter 6 below.

who help others of the species, and in so doing their natures are fulfilling their potential.

Finally, another cause of the natures of animals interacting is intelligence. Aristotle has no hesitation about attributing intelligence to some animals, although of course he would not equate it with the divine and rational part of the human soul. The hind, 'pre-eminently intelligent'[169] bears its young near a public road, where other wild animals, afraid of man, will not approach. The ichneumon (Plate 4) will not attack a snake until it has summoned others of its kind and they have all covered themselves with mud as a protection.[170] Most generally Aristotle's examples of animal intelligence involve wise use of natural medicines. Stags bitten by the venom-spider cure themselves by eating crabs; Cretan goats attacked with arrows seek out dittany, which makes the arrows drop out; tortoises seek marjoram to help their digestion after eating snakes; the weasel eats wild rue before joining battle with a snake, for the snake cannot stand the smell.[171] There are many more examples, mostly country lore and travellers' tales, collected because they are interesting and perhaps because they might illustrate a point in the Lyceum's philosophy of nature. But Aristotle heaps them up and does not make much use of them. The story of the man in Byzantium who made a huge reputation for weather-forecasting by watching his hedgehog is an interesting enough *historia*[172] as is the assertion that the hoopoe builds its nest out of human excrement,[173] but neither in fact add very much to a philosophical appreciation of the intelligence of animals. Nevertheless, Aristotle discusses the 'personalities' of animals, which underlies this whole discussion, in language that recalls that of the *Eudemian Ethics*, where we are told about the essential and accidental attributes of mind.[174]

THE PROBLEM OF THE SHARK

It has now been stressed that 'nature' for Aristotle was the nature of the animal; when it did 'nothing in vain' it did it for the benefit of the animal. We have looked at how different natures of different animals interacted in the absence of a transcendent 'Mother Nature'. Only in one case does Aristotle appear to accept that there is an external guiding principle that governs the relationship between animals.

As a general rule the larger fishes catch the smaller ones in their mouths by swimming straight at them in the ordinary position;

but the selachians, the dolphin, and all the cetacea must turn over on their backs, as their mouths are placed down below; this allows a fair chance of escape to the smaller fishes, and, indeed, if it were not so, there would be very few of the little fishes left, for the speed and voracity of the dolphin is something marvellous.[175]

So here apparently the nature of the predator is doing something not advantageous for it. Here is a circumstance imposed upon an animal for the benefit of others. It would be a good example to use to illustrate the providence of an external nature or creator, and was used in such a way down to immediately pre-Darwinian biology. Certainly there are problems with the passage, for the mouth is not so placed in the dolphin (Plate 5) and cetacea, and it has been attacked on these grounds by some of the commentators. Had Aristotle never seen a dolphin? Did he really believe their mouths were placed thus? Perhaps it is an interpolation; but nevertheless it is repeated in the *Parts of Animals*. More puzzling than the dolphin's mouth is the action of 'nature': in the *Parts of Animals* it is again said that nature in this way allowed the small animals a chance of escape. It is also said there that by this device nature prevented the predator from satisfying its gluttony. This may be in the interest of the 'dolphin' and sharks and so look like the nature-of-the-animal doing its best for the animal, but it also implies that the soul or nature of the animal was at root so imperfect that corrective steps were needed as it came

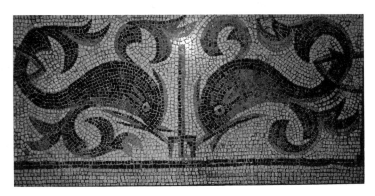

Plate 5 Dolphins in a Roman mosaic (in the British Museum). Dolphins were also a common pattern on tableware, including some from Greece, and so were presumably well known. These Roman examples have well-marked mouths which do not follow Aristotle's odd description.

to expression in the adult. The whole is quite at odds with Aristotle's general position, and must be the only time that the danger of extinction – of the small fish – is mentioned. D'Arcy Thompson did not know of any other place where Aristotle says that a structure of an animal is intended for the benefit of animals other than itself. Rather than face the 'horrendous consequences of overall finality' Balme thinks Aristotle is simply politely correcting a popular but mistaken teleology.[176] There is a good possibility that the passage in question is not from Aristotle's hand. We have already seen that the *History of Animals* is a collection, badly edited and repetitious, with material from a wide range of sources. It was obviously impossible for Aristotle himself to have seen all the phenomena that are reported here and the question must be how far he supervised the assembling of the second-hand facts. Very unusually among Aristotle's works the *History of Animals* does not make an argument, apart from some generalisations, and deliberately avoids doing so, in order to leave them for the *Parts of Animals*. This is why, again unusually, Aristotle does not mention his predecessors, for the destruction of their arguments is usually the first stage in the construction of his own. Nor does Aristotle in the *History of Animals* say much about the 'earlier' or 'later' books in the whole undertaking, which makes it look as though, like the *Dissections*, it was a collection of material for research rather than an argued part of a philosophy of nature. The passage about dolphins and sharks looks very much as though it was inserted into the collection by someone else, as many other items must have been, and that it passed, as such items were intended to pass, into the arguments of the *Parts of Animals*. It is more difficult to argue that it escaped Aristotle's eye there, where he *was* making an argument. Maybe it happened after Aristotle's death; certainly it reads like a later fragment from someone who believed in some form of external providence.

VARIATION

Although the nature of an animal is generally stable in Aristotle's perception of it, there are occasions where it can vary. It varies partly because the 'material nature' organised by the soul, like all matter, can introduce defects into the way the 'formal nature' (the soul) expresses itself. We shall see, when dealing with the generation of animals, that it was routine for Aristotle to see the female as defective from the male norm in this kind of way, and monstrous animals had even greater defects of the same kind. In general female animals were thought by Aristotle to be less hot, less concoctive and less perfect: their natures reached a lower level of expression than that of the male.

The natures of some animals included the ability to change their environments by migration to avoid extremes of temperature. Of the birds Aristotle notes the crane for the distance it migrates, almost across the world, from the steppes of Scythia to the marsh-land south of Egypt, where it was thought that the Nile rose. Here, it was believed – and Aristotle credited the story – they fought with the pigmies, a race of men who lived in caves and kept tiny horses.[177] Both topics were traditional in Greek literature, and we met above Aristophanes' whimsical account of the cranes building the founda-tions of the city in the sky with far-fetched stones. Aristotle knew of some fish that migrated and says the same thing about them – that they seek cool in the deep sea and warmth in the shallows – twice in different places.[178] This again looks like poor editing of a compilation.

Animals also vary according to the locality in which they are found. Sometimes they are simply not to be found at all, even in localities close to others where they thrive. In Cephalenia there is a river, reports Aristotle, on only one side of which are found cicadas. In Pordoselene weasels are found only on one side of a road.[179] Or the same animals may vary in form according to their location. Syrian sheep have a tail a cubit in width, reports Aristotle,[180] and the ears of some of the goats reach the ground. Many Egyptian animals were thought to be bigger than their Greek counterparts, and Aristotle attributes it to the quantity of food available. He is talking of domestic animals, for example the cow and the sheep, and so perhaps is making a reflection on farming practices. But the wild animals of Egypt – wolf, hare, fox, raven and hawk – were thought to be smaller because of the comparative lack of prey. The nature of the animal also responded to climate, so that animals in hot countries are reported to be bigger. The Arabian lizard was said to be a cubit in length and the mouse there grew much bigger than the Greek mouse, especially in the rear legs.[181] In general, says Aristotle, animals are at the wildest in Asia, boldest in Europe and most diverse in Libya; even in the same country, mountain animals are fiercer than those living in the valleys. The modern natural historian can hardly help wondering whether only animals with fierce natures survived in the mountains or whether the mountains made their natures fierce; but it is not a question for Aristotle and he concludes by advising the reader how variation in animals makes them particularly good to eat at certain seasons (normally the breeding season).

THE PARTS OF ANIMALS

In the Lyceum programme, the *Parts of Animals* follows from the *History of Animals* and the book on dissections because Aristotle is now handling the matter of these works in a philosophical way. This is clear from the opening of the *Parts of Animals*, where Aristotle's words are weightier than those with which he discusses the similar and dissimilar parts at the beginning of the *History of Animals*. In the *Parts of Animals* Aristotle starts with a reflection on education which might well represent his own entire undertaking as a teacher to the Athenian upper classes, and it moves to the nature-of-the-thing as the goal of this undertaking.

He begins by distinguishing detailed expert knowledge of a subject from 'a kind of educational acquaintance with it'. The former is the mode of exposition which may be adopted by the expert and which can be judged by the educated man independently of the truth of the contained facts. 'To be educated is in fact to be able to do this', says Aristotle.[182] His teaching was directed to the 'universal education' which he says we see in a man who is able to judge in this way. That is, the educated man was not a specialist, achieving great proficiency in one field but ignoring others, and he was certainly not a man who professed productive knowledge, like a doctor or a carpenter. He was in contrast a man who could distinguish, over the whole range of knowledge, an inappropriate from an appropriate form of exposition. Again we are reminded that a 'liberal' education of this kind not only served as a feature – by marking him off from those with productive knowledge – of the free man who took part in the government of the city-state, but that it was a suitable education for those who needed to be able to assess one argument against another in the political arena and act in what we would now call a management role over those with different kinds of knowledge and skills.

It is immediately clear that what Aristotle means by an educated approach to animals is how to discuss them: it is clearly inappropriate to describe them, kind by kind, when natural groups of animals have many features in common, each of which would be unnecessarily repeated as each kind was described. His examples of such things are sleep, respiration, growth, decay and death, shared by horse, man and dog and indeed all animals. Likewise swimming, walking and flying, although distinct, yet are all forms of locomotion, a topic that can be discussed separately as applicable to all animals. In his general scheme of education, this is what Aristotle did, in the treatises on these topics from sleeping to animal locomotion. His words here[183] make it clear that he was not yet prepared to compose such works: they came after the completion of the *Parts of Animals.*

Aristotle was conscious of the novelty of his position here, and sees himself[184] as taking up and improving the study of natural things that had been dropped, when finally showing promise at the time of Socrates, in favour of a study of politics. He claims that no one had previously discussed these issues of procedure. It is clear that Aristotle is directing this procedure first towards 'the phenomena presented by animals' (that is, in the *Historia Animalium*) and then towards causes. The only model he gives for this is the method of the astronomers, who first observe and then make mathematical demonstrations of causes. Aristotle at once launches into a personal statement of the proper procedure to be followed in investigating animals. It is personal because it was novel and because it involved the principle that Aristotle elevated to a dominant position in his thinking, the final cause. It is illustrated by analogies that tell us a great deal about Aristotle's thinking and which we have met in part before: they will bear repeating. Thus he compares the actions of 'nature' with those of the builder, who begins with the notion of a house. This notion is 'final' in the sense that its ultimate realisation is the guide for every action taken by the builder. 'Nature' acts in the same way in giving motion to the materials that constitute the growing and complete adult animal. These are *necessary* stages in the completion of the house and animal and Aristotle again emphasises the novelty of his position, in that his predecessors did not recognise the different kinds of necessity. Broadly Aristotle criticises them for relying solely on material necessity, that is, in arguing that the appearance of things depended only on the characteristics of the matter out of which they were made. In arguing against them Aristotle distinguishes first absolute necessity, that of the motion of the heavenly bodies. These are 'necessary' in the sense that they always have moved and always will. Aristotle's 'hypothetical necessity' is the series of steps that have to be taken to reach the final cause, the house or the animal. Aristotle also uses the image of the house under construction, in order to show what hypothetical necessity is, in Book 2 of the *Physics*, and it may be that he uses it again here because now, with complex organisms as the subject matter, the 'original undertaking' of the Lyceum programme, with the final cause, could be demonstrated fully.[185]

We have to remind ourselves about what Aristotle means here. It is not the case that given the existence of these steps, whether they be matter or motions, the animal necessarily appears; the necessity is that they have to be undertaken *in order* that the animal has its final and best form. He attacks the materialism of his predecessors in a number of ways. First he asserts that the method of treatment of questions that are concerned with 'nature' is to look at what *is to be*: the final and best form of the animal (like the house to the builder or health to the doctor). Purely intellectual questions in contrast are concerned with what *is*.[186] What is to be does not depend upon some eternal and necessary motion that of necessity produces it, for absolute necessity lies only in the circular motions of the heavenly bodies. Earthly, material motions are not circular and do not have this kind of necessity but have the hypothetical kind instead. Ultimately, in opposition to the materialism of his predecessors, Aristotle does not treat 'matter' as the universal stuff of things (which later ages came to call *materia prima*) but as matter of this or that kind of thing, something which only became recognisable as matter as it took on the attributes of the 'nature' that formed it in the steps necessary for the production of the natural object.

All of this is used by Aristotle to explain how he is to proceed in describing and accounting for animals. He is to begin with the final form of the animals, their appearances as gathered in the *Historia Animalium*. As one may see from a finished house what the necessary steps in its construction were, so an investigation into animals reveals, from the nature of the animal, what were the antecedents necessary for its final features. This scheme enables Aristotle to avoid what he saw as the errors of earlier nature-philosophers. He can avoid chance as a kind of causation, used for example by Empedocles, who claimed that the vertebrae were formed by the breaking of the spine in the foetus's contorted position in the uterus.[187] He can avoid the materialism that he credits to Democritus: that everything consists of the four elements, which have irreducible properties, so that fire is always hot and light, earth cold and heavy. In such a materialist scheme it is the action of water, for example, which creates the stomach in the foetus[188] and air that forms the nostrils: matter is both the efficient cause of the body and its substance.

We here return briefly to Aristotle's 'nature'. We have seen that Aristotle's *physis* was the nature-of-a-thing. The natures of animals was that they were alive, that they perceived, moved, nourished themselves and generated their kind. These are the actions of life, at least of animal life, and the nature-of-the-animal is for Aristotle its soul. He acknowledges that there was a sense in which animals had a material nature, but asserted that it was the soul that enabled the matter to participate in the nature of the animal, not the other way round. His enquiry is therefore centred on the soul as the essence of animality. The actions of animals are therefore for Aristotle actions of their souls. He is now in a position to return to those characteristics that animals have in common and which ought to be discussed in general and not repeated when different animals are described: what they have in common most of all is that they are actions of the soul. Aristotle gives an example, respiration. To give an account of this action of the soul, we first enquire what it is *for*, its final cause. We then look at the stages by which this is achieved, and the kinds of necessity involved in those stages.

THE KINDS OF ANIMALS

A traditional topic in Aristotelian scholarship is how Aristotle 'classified' the animals he discusses. It has been of interest to historians because it has been a major topic in natural history or biology both before and after Darwin: before, because it displayed how God had ordered His Creation, and after, because relationship of form indicated relationship in descent. It has been difficult for historians to shake off this modern question. But when we recall that for Aristotle each animal kind was an expression of its immanent nature, it is clear that relationships between different kinds of animals were less significant than for later historians or natural historians. Indeed, Aristotle is concerned with 'classification' mainly as a means of procedure of *exposition*, so that common characteristics can be dealt with efficiently, in a once-for-all discussion. Aristotle is interested in features animals have in common and the categories into which animals might be put as a logical exercise that makes a clear discussion possible, rather than as a representation of biological reality.[189]

This is why he discusses and rejects the method of subdividing animal life by dichotomy, in which groups were formed by dividing larger groups into two on the basis of possessing certain common characteristics. Thus in dichotomous tables which Aristotle read, animals with feet formed a 'footed' class, which was divided to form a smaller class of 'two-footed', itself divided (apparently)[190] to produce a class of 'cloven-footed'. Aristotle complains that the last term is all-expressive on its own and that to present the whole dichotomous series is to make the higher classes an unnecessary repetition (as in the case of his discussion of procedure at the opening of the *Parts of Animals*).

Another objection that Aristotle had to the method of dichotomy was that it broke up natural groups like birds, some of which ended up grouped with fish because they swam.[191] This looks eminently sensible to a modern biologist, but again we have to remember that for Aristotle a 'natural' group like birds was simply a number of animal kinds whose natures used similar ways of expressing themselves. To talk of them as a group was convenient for clear discussion. The point of the dichotomous method also seems in this way to have been to arrange animals in a logically clear way so that each ultimate kind fitted into a category and the categories into categories of the all-embracing term 'animal'. That both forms of 'classification' were primarily logical instruments is also shown by Aristotle's further criticisms of dichotomy. This was that such schemes used *privation* as a category, for example by dividing animals into feathered and non-feathered, or footed and non-footed. But Aristotle says there can be no further subdivision of a category with a negative characteristic: 'non-feathered' is as far as you can go in terms of the character (feathers) that define the group. One had either to bring in fresh terms that did not exist in the categories higher in the hierarchy (which spoiled the logic)[192] or admit that the method could not descend to individual kinds of animals (which was its purpose).

So for Aristotle the principal objection to the dichotomists was that they used a single *differentia* to subdivide their categories. He sees that such a *differentia* as 'wild' or 'tame', or 'flying' or 'walking' would divide his 'natural' groups, because, for example, some ants fly and others do not, and in India dogs may be tame or wild. His answer is that 'natural' groups are those seen as such instinctively by men, like Fish or Birds. There is logic even in the instinct however, for Aristotle claims that this judging by means of the many *differentiae* characteristic of natural groups is superior to that by the single *differentia* of the dichotomies. Moreover, when the dichotomies ultimately descended to single kinds of animals, they too were defined by a single *differentia;* but for Aristotle the essence of a kind of animal could not be expresssed in a such a limited way. The defining characteristics of a group had to belong to and express its essence. Ultimately a natural group of kinds for Aristotle is where the kinds differ only in the proportions of their homologous parts, such as the beaks, feathers and so on of the birds. Resemblances between animals of different groups were in contrast analogies rather than homologies, like the spines of fish and the bones of man.

In short the physical reality of animal life for Aristotle was the way in which the nature of the animal achieved its final cause, the best life for the adult animal. To consider groupings of individual animals into kinds of greater or lesser inclusiveness was to make possible a detailed discussion about the ways in which the nature-of-the-animal did this, but did not of itself reveal any physical significance about the relationships of larger groupings. It is not a question whether Aristotle or the dichotomists achieved a more 'natural classification', for that would be to ask modern natural-history questions of the ancient world. Aristotle's scheme, whether logical or instinctive, was explicitly artificial.

Some animals did not seem to Aristotle to fit naturally into any of the large and instinctively perceived groups. Some seemed to be half-way between the terrestrial and aquatic.[193] Others were between the flying and terrestrial.[194] Such animals seemed to fall between two major groups because they had some parts in common with one group and others with the other group. For example, seals regarded as sea-animals are anomalous in possessing locomotory organs that look more like legs than fins; as land-animals they seem rather to have fins.[195] As winged animals bats are rather odd in having fore-feet. As quadrupeds they are unusual in having wings. In a similar kind of way, says Aristotle, ostriches have some features of quadrupeds, and apes fall between men and quadrupeds in having neither tail nor buttocks.[196] Such 'dualising' animals have provided material for comment amongst Aristotle scholars in being exceptions to Aristotle's classification of animals.[197] But Aristotle does not give any significant discussion of them as exceptions. They do not, to be sure, belong easily to the big and instinctively recognised groups, but it seems likely that Aristotle simply means that the 'educated man' whom he targets at the opening of the *Parts of Animals* would need more than instinct[198] when grouping the whales, dolphins and so on (which live in water like fish but breath air like quadrupeds). It is precisely these animals that have affinities to two different groups that would be badly located in a dichotomous scheme of 'classification'; and Aristotle's educated man would also need to be able to rise above the groupings of the dichotomists and the vulgar.[199]

PERFECT AND IMPERFECT ANIMALS

Aristotle thought about animals in two ways, which we must disentangle. First, the nature of the animal expressed itself as well as posssible in the matter of the animal, and did nothing in vain in securing the best for the animal and immortality for the species. Yet, second, the adult nature of the animal is compared favourably or unfavourably with that of other animals. It is not that the natures of some animals have done their job badly – 'in vain' – but that the animal is naturally imperfect. The scale of nature has man as its high point, and it is in respect of him that, for example, fish are 'stunted' in having fins rather than limbs,[200] and that the seal is a stunted quadruped.[201] River crocodiles and some fish have 'a kind of shabby representative of a tongue'.[202] Indeed, in comparison to man, *all* animals are for Aristotle dwarf-like.[203]

In other words, here Aristotle is not looking at animals causally – that was a business of their *physis* and their matter – but historically, where their *historiae* are events that have their place in a hierarchical world. Aristotle's world was hierarchical, in living things from plants to man, and more widely from non-existence to divinity. This scale of natures was in some ways analogous to the coming-to-be of the individual natures, for both were made meaningful by final perfection. It is not surprising then that both feature in Aristotle's work on *The Generation of Animals*. Aristotle finishes Book 1 with how simple sensation in animals is preferable to a mere plant-like life, for sensation is a kind of knowledge. Book 2[204] shows how the scale continues up to eternal, divine things. Animal species share in the eternity of the world and so are more perfect than the individuals; what shapes the individuals – their natures – is more divine than the matter it works on, and the passive, material female essence is always lower on the scale than the active informing male.

We shall in a later section look at the mechanisms at work when the natures of the animals continued the species by generating new individuals. We need to note here that an important diagnostic feature, by which the place of an animal on the scale of natures could be judged, was the nature of the immediate product of generation, whether an egg or something at once mobile. Here Aristotle uses empirical observation more than in other aspects of the scale of natures, but his organising principles are tightly bound to his underlying philosophy. His basic principle relies on the relative perfection of the natures. This is judged by the extent to which they take in the pure (and divine and life-giving) element, air. The more perfect natures do this by special organs, the lungs; possession of lungs also implies a greater degree of heat, the possession of blood (and a brain to cool it). The heat of the more perfect animals allows them to fully concoct the parts of the offspring in generation, and they are accordingly viviparous. 'All vivipara have blood' is an axiom for Aristotle, but whether it was derived from, or prompted, observation is not clear. Likewise Aristotle asserts that all animals with blood are either viviparous or oviparous. It looks like an inductive statement, but Aristotle's explanation is that the egg-laying blooded animals have less heat than the viviparous, and are consequently unable to fully concoct the parts of the offspring – the eggs have to be incubated after 'birth'.[205] The eggs of birds and egg-laying quadrupeds are perfect eggs in having a hard shell and not growing after birth. But below them are four groups with imperfect eggs,[206] including the bony fish, crustacea and cephalopods. Less perfect still, according to Aristotle, are the insects, which produce a sort of pre-egg, the *scolex*.[207] This is the grub or larva and in due course it turns into an 'egg' or what we call the pupa. True eggs, says Aristotle, contain a part intended as nourishment for the developing animal, but the *scolex* wholly turns into the adult. It had been born, that is, at a very early stage because of the imperfection of the concoctive powers of the nature, and was obliged to feed on external food before reaching the egg stage. The caterpillar eats voraciously but stops on becoming an egg.[208] By making the scale one of descending moisture as well as descending heat, Aristotle can explain how it is that cartilaginous fish, naturally moister than land animals, can sometimes produce viviparously live young from internally hatched eggs.(But the coldness of the fish means that a perfect shell cannot be formed, and they are soft. And rather indirectly, Aristotle argues that the eggs are nevertheless perfect in not growing after having been laid: they are *not* laid, so cannot grow, so must be perfect.)[209] This natural scale in its various forms is often little more than a series of examples of the principles of heat and moisture in the natures' self-expression[210] and Aristotle is not using the scale to illustrate some different principle of 'classification'; indeed he shows that such a scale cuts across other useful criteria for judging animal groups, like limbs and locomotion.

Aristotle also gives an account of how the occasional monster is produced in animal generation. The problem was that such things were in some sense against nature,[211] yet were clearly the production of a nature. Aristotle says that nothing can be contrary to nature as eternal and necessary, and he means the eternal cycles of the heavens and the perpetual generation of the species, both of which are necessary because eternal and perfect because eternal. Monsters occur when individual natures are defeated in their usual operations by matter, where the 'formal nature' fails to overcome the 'material nature'. Monsters are therefore *materially* natural and *formally* unnatural.[212] Monstrous changes are not random, but often involve similar deficiencies and occur regularly and in a sense are less monstrous in doing so. The philosophers knew of a particular grape vine that normally produced green grapes but occasionally black. This, said Aristotle, is not a violent or unnatural change; nor is it a change of natures: since natures are different from each other, a change from one to another would be a change of category. Monstrous variation in animals included changes in or absence of some of the viscera. Because of the importance he gave to the heart, Aristotle held that this alone could not suffer monstrous change: if a monstrous animal had two hearts, it was two individuals fused together. We may guess that one form of monstrosity that he had in mind was duplication of organs, and the implication is that for Aristotle, a two-headed sheep remained an individual if it had a single heart. Aristotle is on familiar ground in rejecting the materialist views of his predecessors, for example Democritus, who maintained that monsters were the result of the meeting of two different emissions of semen in the uterus.[213] Aristotle has some special explanations of the generation of monsters, as for example when a large number of foetuses in the uterus may impair each other's development, or where the need to produce large numbers of young leads to the occurrence of errors. His general explanation however once more returns, in rejecting the materialism of his predecessors, to the imperfect role of the female matter in the end-directed process of generation. In the *Parts of Animals* he had accounted for monsters partly on the basis of material necessity – in general that matter was refractory and unpredictable. Its shortcomings were likely to be of the same kind on many occasions, and this is no doubt what Aristotle meant by saying that monsters were of recognisable kinds. He probably also had this in mind when he said that monsters did not happen by chance or accidentally, and he certainly meant by this that they were not goal-directed. Finally, when Aristotle rejects the old opinion that monsters were provided in order to help men prognosticate the future it reminds us of the not insignicant part played by augury in

Greek life. The men who inspected the entrails of the sacrifice must have known what was normal and what monstrous. Augury from inspection of this kind suggests that regular variants of form (which Aristotle mentions) were routinely associated with kinds of prognostication. In a world where some animals were regarded as under the special protection of some gods and where the gods frightened people, then the animals and their insides held a significance greater than satisfying intellectual curiosity.

NATURAL-HISTORICAL KNOWLEDGE

For most of the first book of the *De Partibus Animalium* Aristotle has been doing what he said he was going to do at the outset, that is, providing a guide for a critical appraisal of the methods of gaining natural knowledge. He now justifies the status of this knowledge.[214] The passage in which he does so is a famous one. Its significance has been pointed out by modern commentators and it was an inspiration and justification for those in renaissance and early modern times who dissected or vivisected animals. In the passage Aristotle extols the excellence of the heavenly bodies which makes knowledge about them valuable and pleasurable, but difficult to obtain because of their distance. In contrast the accessibility of the plants and animals of the earthly world make it possible to obtain very much more knowledge about them than about the celestial bodies. The charm of such knowledge lies in its certainty and abundance, says Aristotle,[215] and even if some animals do not appeal to the senses, there is great intellectual pleasure in seeing how they are constructed. What Aristotle means of course is that the animals should be inspected with an Aristotelian eye, and Aristotelian causes looked for. Then the order and design by which the nature-of-the-animal achieves its ends will become apparent and the intellectual heart will warm with the vindication of the Aristotelian method.

But Aristotle is also defensive about his dissections. He recognises that the 'primordia of the human frame',[216] its blood, flesh, bones and vessels, are repugnant to a degree, but urges his readers to drop their childlike aversion to such things and to the humbler animals. He encourages them with the story of Heraclitus warming himself at the stove and welcoming hesitant visitors with the remark that there are gods even in the kitchen. For Aristotle is aware that he is doing something novel. We have seen that he saw himself as breaking away from the philosophy of Socrates and Plato, which was concerned with moral and political issues, and returning to the physical interests of the philosophers before Socrates. But to Aristotle, the views of such men were vitiated by their gross materialism. Nor does Aristotle report that they made extensive investigations into animals. His own programme was therefore clear: to investigate extensively, and with a correct method; to find in the natural world teleological final causes which had been dismissed by the materialists and the atomists; to dignify the knowledge so gained to people inclined to turn up their noses at the objects it was gained from, and to teach.

So now, in what follows, the Aristotelian method is in full flow. His search for and demonstration of causes begins[217] with the similar parts, with the description of which he had opened the *Historia Animalium*. He prefers to begin with elementary forces rather than elements, no doubt as another move away from materialism. The cause of similar parts is, then, the final form of the animal which makes similar parts a necessary step. 'Now the order of actual development and the order of logical existence are always the inverse of each other.' That is, the final form of the animal determines the antecedent steps, but they must start at the simplest. It is by 'the order of actual development' that Aristotle can most clearly and emphatically state his main theme, the expression of the nature of the animal. His studies of animal generation are designed to be the vehicle of this theme.

THE CAUSES OF ANIMALS

(i) Pangenesis and potentiality

The fields of study laid out in the curriculum of the Lyceum were not wholly new. While Socrates had explicitly turned his back on the study of natures, and Plato had largely followed him, Aristotle was to a certain extent following paths trodden by the pre-Socratics. We have seen that his refutations of them are very often the starting point of his arguments, and while the substance of his arguments is shaped by his belief in the superiority of his own causal method, there is a clear sense in which he is being directed by earlier work. Here he is tackling a question, for example, that had been faced also by Empedocles.[218]

This is clear when, in dealing with sexual generation, he refutes the notion of pangenesis, which had its roots among the pre-Socratics and the medical men.[219] This theory sought to explain why it was that animals and men resembled their parents in many of the parts of the body. It argued that male and female semen was produced by the coming together of representative particles from all over the body of both parents. The mixture of these two semina produced the offspring.

For Aristotle this was yet another materialist view of things from his predecessors. He thought it was an attempt to explain the final form of things merely by identifying the matter that went into their material structure. It was materialist too in asserting that the particles that derived from the parts of the body were 'seeds' resembling the parts they had left, and that the subsequent generation of the embryo was a rather mechanical process of reassembling these intact qualities and similarities. He appreciated that the theory tackled the question of the resemblance of the young to the parents, even of mutilations acquired during the life of the parents. But for him the whole matter needed re-examination in the light of his own views on coming to be.

His attack on the theory of pangenesis characteristically consists of pointing to things that it does not explain. It is not possible to imagine, he says,[220] that the hair and nails of the body contribute seed, yet children are often seen to resemble their parents in these features. Nor does the theory explain why in some features the children may resemble the grandparents more than the parents. Another difficulty was in identifying where the seeds came from: was it the homogeneous parts or the organic, the compound? The homogeneous parts looked like the better candidate, yet the resemblances between offspring and parent were clearest in the compound parts.

Aristotle's major objection was of course that the theory did not posit, as he did, the adult individual as the final cause. Since for him this was the full expression of the nature of the animal it followed that all of its parts were subordinated to that purpose. Some of them were there by material necessity, some because they were directly concerned with the final cause. All parts had their own action or use that could only be understood if the whole was taken into account. It therefore made no sense at all that particles of these parts, said to act as seeds by virtue of a physical similarity to the part from which they had come,[221] could have an independent existence. For Aristotle they could meaningfully exist only as parts of a correlated whole – as parts of the adult they were *final* parts, the end of a process, not its beginning. He claimed that in the theory of pangenesis all would be confusion as the isolated particles mingled in forming the male and female semen. If they were real parts in a proper relationship, he said, they would form little animals in the semen, and when the two sorts of semen mixed, there would be two animals because there had been two parents. And as we have seen, Aristotle did not believe that the female generated semen. Indeed, it was the chief characteristic of femaleness that concoction could not produce semen and that the female supplied the matter to the male's form. That pangenesis did not explain the difference of the sexes at all[222] was enough to condemn it in Aristotle's eyes.

So the thrust of Aristotle's argument is the characteristic one that the process under review is not driven by the end to be achieved but by the materials involved. For Aristotle the smaller and more isolated the particles the less they could have a part in processes as he saw them and the more akin they were to atoms (which he believed explained nothing at all). To explain the formation of the embryo by materialistic pangenesis, says Aristotle,[223] would be like saying a statue came to be from the stone, rather than by the sculptor. It was essences, not merely material qualities, by which a child resembled his parent. A boy being essentially like his father might choose to wear the same kind of shoes; but no one would suggest that semen came from the shoes.

Finally, the centre of Aristotle's attack on pangenesis is that it took no account of the nature-of-the-animal in his sense. Aristotle's preferred image[224] for the generation of animals is derived from plant life, where a cutting from one part of the plant takes root and grows into a whole plant. This is the process of realising potential as Aristotle saw it, with the semen coming from one part of the body and being potentially the whole body. Pangenesis could not explain the rooting of cuttings. It could not explain how insects produced not young copies of themselves, but grubs. Nor could it explain how animals arose by spontaneous generation.

(ii) Spontaneous generation

Aristotle's natural history passes from the lifeless to the living without change of the underlying physical principles. 'For nature passes from lifeless objects to animals in such unbroken sequence, interposing between them beings which live and yet are not animals, that scarcely any difference seems to exist between two neighbouring groups owing to their close proximity.'[225] Natural motion in all cases was the realisation of potential through necessary stages. The difference between animals and non-living things was that the nature of animals included provision for ensuring generation of more animals of the same kind. But this was a property of only the more elaborate souls of animals. Closer to the boundary with the non-living, animals – generally those not posssessed of locomotion[226] – could arise from sources other than their parents. Indeed, they do not have parents, for in animals that are generated spontaneously, says Aristotle, there is no differentiation of sex.[227] Such animals may arise from corruption, where this is to be understood as the opposite of concoction. Concoction is the production of something useful and good, and what Aristotle means is that corruption is the removal of waste and useless matter so that generation can proceed.

Some plants too arise spontaneously and in being devoid of locomotion resemble the bulk of spontaneously generated animals. The most complex of animals to arise spontaneously, according to Aristotle, are some insects. This must happen every generation, because if they could copulate and reproduce, a new line of similar animals sexually generated would begin. If they copulated and produced something different, then there would be an infinite variety of different forms, and nature avoids the infinite.[228] In all cases it is 'nature' bringing these creatures into existence: are there difficulties here for Aristotle's 'nature of the animal'? The question arises because one of the principal actions of the natures of the more perfect animals is the provision for sexual reproduction and the transmission from one generation to another – in the semen – of the 'motions' by which generation takes place. How can we speak about an enduring nature of an animal that arises spontaneously?[229]

There are several degrees of answer. The first is that Aristotle sometimes means by 'spontaneous generation' the generation of animals that do not copulate. This means that they are not to be understood by Aristotle's theory of why animals have sexes. We must examine this very briefly. It is well known that Aristotle held that the male animal was hotter, more concoctive and more perfect than the female. This enabled him to understand maleness and femaleness in terms of his wider theory of form and matter, for the female supplies the matter of the child and the male the motions by which the form is enabled to inform that matter. There is thus a 'formal nature' and a 'material nature' of the animal so generated.[230] In some animals, however, such as the purple murex,[231] although there are no sexes and no copulation, yet some material is given off by the adults which has some bearing on the generation of young. Aristotle says the murex gather together in the spring and deposit a substance called 'honeycomb' and a mucoid substance. These play some part in the generation of the young, but it is not entirely clear what, for the young spring up where these are deposited, although Aristotle says their material component is mud and rotting matter. Cockles, clams, razor-shells and scallops are all said to arise spontaneously.[232] Aristotle groups them with the murex as testacea, the group that also includes the mussel and ceryx. While the latter two also behave like the murex, it may be that it is only the mussel that also sheds the 'honeycomb'.

Where no such aid to generation is mentioned, Aristotle simply says that the differences between the spontaneously produced testacea arise from the kind of mud that generates them. Oysters grow in slime, cockles in sand and barnacles on the rocks.[233] Other animals to arise spontaneously are sea-anemones and sponges, which are again, like plants, immobile.[234] Of mobile animals the hermit-crab is said[235] to arise spontaneously from soil and slime, and various insects from dew falling on leaves in the spring; in decaying mud or dung; in timber; in the hair of animals; in flesh, and within the intestine of animals (although the flatworm is seen to eject seedlike parts).[236] Here it is implicit – it is in the *Historia Animalium*, so Aristotle is not discussing causes – that it is the matter in and from which they arise that determines what kind of insect will appear. This matter is intended by Aristotle to be the equivalent of the female matter of the sexual animals. To make such a correspondence, he says in the *De Generatione Animalium*,[237] is to follow the right path of investigation, that is, in essence to go back to the principles of natural change, with form and matter. He adds that it is the heat of the season that concocts this matter, just as the native heat of animals concocts the generative residues. The male action is also present in this macrocosm–microcosm analogy: it is the air, says Aristotle, which imparts a 'motion' to the matter. The text is a little corrupt here, and some of it is missing; otherwise we *might* be better informed on just how the air represents soul and how the specific characteristics of the spontaneously generated animals remain constant from one animal to another when they share only such an unspecific thing as air. But it is clear from the tenor of Aristotle's words that this was not a major problem for him and whatever is missing from the text would not be an answer to it. He is close to what for a Greek was the self-evident fact that air is vital,[238] but this is not so much a genetic cause of the developing animal, but a necessary condition for the existence of the adult. As he reiterates a little later, it is the individual that exists in the truest sense, and individuality that is the principle cause of its coming to be. Given that it is prior in nature to the steps necessary to construct it, the individual takes Aristotle's interest more than the initial steps of its development.

Another reason for Aristotle to be less than comprehensive about the nature of spontaneous generation was his ignorance. He more than once announces that not enough is known about such things to warrant conclusions being drawn.

> Such appears to be the truth about the generation of bees, judging from theory and from what are believed to be the facts about them; the facts, however, have not yet been sufficiently grasped; if ever they are, the credit must be given rather to observation than to theories, and to theories only if what they affirm agrees with the observed facts.[239]

The problem with bees was that there were three kinds of them living in one society, the 'king', workers and drones. It was in Aristotle's eyes quite possible that the generation of bees was spontaneous or sexual. But which process produced which kind of bee? Which kind of bees paired sexually to produce others? And did they generate their own kind or the third? The workers looked like females because they cared for the young, but they carried weapons of defence, which was a male characteristic. The single leader of the entire hive was naturally a male for Aristotle, and as more perfect should have had a role in generation: perhaps the kings generate their own kind and the workers.[240] Perhaps the drones do not arise by sexual generation – some people thought that they arose spontaneously in flowers and were imported by the workers – or are derived from the workers by some means other than copulation. Pretty clearly the drones produce nothing.

Aristotle was much taken with bees. Not only were they at the limits of knowledge, but the complexity and the harmony of their society meant that there was something divine about them, not present in other insects.[241] When he speaks of the due order of nature[242] in harmonising the lives of the three kinds of bee, he is still in a sense discussing the nature-of-the-bee; but since the individual, the adult, the final cause of its own existence, is constantly of three kinds, 'nature' is either threefold, or as single covers all three. Apart from the dubious example of the shark this latter situation is the only case where Aristotle has 'nature' achieving its ends by ensuring harmony between different animals. Or perhaps Aristotle wanted the nature of the bee to be expressed in the king, as the 'father' of the whole tribe. The workers attend him, as sons might, and punish their own children, the drones, as a father might.[243]

(iii) Sexual generation, purpose and necessity

Having seen the nature-of-the-animal at its simplest in those animals that arose from the matter of the earth, the heat of the sun and the motion of the air, let us look at the nature of the more perfect animals. Animals that reproduce sexually have the capacity to resemble their parents, both in being sexually differentiable and in personal characteristics. They also have the ability to occasionally show features of more distant ancestors. Aristotle is not thinking about long-term change but of present reality. As mentioned above, for Aristotle it was the individual that was the reality and that needed explaining. With sexually generated animals, part of that explanation was the parents, and a smaller part *their* parents. Aristotle is thinking also logically, in terms of categories: the individual is of this or that sex, more widely of this family and still more widely belonging to humanity and animalness. This is a scale of perfection for Aristotle, with an adult male human at the top. We shall see that perfect reproduction generates another like him, and imperfect produces a female. If anything should go further wrong and the child resembles a distant ancestor more than its parents, its category is 'family'. Ultimately the failure of the process produces monsters, which may be recognisably human or merely animal.

In all this is presupposed the transmission of characteristics from generation to generation. In explaining this let us start, as Aristotle would wish, with the adult male. The male human or animal is hotter than the female. Only he has the power to concoct the nutriments of the body into a final form, the semen: his nature has given him the faculty and the organ to perform it with.[244] The female in contrast prepares the matter of the future offspring with the degree of natural heat she has. She is providing potentiality in the form of the 'material nature' of the foetus. The actuality is provided by the male. The semen is water and spirit, *pneuma*,[245] and resembles ether, the fifth element in which the stars move.[246] But its material nature is not important, for it has its effect by passing certain motions to the female matter, which thereafter continues to develop automatically, like the wheels of a machine.[247] The motions of the male are the equivalent of the sensitive soul, which the female on her own cannot provide; sterile 'wind-eggs' in fowls are the female's attempt to generate a whole creature herself.

What makes all this possible, the greater heat of the male, originates in his heart. Aristotle works characteristically round in a cycle: the adult male, the definition of the animal and therefore its goal, is, by definition, the full actualisation of potential. He has Form – in the case of the animal, soul – to the highest degree. The soul, as the nature of the animal, wishes to perpetuate the kind and therefore has close control over nutrition, motion and generation. Nutrition is carried out in the midddle region of the body, midway between where food is taken in and where excrement is voided. This will be the hottest part of the body, because heat is a tool of the soul and is needed for nutrition. The result of concocting the nutrition is blood, which is the cause of the viscera. The final product of concoction in the male is semen; in the cooler female, menstrual blood. The native heat that characterises the male is akin to the generative heat of the sun (as we saw in spontaneously generated animals) and is quite unlike element-ary fire.[248] It persists in the semen as the agent of the actual and potential soul, and so when this begins to act in the female matter, it first[249] produces the heart, the hottest organ, the seat of nutrition,[250] the first to live and the last to die.[251] Between its first appearance and its death it begins to repeat the male cycle.

Much of what Aristotle says on the causes and parts of animals can be explained in the basis of this cycle, and we shall need to refer back to it a number of times. Let us examine some of the things that it implies. We can start the cycle again with the adult male, the full nature of the animal. Aristotle is here as elsewhere anxious that the novelty and superiority of his method should be appreciated. It is the adult animal that is to be explained, so it is prior in nature, but not chronologically. Therefore the old philosophers who tried to *begin* with the embryonic rudiments and so build up a picture of the adult were for Aristotle too materialist in seeing the material causes of the animal only. Aristotle characteristically demolishes the opinions of his predecessors in making his own case stronger. Although Aristotle firmly believed that right was more perfect than left, he could not agree with Anaxagoras and Empedocles[252] that male embryos were conceived in the right hand side of the uterus. His own notion of goal-directed process in sexual generation overrode such a view. He had, moreover, seen by dissection embryos of both sexes in the same part of the uterus. Nor would his own theory agree with that of Democritus, in which maleness was the result of a predominance of male semen.[253] These are materialist explanations for Aristotle, and do not explain how boys can resemble their mothers or distant ancestors. Aristotle explains these things by taking the mother and ancestors to be *causes* of different significance in the goal-directed process of development. The 'motions' of the ancestors remain, potentially at least, in the semen and variations in the matter associated with the process can allow them to become actual.[254] This is to an extent unnatural, more so than the formation of a female.[255]

But of course female offspring, although to this extent unnatural, were necessary for the generation of the animal kind. This kind of necessity is an important part of Aristotle's account of the generation of the body. Females are means to an end, not the end in itself. In *De Generatione Animalium* he gives a little homily on 'priority', distinguishing temporal priority from that involved in 'for the sake of which' relationships. It is for the sake of the grown man or animal that the early stages are gone through, and these may be merely necessary, often with a material necessity, or may be directly related to the final cause. Thus in the developing embryo, says Aristotle,[256] the bigger organs appear before the smaller and the upper before the lower, because more important in the final adult. The lower organs (nutritive and motive) are necessary for the upper (heart) but are not themselves part of the purpose, *telos*, of the nature.

The interplay between purpose and necessity is evident throughout Aristotle's account of development. After the heart is formed as the first part of the embryo, there follows the brain, together with its vascular connections to the heart, in order to moderate the heat of the heart.[257] But both brain and eyes, being cold and wet, take longer to bring to completeness, and so are comparatively big at first, but shrink (either relatively or absolutely) as the embryo grows.[258] An eye is not an eye for Aristotle of course until it is open and can see, and in some animals this does not happen until after birth, so long does the process of forming it take.

Often, according to Aristotle, parts of the body appearing by necessity are employed for a useful purpose by the nature of the animal. Thus the omentum[259] is formed of necessity since it receives the greasy parts of the food in circumstances (the heating of a liquid and a solid) that Aristotle says always result in the formation of a membrane. But once formed, the nature uses the heat of the omentum heat to promote digestion. The mesentery too is formed of necessity[260] but here the case is rather different, for upon reflection it has a use, even a final cause (to act like the roots of a plant in extracting nourishment from the intestines). A better example of the nature taking advantage of a necessity is the sepia, the ink of which is as excremental as urine or faeces (and therefore necessary) but which the nature makes use of in defence, to hide the animal from its predators.[261] Aristotle has similar discussions about the relationship between material necessity and final causality in the cases of the diaphragm and the fat around the kidneys, and the hair on the head.[262]

NATURE DOES NOTHING IN VAIN AND 'GROUP NECESSITY'

As we have seen from Aristotle's account of generation, the nature of the animal uses female matter to construct the primordium of the embryo. The embryo in Aristotle's words is then a potential animal but has to nourish itself, which it does in the uterus like a plant, absorbing nutriment from its mother.[263] The process of nourishment is largely one of addition of similar parts to similar in the process of growth, but some nutriment is 'creative'.[264] In doing this the nature of the animal is like a good householder, says Aristotle,[265] throwing nothing away but reserving the best food for the free men, the next best for the slaves and the worst for the animals. Nature uses the best for the sense organs and the flesh, while the residues form bones, sinews, hair, nails or hooves, depending on which animal it is the nature of.

This helps us understand a common feature of Aristotle's treatment of animals. It is fundamental to the whole of Aristotle's work on nature that matter is capable of imperfection. Matter, not form, produces females and monsters, and here it is the matter of nutriment that is sometimes wanting in attributes needed for the growing embryo. For example, the earthy part of the nutriment of the embryo is always secondary in coming to the embryo externally – from the mother in the viviparous animals and from parts of the egg in the oviparous.[266] Sometimes it will be in short supply, and the nature of the animal has to use what is available wisely and distribute it fairly in the animal's body. This is why in the *History of Animals* we are often told about correlations between bone, teeth and horns – all earthy parts – in different animals. For example, in some animals the earthy matter is used up in the horns, leaving none for the front teeth of the upper jaw (but Aristotle says their fat and marrow is like suet because of the presence of earthy material).[267] Animals with teeth in both jaws are said to have had too little earthy matter to make horns (and have fat like lard from lack of earthy matter).[268] Again, when the nature used earthy material for the hard skin of some selachians, there was not enough left over to make rigid bones.[269]

The three major works on animals are thus seen in their most important relationship to each other: the *Historia Animalium* presents apparently empirically gathered facts of observation and makes correlations between the appearances; *De Partibus Animalium* offers causal explanations in terms of nature fitting out the body of the animal with the matter that is available and with a view to expressing its final form with the habits and habitat proper to it; and *De Generatione Animalium* is more deeply philosophical in being devoted wholly to the process of reaching the final cause. Final causality could be found in the smallest of parts, and one example used by Aristotle is of interest, since it survived in the literature to be discussed in a very different context, as we shall see. It is the question of eyelashes. Aristotle maintains that man alone among the animals that have hair has eyelashes on both upper and lower lids.[270] His reason is that hair in general is a defence and so occurs more often on the front of the animal than on the back. But quadrupeds, because of their inclined gait, are less exposed on the under side and so have no lower eyelids. While eyelashes in this way have an express final cause, to keep objects (and descending liquids) out of the eyes, it is also the case that the nature is making use of something that *necessarily* occurs, for as Aristotle observes,[271] the lashes grow at the superficial termination of blood vessels, where a corporeal emanation always produces hairs (unless diverted by the nature elsewhere). Final causality is also involved here in the nature taking care to protect first the more noble parts. Noble parts are those both Up and Front: this seems partly axiomatic with Aristotle, but it is also because up and front parts are the first to meet the good and the bad in the external world and so are endowed with the senses and have the most direct connection with the centre of the body, the sensorium and the place of the most intense concoction. This is the reason why man is hairier in front and animals hairier on their backs.

An important way in which the nature does nothing in vain in Aristotle's view of the world is that two kinds of final causality can be achieved by the use of a single organ. This is akin to the nature making use of something which is, by necessity, there anyway, like the ink of the sepia. Nowhere was this double usage more apparent than in the trunk of the elephant. The trunk is, first, a nostril, serving to allow the elephant to breathe when in deep water. Aristotle thought of the elephant as in some way being between land and water creatures (like other 'dualising' creatures), getting its food from the water but being structurally an air-breathing land animal.[272] Second, the trunk is also a hand, conveying food and drink to the mouth and tearing up trees. In a sense the trunk too has a third function in replacing the forefeet of other quadrupeds which act as hands (the forefeet of elephants being unsuitable).[273] Clearly Aristotle does not have far to look for further examples of the principle. There are mouths that eat, talk and bite in defence. There are tongues that taste and speak, and teeth that chew and are weapons.[274]

While the nature of the animal was clearly being ingenious and economical in serving two final causes in a single organ, yet where possible it gave separate functions to separate organs for the sake of their being performed more perfectly.[275] What is behind this basic principle is that Aristotle held that the nature of the animal was prior in all respects to the material form in which the nature ultimately expressed itself in development. The nature of insects is fierce, but only the larger ones have four wings and are able to carry the sting that fits the fierceness that suits them especially. The nature is instinct with abilities that call into being corresponding corporeal structures. In an analogy that Aristotle was fond of, he says that the nature gives an organ to the animal that can make use of it, as one would give a flute to a flautist, rather than teach a man with a flute how to play it.[276]

This particular expression of Aristotle's doctrine was prompted by his examination of the opinion of Anaxagoras, who said man was intelligent because he has hands. No, says Aristotle, he has hands because he is intelligent. This introduces the enduring theme (which can be met with throughout the period covered by this book) of man's defenceless nature, born naked and helpless. Aristotle denies that he is for this reason inferior to animals and argues that man's hands are many instruments combined, and indeed can manufacture instruments of defence in great variety, while animals are limited to one means of defence only.[277] Perhaps it is reading too much into Aristotle to say that he saw that the human hand, with its short, strong opposable thumb (which he notes) was *potentially* any instrument of defence.

In these ways, the nature doing nothing in vain for the animal can use a single organ for more than one purpose, or perform operations more perfectly by using one organ for each purpose. In one case however the nature seems to have given an animal an organ that in some sense has no purpose. The case is that of the horns of the deer. Aristotle is quite explicit that the deer's means of defence against predators is its speed.[278] The horns are without function. This seems to go against Aristotle's general principle that nature does nothing in vain, and it has been a problem for Aristotle's commentators from Theophrastus (where we shall meet another aspect of the problem) to the modern philosophical scholars who are upset at an apparent anomaly in the integrity of Aristotle's philosophy of nature. It does not, however, seem to have been much of a problem for Aristotle. Nevertheless we should not gloss over it on that account, for by examining our own problems about understanding Aristotle we may learn more about his philosophy of nature (Plates 6 and 7).

Plates 6 and 7 With and without: For Aristotle deer were by definition horned animals, although females and small varieties regularly did not have them. Even the adult males shed theirs once a year to lessen the disadvantage they conferred. Aristotle believed that the antlers had final causality because they were part of the definition of deer; Theophrastus did not agree. One of the most enduring stories of ancient natural history was that the stag buried one of its antlers, useful in medicine, in order to prevent it being used by men. It did so in places so hidden that they became proverbial.

The deer without horns, in marble, has been seized by Diana. That with horns is a bronze from Herculaneum. (Museum of Classical Archaeology.)

Why, then, did the nature of the animal give deer useless horns? Rather than useless, large branching horns are actually a disadvantage, says Aristotle. Moreover, some horns in some animals curve inwards towards each other and so – by implication – are useless in defence and attack (which the nature has provided for in different ways). In addition to this, Aristotle argues[279] that it is actually necessary that the deer should shed its horns regularly so as not to be disadvantaged all the year round. Why is the nature of the animal apparently doing something in vain?

There seem to be two main answers. Running through Aristotle's text there is the argument about material necessity and he is giving at least as much attention to it as to final causality. The case seems parallel to that of hair, a necessary product of the body (but one which the nature can turn to good use). Both hair and horn are also similar parts and so much closer in their nature to the elementary qualities that were so basic to the structure of the body: material necessity (such as the production of earthy matter) clearly applied much more to the similar parts than to the organic. Aristotle argues that in making the bodies of large animals their nature uses a great deal of earthy matter for strength, for example in the bones. This, he says, is a 'general rule' and no animal of the deer kind smaller than a gazelle has horns. In the larger animals the earthy matter is in excess. It 'necessarily' flows upwards, says Aristotle, and is used by the nature for the production of teeth, tusks and horns. This is an example of 'the material nature whose necessary results have been made available by rational nature for a final cause', that is, in most animals the materially-necessary earthy matter is used for instruments of offence and defence. Aristotle repeats his generalisation about no animal with horns having a complete set of teeth, for which his general rationalisation is that the nature has insufficient earthy matter to make both. Our problem is that the deer has earthy matter to such excess that the deer has to shed its horns, and the argument about insufficiency of it does not seem to work. Perhaps Aristotle held that the earthy matter was necessarily drawn preferentially[280] to the horns and so was not available to furnish the deer's missing teeth.

The second answer to the question of why the deer's nature seems to be doing something in vain is that *by definition* deer are horned animals. All of Aristotle's sources – the material gathered in the *Historia Animalium* – agreed that deer had horns. Horns were a characteristic feature of deer. As such, they formed part of the definition of deer. We can recall that Aristotle, arguing against a dichotomous manner of arriving at animal types, insisted that types were recognised by many rather than by progressively fewer characteristics. Aristotle's thinking on this point is clearer to us at the beginning of the fifth book of the *De Partibus Animalium*, where he is discussing accidental attributes of animals. Eye colour, he says,[281] is often purely accidental, as in man. Clearly the eye itself has final causality, but eye colour has not. But, Aristotle adds, eye colour *can* have final causality if it is characteristic of the animal type. Man can have brown or blue eyes, but *all* lions have brown eyes. Brownness is essential to the eye of a lion: its final cause is to contribute to the definition of the animal. As he says a little later,[282] all things included in the definition of an animal partake of full causality. So here is Aristotle the logician, wanting to identify and define natural kinds, battling against the dichotomists. It is this Aristotle too who often begins his account of an animal with a rather dialectical definition of it as the goal of its development. Again, in the book on the generation of animals[283] the definition of an animal is said to be the same thing as the final cause. Brownness of eye in the lion and large horns in the deer are *logically* final.

Aristotle's doctrine was also moulded by the materialism of his predecessors. Eye colour was a topic that had been discussed by Empedocles[284] and Aristotle wanted to refute his opinion that the colour of eyes was due simply to the predominating element in their physical make-up. Aristotle once again insists that things develop because they are, not that they are because they develop, and so no materialist explanation without final causality can be sufficient. Here was another reason for Aristotle to say that even eye colour had final causality.

There is a parallel case of 'group necessity', the equivalence of definition and final cause, in the example of the lobster. Aristotle held that most natures of animals were right-handed[285] (it was the more noble side). In general the right-hand side of animals was the more perfect and for example the right front claw of crabs was bigger. But in lobsters, Aristotle asserts, it is a matter of chance whether the right or left claw is bigger. They *have to have* claws because they belong to a group of which claws are a common and constant characteristic; but the indeterminacy in form arises because the lobster uses them for locomotion rather than grasping.[286]

ANIMAL MOTION

We have seen that Aristotle considered that the nature of the animal reached its full expression in the adult male. The presence of the sexes, in all but the least perfect animals, allowed Aristotle to employ his principles of form and matter, of the process of coming to be, in his explanation of the animal's reaching its goal, the adult. Motion was essential to this full expression of the creature's nature because it allowed both nutrition and copulation. This is why the motion of animals and the organs responsible for it was one of the things that Aristotle looked for in animals.

Animal motion also reflected Aristotle's scale of nature. Animals whose natures are not mobile, says Aristotle, do not have sexes.[287] Their generation is therefore closer in kind to spontaneous generation, where Aristotle's basic principles of coming to be are less clear and where the continuity of the animal's nature from one generation to another must be in question, especially when animals are said to arise from corruption. Slightly higher in the scale are those animals that are fixed, but which have some sexual differentiation; but the principles that link motion, sexuality and nutrition to the nature of the animal are most clearly seen in the higher animals.

This link is again Aristotle's conception of change as process, of coming to be and the achievement of a goal. All motion is in this way directed at some end which will benefit the animal by expressing its nature. The ultimate objective is the Good, that is, conditions that favour the continued existence of the animal and its kind. How this is achieved depends upon the powers of the nature of the animal. If it is rational, like man, it can by its intellect seek the Good and avoid the Evil. Irrational animals may nonetheless have imagination, which acts in the same way. All animals that move have at least senses and it is largely by the operations of these that the external Good and Evil act upon the instinctive appetites of the soul and move the animal accordingly. The importance of the soul and the senses in this process is why Aristotle devoted a series of treatises to them. We should note here that while Aristotle marked off the power of reason as a strictly human category, it was but part of a scale of soul-activity in which animals largely shared. Their appetites were instinctive, but man's rational appetite steered him in the same directions. Animal motion was the result of thought in some sense, whether sensory and imaginative or logical. In the latter case motion was for Aristotle a sort of practical conclusion to the logical process.[288] (The process arose from two premises, the Good and the Possible.) In all cases motion to the desired ends made certain steps necessary, and Aristotle has another opportunity to bring in a fundamental principle – Necessity – and show that all change is Process, towards an end.

Aristotle also employs another fundamental principle, that of the unmoved mover (which we can read about in the *Physics, Metaphysics* and *De Anima*). Indeed, *De Motu Animalium* is presented as an extension of this principle.[289] The principle is presented at various levels. It is given in the form of an analogy with the unmoved mover of the heavens.[290] There is a clear sense in which the external Good and Evil are unmoved movers of the animal's senses, imagination and appetite[291] and resultant motion. Most clearly, the soul of the animal is the unmoved mover, and Aristotle is developing a theme that he says[292] had been broached earlier in *De Anima*. Even the necessary conditions that have to be met before motion in an animal is possible require an unmoved mover. Where the motion of a bone in a joint is relative to another, it is as if one is fixed and the other moves against it: what resists must be different from what moves. Men cannot walk in shifting sand, nor mice in loose grain; Boreas in the pictures cannot move the boat in which he is himself sitting by puffing into the sails. Ultimately, the firm earth (and the resistance of the air in the case of birds) is the Unmoved which makes possible the motion of animals.

In these ways the motions of animals are linked directly to Aristotle's first principles, and the machinery by which action occurs takes second place in Aristotle's scheme. It is primarily concerned with the connate spirit[293] which is located at or near the soul and which does its job by pulling and pushing the mobile parts of the body.[294] The soul controls the connate spirit and the well-ordered body runs like a city, every part performing its function. Some motions – the involuntary – are not under the direct charge of the soul, but are simply in some sense necessary.

Although the text of *De Motu Animalium* ends with a forward reference to the work on the generation of animals, as though Aristotle wanted next in the curriculum to explain how motion makes sexual generation possible,[295] the text of the modern edition runs on into another work on the motion of animals, *De Incessu Animalium*.[296] This text is best thought of as part of the *Parts of Animals*,[297] and is like it in drawing on the *History of Animals*[298] and in comparing different animals. Its subject matter is locomotion – from place to place – and can reasonably be seen, then, as the particulars that derive from the general principles of *De Motu Animalium*. It would perhaps be possible to argue that *De Incessu Animalium* was a collection of particulars from which general principles were inferred, in the way that the *Historia Animalium* has been taken to be the empirical collection on which the *De Partibus Animalium* was based. But in both cases, and especially here, it is clear that Aristotle knew what the general principles were before deciding which observations to report.

Motion from place to place, observes Aristotle,[299] implies front, back, up, down, right and left for the moving animal. Front is where nourishment is taken from, and as we have seen, the taking of nourishment is one of the two reasons for motion. It follows for Aristotle that the 'front' of plants is down, for they take their nourishment from the earth. Front for quadrupeds is fowards: not only from their direction towards their food, but because it is more noble than the orientation of plants. Aristotle is here very conscious of natural hierarchies of nobilities: right is better than left (and is the source of all motion), up more noble than down, front than back. These are topics he had dealt with also in the *Parts of Animals*[300] and all are characteristics that can help us put the natures of animals in their place in the natural scale.

De Incessu Animalium also agrees with other of Aristotle's works on animals in asserting that the heart is the centre of motion, equidistant from all moving parts.[301] It is indeed the centre of the body, and part of the argument that motion implies front and back is again to make the case that the heart is midway between the front, where food is taken in, and the back, where its useless parts are ejected. The heart is therefore the part of the body, according to Aristotle, where the digestion of food is at its most intense: the hottest part, the most obviously mobile (the heartbeat), the centre of sensation (so placed to receive equally from all parts). Aristotle knew of opposing arguments that the brain was the sensory centre of the body, but had already argued that the brain was cold and immobile, and so lacked the two most important characteristics of the soul. Moreover, it produced no sensation when touched.[302] Its reason for existence was its very coldness, for it served to cool the heat given to the blood by the soul in the heart, and its presence was therefore a defining characteristic of sanguineous animals.

The centrality of the heart on these and other grounds had been for Aristotle a structural principle of exposition in the *History of Animals*,[303] where he makes it clear that man is the model, a divine animal with a true upright position (and therefore with all directions of motion – like up and forward – correct) and with all internal organs in the right places, especially the heart. In lower animals without a heart what corresponded to it was defined by being midway between intake and expulsion of food.[304] Animals too simple to have a single controlling centre have a number which collaborate (and which enable the parts to go on living for a while after separation from the whole). The imperfection of some animals was defined by the extent to which they depart from the model of man and his central heart: in particular some cephalopods are twisted so that their mouth is close to their anus. This meant to Aristotle that the heart was no longer central, a principle important enough to warrant a series of diagrams marked with indication letters.[305] These diagrams seem to be those of the *Historia Animalium*, or derivations from them. They are referred to again in the text on the generation of animals,[306] where the proximity of the mouth and anus of the young sepia is referred to. Not only are Aristotle's general principles evident throughout the works on animals, but also in his teaching devices.[307]

NATURAL HISTORY, NATURAL PHILOSOPHY AND THE GODS

This chapter began with Aristophanes making coarse fun of Socrates' reputed denial of the existence of Zeus and the other gods. This may well have been a common perception by non-philosophising Greeks of the natural philosophers – represented by Socrates – who had sought natural rather than divine causes of things. But it is unlikely that the philosophers were in fact atheists, at least explicitly. Most philosophies that we know more than fragments of have an important place for the divine. It was not the business of Aristotle's *libri naturales* to discuss divine beings and while we may guess that he shared the philosophers' rejection of the traditional gods of the pantheon performing certain natural actions, it is clear that his philosophy in an important way incorporated the idea of divinity.

Human reason indeed, the very means of philosophising, was divine for Aristotle, the only element of the developing body to enter it from outside and the only function to have no necessary connection with a part of the body.[308] We have also seen that there was something divine too in the intricate behaviour of bees, at the limit of Aristotle's knowledge and admiration. In the sublunary world the pure air came close to the divine for Aristotle, accounting both for

the perfection of the higher animals and for the spontaneous generation of the lower.

But it can be argued that the major presence of the divine in
Aristotle's natural philosophy is in the unmoved mover, the ultimate
source of all motion.[309] Quite apart from the *Metaphysics*, which is
a study of the nature of existence (but hardly of the natural-history
kind) and which could be called a natural theology, Aristotle could
claim support for his philosophy by including an element of divinity.
Study of the unmoved mover, because it is unmoved, was not for
Aristotle a part of the study of motion: the unmoved mover was an
arche different from what it causes, and so fitted with Aristotle's
notions about the relationship of different branches of knowledge.
The arguments for an unmoved mover were that every motion is
caused by something else moving and that there cannot be an infinite
regress of causes. The later Christians argued for the existence of God
in very much the same way: this has nothing whatever to do with
Aristotle's use of the argument, but does serve to signpost a location
in Aristotle of one of the reasons why the Christians could accept
his doctrines. The same may be said of Aristotle's rhetorical question: if there was a time when there was no motion, what could have
caused it? Aristotle thought that this proved the eternity of motion
(and the Christians thought it proved the existence of the Creator).

Aristotle does not explain how the unmoved mover moves the first
mobile[310] but is perfectly clear that it is a business of the divine. It is
the circular motion of the heavens that is the divine first perceptible
result of the unmoved mover; our old beliefs about this divinity are
right, says Aristotle,[311] but we must not believe in an Atlas[312] (that
is anthropomorphically, as holding up the world) or that the
heavenly bodies move by voluntary effort. Nor should we think with
Empedocles that they are moved in the cosmic swirl. This is surely
the Cosmic Whirlwind that Aristophanes attributed to the atheistic
Socrates, and we see Aristotle very much as the philosopher avoiding
the named gods of the pantheon and their supposed actions in the
natural world, but avoiding too the materialism of the natural
philosophers of an earlier period by means of a causality that was
ultimately linked to the divine unmoved mover. We shall see in later
chapters, as we have seen in this, that philosophy, of which natural
history was part, was not a pure intellectual enquiry but a practical,
even political subject, and a religious one.

2

THEOPHRASTUS, PLANTS AND ELEPHANTS

Aristotle's successor as head of the Lyceum was his clever pupil, whom Aristotle named Theophrastus from the divine way he argued. But he did not argue in the same way as Aristotle, especially about final causes. Since his enquiry into causes was what Aristotle thought made his own natural philosophy so much better than that of his predecessors, and since it was all closely connected to Aristotle's notion of nature, we must ask how Theophrastus saw causes, nature and *historia*.

Theophrastus had abundant opportunity to learn from and work with Aristotle. Born about 371 BC (in Eresus on Lesbos) he travelled and worked with him at Assos and Stagira between 347 and 344. These are traditionally the years of Aristotle's books on animals, and perhaps it was during them that Theophrastus began to differ from his teacher. It is probable too that he began to write while still a colleague of Aristotle, and it has been suggested that his *Metaphysics*, where he has some reservations about Aristotle's final causality, was written before Aristotle's *Parts of Animals* and *Generation of Animals.* At all events what he thought about the natural world was of great importance for those who came later. Theophrastus was head of the Lyceum for thirty-six years (he died in about 287 BC) and is said to have had two thousand students.[1] If it is true that he had also heard Plato and had gone with Aristotle to the court of Philip of Macedon when Aristotle taught the young Alexander, then there are more reasons for thinking of Theophrastus as being at the centre of Greek intellectual and political life. Although he is said to have been of a retiring disposition, as an important teacher he could not avoid contact with and evaluation by political leaders. Cassander, son of Antipater and a man with whom it was necessary to get on, welcomed him to Athens, and Ptolemy extended overtures of friendship to him. When (like Aristotle and Socrates) he ran into political/philosophical difficulties (on a charge of impiety) in Athens, his popularity saved the day. But even then he had to leave Athens for a while for the duration of a decree that no philosopher should be in charge of a school unless approved by the council and the people. Clearly, the Athenians wanted their philosophers and what they taught, and the philosophers wanted patronage and approval as well as their philosophy. But as we have seen the constant danger of displeasing the politically powerful shaped what the philosophers had to say. Men like Socrates, Plato, Aristotle and Theophrastus, who wrote on politics, the best political and social organisations, on kingship and on why non-Greek people were most suited to slavery, and who reached a large and influential audience, necessarily taught what was acceptable within the polis as a whole,[2] and we may guess that the same constraints acted upon him as upon Aristotle.[3]

Theophrastus' teaching was vast.[4] He covered most if not all the subject areas dealt with by Aristotle, largely by way of picking up a much larger number of smaller topics and devoting separate works to them. But a much greater proportion of his works than of Aristotle's have been lost, and we have only his *Characters,* the *Metaphysics,* two works on plants, some physical works and another on sense perception. But enough survives to suggest that the intellectual habits of the Lyceum continued as they had been under Aristotle. The investigations into plants seem to have been collaborative enterprises, just as were Aristotle's projects on animals. The empirical nature of many of the collections of observations was retained. Aristotle's library remained in the Lyceum and was clearly a model and a tool for the peripatetics who worked there after his death.

But despite these similarities, Theophrastus' ideas about the history of nature, as mentioned above, were different from those of Aristotle. To understand Theophrastus' conception of nature, and how it found expression in the physical works, including those on plants, we must return to the *Metaphysics.* Whether or not it was written before some of Aristotle's works on animals, it is certainly the case that it is in this work that Theophrastus shows most clearly his disagreements with Aristotle. He shows them too with the use of examples drawn from the animal world, in fact, from Aristotle's *Historia Animalium.* Given the nature of Aristotle's work on metaphysics, it might seem a little odd that Theophrastus is so ready with such concrete examples; but without Aristotle's total commitment to final causality Theophrastus' metaphysics was bound to be different and the animal examples are in fact a useful way of illustrating the finality question. The question has attracted the attention of a number of scholars and has puzzled several philosophers who have tried to assess Theophrastus' philosophical position. Here, in contrast, we must be as historical and concrete as possible. In the *Metaphysics*, then, Theophrastus raises a number of problems about final causality. What is the purpose, he asks, of men having breasts? What purpose does the female emission have? What are beards for? Why is it good for deer to shed their antlers? How can one part of the body be said to be more 'honourable' than another? What is the purpose of an insect living for a day only?

PERIPATETIC PROBLEMS

In finding out why Theophrastus was asking such questions, and what his answers tell us about his view of natural history, we are led back to the nature of Aristotle's works on the natural world. We will recall that most of them were unfinished and poorly edited and that many of them show evidence of collaboration. In particular the *Dissections* and the *History of Animals* as collections of data seem to have served primarily as reference works rather than as monographs structured by an argument. Certainly these two in particular and to an extent all the natural works could readily be modified as new information was received and if (as suggested in the previous chapter) the extant works represent not a sequence exhibiting the growth of Aristotle's thought, but a cycle of teaching with internal cross-references and open to modification, then a pattern begins to emerge in respect of Theophrastus' relationship to Aristotle.

Let us begin with the notion of the Aristotelian works as a cycle, the structure of which is suggested by internal cross-references. Some cross-references in fact do *not* make a link between the different works. Quite apart from references in the works we know to those that have not survived or were never written (the four on dissections, plants, nutrition and medicine)[5] there are references to works in versions that are *not* those we have. Three references[6] to what Aristotle calls his *Problems* contain topics not in the work that we know by that name. One explanation of this may be that the *Problems* was a working collection that was added to and subtracted from. Perhaps discussion threw up new problems, and the development of extended works solved or replaced old problems. The same can be said about other references within the Aristotelian corpus to things that cannot now be found. In the *Parts of Animals* he refers back to *De Sensu et Sensato* about loss of sensation, the brain and cooling blood.[7] No such topic exists in *De Sensu* as we know it. The *Parts of Animals* also contains an internal reference (to sea-urchins)[8] which is not in our version. In the *Meteorology* the question of the heat from the sun is said[9] to have been discussed in *De Sensu et Sensato*, but is not in our version. Of course loss of text from manuscripts and interpolation of glossses by scribes is a recognised cause of such things, but it is entirely possible that the texts were brought up to date in the Lyceum by editing in new material and editing out old (and forgetting to alter the cross-referencing).

Another case is in the *Generation of Animals* where Aristotle refers back to the *History of Animals* for further details (on embryonic membranes).[10] He often does this, and it may be that he sometimes meant that the illustrations in the latter work gave a clarity that words could not supply. But apart from this, the words of *History of Animals* give no greater detail than those of the *Generation of Animals*, where Aristotle makes the reference. For this reason its modern editor is inclined to think[11] that the reference in *Generation of Animals* was an early note made during the compilation of *Generation of Animals* and was retained fortuitously when the detail of *Generation of Animals* had made such a reference in fact superfluous. The same editor also feels the need to supply a table of contents to explain the structure of the 'confused and repetitious' *Generation of Animals*. We have already noted that in particular the *History of Animals* too is repetitious and poorly edited: the process of compilation was still going on when Aristotle left Athens. Where the modern editor says that a chapter of *Generation of Animals* is 'much mutilated' the implication is that it has been handled roughly during the history of the manuscripts; but presumably a chapter poorly edited from notes would look much the same. The same editor thinks that Aristotle had confused his notes[12] (on the topic of the uterus of the sepia). Aristotle has a comparison of the motion of fish and serpents and refers to the *Motion of Animals* where the expected details do not in fact appear. The *Meteorology* is repetitious and contains two mutually inconsistent accounts of the south wind;[13] one chapter at least is 'confused'.[14] Another paragraph is so 'incoherent and disorderly'[15] that the editor wants to reject it as non-Aristotelian. Perhaps it is not Aristotle's, and may be much later; but it might also be a Lyceum interpolation of the same nature as the other contributions Aristotle received from his collaborators and failed to give a final editing to.

So if our picture of the work of the Lyceum is that the Aristotelian texts grew slowly, perhaps in parallel, and that they were to an extent collaborative, we can see why some of Theophrastus' questions about Aristotle's causality (listed above) do not seem quite fair. Aristotle, after all, *does* give a final cause for male breasts: they help protect the heart. It looks as though Theophrastus should have asked why men have nipples, for to that Aristotle does not have an answer. As for the final cause of the beard in certain animals, modern scholars have been unable to find the relevant passage in Aristotle.[16] Theophrastus does not make it clear whether the female emission he speaks of is a theoretical female semen, which Aristotle flatly denies, or menstrual blood, to which Aristotle *does* assign a cause. When Aristotle says that the windpipe is placed in front of the gullet because 'in front' is more honourable than 'behind', Theophrastus seems to have forgotten (or never saw) that Aristotle also uses here an argument of physical necessity. Where Aristotle says that the centre is the most honourable position, Theophrastus objects to his arguing that therefore the middle ventricle of the heart contains 'the best' blood. But Aristotle did not say that the middle ventricle holds the best blood, but simply different blood. Likewise when Aristotle said that it was good for the deer to shed their antlers, because it increased their speed and therefore safety, he was in fact admitting that the antlers were without purpose, and so Theophrastus was not in fact disagreeing with Aristotle.

The question of whether these were fair questions to ask disappears if we return to the chronology of the growth of the Aristotelian works. It is not only that Theophrastus was probably using early versions of these works, to which his questions were pertinent, but it may well have been the case that Theophrastus was one of those who collaborated in the Lyceum's programmes, even if only in raising questions on what was being taught and written. The problem that Theophrastus seems to misunderstand Aristotle might be neatly solved[17] by assuming that the material was drawn from the *Historia Animalium* during teaching or research, when, as Theophrastus himself says, questions were asked, and that the *Parts of Animals* was put together *later* and incorporated answers to such questions. No doubt the teaching and the texts were discussed in the Lyceum, perhaps at an early stage, and additions were made.

Theophrastus wrote to Phanias,[18] observing that public readings led to revisions. More private readings, before a select few[19] who were probably also collaborators, would *a fortiori* be followed by revisions, no doubt after further work had been done (both Aristotle and Theophrastus often point to areas that need attention). If in this way we think of the peripatetic treatises as examples of a process rather than as finished works we can see what was different about the Lyceum. Earlier philosophers had taught by way of personal statements and arguments. Although the personality of Aristotle is stamped over most of what bears his name, yet the collections of empirical fact that characterise the physical works, especially those on animals, is good evidence of teamwork. We are reminded that the Lyceum housed a library, perhaps the first in the Western world, and it acted as semi-religious philosophical workshop. Theophrastus (who was able through a pupil to purchase property for the Lyceum[20]) instructed that Aristotle's statue should be put up in the shrine, where there was an altar and votive offerings (there were also tablets bearing maps of the earth). The gardens and its dwellings were left in Theophrastus' will for the common use of the philosophers, as if a shrine. The oldest of them were instructed to take care of another Aristotle, the young son of Metrodorus and Pythias. We can well imagine long-term collaborative projects under way in such a home of the muses.[21]

Let us look in a little detail at two problems that might look clearer in this light. They relate to the topics of Theophrastus' criticism of Aristotle's finality and are therefore important if we are to consider the possibilty that Theophrastus may have played a part in the Lyceum's work before he took over as its leader. In *History of Animals* and *Parts of Animals*[22] Aristotle mentions 'female sperm', *gone* and *sperma*. This is in addition to the menstrual discharge, and it is possible that this is what Theophrastus had in mind when criticising the finality of the ambiguous 'female emission'. Certainly such a thing would be without purpose in Aristotle's *developed* theory and Theophrastus' critique would in that case have been justified. At all events, Aristotle in *Parts of Animals* promises a more accurate account later, and when he came to deal with the matter in *Generation of Animals*[23] he was resolutely against the notion of a female semen and is emphatic that menstrual fluid is the female equivalent of the male semen. It is thus possible that Theophrastus' critique was of Aristotle's mention of female sperm in the earlier stages of the enquiry represented by the *History of Animals* and that his later and more precise account in the *Generation of Animals* was partly in reply to Theophrastus.

The other example is the relative position of the windpipe and oesophagus. Theophrastus objected that Aristotle had used a concept of 'nobility' to explain the precedence taken by one organ over another. In *Parts of Animals*[24] Aristotle describes the relative position of the two organs and refers back to an explanation that does not appear in our version of the work.[25] Had it been edited out? Was Theophrastus' criticism anything to do with it?

THEOPHRASTUS AND FINALITY

Whether or not the explanation outlined above is adequate, it remains undeniable that Theophrastus was unhappy about Aristotle's notion of final cause.[26] That things existed or changed for the sake of something else seemed to him impossible to assert in every case. Much more than Aristotle, he saw things happening by necessity and coincidence or chance and even that 'most terrestrial phenomena'[27] seem to fall into these categories. It is with terrestrial phenomena that most of Theophrastus' surviving works deal: plants, minerals, fire, odours and even winds, and here it was perhaps more difficult than in the case of animals to follow through a thoroughly Aristotelian search for causes. Theophrastus scarcely tries.[28]

(i) Fire

Probably the beginning of a typical collaborative project is represented by what we have of Theophrastus on fire.[29] Like others it is described by its modern editor as a scrappy collection of lecture notes without a central argument. Theophrastus' notes are physical in an Aristotelian way, but Theophrastus differs in making fire unique. It is not (as the Aristotelian elements were) capable of being generated from the other elements, but generates and destroys itself. Indeed, fire is said by Theophrastus not to be an element (he also said that it had particles). Like Aristotle, Theophrastus collected some of his information from craftsmen; and although the differences from Aristotle may indicate that Theophrastus wanted to extend and bring up to date the Lyceum's programme here, this collection of notes on fire is not far enough developed for significant lessons to be learned from it.

(ii) Winds

A similar collection of Theophrastean notes on winds seems to be further developed.[30] But here too its modern editor views it as a disjointed series of lecture notes, which often point out where further work needs to be done.[31] The starting point is the section in Aristotle's *Meteorologica* where he claims that winds are the result of exhalations from the earth moved horizontally by the circulation of the heavens. Theophrastus in contrast favours a view explicitly denied by Aristotle, that winds are merely air in motion. Theophrastus' purpose seems to be that this explanation enables him to assimilate the further information that had come to light since Aristotle died (Theophrastus was writing about a quarter of a century later).[32] That this was a common programme is borne out by the many cross-references to other Theophrastean and Aristotelian works, the historical evaluation of older works, the evidence of information from sailors and farmers coming by way of 'trained colleagues'[33] originally from the Lyceum. Modern studies suggest that Theophrastus' wind-lore must have been collected over a period of years.[34] Characteristically Theophrastus' teleology is less well marked than Aristotle's and his system of causality is alternative to rather than a development of Aristotle's (he gives attention to the action of heat as a physical force and uses antiperistasis and *horror vacui* as physical principles[35]). Theophrastus agrees with Aristotle that winds are like rivers, flowing to and from recognised places: they are individuals, are named, can be reduced (like Aristotle's) to a diagram and bring all the varieties of weather. Such a study was of obvious interest for a maritime and agricultural nation and there must have been real utility in a largely chronological wind-lore. Theophrastus is again less theoretical and more mechanical than Aristotle in his account of the relationship between winds and mountains, seas, and their ultimate cause, the sun.

(iii) Tastes and odours

Another indication that Aristotle's and Theophrastus' programmes were closely linked is the latter's work on tastes and odours. It seems in fact to have been a topic that it was necessary for the peripatetics to address, because it had been discussed by one of the pre-Socratics, Empedocles, and so was seized on for revision. Aristotle deals with the topic as part of his work on the senses and the sensed[36] and bases his argument on fruit, for which he invented the term *pericarpion*[37] to indicate more precisely what he meant by 'fruit'. Because it relates to fruit, Theophrastus deals with the same topic, using Aristotle's word for fruit, in the last book of his *Causes of Plants*.[38] He had already touched on the matter in his own text on the senses[39] but here deals with it more extensively. Aristotle's treatment is characteristically part of a great rational scheme: *De Sensu* follows *De Anima* in describing how the soul perceives what is good or bad for the animal and so provides for pursuit or evasion. This – perception and motion – is the characteristic of the animal soul, distinct from those of plants and men. Perception and motion are the operations of a nature that is seeking the best for its animal and are ways of ensuring that the final cause, the adult, is achieved. In contrast Theophrastus' own work on sensation is largely an historical judgement on the predecessors common to him and to Aristotle; and when dealing with flavours and smells in the work on plants his business is to present in a much more empirical way the active qualities of plants that are much more often due to 'necessary' causes, largely material,[40] than to the final cause and the rest of Aristotle's scheme.

(iv) Minerals

Here Theophrastus takes as his starting point Book 4 of Aristotle's *Meteorologica*. Many scholars have discussed the question of whether this book is genuine, that is, from Aristotle's sole hand. But such a thing is unlikely, from what we have seen, and the question must be to what extent the book was revised after Aristotle. Perhaps it did indeed attract further work and the fact itself of Theophrastus' taking it as a point of departure may be evidence of this interest.[41] One reason for revising part of a Lyceum project would have been the receipt of new empirical information, and Theophrastus is dealing with details made available by the conquests of Alexander the Great.[42] (The same may be said about the *History of Plants*, where the descriptions of the cotton plant, banyan, cinnamon, myrrh and frankincense all follow from Alexander's campaigns.[43]) Theophrastus' programme here is the peripatetic one of listing differences; but because he is Theophrastus and not Aristotle, he is hesitant even about making generalisations and very loath to give causes. In order not to get involved in questions of causality, he is content to believe that a single mineral, like pumice,[44] can have a number of causes. He discusses stones that burn, smell, give colour to water, melt, resist cutting and so on. He deals with the manufacture of verdigris, white lead and cinnabar.[45] He argues that minerals are generated within the earth in a way that differs from Aristotle's account but he does not pursue the matter because it is again a question of causality.

Just as we found it useful in an earlier chapter to see Aristotle's works as being part of a cyclical programme of teaching and each a process of bringing up to date (rather than being chronological evidence of the development of Aristotle's thought) so it might well be useful to look at these physical works of Theophrastus in the same way. We have seen that if his own thoughts on metaphysics were developing while he was one of the colleagues listening to and commenting on Aristotle's earlier lectures on animals, then we have a neat explanation of his apparently misplaced critique of Aristotle's final cause in those lectures. The explanation would also fit Theophrastus' selective use of Aristotle's material on bees, which we shall meet below. It was not part of the Lyceum's programme to avoid problems like the shedding of the deer's horn or the generation of bees. Indeed it was the purpose of giving readings of lectures and projects in their early stages to identify and tackle such problems.

THEOPHRASTUS' PLANTS AND THEIR NATURES

We should remember that for Aristotle the nature of an animal was fully expressed in its adult form, the goal that determined the stages necessary to its achievement. It was the nature of the animal that did nothing in vain in doing its best for the animal. But Theophrastus greatly reduces the sense in which 'nature' is nature-of-a-thing. Much of what happens on earth is of necessity or coincidence, he says. For the 'essence' of a plant he often uses the term *ousia*[46] in place of the *physis* that had such ramifications in Aristotle's system. The new and lesser meaning given to 'nature' by Theophrastus is an important part of the story being told in this book. Let us see how his general position, made clear in the *Metaphysics*, was expressed in the detailed work on plants.

Theophrastus wrote two works on plants, the *History of Plants* and the *Causes of Plants*. The two works of Aristotle with similar titles in regard to animals at once come to mind, and it naturally looks as though Theophrastus was doing a peripatetic exercise. To a large extent he was, searching for differences and then arranging them in significant ways. He was looking for *historiae* of things worthy of report, as well as the regular natures of things. Some of these were (as Aristotle reports of animals) things noticed and used by soothsayers, like a sweet pomegranate appearing on a tree that normally bore only acid fruit, or the change of colour of a fruit tree, such as a fig turning from white to black. Some of these wonders were commonplaces to the people of the country of origin of the plants, and were indeed in the nature of the plant. No one in Greece, pointed out Theophrastus, marvelled at the way in which the 'smoky' vine sometimes had green grapes and sometimes black.[47] (We have seen that this was acknowledged as a routine natural change also by Aristotle.)

It may be too that Theophrastus' work was a Lyceum exercise in that plants had been given a place in the Aristotelian programme. If Aristotle wrote on plants the text has not survived (but we shall see that there are several Aristotelian features of the pseudo-Aristotelian text on the subject); if he intended to but did not do so before leaving Athens for the last time, it may be that the Theophrastean text was intended to fill a gap. Like so many other peripatetic treatises the *History of Plants* is unfinished, condensed and elliptical, and may be notes for (or of) lectures.[48]

Like the *History of Animals,* Theophrastus' *History of Plants* is an exercise in discovering *differentiae* between the collected *historiae.* As in Aristotle's case, reports had come in from newly available sources in the East and perhaps from 'representatives' of the Lyceum in different parts of the world.[49] Like Aristotle, Theophrastus wanted to look for the parts and the qualities of plants, and how they begin and conduct their lives. But at once there are difficulties in taking Aristotle's *History of Animals* as a model.[50] What is a *part* of a plant? asks Theophrastus. A part belongs surely to the nature-of-the-thing and once having appeared in development is permanent. But this cannot appply to plants, for such noticeable and useful parts of plants as flowers and seed are transient and are shed every year.[51] Yet are they not parts? Theophrastus argues that plants are at their most perfect when blooming and fruiting (and later takes it that the provision of fruit for man is among the most valuable *purposes* of plants) and that flowers and fruit truly are parts. The break with Aristotle is clear, for he would never have accepted that seed, *semen,* or embryonic structures were parts of the animal, which was defined by its final adult male form. Theophrastus in contrast is from the outset not looking for definitions or final causality. He is not really looking for the *physis* of plants in the way that Aristotle looked for the nature of animals, and does not treat philosophically of their generation (as Aristotle did of the generation of animals). Nor does Theophrastus arrange his *historiae* of plants in the way that Aristotle arranged those of animals, so that they looked empirical but were partly at least determined by the rational method he was later to employ on them. Although like Aristotle he wanted to see what parts were held in common by groups – proceeding on analogy with animals – yet in comparison to Aristotle, his lessened emphasis on the nature-of-the-thing leads him to a wider but less detailed conception of what groups are. Plants as a whole, he says,[52] have no parts common to all, like the mouth and stomach of animals. (Fungi have neither.) So Theophrastus decided to take a single kind of plant as an examplar for the rest, choosing it apparently for its perfection. He chose the tree.[53] Its parts were then the standard by which the parts of other plants were judged, and their differences are absence or presence, arrangement and shape.[54] In practice his mode of exposition is to take a broad kind of part, such as 'leaf', and subdivide his category into – first – the plants' habit of shedding or keeping them, and – second – shape. He proceeds by taking a number of examples, but does not attempt to categorise plants on the results.[55] Even such natural groups as evergreen and deciduous are entirely relative to location and Theophrastus does not attempt to establish boundaries when discussing such a category as 'time of shedding leaves'. Within the category of 'shape of leaf' Theophrastus has groups of whole, divided, fleshy, spinous and so on. His discussion[56] ranges from oak and juniper to asparagus. As with the parts of plants, so with other topics, the method is the same.[57]

We also seem at first to be firmly on Aristotelian ground when Theophrastus begins his account of the *Causes of Plants* with the maxim that nature does nothing in vain and that its purpose is to produce a seed capable of germination. Here 'nature' is the nature of the plant, and is a constant meaning of the term in Theophrastus,[58] as close to Aristotle's meaning as he comes. We should recall that nature's main aim in animals for Aristotle was the perpetuation of the adult by the processes of generation, and similar thinking accounts for the importance of the seed in Theophrastus' work on plants.

But it is soon apparent that Theophrastus has distanced himself from Aristotle. He does not use Aristotle's language of causality and does not have Aristotle's little homilies on what it is to be 'for the sake of something'. Nor does he base his argument, as Aristotle so often did, on the destruction of the schemes of his predecessors: as we have seen these attacks were the results of Aristotle's crusade against the limited materialism of the pre-Socratics and his promotion of his own final causality. Theophrastus, cool on final causality, has less need for such attacks. So the *Causes of Plants* is not really about causes in the way that the *Parts of Animals* is about causes.[59]

An example is Theophrastus' treatment of an opinion of Democritus, who said that the shorter life and earlier sprouting of tall straight trees was due to the open texture of their vessels, which allowed the rapid transportation of food.[60] It was just the kind of theory that Aristotle had objected to in the *Generation of Animals*, were he attacked Democritus for giving a physical cause and omitting the final cause. But Theophrastus' response to Democritus is simply to give a number of examples of plants that illustrate the opposite of Democritus' opinion, and then to say longevity depends on some aspect of structure, such as density and oiliness. It is clear again that Theophrastus does not share Aristotle's crusade for finality, nor his constant rejection of materialism.

What Theophrastus *did* worry about in Empedocles' natural philosophy was the latter's apparent denial of the reality of the objects of sense.[61] Democritus had argued that sensation was the result of the interaction of the sense organs with 'effluvia'[62] emanating from the objects of sense, and that sensation was consequently a local bodily phenomenon and not a direct perception of the objects. This no doubt looked threatening to the kind of empirical research done in the Lyceum, which relied on sensory perception. Theophrastus was accordingly anxious to establish a philosophical consensus that things could be directly perceived. Even Plato, he says, did not deny the reality of the perceptibles. The consensus is to be reached by examining the opinions of the philosophers, and Theophrastus gives a historical account, rather as Aristotle often did, but in an un-Aristotelian way he says that it is not his first intention to discover truth but to comment on Plato and Democritus. His account of opinions about the senses is fuller than that of Aristotle and although he has less on the nature of soul, it seems he has much more on its actions from the historical literature.

But much more general a matter than attacks on the predecessors, and one which structures the *Causes of Plants*, is that the plants' 'nature' of the kind discussed above is only part of Theophrastus' topic. He does, to be sure, study and report on the natures of plants and how they achieve their purpose of generating more of their kind, but it is also an important part of their natures that plants provide food for man, most notably in the form of fruit. There is no break in Theophrastus' treatment here, no disjunction (which we would make) between the natural and the artificial. In Theophrastus there is a strong sense in which it is part of the nature-of-the-plant to be food for man. Fruiting plants (he says) have two different concoctions, producing the seed and the fruit. These concoctions have different timetables, that making the fruit being determined by the fruit's service to man, and that generating the seed by the demands of the nature of the soil or climate.[63] The concoction of the pericarpion is easier and happens before that of the seed. The sun, air and season lend a hand in ripening it, 'while the seed is more the private work of the nature of the tree'. The nature of the tree aims at giving both concoctions the same amount of development (but we try to breed in favour of the pericarpion, like growers who grow seedless grapes).[64]

Even more than this, Theophrastus says that the *natures* of cultivatable plants are best expressed by *cultivation*. Here again, where we would want to make an absolute distinction between what is natural and what is artificial, Theophrastus does not. He recognises that art follows nature,[65] but sees no major difference in kind between generation by seed and by cuttings. The nature of a cultivatable plant needs man's help. This includes 'artificial' modes of propagation, such as layering, cuttings and grafting. These devices enable the nature of the plant to be fully expressed; moreover, if left to itself to reproduce its kind 'naturally', as we would say, by seeds, the result according to Theophrastus is degeneration.[66] Part of his explanation for this is that cultivation, by granting abundant food to plants, spoils their seeds.

What is of great importance for us is the ways in which Theophrastus departs from the Aristotelian conception of the natures of things. It is partly that receptivity to cultivation is part of the nature of the plant (and by implication that not to receive it is a privation). If like Aristotle Theophrastus believed that the world was eternal, then somehow this part of the plant's nature has always been there; if not then it still must have pre-existed cultivation. Moreover, cultivated plants that are neglected become inferior to such a degree that their natures change; indeed they become quite different plants with a quite different nature. This is due partly to degeneration of the seed and partly to the lack of proper food and perhaps pruning. In general 'wild' and 'cultivated' plants for Theophrastus are *different* plants, so that a wild fig has no greater relationship to a cultivated fig than to any other plant,[67] sharing only the similarity of name.

Wildness is the furthest degeneration can go. This is why, says Theophrastus, wild plants generate their own kind – they 'breed true', unlike cultivated plants allowed to have seeds. There is even a sense in which wild plants, like wild figs and the 'mad vine', are 'unnatural': their natures are so different from cultivated plants that they *fail* to ripen their fruits. This was of course the part of their 'natures' with the purpose of serving man, and again shows how man's intervention is seen as natural rather than 'artificial' in fulfilling that part of the nature of the fruit.[68] It is a general principle with Theophrastus that strength in the body of the individual is quite distinct from fecundity in generation, and so although wild plants are often stronger than cultivated ones, and often bear a great deal of blossom and young fruit, they may yet fail to provide a ripe crop. For 'concoction is in the pericarpion [fruit]; and this must be produced and must acquire a savour that agrees with our human nature'.[69] Part of the trouble with wild plants was that the two concoctions, leading to human food and plant generation ('this being what fruit and seed are for'[70]) interfere with each other, and a big seed meant a small, ill-tasting and hard fruit. (The job of husbandry was to enable the fruit concoction to come to completion.)

Part of what was in Theophrastus' mind when discussing the effect of cultivation of plants was that many of them were cultivated at a distance from their native habitat. There were in fact foreign plants. The places to which they were native supplied them with the right kind of food in the right quantity, together with climatic conditions appropriate for the full expression of their natures. In foreign parts they needed cultivation to provide things lacking in the 'nature' of the place, and to remove any new impediments to full growth. While uncultivated growth was for Theophrastus natural in having internal starting points ('nature' as an internal principle of motion in a rather Aristotelian way) the starting points of cultivated growth were external. But then, continues Theophrastus, the circumstances of the plant's native habitat – the habitat's 'nature' – were external to the plant's nature, in just the same way as the 'starting points' of cultivation. And just as the plant's nature 'demanded' these external starting points in its original habitat for the full expression of itself, so it demands them of cultivation. In this sense cultivation in Theophrastus' eyes is natural. Not only that, he argues, but cultivation can make *internal* changes to the plant, again demanded by the plant's nature. This makes cultivation even more natural, for it is by cultivation that the nature of a foreign plant can fully express itself, in reproducing its kind. What is *unnatural* is the degeneration into another nature of a plant once cultivation ceases.

Theophrastus generalises here with a distinction upon which, he says,[71] his whole study rests. This is the distinction between the two kinds of nature that a plant can have. Some have a nature that is best left to itself, and which indeed refuses cultivation. (Medicinal plants in particular lose their virtues under cultivation.[72]) Others have a nature that is best expressed in cultivation. He has partly in mind that some plants have a dual purpose, that of providing food for man and of generating their kind. The two concoctions he has already described (of the fruit and of the seeds) are therefore related to the two natures of plants. The distinction is indeed fundamental to his work, for having discussed the natures of plants in a philosophical way in the first book of the *Causes of Plants*, Theophrastus goes into a great deal of detail about the operations of cultivation; so much so that the work assumes the nature of a practical handbook. But of course the Theophrastean farmer *understands* the reasons behind the various operations that other farmers did empirically, by tradition or trial and error. Thus while the occasionally forgetful countryman who neglected to prune his scarabeus vine knew that it would not bear ripe fruit, it is Theophrastus the philosopher who knows that pruning prevents the material of the vine from going into too much woody growth and directs it instead to the fruit: the vine has recovered its 'nature'.[73] Much of Book 3 in particular is given over to the operations, such as digging, planting, grafting and pruning, that are necessary for the practical art of agriculture and intelligible on the basis of allowing a plant to express its nature.[74] This technical advice is not the sort of thing that Aristotle would have considered part of philosophy, and it is a major way in which Theophrastus departs from him. It relates to Theophrastus' suspicions about the universality of final causes; we will see how later on.

Change of kind

We have seen that both Aristotle and Theophrastus accepted that a certain kind of vine (the 'smoky' or 'mad' vine) could sometimes and quite naturally produce black grapes when the normal fruit was green. For Aristotle this was part of the nature-of-the-plant and he is quite clear that this is not a change of *kind*. The nature of the plant was, like that of animals, the definition of the adult and the goal of development. This made each nature very special, the essence of an eternal kind. Little of this applies to Theophrastus' notion of *ousia*. Although sometimes sceptical about complete changes of natural kind, such as that from white to black poplar, or wheat to darnel,[75] he elsewhere accepts that cereals can change from one kind to another,[76] and raises no objection to the change in poplars.[77] In producing seed, all plants are weakened to some extent, having put their natures into the seeds, but annuals, like wheat, put all their natures into the grain and so die at the end of the season.[78] This seems to have made the nature vulnerable in the stored grain. The reasons for this that Theophrastus gives are somewhat diffuse, but they often are inclined more to the materialism of Aristotle's predecessors than to Aristotle's nature of a thing. The wheat plant 'necessarily' dies, and this necessity is often of a physical kind, related to the physical construction of the plant, its density and rarity, how easily fluids pass through its parts and so on. It seems to be through such things that the external circumstances of cultivation and so on have their effect. If it is true that wheat can turn into darnel and even back again, then the cause is wet weather, which causes change in the parts, or disease, in the seed.[79] In the *History of Plants* he argues that physical treatment of the grain (for example bruising it) will change rice-wheat to wheat.[80] It is part of Theophrastus' approach that a change in natural kind can be produced by cultivation (and is accordingly natural). Bergamot-mint changes into mint if left uncultivated, when its roots penetrate more deeply and its upper parts lose their pungency. Basil tends towards tufted thyme, but the change is not complete.[81]

THE NATURE OF THE WORLD

We have now seen a number of ways in which Theophrastus has departed from Aristotle's use of the 'nature' of the organism and made it wider and looser. Ultimately this was because Theophrastus could not agree that the nature of the thing was a goal that determined the stages of a process of development, in animals that the adult was the final cause of growth, motion, sensation and generation. In any case there was less evidence for Aristotle's highly structured teleology in the world of plants, which did not move or perceive. In Theophrastus' words, the nature of plants was simpler, more irregular and confused than that of animals.[82] For these reasons it behaved in other ways which distanced it still further from Aristotle's 'nature' and which ultimately encouraged Theophrastus to think about the cosmos in a radically un-Aristotelian way.

Let us first look at some of the other meanings of Theophrastus' term 'nature'. The nature of the plant is changeable not only by cultivation, but by habit. Heavy training of plants over a period changes their nature.[83] Trees that have become habituated to little water change their nature so that abundant water is bad for them.[84] A habit of sprouting (in wheat) at a certain time, appropriate for a certain locality, persists for a time in a new place.[85] In other words the natures of plants can change by the acquisition of habits. This is related to a new locality 'taking away' from the nature of plants (and animals: Theophrastus is using the *History of Animals*).[86] The causes are material, or necessary, the air, water and food.[87] Habit could also include relationships between the natures of plants. Theophrastus recounts the story of a man who grew figs and vines close together for a long time. When he took the figs away, the vines died, for by then they had almost become a single nature with the figs.

Figs and vines were in any case 'good neighbours': there was something in their separate natures that attracted each other. Myrtle and olive were another sympathising pair. Theophrastus names plants that by reason of the complementary (rather than competitive) need for water and food, can be usefully planted alongside young vines; again there is no sense that this is a sympathy of an artificial kind: it is in their natures. Likewise vetches were sown among radishes, says Theophrastus, to keep the flea-spider down: such relationships belong to nature, for art follows nature.[88] Other plants were bad neighbours, generally when competing for food or sun, or where their fruiting times coincided. Antipathies were more frequent, because many plants had the same requirements and so competed. Theophrastus says that the vine is antipathetic to the cabbage and bay, and is damaged by their smell (but no cause is given).[89] Aristotle had made the same point about animals in the *History of Animals*, but Theophrastus goes beyond him in an important particular. With the possible exception of the case of the shark's mouth, Aristotle never speaks of *collaboration* between animals, for the nature of each was concerned only with doing nothing in vain for the animal in question. But Theophrastus has no hesitation about the nature of one plant contributing to the welfare of another. Thus climbing plants need the physical support of another plant to express their natures.[90] More important is the case of mistletoe, the seeds of which require to pass through the digestive tract of a bird in order to be able to generate. It begins to look as if the natures of the bird and mistletoe co-operate. Theophrastus recognised of course that he was departing from Aristotle's opinions and is prompted to conduct a discussion about apparently co-operating natures. Its starting point is the *History of Animals* which Theophrastus reads as evidence of animal co-operation. Thus, he says, it could be argued that there would be no cuckoos but for the wheatear, in whose nests she lays her eggs, and no pinna without the crab.[91] Related to the case of mistletoe is that of the oak, which often grows from caches of acorns buried by jays for food. Is this collaboration between natures, or merely accidental? Theophrastus implies that this is the wrong question to ask. It happens; it looks accidental; but we should not argue that 'but for the bird there would be no mistletoe'. His point is that we should not attribute such things to accident, for there is more behind it than that. Since co-operation happens between animals, argues Theophrastus, then it should happen in plants too. One example he gives is that the leaves of deciduous trees form a mulch for conifers.[92] Others are the climbing plants and vine-helping plants already mentioned.

Although the *History of Animals* is a point of departure for Theophrastus in this matter, either he read it very selectively or knew it in a form different from that which we have. For example he refers to the theory that the generation of bees is accomplished by the adults fetching to the hive grubs generated elsewhere (perhaps spontaneously in flowers: Theophrastus is not specific).[93] The argument is then 'were it not for the grubs there would be no bees'. But it is precisely here that Aristotle declares that theory cannot deal with the matter and that more observation is needed. This methodological point was not lost on Theophrastus, who often asserted that more empirical work needed to be done (for example on the fruiting of the date palm[94]) but he ignores it here. Perhaps it was not in the version he had. Perhaps even the *History of Animals* reached its final form only after the comments of people like Theophrastus.

But the overwhelming reason why Theophrastus departed from Aristotle's nature-of-a-thing is that he had a very different conception of the cosmos. Ultimately plants and animals sympathised and antipathised because they were part of the same cosmos. The very diversity of the parts of the world meant for Theophrastus that all things were connected and that there was no simple chain of causality ultimately depending on an unmoved mover. It is in the first place, for Theophrastus, simply too difficult to see the final cause of all things, and second, unnecessary to invoke it when the interconnectedness of things gives reasons for their mutual actions.

Some changes are merely symptoms – *symptomata*[95] – of changes happening elsewhere and do not imply purpose. Theophrastus thought that if some things were 'for the sake of' other things, they would always be the same, whereas what is so striking about the cosmos is its changeability and variety. In particular, while the sun and the seasons are the cause of many things, especially animals and plants, they are the *source* of motions, not a goal.

Thus for Theophrastus the universe is a whole, marked by the interconnections of its parts and by the revolutions of its higher parts, which affect the whole. The higher parts have order, the lower diversity. Change is not an Aristotelian process of becoming, with an active and formal part being impressed upon a passive and material with a hierachy of causes, but a partnership between matter and order. Some parts of the cosmos are less ordered than others, necessarily so; but there is a sense in which the whole depends upon all of its parts as well as the parts receiving the motion of the whole.

Significantly Theophrastus compared the cosmos, perfect and complete in itself, to an animal. The origin of motion, that most basic of all natural changes and the source of Aristotelian 'nature', is not a problem for Theophrastus. An animal is self-moving and the universe has always moved; by that act alone it has a certain life. So there is no unmoved mover and the rotation of the whole causes motions in the parts by making operative their innate power, *dynameis.* The relationship between the parts is partly of necessity (for example material necessity) and partly *sympatheia* by which the part adjusts its innate powers to its surroundings, the other parts. This is ultimately for Theophrastus why plants and animals sympathise and antipathise. Whatever had been Aristotelian in their natures has been swallowed by their roles in a living and sympathising cosmos.

Such a world picture is consistent with what we know of the rest of what Theophrastus wrote. In dealing with minerals, for example, his interest is not in causality or generation, but in their properties, such as whether or not they melt.[96] We have seen that he is content to accept that a substance like pumice might be formed in a number of ways, and indeed this was an example that showed that among such things where matter predominates, natural change might be fortuitous, prompted originally by the rotation of the cosmos, but not imbued with purpose. This meant that Aristotle's scale of perfection from matter to form was inappropriate, as was its counterpart, the downward direction of causality. For Theophrastus it was the very interrelatedness, the 'organicity' of the parts of the cosmos that gave it some measure of divinity[97] and this in turn meant that an Aristototelian search for causes must ultimately fail, either because there is no ultimate causality or because the human mind is incapable of perceiving the ultimate: we cannot see the most luminous of all things.

But this is not to argue that Theophrastus denied teleology. We have already seen that parts of the cosmos, the natures of plants, could act for the benefit of each other, and Theophrastus often enough expresses the belief that the natures of plants do nothing in vain. His hesitation is about Aristotle's conviction that final causality is everywhere. But Theophrastus is far from entering a polemic and his criticism of Aristotle is muted. Indeed it has been suggested that Theophrastus was attacking primarily the Academy and in fact defending a rather Aristotelian teleology. The point at issue was that the purpose in the world as announced by Plato was an *imposed* purpose, for the One was the active controller of the Indefinite Dyas (the substrate of the physical world). This gave no role to a teleology of 'natures' and was inconsistent with Theophrastus' view of the cosmos *itself* moving and ordering its parts.[98] It may indeed also be that where Theophrastus is apparently attacking Aristotle's final causes in the cases we have met where Aristotle in fact seems to have an adequate answer (male breasts, presence of hair, female emissions and so on) that the real target is the Academy and the Pythagoreans.[99]

This is an important moment in the story that this book tells. The Platonic demiurge was not omnipotent and could not create *ex nihilo*. It functioned by rearranging extant matter, which had irreducible properties. The skill of the demiurge lay precisely in getting the best result from imperfect matter: the demiurge did its best and *did nothing in vain*. In this it acted exactly like the Aristotelian nature-of-a-thing but on a cosmic scale. It was clearly incompatible with a peripatetic world picture and a natural enemy of Theophrastus' formulation.

ARISTOTLE, ALEXANDER AND ELEPHANTS

Some of the plants described by Theophrastus came from parts of the East that had been made known to the Greeks by the campaigns of Alexander the Great. The wonders of the lands he had thus opened up to Western inspection formed a staple part of the literature on natural things that varied from the fabulous to the philosophical. His navigators, pilots, surveyors and philosophers supplied a market for bizarre stories from the East. Alexander himself became the subject of a corpus of legends.

The strangeness of the new lands of Alexander's is caught in reports of how – over there – the very constellations of the sky are in different positions. Or the sun might be directly overhead and shine down right to the bottom of wells.[100] Alexander took historians with him, for the sake of appropriately recording his actions. He also had surveyors, guides and generals, all of whom could add to the flood of 'Alexander history' that followed his conquests. Onesicritus reported where the Great and Little Bears were just visible, and where not at all; and where the shadows fell in the wrong direction. Others reported that India covered one-third of the land mass of the earth and contained 5,000 towns, and that Alexander, sailing down the Indus at 75 miles a day, took five months to reach its mouth.[101] Onesicritus and Nearchus encountered races of men who lived on fish, sea serpents 30 feet long and an area of red soil that killed all animals.[102]

The sun reputedly shone directly down the wells at Ptolemais, a town established on the shores of the Red Sea in the country of the Cave-dwellers for the purpose of hunting elephants. This was the first of such hunts, according to Pliny. Other reports said that on the banks of a tributory of the Nile, not far from Ethiopia, lived a race of elephant-eaters, the Elephantophagi. They pursued their prey with knives, hamstringing the stragglers of the herd. Or they shot the elephants with poisoned arrows from a bow so big that it took two men to hold it and a third to draw back the string.[103] Most stories about elephants were indeed about how such vast creatures were captured. Pits in the ground and circular ditches are often mentioned. A story both endearing and enduring in its improbability was that the Elephantophagi carefully noted in the forest which trees the elephants habitually leaned against. In the elephants' absence the men cut partly through the tree, which accordingly collapsed when an elephant next leaned on it. The animal was as good as captured, for (the story assures us), having no joints in its legs, it could not get up from the ground.

There is a traditional link between Alexander the Great and Aristotle, a story that Aristotle's works on animals were based on information or even specimens sent to him by Alexander. Here is Pliny's version of the story.

> King Alexander the Great being fired with a desire to know the natures of animals and having delegated the pursuit of this study to Aristotle as a man of supreme eminence in every branch of knowledge, orders were given to some thousands of persons throughout the whole of Asia and Greece, all those who made their living by hunting, fowling and fishing and those who were in charge of warrens, herds, apiaries, fishponds and aviaries, to be at pains to make sure that he [Aristotle] should not remain ignorant of any [animal] born anywhere.[104]

The story has been rather sneered at by historians,[105] for whom the conjunction of the great philosopher and the great king looks like invention.[106] Yet there are a number of reasons why we might accept some form of the story. Aristotle had been after all Alexander's tutor, and might well have taught him something of his beliefs about the natural world. He had also addressed a tract *On Kingship* to him and came to suffer banishment from Athens for his Macedonian sympathies; he also recommended to the artists that they should paint Alexander's battles as being of lasting worth, so we may imagine that there was a special relationship between the two men. It would also have been natural for Alexander to take an interest in the nature of the countries he controlled. If nothing else, a general planning the logistics of an advance would need to know the nature of the country, its internal distances, and its peculiarities; a conqueror hoping to build a lasting empire would undertake a listing of resources, marvels worthy of *historiae* and tales suitable for his historians. Victorious generals often enough sent strange animals and even trees back for the Triumph, and although it would be rash to assert that any such specimen reached Aristotle, it is entirely possible that Alexander's lines of communication and administration, which must have amounted to a sort of civil service, could have handled some sort of questionnaire from Aristotle, on the lines suggested by Pliny.

Elephants had a special place in the Aristotle–Alexander story and indeed in natural history as a whole. Not only were they the largest land animal, but because they lived in Africa and India, were only indirectly known to the Greek and Roman world. On both counts they were worthy of *historia*. The treatments they received at the hands of Aristotle – and, as we shall see, Pliny – were characteristic of these authors and in general they serve as an example of the subject matter of natural history. To deal with them separately also serves to highlight some of the features of classical life that gave shape to its histories of nature.

There are one or two points in Aristotle's account of the elephant that support the story of the connection between Alexander and Aristotle on the topic of animals. The first is that the quantities that an elephant eats and drinks – fodder, wheat, wine and water – are given in Macedonian measures.[107] Probably the most likely explanation of this is that the quantities were noted down by a Macedonian somewhere in or near India where elephants were kept. Second, all of Aristotle's references seem to be to Indian elephants. At least, African elephants are not mentioned.[108] Again, it seems most likely that the information was derived from Macedonian expansion. (In contrast the Romans' experience, from Hannibal to Juba and Scipio, was with African elephants.) When Aristotle says[109] that the elephant is easily tamed and can be taught tricks, the trick he specifies is kneeling before a king. It would be a bold guess to think that Alexander was such a king, but it would have been an eminently suitable story for the historians to send home.

Some of Aristotle's information is expressly from India, as when he describes how the male elephants are kept from the females to maintain peace.[110] Again he says that the Indians use both male and female elephants in war (and that the males are more aggressive). Aristotle must be quoting a report from the elephants' native country when he describes how they fight in the wild, and how domesticated elephants help to tame wild ones.[111] That a full diet was said to keep Indian elephants peaceful may add weight to the story that the elephants being fed in Macedonian measures were living in India. It is surely also a report of those who had the care of them that elephants (no doubt because of their full diet) were occasionally prone to flatulence (olive oil, salt, honey and roast pork were variously used for their digestive upsets and insomnia).[112]

What are we to make of Aristotle's reports on the insides of elephants? He says they lack a gall-bladder, but that the liver, when cut, discharges gall. He also notes constrictions in the elephant's gut, which makes it look as if it had four stomachs, that its viscera are like those of a pig and that its spleen is comparatively small.[113] It is probable that the number of the elephant's teeth and the nature of its tongue could also only be seen in a dead and dissected animal.[114] Now, it is quite possible to imagine that the Indians of Aristotle's day cut up and disposed of the corpses of elephants, perhaps for food for other animals, and were as familiar with its insides as a butcher is with those of other animals. It is less easy to imagine that they wrote about them in any meaningful way. What would they have to say about them, unless, for example,to describe their unnatural and portentous appearance (as the Greeks and Romans looked at the insides of animals)? Yet Aristotle had answers to the questions that, as we have seen, he considered important in considering all animals. He has *differentiae* of the digestive organs and teeth, of the sex organs, of the mode of locomotion and its organs.[115] Very much part of his programme is the age of maturity, the mode of coupling and the length of pregnancy.[116] Is it possible that Aristotle gathered these details from something written – presumably in India – for other purposes? Or can we guess that he sent out via the Alexandrian civil service a rote of questions to the men in the occupations mentioned by Pliny, including those who kept elephants?

No certain answer to such a question is possible, of course. But it is possible to see how Aristotle's understanding of elephants was formed by the nature of the reports he read. The principal thing to be understood and explained about the elephant was its unique feature, the trunk. When Aristotle came to explain the parts of animals in *De Partibus Animalium* he characteristically makes a correlation between the life-style of the animal and the nature of its parts. For Aristotle the trunk is part of a nexus of necessity that determines the elephant's form. Aristotle makes a start with the report he gives in the *Historia Animalium* of the elephant often being found by rivers.[117] Elephants of course do like water, but here their being associated with rivers is almost certainly because it is by means of rivers that travellers most readily penetrate countries wild enough to contain elephants. The sight, from a boat, of strange creatures like elephants bathing and drinking could well have conveyed the belief that they were in some way water-animals. Likewise the report that elephants copulate only in lonely places, especially river banks,[118] seems traceable to travellers' tales. Aristotle begins with the notion that the elephant was a water-animal to the extent that it had to take its food from the water. But it clearly had the form of a land-animal (having four legs), and having blood and therefore a lung, it needed, said Aristotle, to respire. One function of the trunk was therefore as an extended nostril, enabling the partly or wholly submerged animal to breathe. Moreover, its great weight prevented it from passing rapidly from water to land (unlike smaller and more nimble animals that could briefly submerge themselves without breathing). So here too the trunk allowed land-animal respiration in an aqueous environment.[119] Necessity makes the elephant's trunk flexible, says Aristotle, because one as rigid as those of other animals could not be raised above the water when the elephant was submerged, and could not act as a hand to lift food when the animal was out of the water. Necessity linked this feature too to the weight of the elephant, for – says Aristotle – in most quadrupeds having fingers and toes, the forefeet act also as hands. The elephant for Aristotle was a polydactyl in not being cloven or solid hooved (and we might add in showing the vestiges of five toes) but its weight necessitated that its legs should serve simply as supports. The function of a hand was therefore exercised by the trunk.[120] The bulk of the elephant, so important in this reasoning, was necessary as a form of defence.[121]

This is a characteristic piece of reasoning, in which Aristotle discovers necessities between an animal of a certain kind, its size, its habits and its consequent shape. He has found the causes of the parts. The same applies to the generation of the elephant and its rearing of young. Pregnancy lasts for two years, the time necessary for the foetus to grow to full size.[122] The breasts of the female, he says, are only two in number, because the elephant only has one offspring at a time, and because two breasts are characteristic of the class of polydactyls, to which the elephant belongs. The breasts are placed towards the front of the animal because this is the position of the dominant teats in those animals with many.[123]

In this way Aristotle establishes a causal framework into which he can fit the empirical details of his knowledge of the animal, whether or not these came in answer to a questionnaire. In comparing the *historiae* of the different animals Aristotle seems to have arranged his notes by the size of the animal. In the *Historia Animalium* camels immediately follow elephants in Aristotle's discussion, often enough to make it clear that some principle of organisation is in evidence and that it is probable that he thought that the camel was the second largest animal. Thus the personality, habits and copulation of elephants is followed by the camel's sexual habits;[124] the Macedonian quantities of the elephant's diet are preceded by the camel's drinking habits and followed by a discussion of the life-span of the two animals;[125] the two animals are close together (but not adjacent) in Aristotle's observation of the aggressiveness of male animals in the mating season;[126] the fact that the copulation of both kinds of animals takes place in lonely spots is taken together;[127] the length of pregnancy and mode of birth of both animals are dealt with in adjacent paragraphs,[128] and so are the age of puberty, the extent of the mating season and the period of gestation of the two animals.[129] The flatulence of the elephant follows directly upon the rabies of the camel.[130] Even an apparently passing remark on the elephant as the least hairy of quadrupeds is followed directly by an introduction to the camel and its unique feature, the hump.[131]

Or perhaps the two animals are treated together by Aristotle because they both have a unique feature that is very obvious, the trunk and the hump? Possibly, if the *Historia Animalium* were really a collection of empirical detail, then Aristotle might have wanted to highlight two unique features that were prime *explicanda.* But more likely he knew before writing on the history of animals (and before sending out questionnaires?) what kind of detail he wanted, in order to explain them. It is clear from the details above in the *Historia Animalium* that most of the 'empirical' detail recorded in the case of the elephant and camel related to the means by which the 'nature of the animal' reproduced itself. In other words Aristotle (as indeed we would expect) had worked out his doctrine of causality, and here especially final causality, before seeking and arranging details of the lives, habits, personalities and parts of animals. The occasional duplication of statements of fact in the *Historia Animalium* looks rather as if Aristotle had used two answers to a question and had forgotten to edit one of them out.

Thus, on the one hand Aristotle in Greece received from men in contact with elephants in India reports structured by, or at least intelligible to the demands of Aristotle's natural philosophy; on the other hand men we know to have been associated with Alexander are the clear source of stories about elephants circulating later in the West. It is from Onesicritus, Alexander's companion and philosopher, that the reader learns that elephants can exceptionally live to 500 years and that pregnancy is ten years. (He also says they are bigger than Libyan elephants.) Nearchus was one of Alexander's officers and surveyed the Indian Ocean in the company of Onesicritus: he reported on how elephants are caught (by putting foot-traps where tracks meet), that they are easily tamed and can throw stones at a target and use tools. These are topics that relate to the intelligence of the elephant, worthy of note by philosophers. Nearchus also said that elephants are excellent swimmers, again a view that might be easily gained by water-borne explorers, and conceivably linked to Aristotle's belief that elephants are partly water-creatures.

THE NATURAL HISTORY OF THE NILE

Whether we reject the story of Aristotle, Alexander and the animals or agree with a notable Aristotelian scholar that the *Historia Animalium* presupposes Alexander's campaigns,[132] it is clear that natural-historical details of plants and animals resulted from European expansion. For the men of the classical world the land masses of the globe were divided into three main areas, Europe, Asia and Africa. India was part of Asia, and Alexander's penetration of the subcontinent created an interface between cultures that was – as we have seen – a rich source of accounts of strange animals and plants. Another source was Africa, Libya to the north and Ethiopia further south, proverbial for the novelties that it produced. Here too was an interface, a boundary of European knowledge, partly physical in nature: the desert.

Between Asia and Africa was Egypt. For the Greeks and Romans this was a land of ancient wisdom. Many early Greek philosophers, even Plato, are reputed to have spent time there learning the wisdom of the priests. All visitors quickly learned about the Nile as a thing most worthy of admiration. The Nile was an enduring topic of interest to Greeks and Romans and their accounts of it exemplify many of the features of natural history as a whole. The Nile was above all a worthy *historia*: unlike all other rivers it rose not in the winter but in the summer; it supplied water just when it was needed for the crops, which could not have grown without it; it was vast, of unknown origin; it was extending the area of Egypt at the Delta; and it was full of strange animals, most notably crocodiles. Knowledge about Egypt grew among the Greeks after the Athenians helped Artaxerxes I to reconquer it; again after Alexander the Great conquered it and planted an Alexandria there; and again during the period of Roman power: knowledge followed the flag. Military expansion not only supplied natural-history knowledge but demanded geographical knowledge, and the Nile became a landmark for those who wrote about distances and empires.

For the Egyptians, their Nile was the source and sustenance of their country. Life would have been impossible without it and it is not surprising that the Nile (and its sacred crocodiles) played a central role in their religion: it was associated with Apis, the bull-god.[133] That it flooded, unlike other rivers, when its waters were *needed* showed clearly to the Egyptians that it was providential. Even the kings were not allowed to sail up the river as it was rising.[134]

But when the Greeks made acquaintance with the Nile they brought, of course, their own attitudes to it, and it became a problem to be solved. Just why *did* the Nile flood in the summer?

Many of the features of the Greek philosophers' interest in the Nile can be seen in a text traditionally attributed to Aristotle, *The Inundation of the Nile.*[135] Some modern scholars have claimed that the work is genuinely Aristotelian, while others have denied it. Possibly it had Aristotle's name attached to it when the successors of Alexander established the library in Alexandria.[136] If not genuine then at least the attribution was made by someone who knew Aristotle's 'natural history' books and thought that the book on the Nile expanded or completed Aristotle's enterprise.[137] It could be seen as a part of Book 2 of the *Meteorologica*, added as a particular example after Aristotle's general remarks on rivers.[138]

The work addresses directly the problem that the Greeks saw in the flooding of the Nile, that is, why it happened, uniquely, in the summer. This was a physical event and the author takes it for granted that it has a physical cause, and it becomes the purpose of the investigation to discover it. The author proceeds, Aristotle-fashion, dialectically and historically. The summer flooding, he says, must be due either to an increase of the water from somewhere else in the summer, or a subtraction during the winter. This marks out the areas in which the physical answer will be given, and the author begins his search for it by reviewing older opinions. As so often happened with Aristotle, the search began with Thales, who in the matter of the Nile's flooding had argued that adverse annual winds held up the waters of the river. Diogenes of Apollonia in contrast held that water was added to the river from springs by reason of the attraction exerted by the summer sun, while Anaxagoras held that the cause was distant melting snows. The author spends a little time in refuting this last suggestion, which relies on assumptions about the location of the source and course of the Nile. But no one in the classical Mediterranean world had much information about the course of the Nile, and it is significant that military commanders, to whom great rivers were either barriers or means of transportation, actively sought answers. Our author denies the belief of 'king Artaxerxes Okhos' who, seeing crocodiles in a river in India as well as in the Nile, concluded that they were the same river. This was Artaxerxes III, who re-established Persian control over Egypt and whose severity resulted in his being poisoned in 337 BC. A few years later Alexander the Great was in control of Egypt. He too saw crocodiles in the Nile and in an Indian river, the Indus, and thought that they were the same river, rising somewhere in India and passing through vast desert tracts before emerging in Ethiopia. The idea of course depended wholly on Alexander's knowledge of new territories and in general is part of the story being told here of the expansion of natural history in line with political expansion. Further knowledge of the destination of the Indus made Alexander change his mind.[139] This parallels closely what our author says of Artaxerxes, who later discovered that the Indian river ran to the Red Sea.[140]

The author of the *Inundation of the Nile* also refutes the suggestion made by Nicagoras of Cyprus, namely that the Nile rises in a place where it is winter while it is summer in Egypt. After examining related phenomena, the author concludes that the cause is rain. Other authors in other works offered different causes. We know from Seneca that Euthymenes, having being on an Atlantic voyage, believed that that Ocean was responsible for the rising of the river, an opinion perhaps related to that of Theophrastus, who thought that the Nile was salty. To look forward briefly in time, we see that Juba, the Roman client king in north-west Africa, claimed that the Nile originated in lakes fed by the snows of the mountains of Mauretania and that it travelled below the desert before reaching Ethiopia and Egypt. Lucretius who (as we shall see) was anxious to exclude the supernatural from his philosophy, gave four causes for the flooding of the Nile: sand accumulating in the Delta, the Etesian winds blowing the water back from the sea, rain and melting snow. His principle (announced in the preceding lines) was to give all possible natural causes, one of which was certain to be true (and any of which was preferable to a providential explanation).[141]

Thus we can see that the extent to which the Nile is a constant component of ancient natural philosophy is matched only by the number of different physical explanations offered for its rising. These explanations had in common only that they were natural, and like the explanations of lightning and rain and so on, that they did not rely on the action of divinities. But for the Egyptians the Nile was above all providential and divine and the Greek philosophers were bringing to the phenomena of the river's flooding very much their own style of explanation. If they were tourists in Egypt they noted the *historiae* of the rising of the Nile, and the practices of the priests, but none of them ever suggested that the flooding of the river was providential. That it appeared to flood providentially in the summer only made it more necessary to find a natural explanation, whether it was the

Etesian winds, the motions of Ocean, a collection of sand and stones at the river's mouth, melting snows in the mountains where the Nile rose, rain, or underground caverns. The philosophers adopted a plain 'historical' style of narrative that could hardly carry the meaning of Egyptian religious terms. They even changed the name of the river itself, replacing the Egyptian name by another whose origin is not known. Characteristically, in denying that anything was the gift of the gods, the philosophers argued for the human origin of the arts, and in this case that geometry had arisen first in Egypt as the inhabitants sought to mark out the featureless mud left by the floods of the Nile. We saw in the previous chapter that it was the activities of the Greek pantheon that gave contents and boundaries to Greek natural philosophy, and here we see the same process being exported to the area of the divine in another country. We shall follow the process to India in a later chapter.

3

GEOGRAPHY AND NATURAL HISTORY

MAPS AND LIBRARIES

During Theophrastus' long reign at the Lyceum two new schools of philosophy appeared, the atomist and the Stoic. At the end of his reign a disaster happened to the Peripatetic school: its library was lost. How the Lyceum was deprived of the great working collections built up by Aristotle and his colleagues and the additions made by Theophrastus is a story told in some detail by Strabo and we shall look at it a little below. Here we can note that the loss must have had a paralysing effect on the peripatetics and may well have encouraged the growth of the rival philosophies. It was symbolic of the changes of the time that the Lyceum library finally reached Rome. This was where economic and military power now lay, and in this chapter we are concerned with how the Romans reacted to Greek philosophy, particularly Stoicism. By Strabo's time, Roman expansion had made it literally necessary to redraw the map of the world. The old map, like that carved in stone in the Lyceum, would no longer do. We shall also see in this chapter how the Stoic Strabo was concerned with the new map of the world, both literally and metaphorically, in his text.

Little is known about ancient maps. Fewer images than words have come down to us from antiquity, for a number of reasons. Fewer of them were produced. The skills required to make images are different from those of the scribe, and the scribe, who could handle the bulk of manuscript-copying, perhaps made a bad showing of, or ignored the pictures in his exemplar. Scribal copies of exemplars change in quantum leaps, many of which are recognisable by the scholar, as when the scribe's eye and hand have jumped a line or repeated a line because two began with the same word. The scholar thus has a chance of detecting and correcting the error. But the copy of a drawing differs from its original by imperceptible degrees and often allows its creator to develop his taste for symmetry or style. Undoubtedly the drawings referred to by Aristotle in the works on dissection and the history of animals were a great help in schematising differences in animals and in showing the shape of parts more effectively than could words; but neither function could be maintained over many copyings. There is evidence to suggest that two or three generations after Aristotle, anatomy was taught in Alexandria by the aid of diagrams; and if the strange medieval drawings that survive are in fact evidence of this, it is evidence too of how much mutilated drawings become after centuries of copying.[1] Much the same can be said of the drawings that accompanied the texts of those who wrote about medicinal plants, like Dioscorides: only when we have an unusually old manuscript are the drawings like the plants the text describes. Manuscript maps are rarer still.[2]

The maps of the world cut into stone in the Lyceum in Aristotle's time undoubtedly showed the improvement that the mathematical astronomers had made on the old physical descriptions of the earth, for Aristotle constantly refers to them. But these maps progressively became out of date. After Aristotle (and Alexander) we know from Strabo[3] that Eratosthenes (born in 276 BC) constructed a map of the habitable world, reaching from the Pillars of Hercules to India. We also know from Strabo that the Romans had a chorographic map of distances.[4] Pomponius Mela (*fl.* AD 37–42) wrote a Latin chorography, and Agrippa, a contemporary of Strabo, used maps in planning Roman military expansion.[5] Perhaps he used them in his final subjugation of the Cantabri in northen Spain, which provided Strabo with some new geographical knowledge. In the business of redrawing the map of the world after Roman and Parthian expansion, Strabo expected great improvements. Part of the redrawing (about which Strabo tells the reader) is mathematical, parallels being established by the height of the shadow of the gnomon on the sundial at a certain time of day (generally noon) at different places. Strabo relies on Eratosthenes for most of his mathematical geography, into which he fits his new information. Some of it was also drawn from military and naval reports – not necessarily visual – of distances marched and sailed.[6] If you make a globe to demonstrate the earth, says Strabo,[7] it should be at least 10 feet in diameter; since the habitable part of it is comparatively small, it can be drawn on a flat surface, about 7 feet long, and less across. Draw the parallels along the length of the habitable world (beginning like Eratosthenes in the middle) and construct a grid by drawing the first vertical line across the middle (and widest) width of the habitable earth.[8] The other verticals can be parallel to the first, and serve to show the climates and winds, or they can converge slightly. This final instruction is vague enough, and is probably evidence of Strabo's being unable to follow the more technical mathematical arguments of people like Eratosthenes.[9]

Strabo tells the story of Aristotle's library. Strabo, like some later scholars[10] says that Aristotle's was the first library in the world that we like to look back on as learned in our image. When we think of the volume of reportage of natural questions that came back to the Lyceum, the constitutions, the lists of victors at the games, the shifting nature of the texts on natural things and on problems, in general on the joint Lyceum research programme and on Aristotle's empirical mode of investigation, we can see how a library was necessary. Not necessarily a library of finished pieces, but a working library, of pieces received, lists of things to be done, provisional drafts of results achieved. No doubt the works of Aristotle's often quoted 'predecessors', the pre-Socratics, were well represented. Strabo adds that Aristotle taught the Egyptians how to organise a library: if so, it adds a great deal of colour to our picture of Aristotle as the systematiser and of the Greeks as the assimilators and successors of the immemorial Egyptian learning.

Aristotle left the whole collection to Theophrastus, who, as we have seen, added to it. Both Aristotle and Theophrastus had in mind the common good of the philosophers who shared the accommodation and facilities of the Lyceum, which had been consolidated under Theophrastus as a property-owning group. But it was not long before the joint library of Aristotle and Theophratus was recognised as valuable and therefore heritable, and perhaps therefore as the property of an individual. It was Neleus, the Socratic philosopher of Scepsis, who inherited the Lyceum library.[11] It was expected that he would be the next head of the Lyceum, and it was natural that he should have the books; but Strato was chosen instead, and when Neleus went away in disgust, he took the books with him.[12] He passed them on to his heirs, says Strabo,[13] and so deprived the Lyceum of much of its working material. But by now libraries were becoming desirable.[14] Ptolemy Philadelphus was on the look-out for books. The Lyceum library would have been a great catch, but Neleus cunningly sold to his messengers the 'library of Aristotle' that consisted of the books that Aristotle had owned, not the ones that he had written. His heirs, coming under similar pressure to sell

Aristotle's own works, and who had stored the collection securely but not with much regard to its physical condition, now in a fright put it 'in a kind of trench'[15] in the ground, resulting in physical damage. At last the collection was sold to Apellicon of Teos (who died about 84 BC) who attempted to fill in the gaps caused by the storage and so published a poor edition. Finally, when Sulla the Roman took charge of Athens, the collection became his personal booty. It ended up in Rome in the charge of Tyrannion the grammarian. Strabo does not mention Andronicus of Rhodes, the first reputed careful editor of Aristotle, under whom, it has been conjectured, he may have studied; Andronicus had time to study, copy and divide Aristotle's works into books before the original collection was sold piecemeal by Sulla's son Faustus.

This series of events was disastrous for the Lyceum. Its original programme as envisaged by Aristotle was deprived of the very stuff of its existence – an accumulating corpus of empirical knowledge that could serve the philosophical purposes of understanding and practical action. As Strabo says, after Theophrastus the peripatetics had no books and could only talk bombastically about commonplaces and could do no practical philosophy; and later, because of the bad state of the texts (after Apellicon) could be certain of nothing.

The growth of libraries and awareness of their value was parallelled by an increasing circulation of handbooks and summaries. After Aristotle a great deal of information, philosophical and technical, was relayed in this way. Sometimes the names of the big authors whose works were abstracted from were given, sometimes not. It is difficult to tell whether the older authors were quoted directly or by way of a handbook in the work of later writers. The Romans took over the habit from the Greeks and it ideally suited their intellectual temperament, which did not lie in the direction of detailed philosophical analysis. The preparation of collections of abstracts presupposes a library of some kind, and libraries bred, too, a new kind of scholarship that included comparative studies, refinement of texts and attribution of authorship in uncertain cases.

Libraries often received royal support. Those who had followed Alexander the Great knew that to rule different races their laws and important writings had to be known, that is, translated into Greek and kept securely. The fragmentation of Alexander's empire at his death resulted in the establishment of a number of more local kingdoms, particularly the Ptolemies, based in Alexandria, the Attalids in Pergamum and the Seleucids in Antioch. They competed for a reputation in cultural things and spent generously on institutions, including libraries, and in attracting scholars. Perhaps they wanted to emulate Alexander, whose reputation was being built by the accounts of his philosophers, historians and commanders: a sizeable proportion of his reputation was concerned with natural wonders and resources. Attalus I fought off the Gauls and extended his kingdom eastwards; Attalus II made a reputation for himself as a patron of learning, and Attalus III in 133 BC bequeathed his kingdom to the Romans, who had supported the kingdom in the past. Perhaps Attalus I was also an author, for Pliny cites him a number of times.[16] His son, Eumenes II, was also a learned man, and was anxious to have a library in Pergamum. He got one, and a librarian too, Crates of Mallos. Crates (who flourished about 160 BC) conducted fierce debates with Alexandrian critics over the interpretation of Homer, and came to see Homer as almost omniscient in matters to do with the physical world. Where Homer was not clear, thought Crates, he was using allegory, which a good commentator could penetrate. Crates was a Stoic and used Stoic physical theory in his Homeric commentaries; the geographical conclusions he came to formed a resource for *mappa mundi* cartography in the Middle Ages.[17] As a learned man, he was an ideal choice for Eumenes to send to Rome, when the time came to parley with the Romans. Other Greek states also used philosophers to petition the Roman Senate.

A case parallel to that of the Attalids is that of Juba I and II, kings of Mauretania, in North Africa.[18] This too is a story of Roman expansion. Juba I backed the wrong side in Rome's Civil War and after an early victory was killed. Caesar led his son in chains through Rome in his triumph, but this second Juba soon ingratiated himself in Rome, became learned in the Roman manner (he wrote a history of Rome in Greek) and was restored to his throne by Augustus. Juba II wrote on the geography and natural history of North Africa from Arabia to the Atlantic. He reported on the Cave Dwellers (*Trogodytae* in Pliny) and amongst them the Jackal Hunters and Fish Eaters, who swim as well as their prey, all of whom are variously located near Ethiopia and Arabia.[19] He wrote about the Canary Islands and their trees that resembled fennel, and their juice, and on giant dogs, of which he received two specimens. Alexander had also received two great dogs from the king of Albania and a conscious parallel may have been intended by Juba or Pliny, in whose book on natural history we read about Juba, and who treats him in much the same way as he treats Bion, one of Alexander's men.

It is well known that the Ptolemies encouraged learning and developed the Library and Museum at Alexandria, where Strabo probably studied.[20] Above all, Ptolemy Philadelphus had decided to create a 'universal' library, no less than the 500,000 scrolls he thought would be needed to contain all the books of the races of people in the world.[21] The Museum was part of the Royal Palace and the men of learning who shared it (says Strabo[22]) have a common dining room. (So did the philosophers of Croton, as we learn from Strabo's story of how their building collapsed, but was supported long enough by Milo the athlete to allow the philosophers to escape.[23]) These men in Alexandria had property in common and a priest was in charge of the Museum, appointed once by the kings, now (in Strabo's time) by Caesar.

Roman power was exerted over all three kingdoms. After the Romans had intervened in Ptolemaic Egypt, Augustus arranged that Juba should marry Cleopatra Selene, the daughter of Antony and Cleopatra. Pliny links Juba's son with the Ptolemies: the Romans were arranging dynastic traditions to suit themselves. They had, then, control over the major libraries, in Alexandria, Pergamum and Rome. According to Strabo, not many other cities gave much thought to education. Tarsus was different, having more philosophers, schools and lectures than even Athens, but mostly directed at the native inhabitants who often then went to live elsewhere (presumably to teach).

Stoicism became a major philosophy. It was attractive to Romans as well as to Greeks, although in different ways. In contrast to Athenian philosophy, Stoicism did not teach the causes of things or how to discover them or what the first principles of the natures-of-things were. Instead it discussed behaviour and the training of the mind. Its purpose was to enable the Stoic to live well, free from fear. The gods were neither capricious nor vengeful and had no effect on men's lives. Freedom of fear was achieved in part by showing that the natural world was intelligible and rational and that nature's laws should be followed with acceptance. The Greeks' 'love of knowledge' is here also, particularly for the Romans, 'use of knowledge' for a moral purpose and a mental state, that of Stoic resignation to the inevitable. The Stoic had to know about nature even if his duty did not include investigating nature. He knew that the governing principle of nature was the *logos*, the reason of nature that governed all. It has some aspects of divinity, and the common people equated it with Zeus; but it was far from the caprice of the gods of the pantheon.

The Stoic philosophy of nature, reconstructed from a number of sources, was something of this kind: the cosmos was a unified body, that is, it differed both from bodies that were combinations of things for a single purpose (like a ship) and from bodies composed of separate parts (like an army, in which parts may be lost without affecting the survival of the whole). The cosmos is like animals and plants, held together by a single binding force, variously *hexis* or *pneuma*; The parts of the cosmos have *sympatheia* like a body that loses one of its parts. Its binding *hexis* is natural – *hypo physeos* – and rational. The binding force is, or is closely related to, *pneuma,* which is the 'heat of life in organic things'.[24]

The important thing for us was the *pneuma,* sometimes represented as physical air, sometimes as a spirit or simply force. It existed at three levels. At the lowest, it gave tension and coherence to physical objects. At a higher level it gave life to animate parts of the natural world. At the highest level it provided man with reason and so was akin to the *logos.* It will be seen that this scheme reflects the distinction in earlier Greek philosophies between the physical, the vital and the rational. While Aristotle had argued that the natures of things could be categorised in a similar threefold way, the Stoic had in mind the 'nature' of the whole world: the world was like an organism with its own 'nature'. This *subsumed* the three kinds of natures-of-things, and the nature-of-the-world became a general thing, our 'mother nature'. Just as earlier natures of things did nothing in vain, neither did the nature of the cosmos: the whole world was balanced and providential.

This physical theory is below the surface rather than evident in the two Stoics we are principally concerned with, Strabo and Seneca; in particular the Roman Seneca (who is dealt with in the following chapter) does not show interest in theory, but both authors rely on *pneuma* in their physical explanations. Strabo does not emphasise so much as Seneca the practical duties of the Stoic; but then he was Greek and his enterprise was different.

STRABO'S WORLD

Strabo was an Asiatic Greek, born in Amasia in Pontus in about 63 BC. The Greek world in which he lived and about which he travelled had been expanded not only by Alexander the Great, but by the

Romans and – says Strabo – Parthians. The Parthians were the Persian group that successfully threw off the control of the post-Alexandrian Hellenistic Seleucid kings and established an empire reaching into India. Like that of Alexander then (but into rather different areas) Parthian power stretched in an easterly direction from Greece, while Roman expansion was to the west. The natural-history *historiae* reported from both directions naturally differed in kind. Strabo was aware of the extent and recentness of these changes,[25] and had written a *History* to give an account of things not dealt with by Polybius. Polybius himself was a Greek with a direct knowledge of the Romans' power, for he was taken hostage by them after the defeat of Perseus of Macedon. He was invited to join the circle of Scipio, and witnessed the Roman destruction of Carthage in 146 BC. When Perseus' library was shipped to Rome, Scipio and the Romans had access for the first time to a substantial body of Greek writings. Polybius' history accordingly had a strong geographical component to accommodate the theatres of Roman action, a matter not lost on Strabo. Strabo's *Geography* (it was finally revised between AD 17 and 23) is an attempt to give a systematic account of the expanded world of the early first century.[26] His aims were largely political, to give useful knowledge to important people, but his world was also a physical world, where nature produced *historiae* that were important for a geographer and a philosopher.

Strabo was then, a Stoic, like Crates, the Homeric scholar and geographer in Pergamum. This helped to determine the way he reported the world. First, although he reports natural and artificial *historiae* it is not his purpose to awaken wonder. The true Stoic did not allow his mind to be surprised and sought equability by accepting the natural inevitability of things. Strabo accordingly lists a number of things that might at first sight be surprising, so that repetition should make them seem more ordinary and less surprising. He is also sceptical about many of the stories of far-off places and people retailed by earlier historians and travellers: not only are recent accounts more accurate and in general more sober, he says, but he saw that the early accounts were often exaggerated for the purpose of generating wonder or aggrandising a reputation (for example of Alexander the Great). A degree of scepticism about such things also helped the Stoic avoid being surprised.

Second, as a Stoic – and despite the teaching of his master Boethus the peripatetic – Strabo expressly denied[27] the elaborate causality of

Aristotle. He was not, then, concerned with finding the natures of things, as Aristotle had been. His world indeed was very different from Aristotle's. Strabo's world had been created and was perishable, while Aristotle's was eternal. For Strabo it was Providence who had ensured that the sphere of earth, at the centre of the universe, had an irregular surface, so that it was not totally covered by the sphere of water and that man would have a place to live.[28] Indeed the whole universe was made for the benefit of Providence's two superior creations, men and the gods. Man occupies the central earth, the gods the highest sphere, and the physical world is enclosed between the two. The sphere of water, the seas, and all animals and plants were made for man's use. Thus natural actions are not, as they had been for Aristotle, the actualisation of potential or the expression of a nature, but imposed from without. It is 'nature' in this providential sense that Strabo the Stoic accepted, the inevitability of which gave the Stoic peace of mind. Strabo held that Providence governed the world by the major changes that we see going on slowly around us, primarily as sea gave way to land, or vice versa. It was no surprise to Strabo that sea shells were found two or three thousand stadia from the sea.[29] He has much on the creation of new land by silting from rivers, and believed that the Mediterranean, once a lake, was filled up by its rivers and finally broke through the Pillars of Hercules, leaving dry areas of sea-bed.[30] Strabo says additionally that by the agency of air (the Stoic *pneuma)* large areas of sea-bed could rise and sink.[31] Strabo's world, then, was not governed by the gods. He saw that, historically, belief in the traditional gods and their means of vengeance like thunderbolts had been politically useful for the control of the people, but as a Stoic he elevated nature or Providence above the gods, whose traditional activities he regarded as myths. Myths, he says, are used by poets, law-givers and those in control of states as expedients because they are attractive to men: as attractive as reasoning. The portentous and the marvellous – myths – make things easy to learn, and children can be spurred on by pleasant myths and deterred, that is, controlled, by unpleasant. But myths, insists Strabo, are essentially childish. Ignorant and half-educated men are as but children: this explains the use of myths by the early historians and even those who looked at *physis.*[32] Only philosophy, says Strabo (meaning of course Stoic philosophy), can rise above myth and the use of it by the politically powerful.

GEOGRAPHY AS A NEW PHILOSOPHY

Strabo argues strongly that geography is philosophy. Since he was a Stoic, this meant that geography was a study of the way in which Providence had disposed the parts of the world and now governed them. The foundation of geography for Strabo was physics, one of the three 'supreme excellences' of Stoic philosophy (the others were logic and ethics). Physics was thus a Stoic *arete*, a kind of knowledge that depended on its own principles and proofs. Physics asserted that earth was heavy and moved to the centre of the universe, and that the heavens revolved around it. Physics settles the poles, equator, tropics and zodiac. The mathematicians and geometers – both philosophers – take up from there; and the geographer accepts their findings.[33]

Let us look in a little more detail at Strabo's arguments about the philosophical nature of geography. He begins with a Greek belief so widely held that it was almost axiomatic. Philosophy, he says, is a knowledge of things human and divine. As a Stoic, by 'divine' Strabo does not mean the gods of the traditional pantheon but nature or providence in the role of creator and controller of both the world and man. Clearly things human and divine were central to geography.

Strabo also argues that geography is part of philosophy because it had been practised by philosophers in the past – Posidonius, Polybius, Eratosthenes, Hecataeus, Anaximander and, ultimately, Homer. To regard Homer as a geographer or as a philosopher is of course special pleading, but it makes a number of points which we should remember. First, it emphasises Strabo's devotion to Homer. For Strabo, there *was* something geographically special about Homer. The Catalogue of the Ships in the Iliad listed the Greek ships at Aulis before sailing for Troy; it includes nearly two hundred place-names, and no other author besides Strabo follows this list so closely. At times his *Geography* looks like a commentary upon it.[34] There was a sense in which Homer, the basis of Greek education, was the source of all knowledge.[35] Certainly, the Homeric poems also gave form to the work of one of Strabo's sources, Demetrius of Scepsis, who wrote historically and geographically (in the second century BC) on the allies of the Trojans in the poems.[36]

Strabo takes a number of things from the resources produced by his authors, early to recent. From Homer, the places associated with the heroes; from Polybius, human history; from Eratosthenes, the astronomical and geometrical techniques that allowed one to measure and divide up the earth into longitude and latitude, zones and climates. Following Hipparchus, Strabo says that a knowledge of astronomy is necessary to locate places on earth.[37] Here too was a powerful reason to think of geography as philosophical, because it was indissolubly linked with the most noble part of philosophy, the study of the heavens.[38] Traditionally the abode of the gods and considered divine by philosophers, including Aristotle, the heavens were 'divine' in the sense intended by Strabo's definition of philosophy. Thus (says Strabo[39]) in philosophical geography there is no separation of heaven and earth, and geography is like a combination of geometry (the measurement of the earth and heavens) and meteorology (all natural changes inside the ultimate sphere). This too is part of Strabo's construction of geography: geography is more than the distance-lists of the chorographers and includes not only political history but what Strabo calls 'terrestrial history' and what we would call natural history: animals and plants and everything useful or harmful produced by the land and sea. The result is a *polymatheia* of philosophical knowledge.

There is another sense too in which Strabo's geography is a new subject, in being constructed to handle the new knowledge made available by the military adventures of the Romans and Parthians. There is a strong sense in which Strabo is in fact inventing the subject of geography, and like other inventors, needed a history of his subject. This is why he announces that Homer was the first geographer. That is, the poems formed a resource that was available and intelligible to Strabo. What he saw in them – names and descriptions of places – was what related to his current undertaking. It gave authority to his own new subject when Strabo showed that much of the subject matter of geography had been known to Homer but not set into a system by him: like Crates, Strabo credited Homer with a vast knowledge which needed to be elucidated by analysis and commentary. Strabo adds that Homer was followed by Anaximander, who drew the first map, and by Hecataeus. Here then is his little history of geography, put together by Strabo as roots for his own subject. The moral of the story for us is that Strabo, like others who write histories, has *constructed* a history out of cultural resources available to him as a Greek philosopher in first-century Rome. These resources were parts of other people's different enterprises, but having constructed a history, Strabo then has an explanation for a 'genetic' transmission of 'geographical' ideas, information and techniques. Historians of science have commonly done the same.

Homer, Anaximander and Hecataeus, the founding fathers of geography in Strabo's eyes, were ancients even to him (Hecataeus flourished about 522 BC). More recent were Aristobulus and Cleitarchus, who had accompanied Alexander, and later still, those involved with Alexander's successors and their purposes: Timosthenes of Rhodes, who commanded the Egyptian fleet under Ptolemy Philadelphus, and who wrote on harbours; and Megasthenes, sent by Seleucus Nicator as ambassador to Chandragupta at Pataliputra on the Ganges. More recent still were Posidonius the Stoic[40] and Theophanes of Mytilene, Pompey's friend. Strabo does not include any except the ancients as part of his history of geography, and often criticises the accuracy of the later writers.

There is another important way in which Strabo's geography is a new and philosophical subject. He says it is philosophical because in general it is *addressed to important men.*[41] These are the men of state[42] who will have been taught the basics of astronomy and geometry in their liberal and philosophical[43] education, and the information he provides is of the kind that would be useful in international military or commercial circumstances. The expansion of Roman power made it clear to Strabo that potentially a great deal of the inhabited world could be governed by a very few people, even by a single command. Geographical knowledge is of immense practical importance in philosophical and military terms: it explains the resources, economic and otherwise, for different forms of government,[44] and Strabo lists a number of military successes achieved by the Parthians, Celts and Germans *against* the Romans by the aid of their better geographical knowledge of the local terrain.[45] For these kinds of reasons, Strabo spends less time on the remote parts of the inhabited world. Their interest is principally the strange men and animals who live there, about which he can report *historiae*, but they are geographically less important because less likely to be of concern to the military commanders whom Strabo sometimes explicitly addresses.[46] And while the geographer is most concerned with natural features, great human works are of interest as enduring and in a sense becoming natural; moreover, learning about great human actions inspires emulation or avoidance. His goal is practical wisdom and he will deal most, he says, with those parts with good government and therefore commerce.[47]

PRACTICAL PHILOSOPHY

That is, Strabo's geography was meant to be of practical use, as well as being 'philosophical'. For us 'philosophy' is one of the least practical of all subjects, and it requires a conscious effort to see it as otherwise. For the Greeks philosophy embraced all knowledge; and since the Greeks were a successful race of people and managed their affairs pretty well, we need not be surprised if their philosophy was practical.[48] They also saw practical philosophy in other lands: a natural part of geography as Stoic philosophy was an account of the different societies of the inhabited world, and how they organised themselves and what they believed in. Strabo consistently reports on 'philosophers' in different societies. He is of course seeing the world through Greek eyes, and we can learn a little more about what he meant by 'philosophy' by seeing what he recognised in other societies as philosophical. This in turn will give us an extra perspective on the natural-historical aspects of his philosophical geography.

For Strabo it was the role of philosophers to give advice to the powerful. He saw himself as a philosopher in this way and he saw other advisers in other societies as philosophers. The Greeks had, or had known, various kinds of government, from tyrannies to oligarchies and democracy. They saw the advantage of strong government, in their own case and in those of others. But the qualifications which equipped a man to assume and handle power did not necessarily bring with them the knowledge that was necessary for the exercise of a sound rule. Those in power needed advisers and the philosophers as professional Knowers sought to give it. In that philosophy was a knowledge of 'all things human and divine' the philosophers could also advise the powerful on the will of the gods, which was also practical knowledge in events of great moment. Strabo is saying that travelling broadens the philosophical mind and that travelled men (like Callisthenes) are a valuable source of advice.[49] But here too there were specialist Knowers, the priests or soothsayers, who inspected sacrifical entrails or the flight of birds for portents.

Strabo routinely recognises these groups of people in other societies. In Babylonia, he says, the philosophers are called Chaldeans; they live separately, study astronomy and some construct nativities.[50] In Egypt the priests as one of the three classes of people study *philosophia* and astronomy and were the companions of and advisers to the king.[51] Strabo had seen the large houses in Heliopolis in which the priests had lived and made their studies;[52] he also saw the houses where Plato and Eudoxus were said to have spent some thirteen years learning from the priests.[53] The Brahmins of India were 'philosophers' as much as the Druids of Britain and Gaul. Strabo saw Celtic society as containing the important divisions of Bards, Vates and Druids. The Vates were *physiologoi*, those who 'read nature'; so too were the Druids who, Strabo adds, also made *philosophia* their business.[54] Strabo uses the term *physiologoi* also for the pre-Socratic philosophers of Greece, and it is clear that a consideration of the natural world was a regular component of 'philosophy' wherever Strabo saw it.

In Parthia, the wise men were the Magi, who formed a council that helped to choose and advise the kings.[55] Here Strabo takes notice of the Parthians not because of notable things uncovered by their recent expansion towards the east, but because of the importance that attached to their indigenous practices by reason of their new political power. According to the slightly later Pliny (who was highly indignant about it) the practices of the Magi were insidiously creeping west, a foreign and malign influence emanating from a people worse even than the Greeks.[56] Pliny, who did not relish, and often did not understand Greek philosophy, saw that the Magi's attempt to manipulate nature and natural things was of a very different kind to Roman practicality and Greek theory: it was, literally, magic.

Strabo saw philosophers in India too.[57] Following Megasthenes, he understood that the highest caste in India consisted of philosophers, who (he says) are few but powerful. They are advisers to the king, and meet together at the beginning of the new year to report what they had seen during the year with respect to the produce – animals and plants – of the country and to offer advice on the governing of the country. It is practical advice, says Strabo, and the philosopher who proves himself wrong three times thereafter is obliged to keep his peace, while those whose advice is useful are exempted from taxes. The same people offer sacrifices to the gods for the sake of the people: we can recall that Strabo was quite clear on the political use of religious fear. It was appropriate for philosophers to know 'things divine' and so be in a position to advise the powerful: it was from Megasthenes that Strabo accepted that an important group of the Indian philosophers were the *Brachmanes* (Brahmins) who were especially (and like the Magi, says Strabo) the advisers of kings.[58] They led an austere life and were in charge of education. This latter fact alone would have made them philosophers in Greek eyes.

In any case (and not surprisingly) Greek enquiries into Brahmin beliefs resulted in answers that the Greeks recognised as part of philosophy. Strabo the Greek found it natural that some of the Indian philosophers should worship 'Dionysius' and others 'Heracles'.[59] When Strabo repeats from Megasthenes that the Brahmins believed that the universe was created and is destructible, with a central spherical earth, it is not difficult to imagine the questions, formed by Greek philosophy, to which these statements were answers. The same may be said of the Brahmins' belief that the universe is ruled by the deity who made it, that it has four primary elements, of which water was fundamental, and that the heavens were made of a fifth element: this, Strabo says, was the Brahmin view of *physis*.[60] A Greek interpretation of Indian thought was also the natural result of Greek investigation when Alexander the Great sent Onesicritus to search out the wisdom of the Indian 'sophists'. Onesicritus naturally expected the 'sophists' to correspond to categories of people he knew about. His interest in Indian 'philosophy' was not merely intellectual, but extended to its practical purposes, and when he with the help of three interpreters interviewed the Indian 'sophist', Calanus, he discovered that the feats of endurance practiced by Calanus were part of the Indian attempt to placate 'Zeus', who, angered at man's indulgence, had once destroyed everything in a perfect world. Onesicritus would have recognised the propitiation of Zeus as also a Greek practice (this is why Calanus' reply is expressed in this way) but declined Calanus' invitation to him – should he wish to learn more wisdom – to take off his clothes and lie on the hot stones. He was extricated by another Indian 'sophist', Mandanis, who reproved Calanus' arrogance and declared that here was a chance to teach wisdom to a philosopher in arms, Alexander. (Mandanis was interested to discover, pursuing the matter with Onesicritus, that his own philosophy shared with Pythagoreanism abstinence from meat and the belief that wisdom is the removal of pain from the soul[61]). Calanus seems to have belonged to the second order of Indian 'philosophers', known to the Greeks as gymnosophists, who (according to Nearchus[62]) investigated natural things.[63]

In short, Strabo the Greek philosopher saw things he recognised about philosophers and philosophy when he looked at other societies. The philosophy was about things human, natural and divine; it was practised by a recognised group of society, often sharing a building; and it was practical, at least achieving something for the soul of the philosopher and very often directing the activities of the politically powerful. His examples are often put in such a way that they illustrate his belief that the politically powerful often used knowledge of 'things divine' to manage their subjects. Strabo has many examples of wise men – potential philosophers – becoming powerful on account of their knowledge.[64] In the new, larger world, he has had to drop the old Greek view that only Greeks were civilised and the rest of men barbaric and enemies. Indians, Arians, Romans and Carthaginians, he says,[65] are refined and civilised (and some Greeks are not). This view allowed Strabo to see their wise men as philosophers and as acting in a philosophical way when giving advice to rulers. He tells the story of Pythagoras' slave Zamolxis, who learned some astronomy from his master and who also visited Egypt; returning home to the tribe of the Getae, he became a partner of the king in governing the country because he could predict eclipses. According to Strabo, this began a tradition of the ruler having a Pythagorean adviser which lasted down to his own day. Another king of the Getae was Boerebistas, a usurper who neverthless raised his people to be a great power, maintaining order among them with the help of Decaenas, a 'wizard' who had been to Egypt, could make prognostications of the divine will and finally, like his counterpart Zamolxis, came to be regarded as having divine features himself.[66] We also read of the peripatetic philosopher Athenaeus of Seleucia, who became the leader of his people;[67] and of Posidonius, from whom Pompey sought advice.

As a philosopher Strabo gave attention to 'things divine' that were part of the natural and human world. Partly his attitude is that of an observer of other people's religions and beliefs (to list and compare, which is for him a philosophical business) and partly to show that there is a divine element in true philosophy. As a philosophical geographer he notes that both Greeks and barbarians have religious rites in connection with festivals, some of the rites being frenzied and others having wild Bacchic dances, like those of the Corybantes in Greece.[68] Some rites are secret, others open.[69] Strabo has something of what we would call an anthropological detachment and notes how the comic writers made fun of strange religious rituals, and how the Athenians were tolerant. Here too as a philosopher Strabo sees the effects of religious rituals, essentially part of the mechanism of social control. If the rituals are secret, he says, then awe is generated. If they are frenzied, they sometimes appear to lead to divine inspiration, like that of the soothsayers. Choral dancing was an important part of Greek religion,[70] and Strabo in noting that Greek education began with music is observing a system where music, dancing, ritual and frenzy form a system from education to religion that had a stabilising social role.

Yet at the same time it is clear that Strabo wants to show that philosophy – Stoicism – also has its divine aspect, and that this is the Providence that manages the physical world. He does so partly by picking up the topic of music. As the basis of Greek education 'music' included verse, and we can recall Strabo's deep attachment to Homer. But – following Plato and the Pythagoreans – the theory of music is also philosophy; and the world has been put together providentially with its parts in harmony. Music (he adds) is divine in being beautiful and the effect of it, of religious rites, and of frenzies is the same, he says: to draw the mind away from ordinary pre-occupations towards the divine. Again, this is not the pantheon, which frightened pre- and non-philosophical Greeks and which the Stoic ranked below nature, but almost man himself, for Strabo observes that it has been well said that man is most godly when doing good to others. (Man is even more godlike when happy, adds Strabo, and music, festivals, and philosophy all generate happiness.)

So there is a sense in which Strabo's philosophy is divine in its subject matter because it looks at the results of providential activity. As a philosophical geographer he is not interested in what he calls the myths of the various peoples of the world, except where they touch upon what is divine. (Many of the myths had been collected by Demetrius of Scepsis,[71] the Homeric 'geographer' we met briefly above.) But Strabo means what is divine in his sense: aspects of nature, whether providential or physical. Thus while the myths of those who dwell on Mount Ida[72] include the story that they were wizards and in attendance to the mother of the gods, it was also part of their mythology that these people were the first to work with iron. Strabo as a philosophical geographer was interested in the iron-working, and in general wanted to separate out the mythical from the natural. He therefore had to gather up the 'early opinion and myths' of peoples precisely because, he thought, the ancients were enigmatic about their natural or physical (*physikas*) beliefs and always added myths. He centres on the 'mountain roaming' of religious zealots who think they are closer to the gods in the heavens and can read their portents. Strabo wants to separate this from the associated search for metals – iron in the case of the inhabitants of Mount Ida – and for other things useful in life.

GREEKS AND ROMANS

Historical opinion has been divided on the question of whether the powerful men to whom Strabo addressed his geography were Greeks or Romans.[73] He wrote in Greek, but at a time when the Romans recognised the cultural value of the language and were using it increasingly. But Greek military power was a thing of the past and Strabo lived in a world where Roman power was actively growing.

His sympathies are Greek, but he is prudently pro-Roman. Indeed his attitude to the Romans may have been more than prudence. Like many Greeks he was impressed with the efficiency with which the Romans planned and did things. Like the major Stoic figure Posidonius, he may have seen the power of Rome, apparently taking control of the whole world, as the fulfilment of the Stoic Providence.[74] If so, then still the Greeks had a large part to play. Apart from an apparently Latin chorography, all Strabo's sources are Greek, and he sees that Roman ventures in the area of history and geography are merely translations of Greek works without any spirit of enquiry. When he says that the Greeks have become the most talkative of all men,[75] the Romans would probably have agreed; but Strabo meant 'philosophical' and the Romans would have meant 'speciously plausible'.[76] He knows that the Romans built splendid roads, aqueducts and sewers, which the Greeks gave less attention to in their own cities. He tells the story that the Tarquins' Great Sewer was broad enough for a loaded hay waggon. He describes the pipes, cisterns and fountains of the private houses of Rome; manifestly, the Romans preferred the useful to the beautiful (but he adds that Pompey and Caesar and Augustus began to beautify the city).[77] Strabo argues that much of this was necessary because of the inconvenient location of Rome, the centre of the Roman world. The Greeks in contrast he says are a nation of many cities, colonising and looking for harbours, strength of position, fertility of soil and above all for beauty in the new buildings. He notes for example some perfectly paved streets where the architect had unfortunately forgotten to make provision for the removal of sewage. He gives the (Roman) Romulus and Remus story about the foundation of Rome, but matches it with a story that the place was originally a Greek colony.[78] His account of Rome itself is comparatively restrained, and he says that its weak defensible position was the cause of the discipline of its citizens, their main defence.[79] He is anxious that it should be known that Cumae and Naples are Greek foundations.[80]

Magna Graecia, says Strabo,[81] the Greek area of the south of Italy, including Sicily, is now wholly barbarised: he means it is no longer purely Greek, but the implication is that the Romans are barbaric. Strabo likes to dwell on the Greek cities of Magna Graecia like Croton, famous for its athletes and philosophers.[82] He is proud of the exploits of Alexander but careful to add that his geography has also been made necessary by the exploits of Caesar.[83]

It is not difficult to see that for Strabo philosophy was an entirely Greek affair, and that his own business was to educate the Romans. Not only were all his sources Greeks, but the *gaps* in his sources were Greek. Do not trust even Greek accounts of places distant from Greece, or small, he says. In contrast, Strabo treats the Romans as innocent of all philosophy; in his view the Romans owed their success to nature, *physis*.[84] To their natural discipline and valour, Providence soon added the rich neighbouring land; it was providential that Italy had few, but good harbours; and that it was defended by mountains as well as the sea.[85] Strabo makes it clear where his allegiances lie by rounding off the entire work with praise of the Romans as the greatest territorial power,[86] but it is also implicit throughout the entire work that the business of understanding the nature of the world that the Romans ruled was a Greek affair. Nature had enriched the Romans, the Greeks understood nature, the Greeks advised the Romans. It was almost syllogistic.

Strabo's Greekness comes out most clearly perhaps in his defence of Homer. Homer was the basis of Greek letters, the early part of all education. The Greek child in learning his Homer was learning to be Greek. As Strabo says, anciently poetry was the first level of instruction, and the Greek states still educate their young first with poetry, for moral instruction.[87] It was a Stoic saying, too, that only wise men make real poets. It was natural then that Strabo should think of Homer, with his abundance of place names and descriptions, as a sort of proto-geographer, both Greek and philosophical. As we have seen, Strabo is making a claim for the relevance of the founts of Greek culture to his own, largely invented, subject. It was accordingly painful that some later philosophers interested in geographical knowledge should claim that Homer was ignorant of some obvious facts, or worse, that his job as a poet was to entertain, not inform. Here his enemy was Eratosthenes, whose mathematical description of the world Strabo was obliged to follow. Strabo defends Homer passionately and at great length. He analyses the poet's words minutely. He indignantly rejects the claim that Homer was ignorant (for example of the Nile) as a mere argument from silence (Homer *did* know of the Nile, but did not write about it).[88] The flooding of the Nile was as we have seen very well known in the ancient world and the philosophers competed to give an explanation of it. Strabo had special knowledge of Egypt,[89] having accompanied the Roman Prefect of Egypt, Aelius Gallus, on an expedition to Upper Egypt (probably in 25 BC). He defends Homer also against Aristarchus, who came from Syria and who, says Strabo,[90] did not understand the spirit of Homer, even when he describes Syria. The clear implication is that Aristarchus had not had a proper, Greek, education, based on Homer. Strabo distinguishes the poet's genuine intention to instruct from obvious poetic licence (and says the Stoics do not expect factual accuracy of every poetic detail).[91] On the distances, directions, places and winds[92] involved in the story of Odysseus' wanderings, Strabo enlists the aid of Polybius and Aristotle to demonstrate the poet's factual accuracy. (According to Strabo Alexander carried with him in a golden casket of Persian origin a copy of the works of Homer in an edition by Aristotle.)

Strabo thought that the habitable world was an island surrounded by Ocean.[93] He accordingly thought that it would be possible to circumnavigate the globe, reaching the east of the habitable world by sailing west; he records that attempts to circumnavigate had been made, but abandoned because of 'destitution and loneliness'. Its fringes were inhabited by plants, animals and men who grew stranger the further away they were from the Greek–Roman centre: the Greeks and Romans were not only physically at the centre of the world but central too in terms of power, wealth and civilisation. What was important in Strabo's reporting was the lands surrounding the Mediterranean, their politics, resources, armies, histories and relationship to Rome. He routinely gives the size of armies that can be raised by the cities and states he describes. He advises the military commander in distant places not to be surprised at the different appearance of the night sky.[94] The political purposes and intended readership of the *Geography* were the same as those of his *History*, which dealt with the famous and powerful.[95]

Strabo's island world reached from Ireland (thought of as north of Britain) to the Cinnamon-lands of the south, and, west to east, from the Pillars of Hercules (the strait of Gibraltar) to Ceylon, beyond India.[96] Reports of a frozen land called Thule, six days' sail to the north of Britain, were denied by Strabo as the lies of Pytheas, repeated by Eratosthenes. Pytheas claimed to have visited the whole of Britain and asserted that near Thule the elements were confused and held in suspension, so that one could not walk or sail. More recent visitors to *Bretaniken* and *Ierne* do not mention this or Thule, says Strabo, dismissing it as a myth.[97] Places like the British Isles, so distant from the centre of the world, did not interest Strabo greatly because they had no strategic importance. The British, he says,[98] are too weak to cross the channel and attack; and the Romans make more money from taxing commerce than from maintaining an army in Britain.

The fringes of the Empire were areas of active colonisation, a process with characteristic features. Necklaces, glass vessels, amber beads and other petty pieces, says Strabo,[99] are exported to Britain, and in exchange the civilised part of the world receives slaves, hides and hunting dogs. The fringes of civilisation are characteristically also seen as the sources of disease, and Strabo talks of recently conquered parts of Spain as a sort of white man's grave, where the abundance of rats gave rise to epidemics which often killed the Romans.[100]

GREEKS AND BARBARIANS

When Strabo says that his purpose in writing was to do better than his predecessors,[101] who did not have the advantage of the material released by Roman and Parthian expansion, this meant a new level of interpretation of sources, mainly because his predecessors had been, he thought, too gullible about strange things. But in being more severe in his criticism of his sources and less credulous than his predecessors, Strabo was in a difficult position. First, as we have seen, his attachment to Homer led him to take legendary places seriously, and to spend much energy on locating them, while the mathematical geometers were inclined to dismiss poetry as mere entertainment. Strabo had to carefully and emphatically distinguish legend from myth, for it was in accepting myth, he thought, that the earlier writers had displayed their credulity or falsity. By 'myth' Strabo meant partly the traditional stories of the activities of the gods, for as we have seen, Strabo the Stoic relegated the gods below nature in importance. But again, his devotion to Homer made Strabo hesitant about denying the gods completely. By 'myth' he also meant marvellous tales told by earlier writers, and he dismissed for example Herodotus and Ctesias as marvel-mongers.

Part of his caution about wonderful things was derived from the Stoic determination not to be surprised at things, which we met above. He tells the reader[102] that Democritus 'and all the philosophers' strove to inculcate the virtue of not marvelling, for they classed this virtue with the freedom from fear which was a widespread aim of the philosophical life. But here the point was to tell repeatedly of marvellous things that were *genuine*, so that surprise would leave them in the telling. So Strabo has to decide which of the wonderful stories he has heard are true. He generally seems to choose those that are the result of the actions of nature in the physical world, in preference to stories of bizarre barbarians.[103] His list of things not-to-be-surprised-at includes the fire that burned in the sea for four days between the islands of Thera and Therasia and created an island; volcanoes that built mountains; earthquakes that swallowed up a Phoenician city and the Achaian town of Bura, blocked springs in Chalcis and opened up new ones; and the destruction of the town of Helice by a tidal wave.[104] Earthquakes were naturally *historiae* of great interest and fear, and philosophers who wanted to achieve *ataraxia* or dispel other people's fears often discussed the nature of earthquakes. Strabo has another list of wonders from Demetrius of Callatis, who had listed all the Greek earthquakes.[105] For Strabo it is all part of the way in which Providence is controlling the earth (by the agency of air) and he is prepared to report those who say that Sicily was once part of Italy, removed by the sea near Rhegium.

In contrast Strabo is not prepared to accept stories of strange people – very strange people – who were said to live in very distant lands. He cannot accept that some men have ears so big they can sleep in them, as one would in a blanket. Nor does he believe there are men with no mouths, who subsist on the fragrances of flowers and roast meats. This is a tall story from Megasthenes, who claimed to have met them: a gentle folk, he said.[106] As for the habits of bizarre barbarians, Strabo is rather less sceptical, and they come second to his accounts of physical events. He repeats the story[107] that the people at the northern limit of the inhabitable world, the Irish, commit incestuous acts in public and eat their dead parents, but he hesitates about the accuracy of his sources. Such things were also said of people at different fringes of the world who had in common with the Irish only their distance from the Greco-Roman centre.

To summarise the question of Strabo's sources and their reliability, it is clear that they derive from three main chronological phases. The earliest are the philosophers and historians of ancient Greece, including the unreliable Herodotus. These were individuals who had opportunity to travel, perhaps with the Persians and generally to the East, and who were able to tell tall stories to the Greeks at home on their return. Second were the historians of Alexander, some of whom were determined to aggrandise themselves or Alexander by exaggerating his achievements and the wonders of foreign parts. But others of them 'began to write the truth', said Strabo, like Nearchus and Onesicritus.[108] Strabo had also given attention to the Alexander-historians in his *History* and said flatly that Megasthenes and Deimachus were liars, describing the men without mouths, ants that mine gold, snakes that swallow oxen and men with one eye. Strabo particularly resented their re-invention of the Homeric story of cranes fighting pigmies, which they located among the troglodytes of Ethiopia. (Plate 8.)

Third, the more recent writers were more satisfactory for Strabo. Their accounts came from three sources: the Hellenised areas con-

Plate 8 Pigmy carrying a crane. Greek figure of *c.* 460 BC. (British Museum.)

quered by Alexander and now under the control of a series of monarchs, the westward expansion of the Romans towards Britain, and the eastward movement of the Parthians towards India. One of the writers using the first source was Patrocles, from whom Eratosthenes had taken some of his accounts of the distances between places.[109] Patrocles had been one of the officers in the fleet of Seleucus, who was one of the post-Alexandrian kings in the Near East. For Strabo, Patrocles' direct involvement with naval and diplomatic missions lent credibility to his account. Strabo also seems to give him credence because he had direct contact with Alexander's treasurer, Xenocles, and indirectly thus from Alexander himself, who, as Patrocles said, was always the best informed because intelligence reports came to him alone, and his companions, including the extravagant Alexander-historians, were less well informed. Egypt was an important Hellenistic state and Strabo knew directly too how much the trade of the Alexandrian merchants with India had increased since the time of the Ptolemies.

Better accounts have also been given recently, says Strabo,[110] of the Germans and British (resulting from the westward Roman advance). Not only were recently conquered races more reliably reported in the literature available to Strabo, but because still barbaric they were almost as bizarre as people on the edges of the world. Strabo cannot bring himself to list the outlandish names of the races of recently conquered northern Spain, near the Cantabrians, and such people were normally named by the Romans from their strange habits: cave-dwellers, floor-sleepers and so on.[111] The inhabitants of the distant Atlantic coast of the Iberian peninsula, says Strabo,[112] are bestial and slovenly. Like the Cantabrians, they bathe in, and clean their teeth with urine, which they age in cisterns for the purpose. They are slovenly too in not cultivating grapes, olives or figs. They are more distant, more recently conquered and so it is not to be wondered at that they did not have these three foodstuffs that are almost the criterion of civilised life. Strabo constantly uses grapes, olives and figs when describing the comparative fertility of different countries.[113] (Plate 9.)

Partly the lack of grapes, olives and figs on the Atlantic coast was a result of the cold. Strabo's geometrical division of the world into 'climates', basically the areas between lines of latitude, allowed him to postulate what could be grown in countries progressively colder as one went north from the equator. This, he thought, enabled him to check the accuracy of reports of monstrous plant or animal

Plate 9 Getting in the olive harvest. Olives (and figs and grapes), so well known to the Greeks, were almost a criterion of civilisation, since they were not cultivated in barbaric and distant countries. Even Italy, according to Pliny, was at one time without olives. (British Museum.)

growth, or surprising lack of it. Some of these reports seem to have come from the third of the sources we identified above: Strabo draws from the writers of Parthian histories like Apollodorus of Artemita, who supplied information on the Albanians and Iberians of the Caucasus. He also reports that in Aria, one of the most powerful countries in Asia, the soil is so productive that wine will keep for three generations in vessels made without pitch. In the nearby Margiana the vines are so big that it takes two men to embrace a single stem; the bunches of grapes are 2 cubits long.[114] The same is said of Maurusia, in Libya.[115] The Romans were moving east too, and Strabo reports that they had recently invaded Arabia Felix: Strabo's friend Aelius Gallus, whom we have met as Prefect of Egypt, commanded the army there.

Strabo can also give credence to the stories of the non-civilised

138

habits of the barbarians when reported from recent colonisation and exploration. It is from recent Roman military exploration too that Strabo knew that the Britons, more barbaric than the Continental Celts, lived in the forests, making defended enclosures. They have milk, he says,[116] but do not know how to make cheese. Even more savage are the people of the mountains of Lesser Armenia, who live in trees and eat nuts and the flesh of wild animals.[117] More disgusting are the Dardanians, who dig caves under their dunghills and live there.[118] The Spanish Vettonians were surprised on seeing a Roman camp for the first time to observe the officers walking up and down its streets for exercise. The Vettonians thought they were mad and tried to lead them back to their tents, thinking that they should either be fighting or sitting quietly.[119] Strabo has reliable information on the habits of the Cantabrians, subjugated by Augustus in 25 BC and by Agrippa in 19 BC. There were those who committed mutual suicide rather than surrender to the Romans, and those who sang victory paeans while being crucified.[120] Just as bizarre to Strabo were the barbarian women. Not only did they wear iron collars that had veil-supporting frames extending over their heads, but as women they had an importance in Vettonian society. The husbands gave their wives dowries, daughters inherited, and brothers were married off by their sisters: woman-rule was not at all civilised to Strabo.

An extreme case of woman-rule was that of the Amazons.[121] Strabo, striving to keep a distinction between history and myth, is puzzled by the consistency of the myth of an all-female society, the Amazons. Who could believe that women could organise themselves without men? Even to fight successfully against their neighbours and send an expedition as far as Attica? The Amazons (he reports) live in the mountains above Albania. Their right breasts are seared as infants. For two months in the year they go up into the mountains to meet the Gargarians, who go there at the same time and share sacrifices and who may originally have been part of the same tribe. The Gargarians in the tradition are either all men, or only the men go up the mountain. They make the Amazons pregnant and female babies are kept by the Amazons and males sent to the Gargarians. Strabo does not believe that Alexander had a sexual liaison with Thalestria, the queen of the Amazons. Truthful historians do not mention it, he says, only those who wish to glorify Alexander.[122] (Plates 10 and 11.)

The scale from barbarity to civilisation was not only a question of distance from the Greco-Roman centre of the world, and of the

139

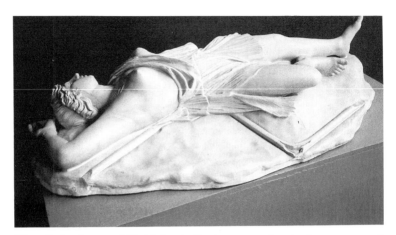

Plate 10 An Amazon killed in battle. Strabo reports that the Amazons seared the right breasts of their female infants, and traditionally some such technique was used for the better handling of weapons. Nothing of the sort is represented here or in Plate 11. This figure was for the memorial of Attalus I. (Museum of Classical Archaeology, Cambridge.)

Plate 11 An Amazon attacks a fallen Greek. From the Mausoleum of Halicarnassus. (British Museum.)

140

recentness of subjugation by the Romans, but of the passage of historical time. We have seen that Strabo's world was not eternal like that of Aristotle, but was one with a beginning and at least a potential end. He takes from Plato the notion that civilisation gradually emerged after a great period of flooding.[123] This was consistent with his Stoic view of Providence forming a place for man on earth by raising parts of the earth above the waters and controlling the interplay of the two elements by the agency of air or *pneuma*. As the waters receded, so men become more cultivated in three stages: first they occupied the mountains and lived wild lives, still afraid of the waters. Second, the foothills were exposed and men began to occupy them; and last the plains were exposed and men descended to the rich valleys. Strabo adds further stages, in which loss of fear of the sea, equated with civilisation, drew men to the coasts and to build towns. This chronological change was reflected in Strabo's view of his contemporary world, and is the difference between the hardy rustic folk of the highlands, the more sophisticated agriculturists of the plains and finally the city dwellers.

NATURAL WONDERS

We saw above that earthquakes frightened people in the classical world and that the philosophers, particularly the Stoics, argued for the naturalness of them. The same can be said of volcanoes, which were frightening and to the ordinary person perhaps were the vengeful action of the gods. When a new volcanic island appeared in the sea near Sicily it was for the Roman Senate clearly a matter of the gods, and they sent a deputation to perform sacrifices on it.[124] The philosophers needed to show in contrast that volcanoes were also natural and need not be feared – provided that one kept to a distance, of course. Traditionally the philosopher Empedocles had not kept to a distance and had ended his life in the active crater of Etna; Strabo is sceptical of the story that one of his sandals was found near by.[125] Pliny too was to find volcanoes philosophically interesting, as we shall see, to his cost. Writing about half a century before Vesuvius destroyed Pompeii, Herculaneum and Pliny, Strabo says that above these two towns 'lies Mt Vesuvius, which, save for its summit, has dwellings all round, on farm-lands that are absolutely beautiful'.[126] Strabo too was interested in volcanoes, and inspecting the rocks at the summit, thought that their porosity and colour indicated that they had been burned through before the fuel of the volcano finally ran out. He noted the fertility of the ground from the descent of volcanic ash, and a number of times observed how good it was for vines; and sheep can grow so fat on it that they choke unless they are bled.[127]

As a Stoic Strabo believed that air was the agent used by Providence for most of the major changes in the natural world. This is the Stoic belief in an active *pneuma*, rather than in air as an element in the peripatetic way (Strabo does not go into the theory of the *pneuma*). But another of the traditional elements, water, does provide Strabo with a physical if not peripatetic background for natural wonders in (largely) distant places. Rivers in particular have the powers to change the colour of things that pass through them. The Celeus and Neleus rivers in Euboea change black sheep to white and vice versa; the water of the Crathis turns yellow or white the hair of those who bathe in it. The Sybaris makes horses timid.[128] Strabo is on traditional ground when describing the petrifying effect of various waters. At Mesogis, on the Maeander river, there are hot springs with such power of petrification that the locals guided the water through ditches in order to construct stone walls. The springs were a tourist attraction and a 'Plutonium' had been dug there to celebrate the springs as evidence of the underworld and its god, Pluto. Strabo was one of the tourists and he threw a sparrow into the Plutonium to test the poisonous quality of the air within it. The sparrow (which died) had apparently been given to him by the eunuch-priests who administered the place. It was said too that a bull led into the Plutonium would die, but that the priests entered it with impunity (but Strabo thought from the expression on their faces that they were holding their breaths).[129]

At other times Strabo does come close to Aristotelian physical thought. He accepts that heat and water are generative in combination, as in the Nile and in rivers in India. Barren women may conceive after drinking such water, and the animals that live in it are correspondingly big.[130] Indeed, crocodiles are so characteristic of the Nile that when Alexander saw them also in the Hydaspes during his Indian campaign, he thought he had found the source of the Nile.[131] (We have seen that in another version of the story Alexander saw crocodiles in the Indus rather than the Hydaspes.) As natural wonders, crocodiles figured large in the experiences of the travelling philosopher. The city of Arsinoe, reports Strabo, who had been there,[132] used to be called Crocodeilonpolis and the priests kept a sacred crocodile there. Strabo saw the priests open its mouth, put in some cooked meat, honey and wine. In the City of Heracles, in contrast, the ichneumon, the enemy of the crocodile, was sacred. According to a traditional story, the ichneumon waits until the crocodile is basking with its mouth open, jumps in and eats its way through the crocodile. Another traditional story is that the ichneumon successfully attacks snakes by first rolling in the mud of a river, allowing the mud to dry as a defence and then attacking the asps and dragging them to the river to kill them.[133] To display strange and ferocious beasts in Rome was to display the power of Roman arms in distant places, and Roman commanders often promoted themselves in this way; crocodiles were accordingly displayed in Rome, attended by natives who had a sympathy with them and were not harmed by them.[134]

Other natural wonders reported by Strabo were not only *historiae* but were potentially important pieces of information for the practical man who needed to know the resources of a tract of land. Strabo's report[135] that all of Iberia is rich in metals is characteristic. A man so practical as Alexander the Great had a mining engineer in his retinue, 'Gorgus the mining expert'[136] from whom no doubt originates the account of the Indians' excellent gold and silver mines. Nevertheless the Indians were reported as being unsophisticated in mining and working the metals. Related to this and from the same vintage of marvellous stories is the account of the 'ant' that mined gold. From Nearchus[137] it appeared that the goldmining ants had skins like leopards. Megasthenes says they are as big as foxes and can destroy both the men who come after their gold and the animals they ride on, so it is necessary to go by night and divert the ants by laying out carcasses. The ants dig holes in winter and pile up the earth like moles; this is where the gold dust is found. The Indians sell it unworked as dust because they cannot smelt it. It is easy to see the charm of these stories of great wealth, not entirely appreciated by its human guardians and defended by monstrous animals. Perhaps (adds Strabo)[138] the legend of the golden fleece is in the habit of the Soanes, near Dioscurias in Asia, of using fleeces to filter out grains of gold from streams. (These people, says Strabo, are as filthy as the Phtheirophagi, the lice-eaters, their neighbours.)

Strabo's reports of other economic resources that come with the framework of natural history or wonders include the copper mines[139] and asphalt springs in Libya and the spring of oil found by people digging near the Ochus river.[140] The tin trade was also of interest to Strabo, and he tells how the Romans learned of it by shadowing Phoenician boats as they approached the 'tin islands', the Cassiterides, off the coast of Britain. The appearance of the inhabitants reminded Strabo of the goddesses of Vengeance in tragedies, for they dressed in long black belted cloaks and walked with sticks.[141] Stories of mines that filled up again after being neglected were not uncommon, and are found for example in the peripatetic *Auscultationes Mirabiles*.[142] Strabo has accounts of iron mines on Elba that filled up after having been abandoned, a salt mine in India, a marble quarry in Paros and a refillable asphalt mine.[143] What lay behind these stories was the belief that minerals were constantly being generated, either by a living earth, or by some natural change like the condensations of Aristotle's 'exhalations'.

INDIA AND AFRICA

India and Africa had been known for a long time, but not well, by the Greeks (Plate 12). There were even stories that the Greeks had made great military conquests in India before Alexander's time. Disregard them, says Strabo; it may be true that Alexander believed them and tried to emulate their heroes, but otherwise the stories are entirely traditional or inventions of the Alexander-historians.[144] This is again Strabo's distinction between the marvel-mongering early historians and the more sober reports of later writers. With India, indeed, Strabo faces a particularly difficult problem of evaluating his sources. India is very far away; not many Greeks have seen it, he says, and those only a part. What they did not see they took from hearsay. Even those on the same expedition contradict each other. The problem was mostly that while some of the Alexander-historians made an approach to the truth, there were few later sources against which they could be checked. While Roman power and presence in north and west Spain in the later period gave Strabo an easy means of communication, there was no corresponding presence in India and it was now a long time since Alexander had been there. There were merchants in plenty from Egypt, but as Strabo says,[145] they did not penetrate the interior and did not write histories. People who did, like Apollodorus in his *Parthica*, were often wrong. But isolated modern reports, like the travellers to India who write of whales, give much less dramatic accounts of them than the sailors in Nearchus' fleet, says Strabo.[146] Nearchus and Onesicritus were commissioned by Alexander to survey the coastline and maritime regions of the Indian Ocean, and much of their written report was available to Strabo. They noticed the shoal-water at the entrance to rivers,[147] a tree whose roots arched out from the trunk and made a sort of wooden tent,[148] snakes 80 and 140 cubits long,[149] how the Indian rainwater changed the colour of foreign cattle to that of the native kind (Strabo agrees)[150] and how the weather changed as the season wore on.[151] Another of Alexander's attendants had been Aristobulus, from whom Strabo has the report that the Oxus is the biggest river outside India.[152] From such sources come stories like that which describes how the Macedonians, catching sight of a crowd of long-tailed apes, mistook them for men and began to move into battle formation. They learned that the apes were caught by trickery: the hunters ostentatiously washed their faces from a bowl of water in the vicinity of the apes and on leaving exchanged the bowls of water for bowls of bird-lime. The apes emerged and attempted to imitate the men by washing with the bird-lime, which stuck their eyelids together and rendered them incapable.[153]

Another problem of reporting a place so distant and strange as India was that of language. Although Alexander had interpreters, translations would have been primarily about matters of strategic

Plate 12 Symbolic figure of Africa and India. From the Piazza Armerina in Sicily, where a long mosaic, the 'Great Hunt', represents the pursuit and capture of animals for the circus in Rome and elsewhere. Sicily was a staging post for the trade between Africa and Italy. (See also Plates 21–23.)

importance. Identification of plants and animals for philosophical treatment by the historians was another matter. We have seen that Greek questions through interpreters to Indian 'philosophers' elicited what were essentially Greek replies; but mere names, standing on their own, were hardly susceptible of translation. Strabo reports that some Indian crops were simply unknown[154] to the Macedonians and so had no names. When Megasthenes reports that wool grew on trees and that the Macedonians preferred the cloth made from it for pillows, we can reasonably assume that it was cotton;[155] and when he found honey in the middle of reeds, yet in the absence of bees, it is not unreasonable to believe that he was investigating sugar cane.[156] But in other cases Strabo uses terms in Greek which must have been little more than guesses as translations of terms in Indian languages. The same thing happens with the huge, strange and effectively nameless vegetables of Libya.[157] It is the same for the Egyptian names of fish in his account of the Nile. He reports that the crocodile keeps out of the Nile all fish but the dolphin (which is stronger), the *cestreus* and the *thrissa*.[158] We cannot translate these names from the Greek (or perhaps Strabo was using Latin terms) any more certainly than we can be sure Strabo had chosen good equivalents of the Egyptian terms. (The *cestreus* is said to have a 'sympathy' for the 'pig-fish', which has spikes on its head and is unsuitable eating for the crocodiles: the *cestreus* shares this immunity.) Strabo tells the same story of crocodile-infested rivers in India, but does not attempt to name the Indian river-creatures. Here Strabo is in the middle of a source-evaluation exercise, giving first an exaggerated story from Nearchus about the size, number and viciousness of Indian reptiles that drive people from their homes when there are floods. Aristobulus more soberly reported (says Strabo) that he did not see any huge animals and that the worst snakes were the smallest; and that the Indian rivers had a fauna like that of the Nile (but without hippopotamuses, which Onesicritus denied).[159] Again it is the stories from the most distant parts that are the least trustworthy, depending on fewer and more exaggerated accounts. Strabo reports with some scepticism on the accounts by Megasthenes of the good country on the far side of the Hypanis, where there are the gold-mining ants, people who live for 200 years, and a flying reptile 2 cubits long like a bat but with corrosive urine and sweat.[160] Strabo struggles with philosophical explanations when he has stories the genre of which he cannot trust. When Megasthenes reports a river Silas, on which nothing floats, Strabo is hesitant because (he claims) Aristotle and Democritus disagree. But it was clearly a matter of the

study of nature, *physiologia*, for it seemed related to known physical facts about atmospheres too thin to support flight, and to the attraction exerted by certain vapours, just as amber and the magnet attracted things. It is very clear here that Strabo the Stoic would have preferred explanations based on *physis* – nature or Providence – rather than on the exaggerations of unreliable historians. As if to make the point he lists a number of tall stories from Megasthenes: unicorns; reeds 50 fathoms long; cannibalistic Caucasians who copulate publicly; pigmies – they of the fights with the cranes – who are as small as three hand-spans. No one trustworthy, says Strabo, claims to have seen pigmies.[161]

Distinguishing the old and unreliable authors from the more personal reports of the moderns also enabled Strabo to solve the interesting philosophical problem of the inundation of the Nile to his satisfaction.[162] As we saw in the previous chapter, this was a great natural wonder, one of the famous *historiae* of the ancient world, 'the best known and most marvellous thing in Egypt and decidedly the most worthy of mention and of historical record' says Strabo.[163] The men of old, he said, had to depend on conjecture, but now there are people who have seen the cause of it (summer rains in Ethiopia); these are those people sent to hunt elephants or on other missions by the Ptolemaic kings. Ptolemy Philadelphus in particular was interested in such things. Sesostris traversed the whole of Ethiopia as far as the cinnamon country. Cambyses went as far as Meroe. Strabo traces the theory of summer rains back though Posidonius and Callisthenes to Aristotle and ultimately to Homer, and so gives the observations of the recents the support of history. Why summer rains are more than winter rains here is still (he says) under investigation, and Ariston the peripatetic and Eudorus have written books on the Nile. Perhaps Aristotle had too; certainly later ages believed so.[164]

Stories about Libya were almost equal to those from India in their exoticism. Libyan rivers too had crocodiles, and Strabo reports that on this account some people believed that the Nile rose here, rather than in India or Ethiopia. The story that Libyan rivers also contain leeches 7 cubits long[165] may suggest, as modern commentary holds, that the original investigators were actually looking at lampreys, or it may be the usual kind of exaggeration, like that which held that there were snakes in Libya so big that grass grew on their backs.[166]

NATURE AND GOD

By Strabo's century, with Aristotle's view of the nature-of-the-thing in eclipse, there was a widespread agreement that the physical world had been made and was ruled by a demiurge, providence or an autonomous 'nature'. Strabo notes a group with a very different view, the followers of Moses. He gives an account of Moses as an Egyptian priest who became dissatisfied with the Egyptian practice of representing the divinity in the shape of cattle, and with the Greek practice of making images of gods. Moses instead stressed the omnipresence of the divinity.[167] So (Strabo continues) Moses led a number of like-thinking people into what is now Jerusalem, which he obtained without much force, because its countryside was too barren to be worth defending. We shall see that Jewish ideas of the omnipresence and omnipotence of the deity were not unknown in the first and second centuries, but hardly intelligible or credible to those brought up in the Hellenistic philosophical tradition. What is important for us is that the Christians absorbed the Jewish account of God into a Hellenistic view of the world. The result was that they understood what the philosophers said about the world, but the omnipotence of God made 'nature' or 'providence' redundant as a governing principle. Observation of nature and its *historiae* ceased to be relevant. Strabo only records that the followers of Moses fell into tyranny (some becoming brigands) and superstition (like circumcision and abstinence from meat).[168]

4

GREECE AND ROME

FROM GREEK *PHYSIS* TO ROMAN *NATURA*

When the Romans, having successfully erased Carthage from the world map in 202 BC, began to interfere in the quarrels of the kingdoms that had succeeded Alexander's empire, they became better acquainted with Greek philosophy. We saw in the last chapter that the Greeks often used philosophers as ambassadors to Rome. In 155 BC, to try to placate the Romans, Athens sent the heads of the three main philosophical schools to Rome, Critolaus the peripatetic, Diogenes the Stoic and Carneades, founder of the New Academy.[1] They gave lectures and began to awaken Roman interest in philosophy. The ultimate Hellenisation of Rome was considerable, but it remains true that philosophy was not as important for the Romans as it was for the Greeks. In the Roman world philosophy was at first practised by Greeks and then by Romans who learned Greek in order to do so. There were also Romans who wrote philosophical Latin. Lucretius wrote philosophical Latin verse, but it was in imitation of the Greek Epicurus. Of all Greek philosophy the one the Romans found most sympathetic was Stoicism, which struck a chord with the old Roman virtues of *gravitas* and *pietas.* In their own past, Cato seemed to be an example of a native Stoicism and so provided a justificatory Roman history of the philosophy. Famously the emperor Marcus Aurelius was Stoical and his example undoubtedly served to spread Stoicism.

But the Romans treated the philosophies they borrowed from the Greeks in a different way. They adopted these philosophies for their moral virtues rather than for their intellectual virtuosity and made philosophy a practical business. They did not seek knowledge for its own sake, or to understand causes. Romans generally did not see the point of the Greeks' wanting to know such things. This had its effect on the Roman perception of 'nature' and what they considered worthy of note in their own world, the *historiae*.

Stoicism had many virtues that appealed to the later Christians. When we say that we are being 'philosophical' about something (generally unpleasant) the term derives ultimately from Stoicism. The patient resignation that it implies was a form of *ataraxia* that did not necessarily depend for its effectiveness on the acuity of the intellect or the active investigation of nature, whose rules the Stoic accepted. Greeks like Strabo pursued natural knowledge more actively that the Roman Seneca, both of them Stoics. Even among the Greeks there were sects whose 'philosophy' and its sought-after tranquillity of mind were *not* intellectual. That *ataraxia* was sought after in these ways as well as by the philosophers serves to remind us how practical a business philosophy could be. The Cynics sought a tranquillity of mind by a deliberate rejection of all the trappings of civilisation and the adoption of a life based on the bare necessities of nature. Wandering and begging, the Cynic regarded all else with contempt. This was not a 'philosophy' in our sense, but a training for life. Beginning in the time of Aristotle with Diogenes of Sinope – he who lived in a barrel – Cynicism lived on into the time of the Christians, many of whom approved of it. The Sceptics had a similar purpose, but claimed that knowledge of nature, important for the Epicureans and Stoics, was (like all certain knowledge) unobtainable. They therefore did not try to obtain it; and their training for *ataraxia*, as anti-intellectual, was no more of a philosophy in our terms than that of the Cynics. Last, the late Academy developed critical methods to the point of scepticism, or what (as we shall see) Seneca called in derision the study of non-knowledge.

Two Greek figures were important in the Roman adoption of Greek philosophy, Epicurus in the case of atomism and Posidonius for Stoicism.[2] The work of neither has survived and we do not have their own words on what their enterprises were. We cannot therefore – in line with the method adopted in this book – afford them much space. For atomism, we rely on the Roman follower of Epicurus, Lucretius, and for Stoicism, the Roman, Seneca, who used Posidonius as his main source. What we need to note about Posidonius is that he shows how Greek philosophy was affected by Roman power. By the time he died in 51 BC Roman supremacy in the world looked inevitable. It also appeared natural to the extent that the Romans looked to the Stoics as if they were ruling in accordance with Providence. To accept Roman dominion was therefore philosophical as well as expedient. The Romans were nothing loath to see the Empire as a Stoic commonwealth. Cicero, a friend of Posidonius, drew on his Stoic doctrines for both the law of nature and for his philosophical treatise *On the Nature of the Gods.*

(i) The atomists

Thus it was largely Stoicism and atomism that entered the Roman world as philosophies which relied on a knowledge of nature to achieve their purposes. Atomism, which denied purpose in the world and the hierarchy of authority, whether causal in the Aristotelian way or of the gods, was generally disliked by the Platonists and Aristotelians with their different teleologies.[3] Epicurus had set up his school in the Garden in Athens in 307/6 BC,[4] and his philosophical aim was the practical one of achieving freedom from pain and fear, largely of the gods. Understanding the nature of life, matter and the soul was an essential part of achieving *ataraxia.* Like Epicurus, Lucretius wanted to banish fear of the gods. But as we have seen, fear of the gods could be politically useful to those in power and atomism was never popular with them. Atomism looked dangerous to the later Christians for related reasons: it denied divine power and championed materialism. The Christians put it about that Lucretius died an unseemly death (he died in about 54 BC) and did little to encourage the survival of his works.[5]

The first principle of Epicurean physics was that nothing is created out of nothing and matter cannot be destroyed. Since there was nothing but causeless atoms and void[6] the Epicurean world view was radically different from the imposed and innate teleologies of Plato and Aristotle. Also fundamentally different was the Epicurean doctrine of the infinite number of worlds, which were fortuitous and not made for the sake of man. The central position of man in the world had perhaps been held universally before and Epicurus' doctrine is directed towards lessening man's fears by making him marginal. The gods were also marginalised, being represented as material, leading happy lives in the spaces between the worlds, with which they did not interfere. The gods, therefore, could not inflict punishment in this life. Man's divine component, the soul, was also material and mortal: there was no interference by the gods after death, either. Epicurus' philosophy was thus concerned with religious matters and was in fact a missionary business, its practitioners striving to save others from fear by personal contact.[7]

The Memmius to whom Lucretius addressed his poem was politically important, and Lucretius may have nurtured a desire to see his system sponsored by the great, and thus widely broadcast; or perhaps he saw himself as a missionary in the Epicurean way. Lucretius' method was to fight the fear that he thought many Romans, like the Greeks of Epicurus' day, had about the gods. There were widespread notions of divine and arbitrary acts of vengeance, both in this life and after death. It is Lucretius' assertion that it is nature that is in control of the physical world, not the gods. To understand how nature works and why things happen is therefore to remove man's fear that he is being pursued by the gods.

Lucretius found it difficult to express Greek philosophy in Latin. The plainness of his native tongue could hardly cope with the intricacies of the Greek original. Yet the fundamentals of the Epicurean world picture were simple enough: atoms and the void. Even the soul was atomic, which is why it dispersed at death and allowed no afterlife: Lucretius, like Epicurus, sought to remove fears of future torment in another life: there is *nothing* after death, he taught, and so no torment. The atoms were not guided by any providential or ruling intelligence, but were simply particles of matter in motion through a void. To have included a ruling intelligence of the universe would have been too close to divine intervention for Lucretius. His system, then, differed radically from that of Aristotle, and the atomism on which it was based had been cordially disliked by Aristotle for its very lack of purpose in the natural world (Aristotle was thinking of the atomism of some of the pre-Socratics).

So Lucretius was trying to remove fear of arbitrary and supernatural action of the gods by demonstrating that all actions in the physical world were purely natural and that nature was lawful and regular. But the nature that operated in the physical world was still, at one basic level, the nature-of-a-thing, as in Aristotle. This is what Lucretius called the poem itself, *De Rerum Natura*.[8] Each thing has its own nature: the soul is 'this nature'[9] and the body-and-soul a 'joint nature'.[10] The sea, earth and sky are a 'triple nature'.[11] Indeed, everything made has a nature opposed to everything else.[12] But what Lucretius meant by *natura* changes subtly and sometimes dramatically. We can recall that for Aristotle the nature of a thing was a special case in animals. It was the nature of the adult that acted as a goal to the natural process of development. In a not dissimilar way

Lucretius speaks of the primordial motions or principles of things that have always been the same and which determine how the growing animal achieves the *natura* of its parents.[13] But Lucretius also uses 'nature' in a generalised way, as Aristotle perhaps never did. Thus animal development is governed by 'laws of nature', *foedera naturai*.[14] Indeed the world is governed by nature's laws in this sense and Lucretius' reason for concentrating on the generation of animals is to show the regularity and lawfulness of nature's procedures. But more than this, Lucretius can use nature in a personalised way, a figure who speaks to man and upbraids him for greediness of life (it is part of Lucretius' attempt to lessen the fear of death). It is still to be sure the nature of things,

> Denique si vocem rerum natura repente
> mittat. . .[15]

but now not only generalised, but an allegorical figure taking, with poetic licence, Lucretius' side in his argument. As a literary device it is effective: a female figure (*natura* is feminine), but not divine,[16] urging a proper morality upon man and concerned with the regularity and laws of the physical world, especially the generation of animals. She is now *rerum natura creatrix*,[17] the nature of things in a different sense, that of being the creator of them: almost our 'Mother Nature'.

It is an explicit part of Lucretius' programme to liberate nature from proud masters, the gods, and allow her to do everything herself.

> Quae bene cognita si teneas, natura videtur
> libera continuo, dominis privata superbis,
> ipsa sua per se sponte omnia dis agere expers.

But his means of doing so is often to introduce a traditional god and then lead the reader away, and back to nature. The whole poem begins with an address to Venus as generative, a device to seize the reader's attention before nature is introduced.[18] A similar device is his reference to the Great Mother of the gods:[19] the earth itself, producing everything from the eruptions of Etna to corn, fruitful trees and mankind. The Great Mother was a cult brought to Rome from Phrygia in 205 BC, and the Great Mother was originally represented with a team of lions.[20] But Lucretius turns the goddess into the natural world.

Lucretius' philosophical purposes, the achievement and propagation of *ataraxia,* were partly religious. He regarded Epicurus as a spiritual leader rather than a philosopher.[21] It was not a question of studying nature or of remembering all the details of a natural world based on atomism; and he concludes the first book by insisting that Memmius would reach the truth with very little work once he understood the first principles.[22] That is, Lucretius hoped that Memmius would give faith to the first principles, as in a religion, and all else would follow. Lucretius' argument includes showing that everything has come to be naturally. Since man was a product of nature his development was also natural, and there is no sense of contradiction when Lucretius speaks of the development of things we would call artificial. His history of how the arts and crafts were discovered by man by trial and error, or suggested by nature, is an argument that these things were not originally the gift of the gods (for example it was commonly held that medicine was the gift of Apollo). This human progress was matched for Lucretius by the slow decline of the world. The chronological component of his account of the world, having dealt in a cosmogonical way with the appearance of the earth and heavenly bodies from the atoms, contains a description of the earth's infancy,[23] with the sequential appearance of herbage and trees, followed by animals. When he says that animals could not have appeared from the skies (and when he says they did not come out of pools either) he is emphasising not so much the element that gave rise to animals, but earth as a mother. The earth in its infancy was rich in moisture and the heat of the sun, and grew as it were wombs in her substance, from which creatures came. They were nourished by her rich pastures as by a mother's milk. This is Lucretius' nature in another sense of the generalised Mother Nature.

But then by degrees the earth grew old and passed out of the child-bearing age.[24] Thereafter the generation of living things was ensured not by the fertility of the earth but by the regularity of nature that ensured the occurrence of sexual generation. Only those animals that could generate themselves in this way survived, and many of the strange products of the once fertile earth vanished, like the hermaphrodites, and the creatures without mouths, or with their limbs bound to their bodies so that they could not feed or move. Survival depended not only on sexual generation, based on the existence of seeds, but on attributes of speed or cunning on the part of the animals, or on man's protection of those that were useful to him. This is how Lucretius presents the traditional view of the personalities of animals, which is so characteristic of ancient natural history. While Aristotle could serve the principles of his philosophy by demonstrating that the bodies of animals were the manifestation of the soul, regarded as the nature-of-the-animal, Lucretius uses the same body of opinion about the natures of animals to show how they have survived from the earth's first productive phase in a wholly natural way. Thus, he says,[25] lions have been protected by their courage, foxes by their cunning and deer by their speed. In contrast the seeds of the dog and domestic animals have been protected by man; but this again is natural, partly by reason of their natures, which made them avoid wild animals and seek man; and partly because man's dominance over them is intended by nature. Other kinds of animals became extinct.

But of all the earth's early productions, explains Lucretius, there were never monsters that combined the characteristics of different animals. That is, literally, Lucretius has said that many kinds of animals, some with random features (such as having no mouth) died out when the earth's generative period ended, and that others died out because insufficiently endowed with self-defensive personalities; yet none of the early monsters were combinations of kinds of animals that *did* survive and were known in Lucretius' world.[26] The moral of what he is saying, however, is that traditional marvellous animals like the centaurs and chimeras were simply myths and should, like the gods, cease to have an important place in men's minds. The argument against centaurs, chimeras and gods is simply that they are un-Natural. Centaurs, with the body and limbs of a horse with the torso of a man, would be entirely impossible, says Lucretius,[27] for a horse is at its most vigorous at the age of three, while a man is still an infant; when the man is in vigorous growth, the horse is senile. Do not believe, advises Lucretius, that the seed of a man and horse can combine. (Plate 13.) As for the chimera, supposed to be a lion in its front parts, a snake in its rear and a goat in between, how could it *naturally* breathe out fire, which destroys all animals?

In the same way in the natural world there were never (as some may affirm, observes Lucretius) rivers of gold or trees that bore jewels as fruit. Nor were there men who could stride through the seas and turn the heavens with their hands; no, all things are fixed in their boundaries by the nature of the seeds and the law of Nature that formed them.

Seeds play an important part in Lucretius' account of nature. It is partly by seeds that nature is so regular, observing the boundaries of natural things. Lucretius emphasises the regular sequence of the seasons, to each of which is appropriated some natural kind: the rose in spring, corn in the summer and grapes in the autumn. It is the

Plate 13 The philosophers denied the existence of mythical animals on the grounds that they did not follow Nature. Lucretius argued that the natures of the man and horse could not be combined because they were so different in matters like life-span, while Galen, in whom were combined a detailed anatomical knowledge and a deep teleology, held that centaurs were structurally impossible. (British Museum.)

doctrine that 'nothing comes from nothing' that makes Lucretius rely on seeds to explain generation on earth after the first flourish of productivity. Since atoms in motion are for Lucretius the *only* explanation of the nature of things, spontaneous generation in Aristotle's sense was not a category of explanation available to him. Aristotle after all held that in any kind of generation the important factor was the immaterial influence of the sun's heat or of the male animal. For Lucretius such organising principles were inadmissible: the organising principles of future generation had to be material and therefore atomic: seeds, the material organising cause of the growing organism, were ideal.[28] The irreducibility of matter, for the handling of which Plato's demiurge earned praise and which was the basis of Aristotle's physical Necessity, was Lucretius' guarantee of the continuity of kind.

Just as life came from seeds for Lucretius, so did things opposed to life, diseases. We know from the rather later Greek doctor in Rome, Galen, that in a technical (medical) sense, diseases were 'against nature', but it is not clear whether Lucretius was aware of any earlier medical tradition. What is quite clear is that diseases were an important category of things that frightened people. Lucretius therefore had to show that they too were perfectly natural and came from natural seeds, perhaps by corruption of the earth, or from the air. Implicit rather than explicit here is the fact that, as historians have often noted, disease has in many societies been seen as a punishment from above and therefore as a stigma, and on both counts as something frightening to the ancients. In insisting that diseases come from purely natural seeds, Lucretius is again arguing that the fear that man has of divine retribution is irrational because un-natural.[29]

It seems that the seeds were produced originally during the earth's first burst of generation[30] and, conceived by Lucretius in atomistic terms, it is clear how they could express the notion of invariability. It is in their slow growth from seeds that living things express the regularity and sequence of nature and the fixity of their own kind. All have not only appropriate seasons, but appropriate food, without which they die.[31] Matter, being atomic, is for Lucretius an important factor in the fixity and regularity of nature. It is because their matter is bounded and fixed that the flowers and fruit appear regularly, so that birds do not suddenly hatch from the sky or trees leap from the earth.

Lucretius' account of the development of civilisation is likewise designed to show that it is the result of nature. In common with other ancient authors Lucretius held that early man was hardier than modern man, but lived a very primitive life. He draws a detailed picture of the growth of physical and political civilisation as a result of man and nature meeting the exigencies of the circumstances. The great men of history were not the heroes or men who traded with the gods, but the kings who founded cities and dealt in cattle and gold.[32] The implication throughout is that man does not owe his civilisation to the gods, either by imposition or emulation. Rather than making the implication explicit, Lucretius neatly handles the matter by arguing that the conventional belief in the gods was a stage through which men passed on their way to a higher degree of civilisation and understanding. Part of his message is his exhortation to man to move to the next stage of civilisation and accept that nature and not the gods are the true causes of things that look so alarming. This is a large section of the poem and was clearly an important argument for Lucretius. Like others in the god-free zone of philosophy his account of the development of the arts looks historical in the chronological sense, its *historiae* being notable events of the past. It is easy to see that the *natural* world and the *nature* of man fitted Lucretius' overall purpose in matching up with the 'history' of man and the physical world.

Quite characteristically Lucretius bemoans the fact that man has made himself miserable by attributing to the gods the motions of the heavenly bodies, the seasons, and all of 'meteorology': lightning and other lights in the sky, thunder, rain, snow and hail. 'O genus infelix humanum!' cries Lucretius,[33] mourning that too often man performs superstitious prostrations and sacrifices before the altars of the gods in attempts at appeasement, rather than surveying all with a tranquil mind, which sees the natural causes of things. As a corrective, Lucretius has to explain the natural reasons behind things that have in the past frightened men as the work and often vengeance of the gods. This is particularly the case in 'meteorological' examples from which men thought the gods in the heavens above were directing all things down to man on earth. This means that Lucretius has to deal with the range of topics mentioned above, from thunder to hail. Greek philosophers had been doing this for a long time, from the pre-Socratics to Aristotle and the Stoics. It does not mean that they were inventing or adding to an early science of meteorology; rather that the practical nature of Greek philosophy meant it had to address topics that forced themselves upon the minds of ancient Greeks. As we saw in the first chapter, the boundaries and contents of at least part of Greek natural philosophy were determined by the things which the natural philosophers were determined to show the gods did not do. It therefore adds less to our historical understanding to examine minutely the way in which Lucretius said thunder and the rest is naturally produced than to see why he was saying that nature produced it. We have now examined some of Lucretius' purposes in this respect. Lucretius' explanations for the now god-free events are various. He explains that thunder comes from the collision of clouds high in the ether,[34] making a noise like canvas or paper flapping and tearing in the wind or exploding like a bladder inflated with air. Or sometimes the clouds rustle and creak as the wind blows through them, like a gale in a forest, and at other times the clouds break like waves crashing on to the shore. Lightning for Lucretius is the finest form of fire, its particles so small that they cannot be stopped.[35] This is why it passes through the walls of a house as easily as sound, and melts gold and bronze; sometimes it will evaporate wine without damaging the vessel. Clouds contain 'seeds of heat' and lightning comes from many clouds piled up on each other, pushed together in the same place by the wind, which squeezes out the seeds of heat.[36] Sometimes there is a thunderbolt[37] ready formed in the cloud and the wind simply bursts the cloud, releasing it. Or perhaps the speed of the wind itself can cause fire as it rushes by things, like a leaden bullet which heats up as it travels. Lightning is most frequent in the autumn, when the change-over from warm, to cold air causes waves and disturbances in the air.

So Lucretius does not have a single or perhaps even a consistent explanation of lightning and thunder. What is important is that his explanations are natural. This has a second purpose, too, to argue against the practice of augury from lightning. This is almost a political attack. These things were in the popular mind because the priests used them to make predictions about the will of the gods. It was an Etruscan practice, for example, to divide the sky up into sixteen areas and observe from which the lightning originated and into which it disappeared. Lucretius is apparently referring to the Etruscan or perhaps to a Roman practice when he says how senseless it is to divide the sky up into quarters: senseless because men, unable to see the natural causes of things, attribute such motions to the gods.[38] Part of the priestly apparatus here was to consult the Tyrrhenian scrolls about the direction of lightning and to purify the places touched and polluted by it by means of sacrifice.[39] If these are Jupiter's bolts used in vengeance, asks Lucretius, why does he waste them on deserted places, the sea and innocent men? Why does Jupiter always wait for dark clouds and never throw his bolt in a clear sky? Why does he often smash structures dedicated to himself?

Lucretius proceeds to other 'meteorological' phenomena with the same intention of showing the natural causes of things. The whirlwind and waterspout, rain, hail, snow and the rainbow are all accounted for on simple physical principles of moisture, wind, and warmth.[40] Earthquakes are said to be due to the undermining and eventual collapse of underground caverns or the action of subterranean winds.

Like other authors Lucretius tells of cities, like Sidon in Syria and Aegium in the Peloponnese, that were swallowed up by earthquakes, and of others that vanished into the sea. (Strabo and Seneca also relate the case of Sidon, which vanished probably in the fifth century BC; more famous were the vanished towns of Helice and Buris, near Aegium.[41]) As Lucretius says, the fear of earthquakes was double, from the toppling houses above and the monstrous caverns below. It is however difficult to see what part an Epicurean understanding of the naturalness of earthquakes could play in lessening such fear. Lucretius' purpose seems to be to remove the *wonder* of such natural occurrences, however spectacular or dreadful, and so to inculcate an attitude of mind that readily seeks a natural explanation.

If earthquakes are natural, so too must be volcanoes, and Lucretius explicitly urges the reader to cease to wonder at such things, since they are such a very small part of the profundity of the whole universe. So very small as perhaps to be unique, for Lucretius speaks of Etna, not of 'volcanoes'. This is our term (which incidentally reflects the common association of the god of fire, Vulcan, with a wonder of nature). Vesuvius was dormant in Lucretius' time, with vineyards on its lower slopes and woods on its upper.[42] Strabo thought that it was a lovely place. Lucretius' explanation of Etna's erupting is not dissimilar in kind from that of earthquakes. The mountain is hollow, and set upon caverns in the basalt. Air set in motion in these cavities becomes heated wind[43] which becomes fire in contact with the rock. Water enters the caverns from the surrounding sea and forces the fire upwards, through the throat of the mountain. The argument is not rigorous and even had he not said so, it would be apparent that it was not particularly important to Lucretius that he had given the correct particular explanation. It is enough, he says, to list a number of causes of such a thing, content that the number included the real cause even if we could not tell which it was. It was like seeing a dead man at a little distance: we can not tell at first whether he has been poisoned, stabbed or has died of exposure or disease.[44] All we need to know is that some such cause has killed him (for there are only a certain number of ways of dying). In the case of Etna, what Lucretius has in mind is that as long as the explanation is natural (and relies on the properties of elements and atoms as philosophical first principles) then it satisfies his philosophical purposes.

Lucretius' position is the same in respect of that other 'meteorological' question, the inundation of the Nile,[45] which we have met before. Probably the Etesian winds, coming from the cold stars of the north, hold back the waters of the river, which runs in the opposite direction, causing them to overflow its banks. Or perhaps the sea deposits sand in the delta, making it more difficult for the Nile to disembogue. Perhaps again the Etesians blow many clouds to the country of the black people and cause much summer rain; or is it the melting of the snows in the Ethiopian mountains? Clearly all such answers are so closely related in being natural that it does not matter which of them turns out to be correct.

Man and the gods had traditional places of interaction, places commonly regarded with fear, or in Lucretius' eyes, superstition. For example a 'Plutonium' was some physical cavity in the earth's surface that appeared to connect to the underworld, the home of Pluto. The lake Avernus was also held to be a gate to the underworld, and was held to be so malignant a place that it caused the death of birds attempting to fly over it.[46] As in the case of the Nile and Etna, Lucretius is pointing to a *historia* with the express purpose of giving its natural cause.[47] In the case of the lake it is a question of naturally poisonous vapours, he says, like charcoal fumes, or the fatal smell of the flowers of a tree in the mountains of Helicon. Such things are simply parts of nature and Lucretius reminds his readers of the dangers of asphalt, which – he says – grows in the earth and like other things there contributes to the short life of miners.

(ii) Natural law

While it may be said of the Greeks that their philosophy tend-ed towards practice, the practical life of the Romans sometimes tended towards philosophy. This appears in their approach to the natural world. We have seen that for Plato the orderliness of the natural world was imposed, by the demiurge. For Aristotle it was innate, the purposeful expression of the natures of things. For the Stoics and atomists, however, the world was ordered by the con-stancy of *nature*. Roman Stoics did not seek to understand causes in the natures of things nor did they look for an imposed teleology, but sought to accept and live with what was natural. Accepting nature meant that nature was lawful, not only in that it was proper to follow nature's precepts but also in that nature's laws were the source of her constancy and the inevitableness of things.

The idea that nature had laws in its operation was familiar to Greeks and Romans from the teaching of the lawyers. For a century before Aristotle[48] the sophists had distinguished between *physis* ('nature') and *nomos* ('law' or 'convention') as a basis for political institutions. *Physis* was the 'nature of man' – his natural instincts and impulses, and *nomos* the artificial constraints placed on his behaviour with a view to achieving the common good. Aristotle treated the matter in a characteristic way and argued that man fully expressed his nature in a polis: he is a political animal (and the state is natural, at least so long as it enables man to reach moral perfection).[49]

Justice, the proper outcome of a law, was also seen as natural as well as imposed. In the *Politics* Aristotle recognised that natural justice arose from natural law, where natural law was universal. Fire burns in Greece as in Persia; by nature the right hand is stronger than the left (we can recall that Aristotle thought that the natures-of-animals were generally right-handed[50]). In the *Ethics* too Aristotle thought of natural law as universal – here it is the nature-of-man (and relates to the common divinity of all men).[51] It is 'natural law' in the form of 'the nature of men' that men are disinclined (says Aristotle, following Empedocles) to kill anything that has life.

So Aristotle's use of 'natural law' is entirely consistent with his wider view of the nature-of-a-thing. The Good that all constitutions aim at, the full expression of man's nature, is exactly parallel to the Good that the *physis* of the animal aims at. But we have seen that others soon abandoned Aristotle's view of *physis* and employed in its place a notion of 'nature' as transcendent, managing the relationship *between* the natures of things. The 'laws' of nature in this sense clearly meant something rather different, and we see the difference as the practices of the Romans began to be affected by the philosophy of the Greeks. As a matter of practical necessity the Romans had to decide how to treat the legal systems of subject peoples. Clearly it was expedient to leave them as intact as possible to avoid unrest; yet there had to be ways in which different legal systems could interact among themselves and with Roman law. For practical purposes, then, the Romans had a *ius gentium*, a 'law of the peoples' that could apply to subject races and to themselves; but at the same time the Roman lawyers thought about Aristotle's 'natural law',[52] for this too was general in application and applied equally to all men: it was *koinon* as well as *physikon*. In Roman terms the *ius naturale* was often the same as the *ius gentium*.[53] Often (as with Cicero[54]) the *ius naturale* was thought of as universal and natural because it depended on the natural reason of man.[55] But here too the discussion of exemplars often hinges on the natures of things and so remained open to a philosophical contribution. It is in the nature of pigeons to return to their loft, and while they do, they remain the property of the owner of the loft. But if they do not return, they are no longer his property. It is by natural law that you are the owner of fish and wild animals that you catch; but if they escape they recover their 'natural liberty' and you have no claim on them.[56]

(iii) Cicero

In the summer of 45 BC Cicero found the leisure to present to the reading public a summary of the beliefs of the chief philosophical schools about the gods, *Deorum Natura*. He worked from handbooks, although he had had a not inconsiderable philosophical education, and his intention was to make Greek philosophy available for his fellow countrymen. For our purposes such a summary is useful as a contemporary survey by an educated Roman who was not writing to proselytise.

'Nature' had a central place in discussions about the gods. Cicero was important in providing a resource which later Romans could use in deciding what *physis* meant and how far it covered the meanings of *natura*. In Cicero's time this kind of philosophy was still very much a Greek thing. Cicero has to borrow Greek terms and select Latin words to act as equivalents and explain them.[57] The authors he quotes are Greek, and although he wants to conflate their wisdom with that of his own Latin ancestors, there are few of them to draw on.[58] Cicero puts the question of what nature is into the mouth of Balbus, the Stoic speaker in the dialogue, and an idealised Roman.

Balbus first orientates his own position in respect of the other philosophies available. He explains that some say that *natura* is a non-rational force causing necessary motions in natural objects.[59] This is perhaps an adequate summary of the Aristotelian nature-of-the-thing, if we can assume that the force is internal. Others, continues Balbus, say that nature is a rational and ordered force, acting like a craftsman, displaying both method and product. Such a description would apply to the demiurge of the Platonists. In the third of his examples, Balbus tells his hearers who he is talking about: Epicurus. He, says Balbus, gives the name of nature to everything, because the nature of everything that exists is the atoms and the void. It looks as though Balbus is progressing from innate natures of things to a transcendent principle, but it could be equally said that Epicurus' 'nature' is universal because everything has the same nature-of-a-thing.[60] It is only in fourth place that Balbus gives the Stoic view of 'nature': it is not of-a-thing, not an external force imposed upon matter, but the world itself, organised, living, designed and rational.

Balbus' argument rests on the interdependence and co-ordination of the parts that make up the whole world. It is the Argument from Design. Suppose, says Balbus, that a traveller carried the orrery constructed by Posidonius (to mimic the motions of the planets) to Britain: would not even those barbarians see that it was made with reason? As with a model of the world, so with the world itself: Balbus flows with all his Ciceronian rhetoric over the designed and beautiful details of the world, its fountains and mountains, flowers, trees and animals, its veins of precious metals. How rich the produce of the sea, some the fish of the deeps, others from the shallows, more clinging to the rocks! (See Plate 18.)

Balbus' argument is that the physical world has been made providentially for man. He can therefore use as a resource many of the 'natural-historical' details thrown up by other writers pursuing different enterprises. Aristotle is frequently cited[61] and stories we have met before about the behaviour of animals to each other are useful to Balbus. The antipathy of cabbages and the vine; the skill of the spider; the collaboration of the pinna and its guard; the antipathy of the kite and crow; the self-purging ibis; the Cretan goats who remove arrows by eating dittany; the ink of the sepia: all are part of nature's providence, ultimately for man. Balbus, unusually among the philosophers, goes into considerable detail on the structure of man himself, to show that his body too is rationally constructed for his benefit.

Cicero – through Balbus – was unusual in drawing attention to the place of the gods in Stoicism. To be sure, they are not the gods of the old Greek pantheon, with which of course Cicero was familiar. They are rather to be identified with the heavenly bodies, and perhaps this reflects a Roman rather than Greek practice, in which Mars, Jupiter, Saturn, Venus and Mercury, together with Sol and Luna, are gods and goddesses. The speaker who criticises the Stoics in Cicero's dialogue attacks mainly Greek figures, which does not help us to decide whether Balbus' Stoicism is of a particularly Roman kind; but it does reveal that a Stoic like Chrysippus was prepared to use traditional names like Jupiter, Neptune and Ceres for parts of the Stoic world picture.[62] For Balbus, man was linked to the gods primarily through his reason: it is about the gods that man's reason learns when discovering the risings and settings, eclipses and so on.[63]

It is also man's reason which links him to the Stoic 'reason' of nature. It is this, not the gods, that is the source of providence for Balbus. Man has in common with the gods that the world was made for them. Balbus is again lyrical on the fecundity of *natura*, here the generative aspect of 'our Providence', *Pronoea nostra*:[64] the animals were created for the sake of man, whether as draught animals or, like the 'teeming swarms of delicious fish', as food. Did not Chrysippus himself say that that the pig had a soul that acted simply like salt, to preserve its pork from putrefaction?

Man's reason also learns about the gods, says Balbus, through divination. The gods have made religion possible by offering man warnings about the future: Balbus turns gratefully to Roman history to prove the disasters that happen if auguries are neglected. Publius Claudius, seeing that the augurs' chickens did not eat on being released from their cage, as a joke threw them into the water so that they would at least drink. But the result was a great disaster for the Roman fleet in the first Punic war.[65] The College of Augurs was a body that reported to the Senate, and was part of the apparatus of social and religious authority. 'Soothsayers' in general were specialist practitioners, often of Tuscan origin. Fundamental to the operations of both was the notion that the gods foretold future events, and Balbus uses this as an important argument for the existence of the gods.

Just as the diversity, appearance and behaviour of minerals, plants and animals was evidence of the gods for Balbus, so was the gods' less than benign actions on earth, the

> lightning, storms, rain, snow, hail, floods, pestilences, earthquakes and occasionally subterranean rumblings, showers, stones and raindrops the colour of blood, also landslips and chasms suddenly opening in the ground. . .the appearance of meteoric lights and what are called by the Greeks 'comets', and in our language 'long haired stars', such as recently during the Octavian War appeared as harbingers of dire disasters, and the doubling of the sun, which my father told me had happened in the consulship of Tuditanus and Aquilius, the year in which was quenched the light of Publius Africanus, that second sun of Rome: all of which alarming portents have suggested to mankind the idea of the existence of some celestial and divine power.[66]

Here we see the minerals, plants, animals, lightning, meteors and so on in their context. People talked about them because they were interesting and frightening. They were the productions of, the evidence for, the warnings and chastisement of the gods. What is surprising is that Balbus, the Roman Stoic, is *restoring* rather than removing the fear of the gods. Of course, Cicero is speaking through a figure in a dialogue, where the other figures take the views of atomists and Academics, so we are not getting his views directly or at all. By the same token Cicero was not a natural historian. He was doing what all authors did, and that was to use the resources he found in the authors (and handbooks) to construct his own argument for his own purposes. He in turn was treated as a resource and the later Christians found much in his arguments for the existence of divinity that was useful to them. No doubt this contributed to the survival of his work.

SENECA, THE STOICS AND NATURE

Cicero's fictional Balbus presented for Roman consumption what Cicero conceived to be an appropriate Stoicism for his purpose, based on Greek material. The Romans did take up Stoicism, although not in the form presented by Balbus, for which the existence of the gods was important. Roman Stoicism, like the Greek form which we met in Strabo, made the world itself divine, so that *natura* was like a god, ruling everything with reason and necessarily good (the gods existed, but without their old powers). The Aristotelian principle that 'nature does nothing in vain' has been transferred from the individual natures-of-things to the nature-of-the-world. Correspondingly, the three levels of 'soul' in Aristotle (the same as 'nature' in living things) are reflected in the three levels of Stoic *pneuma* that provide material, vital and rational cohesion to the Stoic physical world.

We can exemplify this by looking at Seneca (*c.* 4 BC to AD 65) who was educated by a Stoic in Rome, and so was a home-grown product. Roman Stoicism differed from its Greek original in another way, and for Seneca his own Stoicism was 'wisdom' (of how to live) and he contrasts it with the 'philosophy' of the Greeks which he rightly saw as another business and which he denigrated as being over-intellectual. Nevertheless, to achieve his purposes, Seneca did write about the natural world, and what he wrote survived and formed part of the resource that later writers used, whether their business was Christian exegesis, natural philosophy or natural history. We should therefore give him our attention.

Seneca was at first sight an unlikely Stoic. A successful man from the provinces, he rose to be tutor to the boy who was to become Nero.[67] When Nero became emperor, Seneca became one of the most important political figures in Rome; he also became immensely rich. The high moral tone and a sort of gloomy smugness of his letters, in which he declares the Stoic's indifference to power and wealth, thus appear in contrast with his public life. But then, his first philosophical love was Pythagoreanism, and the virtues of Stoicism may have been impressed upon him only later. Indeed, his life was fraught with danger and it may be that for him like the later Boethius, philosophy became something of a consolation. As a successful lawyer he fell foul of Caligula, and turned instead to his Stoicism. On the death of Caligula he opened a school for the sons of patricians. But as we have seen, being a teacher was not always easy. It was difficult enough in a Greek democracy and could scarcely have been easier under an autocratic Roman emperor. The teacher would have taught some species of philosophy, whether it was the liberal arts or Stoicism. The parents and the political masters would have kept an eye on what was being taught lest it was unsuitable for the future masters of the city, state or empire. Whether the charge against Socrates was trumped up or not, it was a natural one to make. When Aristotle left Athens to prevent its citizens committing another crime against philosophy it was certainly because of his Macedonian connections, but surely also because he was in a position to influence the young men of the city. And the teachers whose philosophy included some political aspects wanted to influence the politically powerful. Plato wanted the political leaders to be philosophers. (It would be interesting to know what Aristotle taught Alexander the Great; it may have been political.[68]) Lucretius addressed his philosophy to the politically important Memmius; it was a Stoic saying that the wise man should take part in politics,[69] and Seneca directed his tide of Stoic propaganda to Lucilius, procurator in Sicily.

At all events, Seneca did not last long as a teacher and in the first year of Claudius' reign narrowly avoided a death sentence and spent eight years in exile. But then he returned to become tutor to Nero, and praetor and consul. But things went wrong again and Seneca retired to the country, trying hard to avoid the anger of Nero. Writing his *Natural Questions* consoled him in his dangerous seclusion until, two or three years after they were complete, Nero ordered him to commit suicide.

In these circumstances it is reasonable to guess that Seneca found consolation in the Stoic view of the natural world, so distant from the world of dangerous political intrigue and so helpful in elevating the mind above the fears of present life. Traditionally indeed, Stoicism had had three parts, logic, ethics and *physica*, the last concerned with the natural world. Here the two important Stoic terms were *logos*, reason, and *physis*, nature. But the relationship between these two terms was complex, and we have seen that a Roman's *natura* might well differ considerably from the *physis* of Greek philosophy. We can explore some of these questions by looking at how Seneca argued for the principles of Stoicism in the letters to Lucilius and how he portrayed the natural world and its moral lessons in the *Natural Questions*.

Seneca is very Roman about his Stoic philosophy. He emphasises its practical nature: it guides one's life and builds one's character. It teaches how to live well, he says, by removing fear.[70] Mostly it is Roman by being not Greek: Seneca has a Roman's suspicion of the plausible Greeks, and we can form an idea of his ideal philosophy partly from what it was not. It was not, says Seneca, concerned with words, but facts, and not concerned with self-advertisement (which must have been how Greek teachers of philosophy often appeared in Rome). Seneca thought that Greek speech was undisciplined (and he preferred not to use Greek medical terms)[71] and he consequently saw Greek philosophy as so much word-play. Thus he claims to be more interested in the moral and practical aspects of friendship than in the definition of its terms.[72] It is Greek philosophy that he means when he talks of the sterile cleverness of other people's purely dialectical philosophy.[73] He pours scorn on the elaborate science of syllogism and asks in a rhetorical and very Roman way what serious consequences would *actually* follow should by chance he be taken in by the argument 'mouse is a syllable, and mouse eats cheese, therefore a syllable eats cheese'. 'Is this what we philosophers acquire wrinkles in our brows for?' he asks in scorn. His Roman answer to such whimsies was the sternly practical one that philosophy gives counsel to the afflicted: the man facing death, or poverty, or wealth, or captivity. To these the real philosopher holds out a hand of help. Show them the shining torch of truth, says Seneca, 'tell them what nature has made necessary, and what she has made superfluous. Tell them how simple are the laws she has laid down, and how straightforward and enjoyable life is for those who follow them.'[74]

A number of things are reflected in this attitude of Seneca's. As we have seen, the notion of 'laws of nature' is partly drawn from the Roman jurists' *ius naturae*.[75] As a lawyer in early life, Seneca was surely aware of natural law, and he expressly contrasts the freedom one has under Roman law as a citizen and that which one achieves by the exercise of Stoic principles and as the consequent gift of the *ius naturae*.[76] But also a 'law of nature' was something that we have met above as part of the natures of things: it is a law of nature that dogs bite, the legal code recognises this, and so man should act accordingly. When Posidonius identified the Stoic community with the Roman Empire, it became obvious to many that the old Roman virtues of *gravitas, pietas* and so on were the same as stoic virtues: this too is behind Seneca's feeling for the naturalness and Romanness of his practical philosophy.

Because it was a practical philosophy, with the aim of helping others and oneself to achieve equanimity, it was important that the understanding of nature and her laws was accurate. Truth about nature was important for Seneca but not a goal in itself. Certainly Stoic truth about nature made other philosophies seem more like linguistic tricks,[77] but Seneca cannot understand the Greek idea that discovery of the truth depends on the rigour of investigation. For him it is another agreeable insult to Greek philosophy to say that it encourages intellect rather than character; and that it teaches how to argue rather than how to live.[78]

The practical use of philosophy in elevating the mind above fear and the study of nature as the means of doing so were two features that Seneca shared with Epicurus. This was largely in the context of the classical pantheon and the unpredictable actions of the gods; but for Seneca the pantheon, in the face of the overriding Creative Reason of the world, is largely allegorical or poetical. Since his reasons for looking at the natural world were different from those of Epicurus, he saw a different world. Atomism, with its lack of a grand design for the world, was unthinkable to Seneca. Nor did it commend itself to him that the atomic soul of the atomists dispersed at death and had no previous or subsequent life. Seneca's physical world was continuous (not atomic) and rational, the soul largely Platonic. But, like Epicurus, Seneca wanted to achieve the mental state of *ataraxia*, peace and freedom. He accordingly found that many Epicurean aphorisms were true and useful. The man who knows how to live is self-sufficient and perhaps does not even need friends;[79] rehearse death to be free from fear of it;[80] follow nature and you will never be poor; to want more than a sufficiency is to be unhappy; reserve the freedom to leave this life at will.[81] To Lucilius, Seneca began to sound like an Epicurean; for us, that Seneca could find so much to agree with in a philosopher with a radically different account of the nature of the physical world is evidence that natural knowledge was to be used for moral purposes and not for its own sake.

In fact in understanding the natural world Seneca goes back principally to Aristotle. He gives a fair summary of the four causes, and claims that in addition Plato described a fifth, the *idea* or Platonic form. Seneca at once extends and simplifies the system of five causes: extends, by adding time, place, motion and Creative Reason to the causes, and simplifies by saying that the real polarity is between Matter and Cause, where Cause is Reason or God.[82]

That the entire universe is matter and God[83] is Seneca's most direct statement. Elsewhere, particularly for a reader expecting to find categories of nature, God, reason, *logos* and *physis,* the picture is less clear. Part of the problem is the ambiguity, which we have met before, of our word 'nature' and which can hardly be avoided in English commentaries. The general position of Hellenistic Stoicism was that Creative Reason manifests itself as physical life in plants, soul in animals and *logos*, reason, in man.[84] The latter is the highest expression of 'nature' and in a general sense nature is *logos*. But it is in men as part of *their nature.* The nature-of-plants is not rational. But Seneca was a Roman, not a Hellenistic Stoic, and although he sometimes uses *rerum natura*[85] he seems to emphasise less the roles of *physis* and *logos* and more the direct relation between God (the universal intelligence and pure reason) and the world he has made. At the beginning of the *Natural Questions* Seneca says he will be concerned with questions like: Is God omnipotent? Or does he work with pre-existing and recalcitrant matter? Are the shapes of created things more determined by their matter or by the ideas? (they are Platonic and God is full of them). Is God always governing the world or has he left it to run on its own? Did he make it perfect or has he since changed it?

At the same time Seneca makes it clear that ethics, a traditional part of Hellenistic Stoicism, had little charm for him, representing the dark world of human political commerce from which his natural studies were a refuge and a solace. He conceived of the soul in very Platonic terms, asserting that its period on earth corresponded to a period of captivity in a prison. The body, thought Seneca, was a burden to the soul, a burden which the soul could lift a little in contemplating the natural world, the work of God. In doing so (he said) the soul yearns to return to its place of origin in the heavens; he suggests that the soul has a higher place to go to after death.[86] In answering a real or imaginary complaint from Lucilius, that such natural questions did little to purge the mind of emotion and make it truly stoical, Seneca gives a rhetorical defence of the study of the natural world. It centres on his desire to know how the world began, and it emerges that he saw God as separating out things from a pre-existing mass of matter, that is, creating by rearranging into categories, supplying form and giving laws. Seneca's interest is in the nature of the God[87] who did this, perhaps close in identity to the source of light. He is also very interested in the origin of man and the fate of the soul, trained to recognise that only the body is vulnerable. As God is to the world, so the soul is to the body, and the matter of the body to the matter of the world. Natural studies are (he concludes) therefore very germane, since they may tell us of the nature of God; at the very least they teach us how to face life properly.[88]

In emphasising the study of the natural world, Seneca also played down the role of the liberal arts. He identifies them as linguistic studies, history, poetry, music, geometry, astronomy and astrology. He is surely thinking of Greek philosophy again when he grumbles about those who think they can calculate the distances between the stars. While acknowledging that the liberal arts are suitable for a free man he asserts that their sole use is to prepare the mind for moral instruction. Hence the superiority of Stoical studies, which are not only directly moral, but which include useful physical questions on natural things and man, including those on time and the soul. Part of the problem was a perceived decline of philosophy in his age. Not only were liberal-arts pedants irritating and boring, but all teachers seemed to take a perverse delight in the inconclusive: Protagoras (says Seneca) argues that it is possible to argue with equal force on either side of a question, including the question of whether one can argue with equal force on both sides of a question. To Seneca, the practical and wise Roman, this must have sounded like the very depth of clever Greek play with words. He was equally depressed by Zeno's declaration that nothing exists and by the scepticism of the Pyrrhonists and Academics, 'who have introduced a new branch of knowledge, non-knowledge'.[89]

THE *QUAESTIONES NATURALES*

It was therefore with relief that Seneca turned to his study of the natural world. To study real things and to discover how they taught man to live properly was infinitely better than to play intellectual tricks with words. But we should not imagine that Seneca was seeking a sort of intellectual seclusion and satisfaction in a series of 'scientific' topics. He turns first to 'meteorology', one of Aristotle's topics and one treated of also by Lucretius and later by Pliny. It has been argued above that the recurrence of the topic (and its adoption in the Middle Ages) makes it look – wrongly – as if this subject was one of the genetic roots of a modern scientific topic. But none of these authors had any reason to look to meteorology except to pursue his own purposes. He introduced into it only what was necessary for this and he left out what was unnecessary for him but what had been included by others for *their* purposes. Thus Seneca turned to meteorology not because it was a recognised part of Greek philosophy (with which he was not impressed) or because Aristotle had written on it. He turned to it in the first place because it centred on one the four elements – air – of which the world was composed. More important, it was air that extended from man's habitation on earth to the realm of the traditional gods. Signs of divine vengeance, whether direct thunderbolts from Zeus or portents of things to come, were likely to be manifest in or through the air. Seneca, like Lucretius, had to show that it was all *natural*, and that man could understand it and lose his fear. Lightning, thunder, winds, storms, earthquakes, strange signs in the sky – these were the stuff of meteorology because these were the things that affected or frightened man. It was more important to Seneca to argue that explanations of such events were natural than to judge between the truth of this or that natural explanation. The similarity to Lucretius is striking.

Let us take a few examples. Seneca takes up the topic of the halo or ring that sometimes appears around the sun or moon and which was sometimes regarded as a portent. His natural explanation of it is that it is caused by light entering the air in the manner of pebbles thrown into a pond, which cause circular ripples on the surface of the water. Halos of this kind are like rainbows, another dramatic appearance in the sphere of air and one which, also possibly portentous, had hints of a natural explanation, for everyone knew that they had something to do with rain and sun. Seneca is determined to provide a thoroughly natural answer. One such could be found in Aristotle, namely that the drops of water act as mirrors. When Seneca found mathematical studies of the relationship of object and image in the mirror compelling, and when he pointed to the rainbows seen in artifical fountains, his purpose is to show that the phenomena can be produced by (and so understood by) man and are not divine portents. Nature's skill[90] in arranging the clouds and their reflecting water is thus intelligible in terms of art. That the clouds act as concave mirrors was a question often discussed by Stoics. Seneca gives Posidonius' account, and he reports two differing theories of mirror images (that they are projected 'species' of the object[91] or that the sight is bent back by the mirror). Seneca only partly agrees with Posidonius and is clearly much more exercised that the explanation should be natural than that one particular natural explanation should be true. It is very characteristic of Seneca that not only does he have natural explanations to free the mind in the Stoic manner, but he also has improving, moral stories based in some way on that explanation. Mirrors show that rainbows are natural; and mirrors serve to show us ourselves: as young men that it is time to study, as old men that it is time occasionally to think of death, as ugly men, to be resigned. Mirrors, like other things in Seneca's work, have also a moral history, in the chronological sense. He talks of the first mirrors, the search for different metals to make them with, the first extravagance and expense of mirrors and how degenerate modern man is in comparison to the stern old Romans of yesteryear – a degeneracy that makes men more like women and leads even soldiers to count a mirror as part of their kit. The ultimate horror story – it ends Book 1 – was the rich man who fitted out a bedroom with distorting mirrors to lend novelty to his sexual encounters.[92]

So the rainbow was part of meteorology and meteorology was concerned with the air. Two reasons have been given why Seneca should have given attention first to this element and an even more important reason appears at the beginning of the second book, where he says that the whole of physical enquiry into the natural world is divided into three, astronomy, meteorology and geography. (Possibly this discussion has been misplaced from an earlier position.) That is, air for Seneca is the *pneuma* of earlier and Greek Stoic thought. It was fundamental to the way the world worked. Its tension and unity (says Seneca) provides coherence to physical bodies, growth and fruition to plants and the transmission of light. In stressing its unity and indivisibility (it extends through things) Seneca is tacitly arguing against the atomists and their discontinuous world. It is air that transmits sounds through solids, causes earthquakes, enables heavy things to float and makes it possible for pumps to move (perhaps suck) water.[93]

Another example of Seneca's treatment of meteorological topics is lightning. This was commonly thought to be Zeus' personal form of vengeance on mortals and it is easy to see that it aroused a great deal of fear. It was also generally held to be a portent. Seneca therefore 'naturalises' it: lightning is simply fire in the sky, driven by (or perhaps consisting of) air driven very fast.[94] He is nothing loath to repeat the strange stories that had accumulated about the effects of lightning, for example of the purse that remained intact when lightning destroyed the gold coins within[95] or the sword and spear-point that melted leaving the scabbard and shaft intact.[96] Seneca's purpose is here not to deny that these are wonderful stories or that they portend things to come. But in an ordered, rational natural world (of the Stoics) there is no chance or random event that can be signified supernaturally by portents, because everything is connected. Rather, everything (because connected) is a portent, and it is only that man has learned to recognise few of them. In this way Seneca believed that knowing enough of the connectedness of the rational and purposeful world would make a natural prognosis of the future possible. His objection to astrology was partly thus that it relied on so few observations (the Chaldeans observed only the five planets).[97] Partly, too, it was because a Stoic who was properly resigned about the future should not be curious about it.[98] Seneca seems to mean the Stoics when he says the Romans thought lightning was produced because the clouds collide (that is, within the rational plan of the world). He contrasts that view with the view of the Tuscans, who argued that an autocratic and arbitrary God makes the clouds collide *in order* that lightning should be a portent. His view of the superiority of the Stoics to the Chaldeans and Tuscans is plain.

So Seneca accepts that lightning can be a portent of things to come or can pronounce on the significance of things that have passed. It is the Creative Reason that binds things up and makes this possible; it also allows some efficacy to prayer, although obviously little change is possible in the Good represented by God's plans. Seneca's 'naturalisation' of lightning allows him to explain in this way a whole classification of the forms of lightning used for divination by the Etruscans (the more usual form of 'Tuscan'). As we have seen the Stoics regarded the Etruscans as being particularly superstitious, and the Stoic Attalus made a study of their beliefs.[99] The freedom that Seneca and the Stoics felt as arising from their natural studies extended to the political sphere, for not only did they feel free to criticise the great and powerful (for their obsession with life and wealth) but Seneca, like Strabo, also believed that the great and powerful, in order to keep them submissive, had encouraged the masses in their belief in the retributive nature of the gods' lightning and thunderbolts.[100]

As a detail of 'meteorology' Seneca gives a comparatively enormous space to lightning. It occupies a very large part of Book 2, which ends up, characteristically, with moral stories derived from it. His purposes are clear. When he says that he supposes his readers will be saying 'prevent us from being frightened by thunderbolts, rather than teach us about them', his answer is more than the Epicurean 'lightning is natural and not divine retribution', and is the very Stoic 'knowing the nature of natural disasters, bear them calmly'.[101] We can gain some idea of the traditional place of lightning in the hopes and fears of the ancient world by taking a forward glimpse at Pliny, writing just a few years after Seneca. The temple of Jove the Thunderer on the Capitol[102] reminds us that lightning was, popularly, the personal weapon of Zeus. It consequently formed a topic for painters and sculptors. Sometimes Cupid or Alexander the Great were also shown discharging lightning, a thing clearly intended to place them on a scale of divinity. The effects of lightning had similar religious and dramatic possibilities, and Pliny gives an account of a painting of Ajax Struck by Lightning and of the myth of Phaethon suffering the same fate.[103] In the popular view there was great significance in who or what was the subject of Zeus' anger in this way. Although Pliny, like Seneca, wanted to make things like lightning natural, there is a reflection of the popular view in his story of how Nero's unprecedentedly large portrait – it was 120 feet high – was struck by lightning and destroyed in the Gardens of Maius. Pliny clearly implies a divine reproval for the vanity of Nero, whom Pliny disliked. In contrast the story of the picture of the Heroes that was struck three times at Rhodes without destruction carried a different implication.[104]

It is these Stoic principles that determine what is included in Seneca's natural questions. Having introduced the work with air, as one of the elements and as the Stoic *pneuma*, he deals with the remaining elements. But he is not about to give a systematic account of the elementary and mixed bodies, for his purpose is only to have a substrate for promoting Stoic wisdom. In short, natural disasters occur as readily with water and earth as with air (his attention to fire is mostly given in connection with lightning). Storms, floods and earthquakes are the Stoic grist to Seneca's mill.

But before examining what his mill produced, let us look briefly at what these natural disasters tell us about the natural world as seen through a Stoic's eyes. Seneca[105] pursues the analogy between the world and a living organism, with blood-carrying veins and air-carrying arteries. The 'veins' of metal and the presence of 'moisture' like bitumen was perhaps meant to signify the homogeneous parts, as in Aristotle. In Seneca's view such things were not only like living things but like them too suffered diseases; wells that become alternately full and dry act like a body with a recurrent fever or indeed with regular bodily functions. Moreover, like a living body, the world, Seneca held, was subject to growth and decay. New islands have appeared.[106] The very natural disasters his account centres on are signs of change over time. The world not only has a chronological history but has an approaching end, warns Seneca. Is it not always so when long and difficult growth is suddenly terminated? Embryos, children, cities and forests, he says, all have a long and sometimes arduous period of growth, and all may come to a sudden end. But at the same time degenerative changes have been going on since the very first day of the world: Seneca points to the constant erosion of certain coastlines by the encroaching sea. At other places, for instance in Egypt, the accumulation of silt has changed the original pattern of the coast in the other direction.[107] Whether sudden or slow, Seneca sees these changes culminating in a final disaster, possibly fire,[108] but more likely a deluge. The doctrine of an ultimate catastrophe came to Seneca from the East, by way of Berosus, the translator of Belus the Chaldean. It seems related to the notion of the Great Year, for Seneca reports that the final conflagration will occur when all the planets are in conjunction in Cancer (so that a straight line will pass through them in their spheres to earth); the same thing happening in Capricorn is the cause of a flood. Whatever its source, the Final Disaster was entirely appropriate to Seneca's Stoic message. It was the biggest thing possible not to worry about. Like all smaller disasters in the physical world, its final end was natural: Seneca says that the world will be destroyed from its own substance, just as the embryo contains the seeds of grey hair; it will proceed according to nature's laws and so will be as inevitable as everything else to which the Stoic was resigned. Indeed, the end of the world was for Seneca part of nature's purpose. As a Stoic he was well aware of the failings of most men. Like the physical degeneration of the world, the character of men, he believed, had steadily got worse,[109] until it was nature's duty to destroy them all. Seneca dwells with morbid satisfaction on the details: the waters will swell up from their vast underground reserves, and the earth will weep like a gigantic ulcer;

all men will be swept away, drowned within a day, perhaps in a hour. The purpose is to start again, with a new race of men, in innocence.[110] But Seneca was too sceptical a Stoic to believe all would then be well, for he believed that vice would soon start once more.[111] In other words, Seneca's history of nature was cyclical. It also had many features, and a moral tone, that were to make it acceptable to Christianity (which may be a factor in its survival).

Because they were not frightening Seneca pays little attention to animals and plants, the flowers and seashells side of 'natural history' which many other writers did consider. An exception is in his account of the Nile, where he is pursuing a topic in the geographical part of 'natural questions'. Seneca knew[112] that it had attracted the attention of the early Greek philosophers. It was worthy of *historia*, a report of its phenomena and of its history. Seneca had a special interest in the Nile. He had spent part of his early life in Egypt (and may have been familiar with the library in Alexandria[113]) and doubtless had first-hand knowledge of the river's behaviour.[114] When he had power under Nero, it was almost certainly he rather than the emperor who sent out an expedition to look for the source of the Nile. Certainly he heard in person the story of the returned travellers, who had secured the support of the king of Ethiopia for their journey through neighbouring states and 'deep into Africa'. They came to vast marshes and saw two rocks issuing great quantities of water, which they took to be the source of the Nile. Seneca takes this as evidence that the river was supplied not from rainfall but from underground reserves[115] (no doubt among those that would provide the ultimate flood). Apart from such 'natural historical' details of the quality of the water of the Nile and the strange properties of other kinds of waters, in which stones float, which petrify things and change the colours of others, Seneca repeats a story of the grand battle between the crocodiles of the Nile and the dolphins of the sea, at the mouth of the river. The dolphins won, by attacking the under-bellies of the crocodiles.[116]

The pattern we have now found in Seneca's *Natural Questions* is repeated in the later books of the work. The element earth is the basis for his account of earthquakes. Book 6 opens with recent news of earthquakes at Pompeii and Herculaneum and Seneca dwells upon the horrors of those who had nowhere to run and were swallowed up by the earth while still alive. These horrors give point to his subsequent efforts to reduce the fear of earthquakes. He does so as we would expect by declaring that they are not the works of the gods but are purely natural. Ignorance is fear, he says; and while his attempt here to teach the ignorant is an attempt to reduce fear, the consolation he offers is grimmer than usual. 'Fear is but folly when there is no escape from it. Philosophy delivers the wise from fear; even the unlearned may derive great confidence from despair.'[117] Ultimately the message is that everything in life is so dangerous that it is best not to worry at all; and the final consolation is that one is just as dead, however one was killed. Seneca had written earlier in life on earthquakes and now gives a little history of the literature on the subject. He prefers Stoic accounts of the cause of earthquakes (it is air) but his point in discussing those of earlier philosophers, who variously said it was water (Thales), fire (Anaxagoras) or the earth itself (Anaximenes) was not the Aristotelian technique of proving them wrong, but to gather explanations that agreed in being natural (if not about the sort of natural cause). For his own explanation, Seneca relies on the activity of the Stoic *pneuma*, largely as developed by Asclepiodotus, who was the pupil of Posidonius and someone else who had also written on Natural Questions.[118]

PLUTARCH: ANIMALS ARE PEOPLE

While Greek Stoicism was a source of Seneca's practical philosophy, other forms of Greek wisdom also offered themselves to Roman interpretation. Greek writers saw the reality of Roman power and accommodated it. One who wrote on animals was Plutarch, born in about 45 AD in Boeotia, and favoured by the emperors Trajan and Hadrian. His well-known *Parallel Lives* were biographical pairs, Greek and Roman: a work that was part of the Hellenising of the Roman world.

But Plutarch did not subscribe to the Stoicism shared by Greeks and Romans. He may have been a Dionysian with a commitment to the doctrine of the immortality of souls – perhaps including those of animals – and he could not accept the Stoic teaching on the laws of nature. We have seen that the ordering of the Stoic world was imposed, there being a transcendent rationality that directed all parts of the cosmos. While Aristotle had been interested in the nature-of-the-animal as the cause of the animal's structure and behaviour, the Stoics and the Platonists argued that animals were parts of the nature-of-the-*world*. They acted and interacted as parts of a whole and with regard to an overall plan (which as we saw was foreign to Aristotle's thinking). To a degree, then, animals shared in the common rationality of the world, but it was an imposed rationality, part of the laws of an external nature, not an individal quality.

Plutarch disagreed strongly. To him, animals were independently intelligent. Rather than resembling the Stoics, Plutarch is closer to Aristotle in seeing the essence or nature of the animal as its soul, the character of which determines the nature of the physical body and the behaviour of the animal. Being of this nature, animals had character traits or personalities recognisable by men: animals were people. But the converse was also true: people were animals. Plutarch is drawing on the non-philosophical traditions of the Greeks since Aesop to extract *morals* from his accounts of (generally good) human attributes in animals and (generally bad) animal attributes in people. The moral purpose of doing such a thing was to point out faults, dangers or temptations, the avoidance of which was as practical an aim as the aims of the Stoics or atomists. Plutarch may also have been drawing on Pythagorean[119] traditions, in which kindness to animals was urged as a model for civil behaviour.

It seems likely that such concerns with morality are not only the aims of a practical wisdom but also relate to a general view of the history of the world.[120] For Aristotle the world was eternal: animals and men had always been there and the working out of the full expressions of their natures – animals in their habitats, man as a political animal in the polis – was good, the actualisation of potential. But as we have seen, others had different views of history, in which the world was growing, or decaying, or both, perhaps in cycles. Corruption was not only physical, but moral, and it was often thought that man was the cause of his own corruption, his life, particularly in the polis, having become unnatural. The remedy – the moral from animal stories – was to observe and copy the animals, either because they obeyed the laws of nature (as the Stoics thought) or because (as Plutarch thought) their intelligence was uncorrupted. So Plutarch's concern with morality was a world away from Aristotle's search for final causes. But then, everyone who wrote on animals did so for their own purposes and even a historian of science must not judge these purposes on some common yardstick. Writers like Plutarch and Aelian (whom we shall meet below) drew from common sources, often Aristotle himself, and ultimately upon *historiae* of the remarkable and wonderful.

Plutarch's particular enemies were the Stoics, whom he presents as making an absolute distinction between rational man and ir-rational animals. The basis for this seems to be the Stoic doctrine of *pneuma*, the active world-embracing principle that gave physical integrity to all things, life to vegetation and reason only to man, but Plutarch's objections are to Stoic arguments that apparent cases of intelligence in animals are simply false appearances. From what he says it appears that the Stoics wanted to deny *purpose* in animal life, on the grounds that purpose implied reason, the unique feature of man. But Plutarch preferred to believe the Aristotelians, who said that animals could distinguish the Good from the Bad, and act accordingly, seeking the one and avoiding the other. So, thought Plutarch, they clearly have sensations, emotion and some rationality, as we do: they are of one stock with us.[121]

In arguing thus, Plutarch is, not unconsciously, projecting human characteristics on to animals. The projection is not only of the general ancient perception of man as rational, but of Plutarch's own evaluation of reason. For him, true higher wisdom was not simply a natural attribute of man – the reason given by nature to man – but was the result of education.[122] True wisdom had to be taught, and its purpose was moral virtue. The point of stories of animal intelligence for Plutarch was the extent to which animals could reach virtue, given their degree of intelligence. The criterion of the moral excellence or turpitude of creatures is explicitly human knowledge – Plutarch means that which has to be taught – of how things should be. So Plutarch's anthropomorphic projection is not merely that of man, but of a man who puts practical morality and virtue above reason: Plutarch himself. His examples of virtue in animals are accounts of how young male storks support their fathers; and of turpitude, how young hippopotamuses kill theirs in order to consort with their mothers.

There is a good sense in which Plutarch is not only anti-Stoic but anti-philosophical. His insistence that animals are rational necessarily destroyed the privileged position of philosophers. Privileged, that is, as seen by the philosophers themselves; we have already seen that non-philosophising Greeks like Aristophanes viewed philosophy and its practitioners in a different light. Plutarch aligns himself with Greek literature rather than philosophy in the dialogue *Beasts are Rational,* a conversation between Odysseus, Circe and the Greeks whom she had turned into animals. Odysseus is horrified at the new status of his compatriots and begs Circe to change them back. He is accordingly chagrined that the animals preferred not to be turned again into Greeks. Gryllus, the swine, explains why. Animal souls, he says,[123] reach their full virtue without effort, and so are better than human souls. If it is a question of fighting, then animals are braver and fight without any aid other than courage (including the females). Simple pleasures are best: satisfy the senses and do not cultivate a desire for gold.[124] Use smell to tell good food from bad: it is better than the elaborate spices of mankind. Animals do not suffer the lust of man, which drives them to elaborate diets and to unnatural acts of sexuality: homosexuality and particularly bestiality, from which are generated monstrous animals like sphinxes, minotaurs and centaurs.[125]

Most of the examples that Plutarch uses here, speaking through Gryllus, are concerned with myths and legends. He also uses *historiae* that the philosophers also used. Both in this dialogue and in that between the hunter and fisherman in *Whether Land or Sea Animals are Cleverer*[126] he argues that in some departments of knowledge, animals are simply more learned than man. One such area was medicine, and Plutarch uses stories that were the common property of folklore, philosophy and moral stories. Tortoises seek out marjoram after eating snakes; dogs purge themselves by eating grass, the ibis by giving itself a clyster of brine, and the she-bear after hibernation by eating wild arum; goats in Crete eat dittany to remove arrows from themselves; elephants practise surgery in pulling spears and arrows from wounded men.[127]

Plutarch's animals were not only sometimes as learned as men, but could equal men's reasoning in a way that left little credit for the philosophers. The fox was traditionally a crafty animal and perhaps Plutarch was being sarcastic about the peripatetics when he observed that the fox who judged the firmness of the ice on a frozen river by listening to the water running below was acting *syllogistically*: what makes noise, moves; what moves is not frozen; what is not frozen gives way.[128] Nor is it complimentary to philosophers when Plutarch presents the mathematical abilities of animals. There are cattle who can count, never drawing more than 100 buckets of water on the wheel they are put to drive, and fish – the tunny – that know better than man when the equinox has come (their mathematical abilities include swimming in a cube-shaped school).[129] As a moralist Plutarch was sceptical about all physical philosophy that related to animals and plants: natural history. The point of the dialogue on land- and sea-animals is that the speaker for each, the huntsman and fisherman, each relies on his own experience and on that of his kind, and so the tomes of Aristotle, it is said, can remain undisturbed.[130] The philosophers were to be classified here with the Alexander-historians as purveyors of marvellous but suspect stories: in the dialogue Phaedimus speaks for fishermen, 'introducing no opinions of philosophers or Egyptian fables or unattested tales of Indians and Libyans'.[131] Of course the fisherman is more inclined to believe surprising things about fish, and the huntsman is readier to credit strange things about animals (which actually include stories from Alexander's India). But on the whole it is clear that Plutarch's orientation in Greek cultural life was, like Aristophanes', away from the professional knowledge-mongers and their tall stories. Neither author attempted, philosophy-fashion, to banish the gods and exalt natural causes. At least, Autobulus, the hunter of land-animals in Plutarch's dialogue, asserts that it is because birds are very sensitive and quick in apprehension that the gods use them to give auguries to men, and so curtail some enterprises and speed others.[132]

To some extent Plutarch's views were shared by philosophers of the New Academy. They had been waging war with the Stoics over the question of the intelligence of animals for some time before Plutarch. At one extreme the scepticism of the Academics – which Seneca the Stoic derided as the study of non-knowledge – denied the possibility of firm knowledge of, or denial of, animal intelligence. A scepticism that denied the possibility of *any* rational knowledge also did away with the traditional business of the philosopher, knowing. Like Plutarch, the Academic sceptic could look non-philosophical. Where not prevented by scepticism, the Academics argued that animals obviously have sense perception, which results in directed behaviour. Clearly then, they also had some kind of understanding and knowledge, for without it sense perception would be meaningless. Animals therefore had a practical kind of wisdom and the Academics, like Plutarch, were not far from Aristotle's doctrine that animals pursued the good and avoided evil by sense perception and natural appetite.

The case for and against the intelligence of animals was also put by Philo Judaeus, writing a generation or so before Plutarch, in Alexandria. (Philo is important in the Christian tradition and has attracted a lot of recent scholarship.) This is another dialogue, the main speakers being Alexander and his relative Philo (whom we will meet again). It is Alexander who uses the Academic arguments to prove the intelligence of animals.[133] His examples are the animal stories that we find in so many authors, but used in a particular way to make his argument. Characteristic is his account of how the ant stores up grain for the winter and bites each grain to prevent germination. Others used the story to draw out a moral for humanity: be provident and wise. But Alexander does not draw a moral, for his purpose is solely to demonstrate the intelligence of ants. Even when he quotes (with approval) Aesop, he is not interested in the morals, only in the evidence for rationality.[134] Alexander has an elaborate version of the story about the stag hiding when it loses its antlers because it – very rationally – feels defenceless without them.[135]

It is also to Alexander's purposes to prove that animals have memory, a faculty closely related to intelligence. Any animal that could be trained would have made the point and Alexander chooses a story of a troupe of elephants, trained for the theatre, who were taken to a party: they first stood neatly in a row, then danced with the music and finally pretended to be drunk. It was part of the celebrations for an imperial Triumph.[136] It was also to Alexander's purpose to show that animals had emotions as people do. He quotes from a verse about an elephant that fell in love with a camel: an extreme form of a traditional association between these two animals that we have noted in Aristotle. Alexander also knew stories about animals falling in love with people: we know them too, for they include that about the ram who loved Glauce the harpist and the dolphin that so loved the boy who rode on his back that it died of grief when the boy died.[137]

The ultimate claim for the intelligence of animals was to assert that they understood logic. We often meet the story of the hound pursuing a hare or something similar and coming to a ditch that runs left and right. Which way did the hare go? Left, right, or straight on? The hound sniffs left – nothing; right – nothing: *ergo* straight ahead. Alexander claims not merely that this is logical, but that it is 'the fifth complex indemonstrable syllogism'.[138] It was a long-lived story: let us for once be unhistorical, and chase the story down to recent times. It is 1614 and James I has come to Cambridge to hear disputations held in his honour. He is bored by them and wishes he was still hunting in Newmarket, whence he has come. But he pricks up his ears when the philosophy disputed question is announced as 'Whether dogs can make syllogismes'.[139] The major proposition in favour is our story of the hound at the crossing of the ways, wondering where the hare has gone. Before the hound is proved irrational, the king interrupts and says that *his* hound, losing its hare at Newmarket, set up a baying to call the others to help him search: surely that was rational? Ah, say the scholastics quickly, but your majesty's hounds hunt not in the common way, but by royal Prerogative.

Philo's reply to Alexander draws from both the Hebrew and Hellenistic traditions. Above all, it was because man's soul was the image of God that meant that human rationality was quite distinct from that of animals. Animal souls were of a different kind, and that of the fish was merely like salt, serving to keep the flesh from rotting.[140] As a Hebrew, Philo believed that the soul of animals was the blood; as a Hellenist, his ideas about the human soul were related to those of Plato and the Stoics. It was Stoical, also, to believe that human reason was superior in framing speech, which none of the animals had.[141] Philo was particularly exercised to deny animal intelligence in their apparently wise use of medicine, like the Cretan goats that ate dittany to heal arrow-wounds, and the tortoises that searched for marjoram to counter the poison of the snakes they had eaten. In all such cases, he says, it is *natural*, not a rational sagacity, where 'nature' is God's tool.

MEDICAL NATURES OF THINGS

The Romans viewed Greek medicine and Greek doctors with suspicion. Their own medicine was a simple affair, largely to do with herbs (a surprising number of which were cabbages) and it could be practised by a slave. The Romans regretted that by the indulgencies of city life they had become so liable to the diseases that had never touched them in their sturdy rural past that they were obliged to have resort to Greek doctors. The Greek doctors in their turn came to Rome as the centre of opportunity in a Roman world.

One of them was Galen. He was born in Pergamum in Asia Minor in 129 AD, a couple of generations after Plutarch. His father was a well-to-do architect and gave him a thorough philosophical education, no doubt helped by the presence of a library in Pergamum. When Galen started to learn medicine, he sought out the best teachers of the time and spent a while in Alexandria, learning anatomy. Like other ambitious young doctors he sought fame in Rome. The competition was fierce (and dangerous) but ultimately Galen became physician to Commodus, the son of Marcus Aurelius. He succeeded because he was able to persuade the Romans that his medicine was more effective than that of others, and his argument was that his philosophical and anatomical training had given him a better understanding of the working of the body than that of the competing doctors. The natural part of his philosophy was largely Aristotelian, and his first successes were among Roman Aristotelians;

Marcus Aurelius was a notable Stoic, and no doubt like other Stoics saw the desirability of understanding and accepting the way in which nature works: he would have understood the anatomical rationality of Galen's medicine. (Plates 14 and 15.)

Because Galen was a medical man, we cannot claim that he was in any sense a natural historian, but he does have things to say on nature and indeed he handles nature practically in being a physician. He also addresses those of his books that concern nature to philosophers as much as physicians, and in general we can learn more about how educated Greeks and Romans thought about nature by looking at medical thinking on the topic.

An important part of Galen's view of nature had an obvious relationship with Aristotle's nature-of-a-thing. Galen's interest, as a doctor, was the body. The body has a nature in something like Aristotle's sense, an innate guiding principle that constructs the growing body and does nothing in vain in its handling of the limited properties of matter. For Galen, the nature-of-the-body in Aristotle's sense are the moving powers of the body and the physical parts of the body that they move. These are what medical theory

Plate 14 The Stoic emperor Marcus Aurelius, father of Commodus. (British Museum.)

185

Plate 15 The young Commodus, to whom Galen was physician. Commodus thought of himself as a reincarnation of Hercules, and became famous for the number of animals he killed in the circus. (Museum of Classical Archaeology, Cambridge.)

revolves round and are the basis of the doctor's understanding of the body. Current medical theory in Galen's day included a category of 'non-natural' things.[142] Galen discusses these only in the context of the causes of disease, but since it related to things outside the body, it probably included also the medically important things that do not form part of the nature-of-the-body. When Greek medicine came to be formalised by the Arabs the non-naturals are of this kind: partly just what we would call nature, thinking of nature as generalised. Climate, winds, diet are non-natural, as well as exercise and sleep. ('Contranaturals' were those things contrary to the nature of the body, not contrary to nature in any general sense, nor of course artifical.)

NATURAL FACULTIES

Galen's interpretation of the Aristotelian doctrine of 'nature' is illustrated in his *On the Natural Faculties*.[143] The Greek title of this work is *Peri Physikon Dynameon,* that is, the powers of *physis,* which is generally translated as 'nature'. Galen means the characteristic actions of the body[144] not the faculties that some external nature imposes upon the body. In fact Galen provides a little *accessus* to the question in the opening words of the work. He says that sensation and voluntary motion are attributes of the soul, *psyche,* while growth and nutrition, features of plants too, are attributes of *physis.* It is indeed true, he says, that some people prefer to say that growth and nutrition are attributes of a vegetative soul (rather than of *physis*) but explains that essentially the two notions are the same, but expressed in different words (and rather unusual ones). By this he is almost certainly referring to the philosophies of both Aristotle and Plato, for it was Plato who said that there were three distinct souls in the human body, the rational, the sentient (responsible for sensation and motion) and the vegetative (responsible for nutrition, growth and generation). Aristotle had largely agreed on the attributes of the souls but had said that in the case of man there was but a single soul with a range of attributes from the vegetative to the rational. The attributes of sentience and motion were shared in common with the souls of animals, and both kinds of soul shared with that of plants the attributes of nutrition, growth and generation.

While Aristotle's words will certainly bear this interpretation, yet because it stresses the similarity of all animals, it slightly obscures the fact that Aristotle was trying to find the nature of the individual kind of animal and the differences between them. As we have seen, his *physis* was not 'nature' as opposed to 'soul', but 'soul' with its varying range of attributes was the central part of the nature-of-the-animal. This is what Galen recognises in pointing to different uses of language. So it seems reasonable to assume that Galen was familiar with what Aristotle intended.[145]

But Galen's expensive philosophical education did not stop with Aristotle, and this suggestion of Platonic doctrine is a pointer to what is in fact Galen's extensive use of Plato. The most significant part of this is his adoption of the Platonic demiurge and part of Plato's concept of nature. Let us first look at the background to this. First, as a medical man, Galen was well read in the Hippocratic texts. From them he put together an idea that the body had three main categories of parts: the containing, the contained and what moved the whole, in the Latin tradition called the *impetum faciens.* This was an internal principle of motion, soul or spirit. This *impetum faciens* exercised its powers (thought Galen) by means of the elementary qualities: heat, cold and so on. It looked to Galen as if Hippocrates was describing the same thing as Aristotle's 'nature'. Indeed, Galen thought that

Aristotle was commenting on the Hippocratic doctrine. But Galen did not read Aristotle in the way that we have done. Galen, although accepting final causality, did not not give much attention to the Aristotelian doctrine of the adult form of the male as a goal that defined the necessary steps of the process that produced it. For Galen what generated the body was the principle that guided it when fully grown: 'nature' as provident, doing nothing in vain with difficult matter and with a much more personalised rationality than Aristotle's 'natural change'. While Galen's interpretation owed something to the Hippocratic *impetum faciens*,[146] it owed a lot more to Plato's demiurge, the divinity who had created the world like a living animal. It looks likely to us as historians that Plato's creative demiurge contributed largely to later doctrines of an external creative 'nature' – or rather of course, that later readers found Plato's demiurge a useful resource. We need to find out whether this is so; and we can start with Galen, whose works the later West found a considerable resource.[147]

Galen mocks those who say that nature has made the kidneys without purpose.[148] There is an anthropomorphic meaning here that involves the notion that a good craftsman's every motion is governed by the thing he is making, and none is wasted – without purpose. This skill is *techne*, the most important attribute of *physis*. But this is not an external principle of creation, rather that 'the living organism is a creative artist'.[149] Thus as with Aristotle, it is the nature of the animal – in Galen's case the human body – that is being given expression. This is why Galen, like Aristotle, concentrates on the powers of growth and nutrition. It may be clearer in Galen than in Aristotle – but it is the same doctrine – that in this process it is the faculties of each of the parts of the body that draws to it from the nutriment what is appropriate to it (and rejects the rest): it is the *nature* of each part expressing itself in its natural faculty in seeking what is similar to itself and thereby growing.[150] It is by 'our natures' that meat is turned almost wholly into our bodies; and the phrase is of exactly the same meaning as *physis,* which Galen continues in the same sentence to say that radishes contain comparatively little that 'nature' can use.

Galen sets out his position on these matters in the twelfth chapter of the first book.[151] There are, he says, two main sects among those of the medical men and philosophers who discuss *physis*. There are first the atomists, who believe in a void and unalterable atoms, the motion and conjunction of which explains all physical appearance.

Second is the group to whom Galen extends his allegiance and who believe that matter is continuous and capable of change in its own substance. Galen, like Aristotle, disapproved of the randomness of an atomic world and reproved the atomists for not believing in any substance or faculty of *psyche* or *physis*. That is, the atomists believed that the natures of things arose from the configuration of the atoms. Galen in contrast held that *physis* in fact was 'prior' to matter, both in time and causally. *Physis* brought about real changes in the essence of matter by using *techne,* productive skill. *Techne* was composed of the various faculties, especially of attraction and expulsion, that Galen's text is about. Again, when Galen describes how *physis* has affection and forethought for the young after birth, it is easy to read into his words the image of a conscious and providential supra-individual 'Mother Nature'. But Galen means the nature-of-the-body, which becomes manifest in parental affection within the body of which it is the *physis*. As with Aristotle, *physis* reaches its goals teleologically but without conscious awareness of them (except in the case of the rational soul). So Galen is not discussing behaviour given or imposed by a providential and separate nature. We can see this when he is discussing the source of such behaviour and is obliged to be clear in his language: rejecting the notion of the atomists that such behaviour as parental affection (indeed, all behaviour) arises in the animal from sensory images, he insists that it is in the natures of the animals.[152]

NATURE AS DEMIURGE

While writing *On the Natural Faculties*, Galen was finishing the much larger *De Usu Partium*.[153] This treatise is an elaborate discourse on the structure and action of the parts of the body and so includes a range of parts and faculties not covered in the former. We can learn more of Galen's notion of 'nature' from it.

The striking thing about *De Usu Partium* is in fact the extension of the meaning that lies behind *physis*. In some of his commentaries on Hippocrates, as in *On the Natural Faculties*, Galen's *physis* is largely that of Aristotle,[154] attributed to Hippocrates (as is Galen's common practice with many things). But in writing a consciously philosophical as well as medical work, Galen in *De Usu Partium* is at pains to develop the teleology inherent in the relationship between 'nature' and 'body'. Indeed it is the thesis of the entire work that the body has been put together with wisdom, foresight and the greatest skill, constrained only by the 'necessity' of the physical limitations of matter. We are wrong here, however, if we retain the word 'nature' to encompass what Galen means. He uses two words, *physis* for the Hippocratic/Aristotelian nature-of-the-body, and *demiourgos* for the 'creator' of the body, a clear echo of Platonic cosmogony. The one is feminine, the other masculine, and although Galen slides easily from 'she' to 'he' in the same sentence it is surely true that the two words retained different sets of connotations. It is rather as if Galen is deliberately trying to forge a new identity for what we must still perforce call 'nature'. He was unusually well qualified to do so, for his medical specialty was anatomy, in which function figured as large as structure, and his philosophical background made available to him the links between function and purpose, the teleological goal of 'nature'.

Not only was Galen well qualified to do this but also he was highly motivated, by his hatred of the atomists, to prove that there was indeed an organising purpose in the construction and growth of the body. His topic was the human body, and it could be argued that the object of his admiration was the *physis* they all had in common: the nature-of-the-*kind* rather than of the individual. That is, while Aristotle as a philosopher wanted to seek out the differences between the natures of many different animal kinds, Galen as a medical man saw the human body as of supreme interest and was interested in animals only as far as they illuminated man. But even taking all the natures of man as a single collective nature (because it was the same in each case) does not explain all that Galen attributed to his *physis/ demiourgos*. In *De Usu Partium* there is little distinction between Nature and the Creator in making the body. It is 'the One'.[155] It is the same skill that has been used in making the heavens,[156] and the same used in the smallest as in the biggest animal.[157] Clearly Galen has moved far from the individual *physis* when he concludes in the final 'epode' to *De Usu Partium* that there is an intelligence abroad on the earth, an intelligence reaching us from above, particularly from the sun, moon and stars, all of which are, in accordance with the purity of their matter, of so much greater intelligence than anything on earth.[158]

THE DEMIURGE AND ANIMALS

Galen's natural-theological epode to *De Usu Partium*, designed to summarise the admirable powers of nature and to conclude the entire natural-philosophical exercise, takes as its first example the elephant. Like other westerners Galen did not often see an elephant. His encounter with one encapsulates many of the things that characterise his approach and that of others to nature. First, the remarkable nature of the animal makes his report of it one of the few *historiae* that he gives and we see in it how Galen the philosopher reacted to something worthy of report. Second, it was clearly an important moment for him. The elephant has this important place in his works because his encounter illustrates the message of the work.

Let us look at this in a little greater detail. On seeing the elephant, Galen says, he was struck, as most observers are, by the elephant's trunk. Galen could not see of what use it was, and thought it must be superfluous. Had that been the case of course, Galen's entire scheme of nature, his passionate dedication to the cause of purposeful natural action in opposition to the atomists, his defence of Aristotelian rationality and indeed his whole argument in favour of his own kind of rational and philosophical practice of medicine, which had brought him to the bedside of the emperor, would have been flawed. It all depended on nature doing nothing in vain, on everything having a part to play, on grand intelligible principles that related the human body in medical terms to the macrocosm: a single established exception could call the whole into question.

But Galen was not really puzzled. He had read his Aristotle and he knew that the elephant's trunk, however strange, had its uses; he is using a rhetorical device to heighten the reader's appreciation of how the answer he now gives resolves the problem. He saw the elephant pick up coins and give them to its rider: direct evidence that the trunk was useful and nature skilful. He saw that the trunk was hollow and he read in his Aristotle that the animal breathed through it: more evidence of nature's skill and ecomomy in giving the same organ a second function. Finally Galen the philosopher and practical man dissected the elephant when it died and found (he says) that as with the human nose, the trunk had connections with the brain and with the mouth: evidence (by implication) that nature had made the trunk analogous in its functions with the nose. Finally, returning to Aristotle, he read that the elephant breathes through its raised trunk when submerged in crossing rivers: this was for him the final demonstration that nature was provident not only in supplying such an organ to animals but in teaching them to use it.[159]

In Aristotle's case we saw that while 'nature' did nothing in vain for the animal of which it was the nature, yet Aristotle had a scale of perfection, with man at the top, which made some animals 'stunted' or defective. Galen has something similar. As a medical man his principal interest was the human body, and he has little philosophical interest in the lower animals. But apes are a curious exception for Galen. On the one hand he has to say that nature does nothing in vain, given the materials. He says the organs are perfectly matched to their function. But he is really thinking (medically) about man, and says that apes are a ridiculous imitation of man.[160] They are defective bipeds because they cannot walk properly and either stagger along or go on all fours. Again, their whole body is ridiculous and their actions are silly imitations of human behaviour: playing instruments, dancing and writing.[161] This argument is partly informed by Galen's arguments against the sophists, who said that parts do not have a use.[162] Galen is at great pains to show that the human opposable thumb does indeed have a use and is good evidence of Design. His whole exercise – *De Usu Partium* - indeed begins with the human hand as a good philosophical way of introducing man's intelligence and the providence of nature. The ridiculousness of the ape's hand is precisely because it resembles a human hand in all respects except the really important one, the opposed thumb.

So are we still to think that nature is doing nothing in vain in the case of the ape? Galen's thought seems to be that nature is still 'just', because it gives a silly body to a silly soul. Galen has derived from Aristotle the doctrine that 'animals have been fitly equipped with the best bodies'; but his own 'nature', with its demiurgic component, is now distant from Aristotle's 'nature', which was the *equivalent* of soul. Thus Galen's demiurge is a *third party* responsible for matching up souls and bodies. The argument about the design of the hand at the opening of the whole work immediately involves the body as the instrument of the soul.[163] So in some sense Galen sees souls as pre-existing – brave, timid, social, unsocial – and that they come to be fitted with bodies to match. Lions and horses are proud and brave, with appropriate bodies. But apes have a ridiculous soul[164] and their bodies are like men imitating a cripple or a clown. Clearly the perfection of a nature that does nothing in vain relates to an external, demiurgic nature whose principal concern was with man.[165]

GALEN AND MOSES

In pursuing the story of the Greek and Roman view of nature down to Galen, we have come a little ahead of ourselves in the chronological sequence of the broad story of natural history (we return to the slightly earlier Pliny in the next chapter). But we can usefully introduce here the first stages of the major intellectual and religious shift that marks the traditional boundary between the ancient world and the medieval. This change – we met the beginning of it with Strabo and Moses – was the slow introduction of Christianity which with a radically different metaphysics totally altered the way in which men looked at nature and described its *historiae*.

The omnipotent God of the Jews and Christians was a feature of their religions obvious to contemporaries. Galen knew about the Jews: their revolt against Roman rule happened when Galen was six,[166] and in his written works he tackled the question of omnipotence. After the suppression of the revolt the Jews turned their culture in on itself and slipped from public awareness in Rome, while the Christians became more obvious. Christianity flourished under Commodus, whose mistress might have been Christian (and whose physician was Galen).

The second feature of these two religions that was obvious to Galen was the power within the religion of revealed knowledge. Galen the Greek philosopher found it unsatisfactory that faith should supplant reason. He said that those who practice medicine without proper knowledge are like Moses, who did not offer proofs of his laws but simply said they were God-given.[167] Galen had made an early name for himself as a logician, and could not accept the validity of an *undemonstrated* law,[168] an acceptance that was a fault of both the Jews and Christians, he says. Last, Galen in a summary of Plato's *Republic* (it survives only in Arabic quotations) draws attention to Plato's use of allegory or symbolism: 'Most people are unable to follow any demonstrative argument consecutively; hence they need parables.' Galen means that parables are stories of reward or gain in a future life, just as he saw Christians drawing their faith from parables.

This is a very Greek and philosophical view and represents Christianity before it had itself seen the need to rationalise and employ philosophy.[169] It has several times been asserted in this book that ancient philosophy was a practical business, and often a religious business. Galen thought so. He admired the Christians' code, for they were self-disciplined, chaste, and eager for justice, and so (he says) live like philosophers. The Christians 'have attained a pitch not inferior to that of genuine philosophers'.

Thus Galen was unable to reconcile the Jews' and Christians' habit of accepting things on faith, and their omnipotent God, with his own natural theology, its demiurge and its irreducibility of matter. Another example of his natural philosophy in anatomy is the apparently trivial one of the length of the eyelashes. Galen is impressed that they are of the right length for their function of keeping things out of the eyes. If they were shorter, they would not function; longer, and they would impede sight. But how do the eyelashes attain the right length? All other hairs after all keep on growing.

> Has, then, our Creator commanded only those hairs to preserve always the same length, and do the hairs preserve it as they have been ordered either because they fear the injunction of their Lord, or reverence the God who commands it, or themselves believe it better to do so? Is this the way in which Moses reasons about Nature?[170]

At least, argued Galen, an omnipotent God would govern the world in a rational and providential way, and so such a doctrine was better than that of Epicurus and his atoms. But Galen aligns himself with Plato and the other Greeks in denying omnipotence by asserting the irreducibility of matter and its qualities. It was unthinkable that any god could make for example (he says) a horse out of ashes; no, God simply chooses the best course of action from among those that are possible. Thus the demiurge chose to keep the eyelashes at the same length by rooting them firmly in cartilage, whose properties allowed the design to be achieved. This matter (cartilage) and its properties correspond for Galen to a 'material principle', rather akin to Aristotle's material necessity; Galen clearly sees that the whole Greek tradition of philosophical teleology is opposed to the new doctrines of omnipotence.

Galen could not accept omnipotence because his entire philosophical and religious scheme rested on his admiration for the way in which demiurgic nature overcame the problems of matter. Nature has left us unable to think of a better way of doing things, he says.[171] Sometimes the result is a compromise: weapons of offence and defence could be made sharper, but they would then by material necessity be more brittle.[172] In all this Galen's demiurge is very much more human than Moses' omnipotent God, and Galen often draws a parallel between nature and the human craftsman. In such techniques as contriving that the same organ should have several functions, or in combining several organs for one function, nature is wiser and earlier than art. But nature like the artist is hampered by the intractableness of matter, and nature cannot, although she would wish it, make her products immortal.[173] Flesh must always be corruptible and so nature gave attention to regenerating the species. The fourteenth book, on organs of generation, opens with nature's three aims in making the organs of the body – for the sake of life itself (served by the brain, heart and liver); for the sake of better life (eyes, ears and nostrils); and for the continuity of the species.[174] So tangible is Galen's religious feeling for nature at the end of *De Usu Partium* that his attacks on the 'enemies of nature' – the detested atomists – is a sort of philosophical *odium theologicum*. As we have seen, even the credulous and unphilosophical Christians and Jews were to be preferred.

5

THE *NATURAL HISTORY* OF PLINY

INTRODUCTION

In looking at Pliny we are looking at the most obvious example of natural history in antiquity, and indeed at the greatest justification for seeing a topic of natural history in the ancient world. We must be clear then about Pliny's historical setting. We are looking primarily at the change that had occurred in ancient thinking between Greek philosophy and Roman and at why Pliny should have wanted to undertake such an enterprise. Pliny (like Seneca) was a Roman of the Equestrian Order, a group of whom it has been said[1] that they were more willing than the old aristocracy to be concerned with practical and financial matters. This may well have contributed to the attention to practical matters that Pliny gives throughout the *Historia Naturalis.* One of his reasons for writing was to urge his fellow Romans back to the simpler and sterner life they had led a century and more before. Pliny held that all work, literary or otherwise, should be for the public good, and greatly admired the attitude of authors like Cato and Varro. Varro's work on farming can be seen as a sort of moral allegory on the virtues of the Romans of earlier times, and Pliny has something of the same message.[2]

Pliny's century, the first Christian century, was also an age of handbooks and summaries, which perhaps also reflects a Roman desire to meet and answer Greek philosophy at an appropriate level.[3] A good mail service and excellent private libraries in Rome would have contributed material resources to Pliny's task.

PLINY, GOD AND NATURE

What Pliny saw in the world, and how he reported it in the *Natural History*, depended on what was in his mind already, and on the

Plates 16 and 17 Nature's wonders. A well-known natural wonder in the ancient world was the (electric) torpedo, which could stun a man even through a bronze spear. Another was the lion's fear of the crowing of the cock. A red-figure fish plate, showing cuttlefish, perch and torpedo, *c.* 340 BC, made by a Greek potter in Italy; and a Roman mosaic. (Both in the British Museum.)

Plate 18 Nature's bounty. Pliny held that animals and plants had been made for man's purposes and throughout the *Natural History* there is admiration not only of Nature's wonders but also of her generosity. Compare the sentiments of Cicero: 'quot genera quamque disparia partim submersarum, partim fluitantium et innantium beluarum, partim ad saxa nativis testis inhaerentium!' (*De Natura Deorum* II.XXXIX). A mosaic of an upturned fish basket, in the British Museum.

culture that had put it there. The physical world he saw had its governing principle, nature, and to this it owed its form and behaviour. But beyond nature there was an ultimate principle, a deity. Pliny is not entirely consistent in dealing with the nature of this deity, but these are the matters he puts first in the *Natural History* and we can assume that the details of physical nature in some way flowed out of these first principles.

Pliny opens his discussion[4] by showing that he is prepared to accept the view – largely Stoic – that the world itself is divine.[5] It is *numen*, which sometimes means divine will, sometimes divinity itself. This world – the earth and heavens – is, says Pliny, ungenerated and without end. It is self-contained and contains all; although finite, men cannot measure it or conjecture what is beyond it. Pliny is using pairs of attributes in a rather rhetorical way to compose an image, rather than to analyse with exactness, but we must nevertheless note seriously his final couplet, 'at once the work of nature of things and nature herself'.[6] What does this mean for the relationship between nature and divinity?

We have to be rather careful about words in trying to answer this question. For writers in the Christian tradition, after Pliny's time, God was supreme and omnipotent, and nature some subordinate principle with the chief duty of the generation of living things. But this was not the case for Pliny. His 'nature', *natura,* was, much more often than English translations allow, 'the nature *of things*', *rerum natura.* This expression is less some universal principle, some 'Mother Nature', and more an expression of some innate force that determines the shape and behaviour of *individual* things; it is indeed, what makes them individual. As we recalled in the first chapter of this book, when we say 'it is in the nature of cats to catch mice' we are defining some essential property of cats as an individual species; and this comes close to Aristotle's nature-of-an-animal.

But, like us, Pliny also uses 'nature' in the sense of a wider principle (and the conjunction of his two meanings in the sentence quoted above is part of his opening rhetoric) and in this case it is meant in a collective sense, the nature of *all* things. Other worlds would have other natures-of-things. This sense of nature as the totality of natures of things is still not quite our meaning. Nor does Pliny have a directly recognisable relation between *natura* and the deity. Perhaps, he says, it is possble 'to attribute this infinity of nature to the creator of all things'.[7] The futility of any human endeavour to measure and analyse the divinity of nature, which is part of Pliny's opening message, is repeated a little later,[8] when Pliny is discussing the sun. Whoever a deity is, says Pliny (provided indeed there is such a thing) and wherever he is, he is wholly sight and hearing, wholly soul and wholly himself. The sun appears as a good candidate for the office of ultimate divinity, about which Pliny was ultimately unsure. The sun is the ruler of the earth and the heavens, he says, and it 'is proper to believe'[9] that the sun is the soul and mind of the world, the principal governor and *numen* of nature, all-seeing and all-hearing. (Plate 19.)

So in a way which is still not quite clear, for Pliny the sun is the divinity, a first principle that governs and has close links with nature. But another purpose that Pliny had in writing was like that of Seneca and Lucretius, to banish the fear of divine retribution in men's minds by banishing the old pantheon and the gods and goddesses with their human vices and virtues, and explaining that things are purely natural. Replacing these divinities with a single (and so apparently more powerful) divinity would not have served Pliny's purpose unless he could show that that a single God was not concerned with

Plate 19 Sol Invictus, riding across the sky in his chariot. The notion of the sun as a deity became increasingly popular in Rome in Pliny's day and to a certain extent he shared it. (Museum of Classical Archaeology, Cambridge.)

mankind. He accordingly argues that it is a laughable notion that the supreme being, whoever he is,[10] has a care for human affairs. Would he not be defiled by so sad and complex a business? Although his concern here is to show the absurdities of people's superstitions, their auguries, sacrifices and their deification of Fortune, this is Pliny, not after all Seneca or Lucretius, and he readily but inconsistently accepts that life's experience makes one believe that 'the gods' do care about human business; and that God (*deus,* perhaps 'a god') will indeed punish wrongdoers, if even only after a long time, for he has much to do.[11] As the Christians came to say, the mills of God are slow, but grind exceeding small. So Pliny was clearly not totally consistent about the nature of the ultimate *numen.* Perhaps unconcerned with human matters, perhaps punishing sinners, the deity was linked to man in another way, according to Pliny, for man was born 'next of kin' to the deity.[12] Ultimately Pliny returns to the Seneca-Lucretius argument – do not be afraid of the gods – and lessens the force of the argument about the deity's retribution. There are after all, he says, a number of things that the deity cannot do: he cannot undo a life that has been lived or the successes of a career; he cannot recall the dead or make mortals immortal. Man indeed has a gift of great value that the deity does not, that of the ability to commit suicide. Once dead, that is, man is immune from the deity's punishment, because the deity has no power, no law – *ius* – over the past, except to forget it. Other things (of less importance, says Pliny) that the deity cannot do include altering the laws of mathematics, 'by which without doubt is declared the power of nature': 'per quae declaratur haut dubie naturae potentia, idque esse quod deum vocamus'.[13] This surely means that Pliny has shown the limitations of the deity and, as a consequence, the powers of nature; and in doing so has clarified what he means by 'God', *deus*.[14]

This then is what we can gather about Pliny's view of a deity, certainly one of the fundamental principles of his world picture. It is not consistent, ranging from the sun's very direct action on the earth to divine punishment. But to try to understand what Pliny meant helps us to understand what he meant by 'nature', another basic principle and closer to his purposes in writing a 'natural' history.

We can also look at Pliny's use of the term *natura* in order to add to our understanding of his first principles. Although Pliny often identifies the deity and Nature, yet he has much more to say on the latter and very often there is much in his description that could not apply to his few unequivocal passages on the deity. First, as observed above, Pliny often has 'nature of a thing' which we are inclined to translate simply, but misleadingly, as 'nature'. The difference is important enough, given that we are here investigating a history of nature. To translate *natura rerum* always as 'nature' is to personalise Pliny's *natura*, almost indeed to slip into the allegorical mode of portraying Nature as a person in a dialogue, common in the West since the twelfth century. When Pliny eulogises the majesty of nature when discussing the strangeness of the Ethiopians,[15] he is praising not so much the fruitfulness of the productions of a mother-figure, as the variety and number of the natures-of-things. Again, when Pliny appears to say that nature has given animals powers of observing the sky and foretelling the weather, he in fact is discussing the *natura rerum,* the natures of the animals,[16] here having a common feature and treated as a singular noun.

But on other occasions, particularly when he seems ready to slide between *natura* and *deus*, Pliny does treat what he still calls the nature-of-things as a person. This takes a variety of forms, and Pliny adopts this mode of expression when discussing nature's providence towards man; her skill as a craftsman; her doing nothing in vain, her games with animals to entertain herself; and her moral lessons for man. Let us look at some of these locations.

Sometimes when Pliny talks of the 'parent of all things' it is not clear whether he means the deity or nature.[17] But it is probable that we can distinguish between two senses in which Pliny uses the phrase, that is, as original creator (or perhaps more simply 'cause') and as a controller of generation of animals and plants. When generation goes wrong, monsters are produced, and Pliny thought that the seeds of monsters came from the sky, the debris of constellations and the zodiac.[18] More precisely, he accepted that the planet Venus was responsible for generation[19] and when it – unusually among the planets – moved two degrees outside the ecliptic, animals were born in otherwise barren deserts.[20] So nature as generative had a celestial aspect in Venus, just as the deity, as the soul of the world was, or was represented by, the sun.

Nature as generative had both powers to use and rules to follow. Some of the laws that nature has to follow relate to the motions and aspects of the planets.[21] Others, less well known, are those that govern the winds.[22] The west wind was of course generative, and Pliny has much on the correlation between astronomical events and the winds: the rules of nature for *venus generatrix* were not unrelated to those for the fertilising west wind. Pliny held that nature, producing her works, did so perfectly.[23] Particularly admirable was the skill of nature – it is still *natura rerum* – in the construction of the very small animals. How does nature find a place in the flea for all the senses? asks Pliny;[24] *quam inextricabilis perfectio!* How much more nature is seen whole in her smallest productions, he adds.[25] Nature's perfection is a result of her skill, generally *artificia*.[26] But sometimes Pliny's nature chooses not to be perfect. Ethiopians 12 feet high were made by nature as toys for herself and wonders for us, says Pliny.[27] Nature plays with her toys – she is *natura ludens*[28] in making so many different kinds of shellfish and flowers. Indeed, nature enjoys games with her toys, and arranges great spectacles for herself by setting giant snakes against elephants. Pliny is full of detail: the snakes, being enormous,[29] are fully capable of tackling an elephant. But they need to attack from a height, and so they keep an eye open for elephant tracks and, having found one, climb an

Plate 20 The story of the enmity between the snake and the elephant served different purposes for different story-tellers. For the Christian allegorist it was a parable of the conflict of good and evil; for Pliny, the fight between the two animals was a game Nature played to entertain herself. From a classical phalera.

overlooking tree. Dropping on the elephant from above, the snake encircles it. The elephant, thoroughly alarmed, tries to dislodge the snake by rubbing up against the tree, but the snake, foreseeing that this would happen, ties its tail round the elephant's legs. The elephant in turn undoes the knots with its trunk, only to find that the snake inserts its head into the trunk and bites it. Suffocated, the elephant falls dead, killing the encircling snake as it does so.[30] As we shall see below, Pliny's nature has a number of human characteristics, and here is a sort of celestial Roman watching games in the circus.

The human characteristics that Pliny attributes to nature include not only skill in constructing living things but long-term plans for their continued existence. Nature, in short, is providential, not only to man (as we shall see) but to all living things. The overall principle, we may see from Pliny's examples, is that nature maintains a balance. It is a balance partly between good and evil, as when the evil of an animal's venom is balanced by its poor sight and the ability of the *ichneumon* to kill it: *natura rerum* has arranged ills together with remedies.[31] More generally, nature has arranged that nothing should be without its match. The dreadfully poisonous basilisk, although only 1 foot long, was once speared by a man on horseback, says Pliny: the poison at once spread up the lance, killing not only the rider but the horse. But the poison of the basilisk was of no avail against that of the weasel, its natural enemy.[32] As in the battle between the snakes and the elephants, both contestants die and 'nature's battle is done' says Pliny.

Nature's providential balance was also seen by Pliny in the structure of animals.[33] An example is the dolphin, so agile and quick that no fish could escape it, had it not been that nature had placed its mouth some distance back from its snout. The result, says Pliny, is that the dolphin has to turn on its back to catch the fleeing fish and this necessarily enables many of them to escape.[34] As we have seen, the story comes from Aristotle, where it looks out of place: it fits Pliny's purposes much better.

But above all for Pliny, nature was provident to man. The dolphin, so aggressive to fish, was extremely fond of boys: Pliny knows of the stories of dolphins carrying boys about as they swim. Not only had nature generated most things on earth for man's material benefit, but had also provided moral lessons in natural things for the higher benefit of man. So full is the *Natural History* with this kind of argument, that only a few examples will be needed to illustrate the point. Nature made trees for the sake of their timber[35] and she made wheat extremely fertile because it was the staple diet of man.[36] The situation is set out when Pliny begins to discuss man as the principal inhabitant of the physical world: by nature have been born all things for his sake.[37] That nature seems to have balanced this favour against the penalties imposed on man in being born of all animals the most defenceless, naked and sad, was probably a current topic of rhetoric, and was taken up also by the early Christians. Although the general thrust of Pliny's argument is of nature's providence[38] yet he allows that man's wickedness could sometimes make even nature seem careless.[39] But that is an exception that Pliny has to insist on because of his emphasis on the modern moral laxity of man. For the greater part he is grateful for nature's gifts – it is *natura rerum* again[40] – not only of food but of perfume and ornament (which he so often blames in his attacks on luxury). Sometimes nature's benefits seem personal, even idiosyncratic, as when she sometimes spares man, alone among the animals, from the fatal effects of lightning[41] as a sort of compensation for being one of the weakest of them.

Nature's gifts to man also include moral examples drawn from animals. Of these, that of the bee is very important to Pliny, as it was to many. Not only was the bee 'born' specially for man (Pliny means by the agency of nature, who is not here mentioned) but their constant toil, their political arrangements and their behaviour to each other[42] are a lesson of nature – once more demonstrated whole in her smallest creatures – to man. Pliny the soldier was greatly impressed by the order and discipline of bees.

To this characterisation of Pliny's 'nature' we should add that he projects human characteristics to her and her products. In a way unthinkable for the distant and austere deity whom Pliny wondered about, nature had her toys, games and spectacular entertainments, and was specially providential to man, as we have seen. One of her joys was the huge abundance of flowers that she playfully produced.[43] Pliny draws a predictable moral lesson for man from the brief life of flowers; but when he speaks of the degeneration of varieties over time[44] he is discussing cultivated plants, where man and nature collaborate. The growth of knowledge and art occasionally meant that man could do things that nature could not, like grafting, for which Pliny has an elaborate set of rules.[45] Grafting indeed was seen by Pliny as a way to correct degeneration of trees that had grown from seed, that is, in nature's own way. He numbered the varieties produced by the human arts of root-cutting, layering, grafting, inoculating (inserting a seed below the bark of the host tree) as almost as numerous as nature's own varieties.[46] Here, thought Pliny, man was repaying a debt to nature.

Not only was nature as man's guide and collaborator given some human characteristics by Pliny, so too were her products. That the female spider spins while the male hunts was a common assumption that Pliny does not deny.[47] That plants like bamboo have male and female forms was an Indian notion that likewise Pliny does not deny;[48] and he asserts that unlike the male, the female mistletoe is infertile.[49] Like man, trees can be civilised by moving them from place to place when they are young: Pliny wonders whether trees too have a nature that is greedy for novelty and travel.[50] But perhaps the most important part of Pliny's anthropomorphic view of natural things is the likes and dislikes they have for each other. These are the natural sympathies and antipathies inherent in the natures of things and which were a source of much of the dynamism in Pliny's natural world. Pliny's medicine is almost wholly an account of such active powers in natural remedies. Sympathies and antipathies are met throughout the *Natural History*. Here are just a few examples. First are unexplained likes and dislikes. Reeds, says Pliny, have a special affinity for asparagus; timber cut from the hornbeam, box and service-tree has a strong dislike for cornel wood. Fig and rue are friendly, radishes and vines antipathetic.[51] The lion is frightened only by a crowing cock.[52] Then there are dislikes between animals that compete for food or prey on each other, like the raven and the golden oriole, which search for each other's eggs at night.[53] Some natural things have antipathies because of the different purposes nature had for putting them into the world: the leaves of the ash tree were made as an antidote to snake bites, and consequently snakes have a strong antipathy for the ash. Pliny claims personal experience of the fact that a snake surrounded partly by ash leaves and partly by fire prefers to escape through the fire. However, nature has kindly arranged that snakes begin their hibernation before the ash leaves begin to fall.[54] Some sympathies are with a lost environment, like sealskin, which bristles when the tide is going out.[55] Pliny opens Book 20 of the *Natural History* with a brief discussion of the principle of sympathy and antipathy (which he acknowledges is Greek). It is partly nature being at peace or war with herself, but in either case it is for the benefit of man, and a basic principle of all things. The sun dries water, the moon replaces it; the lodestone attracts iron; the diamond is broken only by goat's blood: except for nature's intentions, Pliny has no theory of it, no mechanism or explanation. No doubt he preferred to leave such things to the Greeks.

PLINY, MAN AND HISTORY

These then are some of Pliny's ideas on the deity and nature, ideas which must have determined how he looked at the world and how he reported what he saw in the *Natural History*. What would also have directed his collection and writing of facts would have been his notion of 'history'. We have seen in the introduction that this word for the Greeks meant at root an enquiry into what was remarkable, and that it had a strong chronological component. Pliny too treats history as a search after what is remarkable. Some of it was remarkable – that is, his attention was drawn it – because of what he already knew about the powers of 'nature' as he understood the term.

Some of it too was remarkable because of the 'history' of man. In part this was the story of man's progress in the natural world, about how man and nature had mutually influenced each other. But some of man's history as reported by Pliny was civil and political, as well as intellectual and natural. We must not think that civil and political history is out of place in a natural history of the classical period. Pliny was highly aware that at every turn man depended on nature's gifts and that many aspects of political history were founded on man's desire to obtain more of them. It would have been wrong to pretend that the natural world existed on its own. Indeed for Pliny man was at the centre of the story: nature had made all things for him, and Pliny's book was partly a survey of what was available.

But the man at the centre of Pliny's story was not an abstract figure. It was Roman man. It was educated Roman man, proud of the achievements of his race. Here was Pliny, essentially at the centre of the Roman world. His book was addressed to his friend Titus, the son of the emperor Vespasian and soon to be emperor himself. Titus, in technical terms, was Pliny's patron.[56] Pliny had served in the army with Titus; he had written books on cavalry techniques, on the history of Rome's wars with Germany, and on Rome itself. It is not an unreasonable guess that he felt at the centre of the civilised world, which in his view was coextensive with the Roman Empire. He must have felt in his natural history that he was measuring out man's patrimony.

To a certain extent this attitude informed Pliny's writing. He has been accused since the end of the fifteenth century of being a careless compiler of other people's facts; in particular of garbling more precise work by Greek authors. But Pliny's purposes were not those of the Greeks. He wanted to make a complete survey, something, he said, that no Greek had ever done. From a position close to the power centre of the whole world, much of Greek philosophy must have seemed parochial. How important was it that Aristotle's or Plato's doctrine of Form was better? How exciting were Theophrastus' causes of plants? What was the point of academic discussions of ethics when it was the clearly perceived duty of the Romans to impose peace upon the rest of the world? None of these things seemed to offer any intellectual excitement to Pliny and his book has much more the air of a survey of the material resources available in the natural world for the use of man – Roman man.

Much the same impression is given by Pliny's extensive use of literary material generated by the conquests of Alexander the Great. Pliny's account of the geography of the East is based on Alexander's routes, and much of his description of distances, navigation aids, strange places, people and animals, crops and climate quite clearly originated with Alexander's logistics of movement, communication and the surveying of resources. Pliny uses similar material from Roman military expeditions in the same way. His 'history', as we observed above, had a strong chronological component, and he is very aware of the growth of Roman power, the growth of the Empire, and the consequent growth of knowledge, much of it natural, about the strange things found on the fringes of the Empire. Part of the purpose of the *Natural History* is to collect this together.

An important activity at the fringes of the Empire was trade. This too was proper for inclusion in a natural history, for what was traded was, in the case of raw materials, of natural origin. It was man handling nature, and Pliny is full of advice on prices and how to test for adulteration. On luxury items he is ambivalent, proud that Roman trade reaches India and China directly but scathing of the decadant use of exotic spices and perfumes. Let us look at some of these topics in greater detail, for they help us to understand the form and the contents of Pliny's *Natural History*.

(i) Roman power

When Pliny said that the emperor Vespasian was the greatest ruler of all time, who had come to the aid of an exhausted world[57] he perhaps was keeping an eye open for patronage (and he was explaining how such people come to be called deities). But there is a powerful sense here too of how power flowed down from a single individual to the boundaries of the Empire, and defined what was normal and good (at the centre) and what was strange and therefore worthy of *historia* (at the boundaries). For Pliny, that power was 'the immense majesty of Roman peace' that stretched out over the entire world. The Romans themselves, thought Pliny, were 'another light' shining on the world (perhaps he meant, as Rackham translates, 'a second sun' and so deity-like).[58]

Pliny accordingly paid a great deal of attention to Rome, the seat of the emperor and hub of the Empire. It is his benchmark for chronology and the *Natural History* is punctuated with the dates at which the first specimens of some category of novelty were first seen in Rome. He had access to the annals[59] of Rome and his historical chronology has essentially the traditional Roman baseline, 'since the foundation of the city'. The essence of this history was for Pliny the spread of Roman power; in this regard he even found fault with the historian Livy's motives for writing a history of Rome.[60] His regard for Roman power is epitomised in his description of a triumphal arch, erected in the Alps and recording the races from the Adriatic to the Mediterranean that had been subjugated by the Romans.[61] His additional list of other races elsewhere is very extensive, and would seem almost to have been designed for reference as well as for celebration.[62]

Naturally enough, Pliny also gave a great deal of attention to Italy. It is (he says) the mother of all lands, and chosen by the gods. It is Italy that unites scattered empires, makes other races gentle and civilised – especially in language – 'and in a word to become throughout the world the single fatherland of all the races'.[63] Clearly, Pliny was no hesitant imperialist, and saw only good in the spread of the Roman way of life.

The *Pax Romana* was of course spread by force. As Alexander had found, conquest needed careful planning. Pliny records that one of his sources for geography, Dionysius, was sent to the East by Augustus to compile an intelligence report before the Roman invasion of Armenia.[64] Likewise Nero sent an exploration party from the praetorian troops to report back when he was thinking of invading Ethiopia.[65] Military reports of this kind would naturally contain geographical facts about distances between towns, the physical conditions in which troop movements could be carried out and communications set up, where ships could harbour and so on. They would also list the resources of the country in terms of the army's need of food, water, timber, draught animals and a number of things entirely appropriate for Pliny's attention. The praetorians' report to Nero, for example, included the scarcity of trees over distances defined by the boundary of the Empire and named Ethiopian towns.[66] Pliny writes with the air of one who has seen Roman power open up vast and unknown territories, in which there is much of interest, just as Alexander had done. Indeed, Pliny the Roman claims that Pompey's exploits matched Alexander's in brilliance.[67]

It was doubtless satisfying to Pliny that Roman power had eclipsed Macedonian, and that the emperor could routinely be called the 'prince of the world'.[68] It was at the edges of that world that things were strange and worthy of *historia*. It was from here too that came exotic items of trade – also 'historical' in this sense – and Roman power and trade are often closely associated in Pliny's accounts. In their involvement with north-west Africa, for example, the Romans followed the lead of the Carthaginians, who at the height of their power sent Hanno to explore the African coast. Hanno reported back with notes that had perished by Pliny's time, but which formed the basis of other accounts that Pliny had read. Likewise Scipio Africanus *minor* sent Polybius on a similar mission. Polybius sailed beyond the Atlas mountains and reported back on the forests and animals he had found. When a Roman commander crossed the Atlas range he reported on the quality of timber yielded by the trees, on the possibility of making cloth from a fibrous plant material, and on the snakes and elephants.[69] The same sort of resource-assessment in the same area was carried out by Juba, the king of the Mauretanians and an important source for Pliny. Juba gave distances between important points and warns of pirates who prey upon the trade routes. Like Alexander's surveyors and Pliny himself, he gave details of strange people in distant places, like the Jackal-hunters and the Fish-eaters.[70] Like Pliny, Juba dedicated his book to the Emperor,[71] the source of power that began the circle.

(ii) Trade

Pliny gives a lot of attention to the natural objects and substances that formed the basis of trade. Many of them of course originated in strange places and were worthy of *historia*. Often these were objects of luxury and invited Pliny's disapproval, for although the Roman taste for luxury was remarkable, Pliny is sternly moralistic about it. As we have seen, the Romans explored as far as China for the purposes of trade, and Pliny records a commerce in a plant fibre used in weaving, probably cotton, unless there is a confusion with silk.[72] His comment is typically Plinian: how absurd and wasteful that a raw material should be brought half way round the world so that Roman matrons could make translucent clothes for themselves. Pliny also notes the isolationist policy of the Chinese, who waited for the world to bring trade to them. The Romans, of course, obliged. Trade also connected China and Rome with Ceylon which Pliny says was long considered to be another world, peopled by *antichthones*, 'people who live opposite' on a spherical world. But Alexander the Great proved that it was an island, and for Pliny it was another bizarre place at the edge of knowledge. Indeed, he says, nature placed Ceylon 'outside the world'. Apart from Alexander's account of its riches, Pliny's information about it was gained accidentally: blown off course by gales, a Roman ship found refuge after two weeks in one of the island's harbours. On meeting the ship's master, the king of Ceylon (says Pliny) was struck by Roman honesty, because all the denarii carried by the Romans were of the same weight, although coined by different emperors. The result was an embassy to Rome, during which the two sides learned much about the country of the other.[73]

Pliny's account of frankincense contains many of the features of his manner of reporting the natural world. It was a rare, expensive and remarkable substance, worthy of note. It came from exotic places (Arabia and Asia) where the Romans had conducted military operations but had not described the tree. Arabic envoys to Rome carried no certain information about it; the accounts of the Greeks varied. Pliny therefore gives a rounded account, describing the tree and how it was tapped, and explaining how the product differs in quality. He describes how the raw material was taken to Alexandria to be prepared for sale, and the security precautions that were taken (the workers had to take their clothes off before leaving). As so often, Alexander comes into the story, for he was fond of piling frankincense on to the altars when he was young. His tutor reproved him, saying he could worship the gods like that when he had conquered the lands whence it came. In due course Alexander sent back a ship full of it. It is characteristic of Pliny too that he gives the trade routes along which the product was carried, and the distances involved. Here it was about 1,500 Roman miles, divided into sixty-five stages. Almost everywhere some of the frankincense was used to buy fodder for the camels, lodging and water. Taxes, tolls and tithes account for more and Pliny added up 688 denarii per camel by the time the train reached the Mediterranean coast (at Gaza). Characteristically too he gives the market price of the three grades of the material (3, 5 and 6 denarii a pound) and the tests by which its purity can be assessed.[74]

Frankincense was used in religious ceremonies and Pliny does not directly grumble about expensive luxuries. But it is very typical that he has rhetorical passages condemning what he sees elsewhere as needless indulgence. His argument is partly about the degeneration of the Romans as they wallow in luxury and partly that money is leaving the Empire in large quantities to supply unnecessary things.

He reckoned a hundred million sesterces left the Empire every year to bring delicacies and women's adornments from India, China and Arabia.[75] At a time when invested capital brought a return of six per cent[76] the appeal of Pliny's argument must have been strong. Pliny was particularly disturbed that large quantities of perfumes were purchased simply to be burned at funerals; it was thought that when Poppaea died Nero burned more than a year's output from Arabia.[77] Pliny was particularly concerned about the spice and perfume trades.[78] Pearls and jewels were bad enough, he thought, but at least had a money value and could be inherited. But perfumes, at 400 denarii a pound! Not only do they lose their scent extremely quickly, but can only be enjoyed by someone else (for the wearer soon becomes habituated to the scent). All Pliny's stern old Roman virtues were outraged at women who paid large sums on perfume simply to gain attention as they passed; he is sarcastic at the fashion (taken from Nero) of putting perfume on the soles of the feet; and the old soldier in him was highly indignant at the modern practice that in military camps on feast days all the standards and eagles were anointed with unguents and that beneath their helmets the soldiers' hair gleamed with hair oil. Did we conquer the world for this? he asks.[79]

(iii) Roman history

Pliny was aware that Roman control of the world was comparatively recent. His treatment of the question of how man uses the natural world is accordingly historical, in our sense. Nature had made everything for man's use, trade was largely concerned with natural products, and empire and exploration were largely in defence of trade: this was partly the way in which Pliny approached the natural world, as the theatre of Roman power, but he has to give an historical account of other men, their philosophies and power. The Phoenicians, the Greeks and the Macedonians have their place in Pliny's scheme of history.

The theatre of history was the physical world. We have seen above the way in which Pliny considered the world as eternal, but it was by no means immutable, and Pliny's conception of chronological history includes changes in the physical world. The Pliny who was interested in coastlines, distances and routes was naturally interested in major changes in them. He tells the reader that the town of Charax in the Persian Gulf, originally one of Alexander's Alexandrias, was founded just over a mile from the coast. But by Juba's time accumulating silt from the Tigris had pushed the sea back 50 miles, and Pliny had it, from Arab envoys and Roman traders, that it was now in his own time 150 miles inland.[80] Likewise the island of Pharos, joined to Alexandria by a bridge in Pliny's time, was believed by him to have been twenty-four hours' sailing-time distant in the time of Homer. The silt of the Nile, said Pliny, had effectively created Egypt in historical times.[81] He does not speculate on the outcome of these changes, and although mentioning the theory of the Great Year (when, determined by the planets, everything starts again) he does not seem to have had a theory of history. It was natural that he should see the past as the progress of man and the development of Roman power.

Pliny's account of human progress is the story of how man has learned to use the natural world. After all (he says) man is born naked and defenceless, his only instinctive action being to weep. Nature's gifts to him include greed, ambition and all the vices that Pliny was so aware of in his fellows. Man then had to learn how to use nature's other gift, the natural world.[82] Thus, Pliny argued, men first lived upon acorns, before they learned how to cultivate fruit trees.[83] This necessarily meant passing on information down the generations, which ultimately came to be written down. Pliny believed that the Phoenicians had invented the alphabet[84] and is very alive to the significance for civilisation of the written record (as such a writer might be). The story of paper indeed is a very Plinian exercise. At first (he says) man wrote on various productions of nature, like palm leaves and the bark of trees. Progress was made by various arts, so that records began to be kept on sheets of lead, linen or on wax tablets. Meanwhile nature had been making Egypt from the silt of the Nile and papyrus began to grow there. Paper was made from papyrus only when Alexander had founded the Egyptian Alexandria: characteristically, Pliny takes the reader through the process of manufacture, describes to him the different kinds, qualities and sizes of paper and tells him a story from the historians about the great age of some paper books. It is a very Roman story: when the coffin of king Numa was accidentally discovered during the course of digging on a farm, it was found to contain some paper books. They were extremely old, and included some Pythagorean works; after wondering how paper could have lasted so long, the Romans burnt them, because they contained Greek philosophy.[85]

Knowledge of nature and the arts, Pliny held, was continually improving. After acorns, men began to eat corn, which was, Pliny believed, discovered by Ceres, who also invented grinding it to make flour, for which she was judged to be a goddess. Pliny gives similar accounts for the inventors of buying and selling, of bricks and so the first cities, of mining, tools, clothes and so on. It is an extensive list, written with confidence, and the Romans first enter it with the reception of the Greek alphabet.[86] Apart from the paragraph on the alphabet and a passing reference to astronomy, all the discoveries listed by Pliny relate to the practical arts of civil and military life. Pliny, like most Romans, was not interested in the intellectual philosophies of the Greeks, even when it was a theoretical understanding that could have important practical implications. Pliny has a story about Roman time-keeping that illustrates this. Having described two 'agreements' between the various nations (to adopt the Ionian alphabet and to shave off their beards) Pliny describes how observation of the hours, the third common policy, came rather late to Rome. The old Twelve Tables of Roman law spoke only of sunrise and sunset, to which was later added noon. The Romans knew it was noon because the consuls' apparitor said so, announcing it from the Senate House when he saw the sun between the buildings known as The Beaks and the Greek Lodging. When the sun was between the Maenian column and the prison, the apparitor shouted out that it was the last hour of the day. Satisfied with the system (though it did not work on cloudy days), the Romans continued it down to the first Punic war. Then, having captured a town in Sicily, they brought home a sundial. Of course, Sicily being further south, the lines engraved on the sundial did not correspond to the shadow thrown by the sundial's gnomon in Rome. Apparently not understanding the theory of the thing, the Romans continued with a sundial that did not tell the time much better than the consul's apparitor for another century. It was not until 159 BC that a (better) sundial was supplemented by a water clock and the Romans were able to tell the time when the sun was not shining.[87]

Pliny's image of the Roman people was itself defined historically. Like Cato, he had an image of the real, original Romans as a sturdy agricultural race full of *gravitas* and *pietas.* This may have been an old moral code derived from the provincial upper classes, whence Pliny came,[88] and as we have seen he had endless grumbles about the luxury and degeneration of the modern inhabitants of Rome. He recalled wistfully that in the early days of Rome two acres were enough for every man; while today some have fishponds of greater size. Pliny was thankful that no one had yet built a kitchen so big. He recalled too how the earliest religious insignias in Rome were wreaths of corn, how many important Latin words had etymologies with agricultural origins, and how many noble Roman names had rustic origins.[89] The earth, the soil itself, had for Pliny some aspects of the divinity of the world; it was 'mother earth' whose soil had in the early days been tilled by the hands of the noble Romans themselves. But in these days, laments Pliny, the work is done by slaves, and earth resents the fact, yielding ever diminishing crops.[90] Pliny's ideal was partly one of self-sufficiency, so that each man (presumably on his two acres) could grow enough wheat for his bread, which his wife baked. There were no bakers in Rome, says Pliny, for the first 580 years of the city's existence.[91]

But for Pliny, the historical loss of the original rustic virtue of the Romans was somewhat offset by the spread of civilisation. It was of course Roman civilisation, made possible by the 'majesty of Roman power', *maiestate Romani imperii*.[92] It was this that made Italy the parent of all countries and now enabled a flow of information throughout the whole world, says Pliny; a flow indeed, we can add, that made possible and desirable such a collection as the *Natural History*. Pliny dated what he saw as the recent expansion of knowledge and civilisation back some 230 years, to the time of Cato and the destruction of Carthage. Cato was one of Pliny's heroes, because of his stern morality and concern with agriculture. Cato marked the beginning of this development according to Pliny because his works on agriculture were comparatively simple by Pliny's standards. Before Cato – according to Pliny – no one had written on viticulture, and Cato himself had described only a few varieties of vine. Yet Pliny knew of many more varieties, and of vineyards that produced vastly more wine to the acre than had ever been known to Cato. Claiming that life had been transformed since Cato's day by the introduction of new varieties of fruit, here of figs, Pliny has a story of Cato that nicely illustrates the expansion of the Roman world. It is well known that Cato made 'Carthage must be destroyed' a refrain of his speeches in the senate, and on one such occasion (says Pliny) he produced a fig and demanded of the assembly how long ago they thought it had been picked. It was clearly quite fresh and Cato said he had picked it the day before yesterday at Carthage; 'so near is the enemy to our walls!'[93]

Pliny romanticises the Cato story as the fruit that secured the downfall of a city, but it is certainly true that the new power of Rome, as Pliny says, made possible the growth of trade and the introduction of the new species of plants and fruit that Pliny lists. From the literature Pliny recalled the time when not even olives were known in Italy, and he has dates for the introduction of pistachio nuts, cherries and others. The period after Cato saw the introduction of the medlar, almond, new varieties of myrtle, and so on.[94]

Perhaps the most obviously historical way in which Pliny treats natural objects is by the date of their first appearance in Rome. Returning emperors and other military commanders would often stage a triumph in which a display of strange things from distant territories emphasised their success and the military might of Rome. Some triumphs even displayed exotic trees, and the displays of wild animals like lions and elephants developed into a regular traffic for events in the circus (Plate 22).

Perhaps Pliny's historical treatment of nature's creatures in relation to man is best exemplified by his description of the elephant. There are a dozen or so distinctive features of Pliny's natural-history accounts, and they are all found in his elephant stories, which are worth a little *excursus* here. Elephants first appeared in Rome in a triumph in 275 BC and again in 252 BC when a large number were captured from the Carthaginians and brought to Rome on rafts made from barrels lashed together. The Romans displayed them fighting in the circus, but then did not know what to do with them, and so killed them with javelins.[95] Elephants were, then and later, symbols of military power, spoils of war and signs of the geographical extent of Roman influence. As such, they had little use when the public had seen them and the annalists noted down the year of their arrival in Rome. Everyone knew the story of Hannibal and the elephants; and as a symbol of military force, elephants were depicted carrying 'towers' full of soldiers. They remained a potent symbol for Pompey, who arranged for twenty elephants to fight men armed with javelins in the circus. The public much appreciated the elephant who threw its opponents' shields in the air, and marvelled at another who was killed by a single blow below the eye. Their mood changed to panic when the elephants made a concerted attack on the iron palisade that enclosed them. Yet when, in Pliny's words, the elephants lost all hope of escape and turned to the crowd with indescribable gestures and noises of despair and entreaty, the crowd at once rose, burst into tears and roundly cursed Pompey. Both Caesar and Nero also saw the value of the elephant as a symbol, and staged elaborate battles between elephants (some of them carrying 'castles' with garrisons of sixty, says Pliny) and men. Likewise, under Claudius the battle between a single elephant and a single man was the peak of a gladiator's life.

As the largest and one of the strangest of nature's land animals, elephants were eminently worthy of *historia*; like all strange things they came from the edges of Pliny's world, the Empire. They were a resource – ultimately, a gift of nature – that the Romans found they could mobilise in battle. They were also a potential economic resource, and Pliny notes the great price fetched by ivory, used in Europe for making elegant images of the gods (and in Ethiopa as a structural material in buildings).[96] The expansion of the Roman world meant that in addition to the Indian elephants of Alexander's campaign, described by Aristotle, Pliny had knowledge of the African kind. His source was partly Polybius, the friend of Scipio Africanus and historian of Roman expansion.[97] Somewhere in its transmission this information became corrupted, for Pliny held that Indian elephants are bigger than African, except, that is, those of Ethiopa which, standing 20 feet high, rival the Indian in size. As a resource for mankind, Pliny is interested in how the elephants are captured and trained (and in how the cave-dwellers of the border of Ethiopia hunt them for food). Indian elephants, he says, are captured by tiring them out, while in Africa the hunters dig pits. Once captured 'they are very quickly tamed by means of barley water'.[98]

These are characteristic features of many of Pliny's stories, and another is the human attributes that Pliny read into the nature of the elephant. It was commonplace in the ancient world to attribute personalities to animals – the stupid ass, the wily fox and the evil snake are examples – and to use such characteristics to form moral lessons about the corresponding human vices. Pliny obviously approved of the elephant and in projecting human traits to it made it almost a model Roman: the elephant is intelligent, says Pliny, understands and obeys orders, remembers the duties it has been taught and rejoices in glory. Hardly more could be required of the Roman soldier; and in addition the elephants threw their weapons straight and practised mock battles with others. Elephants had other Roman virtues too, and Pliny would have been glad if every Roman citizen had the elephant's virtues of probity, prudence and justice; like Pliny himself, they have (he says) a natural religion and venerate the heavenly bodies. If elephants could not dance very well, it was probably no disgrace that the same thing could be said of a Roman gentleman; and the elephant that went to a dinner party had a gentleman's manners in picking his way to his place through the drinkers without treading on them. It is also entirely consistent with Pliny's outlook that a clever elephant should not know more Greek than was decent. Here is displayed another Plinian characteristic, his uncritical attitude to his sources. The most determined apologist for Pliny must give up when he reads, uncontested in Pliny's text, of four elephants walking *per funes*, which Rackham translates as 'on tightropes', carrying a litter containing a fifth elephant pretending to be a female in labour. It is true that Pliny expresses some surprise, but not scepticism, at the related and ultimate elephant story: it is remarkable, he observes, that elephants can climb up ropes, 'and especially that they can come down again'.[99]

PLINY'S SOURCES

We have now glanced at Pliny's notions about God, nature and history, and we have seen that his history was largely Roman history. These are the principles that would have guided him in selecting what he wanted from the authors he came to read after he had decided to write a natural history. His choice of authors also reflected these principles. As an author of books on military technique and Roman history he was concerned about Roman power and empire. As an advocate he was also aware that a nation's identity was bound up in its laws and their historical development. This is apparent from the *Natural History*.

(i) The Greeks

The importance of things Roman to Pliny put him into a slightly awkward situation. Most of the authors who treated of the things that Pliny thought were parts of natural history were Greek. It was partly that Macedonian expansion had been very much the same kind of thing as Roman and gave Pliny additional information with a strong chronological component. And it was partly that the Greeks practised philosophy and had written detailed and theoretical treatises on things like animals and plants. The Romans were not a philosophical people.[100] According to Galen they thought that Greek philosophy was about as useful as drilling holes in millet seeds, and as we have seen occasionally, thought that the best thing to do with Greek philosophy books was to burn them. Their self-image as a sturdy agricultural race fitted well with their practical successes in engineering, building, military logistics, civil administration and so on. Pliny was clearly a Roman in these ways, and clearly expressed his dislike of the Greeks. The Greek attempt to measure the height of clouds and the moon came close, for Pliny, to an insane use of effort, however infallible the geometrical method. It was partly the uselessness of the attempt that angered Pliny and partly the impropriety of attempting to measure the divine.[101] But what else would one expect of the Greeks? They were, after all, the parents of all vices.[102] When he condemns the utter credulity of Greek writers[103] (about werewolves) he seems to have forgotten the many bizarre stories he himself tells.[104] In an entirely Plinian passage he here upbraids them for using olive oil in the gymnasium; the Romans in contrast *bestowed honour on the olive* by decorating cavalry squadrons with wreaths of it at minor triumphs. This shows neatly how man, even military man, was at the centre of Pliny's thoughts. But despite his dislike of the Greeks, Pliny found that he could not do without their books and indeed their terms. In the historical growth of knowledge, in which he clearly felt himself to be playing a part, one must read what others have written in the past. In astronomy the vocabulary owes much to the Greek (Pliny is explaining 'apsides' and 'poles')[105] and as for animals, local names vary so much that Greek is useful as a standard terminology.[106] In as far as philosophy is concerned it may be that some Romans felt a sense of cultural inferiority to the Greeks. Pliny clearly refers to some sort of Roman resentment when he advises his readers not to be too proud to follow the Greeks, who had, after all, been more diligent of old.[107] It was probably satisfying to Pliny that Macedonian power, which had provided so many details for his own work, had been eclipsed by Roman, which had provided more; at all events he has a rather spiteful story in his description of the Macedonian empire, of how the Roman commander Aemilius Paulus pillaged and sold seventy-two Macedonian cities in a single day.[108]

Of his two hundred or so sources, less than a third wrote in Latin.[109] Of those who wrote on medical subjects, a very big topic for Pliny, the dominance of the Greeks was even clearer, for only one-eighth of this group wrote in Latin. If we divide the *Natural History* up into the topics contained in the different books of the work we find that Latin authors outnumber Greek on few occasions. It is natural that Pliny should find more Romans than Greeks writing about Italy, for example. There are also more Latin sources for Pliny's topic of forest trees, which deals with timber and horticulture.

Perhaps the Romans were interested in timber for structural and engineering reasons; or perhaps their expansion to the west and north was into more heavily wooded country than the Greek east. Disregarding medicines for the moment, the other topics on which the Romans wrote extensively were aquatic animals and the food they provide, and flowers.

Apart from these, Pliny's Greek sources outnumber his Latin comfortably. He has eight or nine times as many Greek authors as Latin on the subject of gems and the medicines derived from them. On wild, and cultivated plants, it is six times as many. In all three cases the weight of Greek works is medical, but even if we put these to one side, the Greek works still outnumber the Latin. In both cases – Greek and Latin – Pliny depends less on small specialist works than on the broadly based works of the great writers. In each case we can recognise characteristic groups of writers. Among the Latin sources the agricultural writers were important, while we see in the Greek sources instead a group of those who were concerned with Alexander, either personally or as historians.

Aristotle was clearly one of the Greeks whom Pliny recognised had been 'more diligent' in the past; he speaks of him as a man of the highest authority in every subject,[110] and he was familiar with Aristotle's books on animals. He also appreciated Aristotle's connection with Alexander, and gives the story of Alexander ordering information on animals to be sent from Asia to Aristotle. Yet it is clear that he did not understand or had no interest in Aristotle's purposes. Pliny represents his own position as that of one who is about to summarise Aristotle's works on animals and add some things of which Aristotle was ignorant. Yet Pliny does not note the *differentiae* between animals, he does not mention the correlation between habit, habitat and form and he is not concerned with causes. The whole of Aristotle's philosophical enquiry is treated by Pliny as material for his own *historiae,* objects and occurrences sufficiently wonderful to be reported. Thus Pliny records from Aristotle that the lioness bears five cubs at the first birth, and one less every succeeding year, finally becoming barren. Pliny then adds on Aristotle's authority how lions urinate, smell unpleasant, drink rarely and at a meal always pull the last lump of flesh from their jaws with their claws (so that they may not be over-full if they need to run). Then Pliny adds material from other and later sources, that is, material of which Aristotle had been ignorant. Thus from Polybius he adds that in the weakness of old age, lions turn to man-eating. Since they were numerous enough to pose a threat to African cities, the Romans crucified the man-eating lions to act as a warning to others. (Polybius was a witness to this when with Scipio Africanus.) From Juba Pliny adds something else that Aristotle was ignorant of, that lions listen to the entreaties of those they capture and allow them to depart if sufficiently moved, as in the case of a woman who was allowed to go from a whole herd of lions after she had declared that she was weak, female, and generally unworthy of being the victim of the lord of the animals.

Pliny draws out from the rest of Aristotle's works on the natural world a number of details appropriate to his style and purposes. In discussing phenomena in the air, he claims Aristotle's support for the belief that several comets can be seen at the same time, which signifies heat or winds to come,[111] and that rainbows are occasionally seen at night. He mentions Aristotle's discussion of the roles of gills in fish and lungs in cetaceans without engaging in Aristotle's search for a common feature of respiration.[112] He records Aristotle's generic name for soft-boned fish (*selache*) and gives his own Latin equivalent (*cartilaginea*) without concerning himself with the logical or philosophical problems of classification, discussed by Aristotle.[113] The central role given to man in Pliny's scheme of things is shown when he extracts from Aristotle's work on animals the human detail that the race called the Androgynes have one male and one female breast, and that pygmies live in caves.[114] What Aristotle may have been ignorant of, but Pliny knew, was that Alexander, out of respect for his tutor, had treated Aristotle's birthplace well during his military campaigns.[115] Perhaps Pliny shared with Aristotle the notion that the sexual reproduction of animals is of interest because it demonstrates nature's purposes in ensuring the perpetuity of species, but it could also be a human interest in the related behaviour of animals.[116]

Aristotle's interest in the historical development of people's ideas, political arrangements and achievements, was a natural resource for Pliny, who was also interested in them and in general in how knowledge was growing. He cites Aristotle on how a particular island got its name; that the primitive alphabet had eighteen letters; that the Cyclopes were the first to build towers; that Lydus the Scythian discovered how to work copper; on who introduced painting to Greece and that the Carthaginians invented the quadrireme.[117]

If we were to draw up a table of the authors Pliny quotes most

often, Theophrastus would come third. Pliny either did not understand or did not sympathise with Aristotle's search for finality and
undoubtedly felt an affinity with Theophrastus' largely pragmatic
descriptions of plants and his hesitation over causality. Pliny's search
for the medical properties of things would naturally have led him to
Theophrastus' description of plants. Pliny the Roman was more
interested, for example, in what plants supply the most appropriate
fibres for the best ropes, rather than in the obscurer corners of Greek
philosophy concerned with the natures and causes of plants. But we
have looked at the natural history of Theophrastus, as of Aristotle,
and it will be plain of what nature Pliny's borrowings were.

What we can usefully – although briefly – look at here is Pliny's
use of authors whose works have *not* survived – unlike those of
Theophrastus and Aristotle. This is the case with the two authors
whom Pliny depends on most (apart from Theophrastus and Aristotle) throughout the entire *Natural History.* These are the Greek,
Democritus, and Varro the Roman (whom we shall consider with
Pliny's other Latin sources).

Let us look first at Democritus. This is the traditional figure
of Democritus *physicus,* 'natural philosopher'. It is not wholly clear
that references to him in Pliny are always to the Democritus who is
such a standard figure in histories of philosophy and science, but
Pliny does not suggest that he is drawing from more than one author.
The traditional Democritus *physicus* as seen by Pliny (and Seneca)
certainly seems to be like our limited historical picture of him. Seneca
says that he believed in atoms (and that their closeness caused the
wind). He had natural explanations for things that frightened people,
like earthquakes (caused by air and water). He was interested in how
quickly different materials heated up, and in the erratic motions of
the planets. Seneca (who largely agreed with him) thought him the
most acute of the ancient philosophers, and it must have been the
same reputation that made Pliny rely on him to such an extent.

But Pliny's Democritean material is of a different kind. He reports
that Democritus had travelled widely in Persia, Ethiopia, Egypt and
Arabia, and to have learned much (with Pythagoras) with the Magi.
It was perhaps from the Persians that he accepted the doctrine that
there are two gods, one of punishment, the other of reward. It was
certainly (says Pliny) from the Magi that Democritus learned of the
magical powers of plants: plants that made Persian monarchs healthy
and made criminals confess; plants that made lions yawn and wild
animals fall into a slumber that could only be banished by the urine

of a hyena; plants that drive wedges out of trees. With the Magi (who made their vows on it) Democritus admired the nyctegreton plant, which had to be pulled up by the roots after the spring equinox and dried by moonlight for thirty days, after which it glowed in the dark. More prosaically Democritus knew that turnips cause flatulence, that radishes are an aphrodisiac and that mint and pomegranate juice cure hiccups. Pliny's Democritus *physicus* was also a practical philosopher. He knew the names of all the kinds of vine in Italy, and gave directions about training them. He knew how to clear forests by steeping lupins in hemlock juice and sprinkling it on the roots of the trees. Knowing the relationship between heaven and earth, he forecast rain and saved his brother's harvest. Knowing that the rising of the Pleiads meant a rise in the price of oil, he cornered the olive market and made a great deal of money.[118]

(ii) The doctors

There are two other groups of writers whom Pliny attacks at least as fiercely as he attacks the Greeks, despite, in all three cases, using their writings extensively. These are the doctors and the Magi. Let us look first at the doctors, because Pliny's arguments against them are an extension of those against the Greeks. This was natural, because most of the doctors were Greeks. But Pliny is not concerned with their vain theorising and intricate philosophy. Rather, he is extremely perturbed about the physical danger to Romans from Greek medical practice. So vitriolic is his attack that this concern might well have been the major stimulus to his general antipathy to all things Greek. Nothing could be more detestable to Pliny than to pose a threat to the moral and physical integrity of those at the heart of the Empire, and this is exactly what he accuses the Greeks of doing.

Pliny begins Book 29 with an account of how medicine came to be in such a deplorable state. It begins, naturally enough, with an historical account that serves to identify what it is that he is complaining of, that is, what is worthy of *historia*: although his topic is the malpractice of a human art, it is an art that centres on natural things and so a proper part of a natural history. He claims to be the first to have written about medicine in Latin[119] and part of his aim is to explain how home-grown remedies (once so dependable) have been forgotten as medicine fluctuated between one fashion and another. Pliny's brief account of the history of medicine, from its divine origins through Hippocrates, Chrysippus, Erasistratus and

Herophilus, is designed primarily to show how, by attaching themselves to royalty, physicians have been able to command very large
salaries. Although he attaches a label to the Empirics and names
physicians traditionally supposed (for example by Celsus) to have
belonged to the Rationalist and Methodist sects, Pliny does not
discuss the principal difference between them, the role of reason and
philosophy in medicine. For him it was a story of how one or other
of the competing physicians had convinced important people, often
enough the emperor, with some new treatment, and so secured great
wealth. Charmis championed cold baths, even in the depth of winter,
and Pliny has it from Seneca that for a while old and important men
of Rome would appear in public rigid with cold. It is, argues Pliny,
all extremely dangerous, and while 'we are being blown about by the
wind of ingenious Greeks',[120] many die.

The Greek wind for Pliny was the hot air of Greeks talking with
plausible arguments. In contrast, the stern old Romans had lived for
six centuries without physicians, but not without medicine: Pliny is
back to his argument that local remedies are best and that foreign
experts are not needed. Did not Archagathus, the first physician to
come to Rome (from Greece, of course) earn himself notoriety and
the nickname 'executioner'? Pliny has this story from his hero Cato,
who in a striking passage forbade his son to have anything to do
with 'those Greeks', whose writings corrupt all things and who
conspire to kill barbarians with their medicine (for a fee, moreover).
Cato was highly indignant at being thought of as barbarian by the
Greeks, a resentment we have seen also in Pliny. And Pliny agreed[121]
with Cato that whatever good was to be had from the Greeks was
got by merely inspecting their learning rather than by immersing
oneself in it.[122] It was a sentiment that Pliny adhered to throughout
the *Natural History*.

In the passage cited above, Cato urged his son to treat his words
as he would those of a prophet. Pliny took Cato to be a prophet
indeed, foreseeing the degeneracy of the Romans of Pliny's day,
which Pliny attributed principally to medicine. Cato was the prophet
of the Roman cause, and for Pliny Greek physicians were un-Roman
and even anti-Roman. To a large extent this also meant that Greek
medicine had to be resisted, and we have seen that for Pliny this
meant the fluctuating fashions of practice – bathing, exercise, diet,
drinking, sleeping and so on, the physical regimen. But Pliny also
refused to see any theory in medicine, even the dispute about the use
of anatomy and reason that Celsus recorded between the Rationalists

and Empiricists: theory was simply too Greek a thing. Accordingly, medicine for Pliny was what it had been to the old Romans, simply a knowledge of what remedies were suitable for which diseases. At such a simple level even Greek authors could be used – and Pliny keeps it at this level, pouring scorn on the complexity of the two famous Greeks remedies, theriac and mithradatium, the latter with fifty-four ingredients. As we have seen the great bulk of Pliny's medical authors were indeed Greek. Pliny uses them extensively, if that is a word adequate to describe the great flood of detail that composes his medical chapters.[123] They are overwhelmingly dense and multitudinous for the modern reader: Pliny has some organising principles (they are discussed below) but the sheer quantity of his material is difficult to deal with. However, Pliny did not write the *Natural History* to be read through as if it contained and was structured by an argument. As he says in the preface, it was to act as a source of reference, to be dipped into. To judge by the later history of his text,[124] it was just for its medical content that the reader dipped into the *Natural History.* Although medical theory is given much attention by academic historians, people in the past were directly interested, rather, in what remedies were available for their diseases. Even learned physicians were always interested to learn new recipes and *materia medica.* What emerges from these dense pages of the *Natural History* is the list of complaints that people suffered from in imperial Rome and the sense of urgency with which they sought relief.

(iii) The Magi

Pliny reserves his major attack on the Magi for the beginning of the next book. The Magi are liars, he says bluntly, and their magical arts are mere vanities.[125] Who were these people? Why was Pliny so antagonistic to them? Were they worse than the very Greeks?

The answers we can extract from Pliny's text reveal more of the features of Pliny's character that we have already met. First, the Magi for Pliny were foreign, and therefore suspect: the magical tradition was very ancient, originating with Zoroaster who perhaps lived, says Pliny (with Eudoxus and Aristotle) some six thousand years before Plato. This was a long time indeed before the Foundation of the City, from which the Romans took their own history, here virtually as newcomers on the world stage. Not only was magic older than Rome, but it was the invention of the Persians, the great power to the east of the Graeco-Roman world, and a traditional enemy. Indeed the first extant treatise on the topic available to Pliny was that of Osthanes, who had accompanied Xerxes in his invasion of Greece. Thereafter, says Pliny, knowledge of the craft infected the whole world, and in particular the Greeks took to it with a huge enthusiasm.[126] Pliny thought that Pythagoras, Empedocles and Plato had all gone abroad the better to learn magic and that Democritus had gone into the tomb of Dardanus the Phoenician to obtain his magical texts.

In addition to being Persian and Greek, magic awakened Pliny's horror because of the elaborate practices involved in its application and perhaps because it had an elaborate rationale. As a practical Roman, Pliny viewed magic much as he viewed the plausible reasons with which the Greeks justified their medicine. So it was a particular source of disapproval for Pliny that magic had first arisen from medicine, and that it continued in some forms of the medical art. He argued that its hold over people's minds was owing to its having assumed the mantle of religion, and second to its adoption of the 'mathematical arts' – predictive astrology.[127] We have seen that part of Pliny's interest in nature was that of Seneca, to argue that in a purely natural world man is not subject to the vengeance or fates of the gods, and it no doubt seemed to him that a traditional religion, a deterministic astrology and a rigid system of divination from natural objects were destructive of a Stoic philosophy and the history of nature that he was writing.

Thus for Pliny magic was self-evidently superstitious and improper. It was the natural enemy of Roman decency and thought. It was accordingly a good thing when the Romans stamped out the Druids of Gaul, together with their prophets and medical men. But, Pliny adds to this, the job was not yet complete. Magic had even crossed the Ocean and occupied the 'void of nature' – *nature inane*[128] by which Pliny seems to mean that nature – his nature – was not working as she should. Even now, he says, magic is practised in Britain, and with so much ceremony that the British might have taught the Persians. The most odious aspect of Druidical magic, in Pliny's eyes, was human sacrifice and its cannibalism. Roman power was surely justified in taking control to prevent such practices: 'it is not possible to estimate how much is owed to the Romans, who destroyed such monstrous things'.[129]

Justifying military invasion by an argument about the spread of civilisation was and is not an uncommon practice, and it must have been a natural argument to Pliny. It informed his detailed arguments against magical writings, which are concerned largely with the details of medical practice. Although Pliny professed to be amazed that something so obviously fraudulent should have become so widespread, there is often little to choose between Pliny's own remedies and those of the Magi. Except for its length, his treatment for jaundice is not unusual:

> Jaundice is combatted by dirt from the ears or teats of a sheep, the dose being a denarius by weight with a morsel of myrrh and two cyathi of wine, by the ash of a dog's head in honey wine, by a millipede in a hemina of wine, by earthworms with oxymel in myrrh, by drinking wine that has rinsed a hen's feet – they must be yellow – after they have been cleansed with water, by the brain of a partridge or eagle taken in three cyathi of wine, by the ash of the feathers or intestines of a woodpigeon taken in honey wine up to three spoonfuls, or by the ash of sparrows burnt over twigs in two spoonfuls of hydromel.[130]

Yet he mocks the Magi for choosing to apply twelve not dissimilar remedies separately as the sun passes through the signs of the zodiac. It was the zodiac that seemed arbitrary to Pliny, not the kind of remedy or the influence of the heavenly bodies. The other main difference between Pliny's remedies and those of the Magi is that the latter often added spoken and physical rituals to the application of the remedy. It was not an unusual ancient remedy for a painful spleen to place over it the fresh spleen of a sheep, but it was the Magi who ritually said aloud what their purpose was. After this, they said, the sheep's spleen should be plastered into the walls of the sickroom, sealed with a ring three times nine, and the same words repeated.[131]

The foreignness that Pliny felt for the Magi extended to the strange names they gave to perfectly ordinary objects to invest them with an air of magical potency. Precious and beautiful stones were part of Pliny's natural world and presented another opportunity for him to extol nature and condemn man's use of luxury; but the *dendritis,* the 'tree stone' which, buried beneath a tree, kept sharp the axes used to fell it, or the *synochitis* that held the shades of the dead when they had been summoned from below, or again the *anancitis*, which was used to conjure divine apparitions in divination with water, were all part of the Magi's dreadful lies.[132] A system which relied so much on the summoning of supernatural powers was necessarily in conflict with Pliny's attempt to portray a natural world. Pliny was less vehement in his attitude to another characteristic activity of the Magi, divination. This may be because there was, as we have seen, a possible mechanism for divination with the Stoics' natural world and because it was a feature of Roman life. Pliny describes how the Magi practiced *axinomantia*, divination by means of axes, on which a piece of jet was burned: if it did not burn away completely, the wish would come true.[133] But he was impatient with the Magi's claim that the 'tortoise-stone', said to be the eye of a tortoise, gave the power to speak prophecies when placed below the tongue, and it was entirely against his natural principles that incantations made in this way could cause storms to diminish.

It is important to remember that Pliny's idea of 'nature' included the older Greek notion of nature-of-a-thing, which in an orderly and regular way revealed the thing's essence and actions. The Magi's world in contrast was one of active powers that could be summoned and commanded by special knowledge relating to key objects and appropriate ritual: they sought to manipulate the natural world, often with non-natural agencies. All of this was foreign to Pliny and the Roman Stoicism that was part of his character. He was indignant at the Magi's claim to be able to cause storms by sprinkling the tortoise-stone with gold and dropping it into boiling water with a scarab-beetle[134] and he lamented that they went beyond plain medicine (of which we have seen a Plinian example) to the supernatural. The rituals of the Magi included not only incantations but inscriptions: for example, amethysts inscribed with the names of the sun and moon and worn as a necklace with baboons' hair were held to nullify spells, to ease the paths of suppliants to kings and, if used with the proper incantations, to keep off hail and locusts.[135] Different kinds of agate were held by the Magi to avert storms, dry up rivers, settle domestic disputes and make athletes invincible. Prayers said over the plant and stone both called heliotrope, Pliny reports indignantly, were held to make the man who wore them invisible.[136]

(iv) Latin authors

Of his Latin authors, Pliny was particularly interested in Celsus, whose medical compilation has survived. Pliny's interest in Celsus was largely medical and parallels between the texts of the two men can readily be made. As in the case of Democritus let us look instead through Pliny's eyes at sources that have not survived. Pliny used Mucianus as much as Celsus. This was Licinius Mucianus, sometime senator, three times consul and a very powerful political figure.[137]

He wrote a collection of wonders (the *Mirabilia)* based on his experiences as legionary legate and provincial governor, and so was an ideal source for Pliny: he was Roman, recent (he survived Pliny) and authoritative, close to the centre of power, helping to expand Roman influence, learning and teaching about the natural world, its wonders and resources. He may have been a Patron of Pliny.[138]

Much more important to Pliny that Celsus or Mucianus was Marcus Terentius Varro, whom Pliny uses more extensively than either. Varro's work on agriculture survives, but the bulk of the material that Pliny read and used has not. Varro's reputation among the Latins was equal perhaps to that of Democritus with the Greeks and as we have seen they were both extremely important authors for Pliny. Varro (116–27 BC) was an influential figure in Roman education. Pliny of course read both authors extremely selectively. He was not trying to be a Greek *physicus* when he read Democritus, which is why we cannot see the Democritus we know in Pliny's use of him. Both authors were after all a *resource* for Pliny, who was trying to produce a Roman coverage of the whole of the natural world. Varro's enterprise was perhaps rather closer to Pliny's from what we know of his works, and he emerges a little more clearly in what Pliny wrote. It was an enterprise more traditionally educational than Pliny's. To the traditional seven liberal arts of the Greeks, Varro added architecture and medicine.[139] Pliny was not concerned with education in this direct way and thought that human knowledge could not be adequately expressed in such a format.[140] What emerges from Pliny's use of Varro's materials is a Varro who reflects Pliny's interests. As a learned man he was also very practical, commanding Pompey's fleet in the war against the pirates; as a commander he knew enough practical philosophy to provide the sailors with fresh water from the Caspian sea when Pompey was fighting king Mithridates. Varro was therefore involved in the extension of Roman power, and Pliny was interested in his account of geographical distances at the outposts of empire. Pliny also found what Varro had to say on particular imports and exports and borrowed other geographical lore from him, including an account of a floating island. Stories that endured in the marvel-literature that Pliny used were those of the very great strength of a very little soldier in Pompey's army, and of the two Romans of the *equites* class who were only 3 feet tall. Pliny the historian used Varro's account of the first barbers and sundials to appear in Rome.

Other very Plinian topics that Pliny naturally found in Varro were the history of paper and some surprisingly old books; the naming of vines and the best wines; the size of edible snails; prices of animals, and the cost of provisions on the occasion of an especially large elephant triumph.[141]

THE PHYSICAL WORLD AND ITS CONTENTS

Pliny's conception of the world was formed from these authors. Let us briefly look at what kind of thing it was and at the kinds of natural category that it contained.

For Pliny the world was everything visible on the earth and in the sky. Its centre was the globe of the earth on which lived man. Pliny's world was anthropocentric and anthropomorphic: man (Roman man) was at its centre and the world and its natural categories had human-like purposes, largely directed to man. The centre of the world, the terraqueous globe, remained immobile, and the sphere of the heavens rotated once every twenty-four hours. (If it made music while doing so, said Pliny,[142] it was inaudible to man.) The globe was the pivot of the world, both upholding and being upheld by the rotating elements. Pliny seems to have held that the 'unlike qualities' of the elements resulted in the continued separation of their parts. This is a source for his doctrine of innate powers of natural things and of sympathies: the four elements of earth, air, fire and water, with active qualities, form a sort of network which together with the rotation of the heavens, holds the world together. Pliny is not clear, and probably does not intend to be, for this is the passage where he is invoking the mystery and divinity of the world. Later[143] he is a little more prosaic and when discussing the rotundity of the earth and the common people's surprise that the people on the other side of the earth do not fall off, concludes that there is nowhere for people or the earth to fall to: each element had its natural place. But Pliny is not consciously borrowing this or that Greek theory, and plainly declares that his purpose is not to theorise, but to give briefly the agreed facts. (It is a jibe at the Greeks to wonder more at any agreement between theorists than at any disagreement.[144]) This is in accordance with Pliny's principles. He is writing in the tradition of encyclopedia and handbooks, which the Romans had taken from the Greeks. He was deliberately abandoning the tradition of education in the liberal arts,[145] which did require theoretical understanding and which, as the education of free men, were not directed to practical ends (they included geometry, arithmetic and music, which together with astronomy, came to be taught in the Middle Ages as the *quadrivium*). But Pliny *was* interested in practical things, and his account of astronomy for instance is structured by its use to man.

This is the outline of Pliny's physical world. We have already seen that the sun occupied a special place in the upper part of the world, and in the lower, air played a not dissimilar role. It was not unlike the Stoic *pneuma*[146] and Pliny can see it as nature breathing life into the earth as though in a womb, the generating spirit of the 'nature of things', *ille generabilis rerum naturae spiritus.*[147] This 'vital air' penetrates all things[148] and in particular, when it blows from the west in the spring, it is the 'generative spirit of the world', with a proper name, Favonius.[149] In a general sense it is nature's enlivening principle, but the special sense of nature is there too, for it is the *natura rerum* in each plant and animal that is awakened and which guides its growth according to its kind, *pro sua quaeque natura*.

The topics of the *Natural History* are the kinds of things that are to be found in this world, in as far as they are of use to or of interest to man. Most of these categories of things are living, the plants and animals that provide material resources for man's complex life. But Pliny has a lot to say too on minerals, from the valuable gems that the Romans liked to wear, to metals, whether gold for coinage and decoration or the different kinds of iron and steel of obvious functional value. It is among Pliny's purposes to instruct his readers morally, and many a major section of the text begins with a rhetorical passage on the moral laxity of modern man, especially in respect of wastage of natural resources. Another purpose is to report the wonderful things that have been discovered by *historia* and it was surely his hope that the Roman reading classes would be entertained by what he had to say. Third, he intended the whole treatise to be used as a reference work, with the first book acting as a detailed table of contents. The lists of authors he gives were probably put there to lend authority, but they could conceivably have acted as a guide to further reading, had any of Pliny's readers been so curious. Also among his purposes were to cover all fields when earlier texts had not, and to avoid theory by reporting only facts that were generally accepted. All this is by way of saying that although many modern subject areas have something corresponding in Pliny's text, it is a mistake to evaluate his 'botany' or 'zoology'. These are categories of modern science, and science does not seek to instruct morally, to entertain, or to eschew theory and rely on the categorisation of consensual 'fact'. All we can say historically is that Pliny's book provided material for those who came to practice a rather different kind of natural history in the sixteenth century and for those who later came to practice science.

Another of Pliny's non-scientific purposes, although it cannot be said to be the driving principle behind the structure and content of the *Natural History*, was that shared with Seneca and Lucretius, namely to show that in a purely natural world one need have no fear of divine retribution. Pliny's message is less about earthly life, where he often seems to imply divine action, than with death. For Pliny, death is total. It is, he says, childish absurdity and a characteristic human greed (here for life) to imagine any kind of physical or spiritual survival after death. All questions about the nature of the soul, its substances, its use of the senses, its location and its immortality were for Pliny, without value.[150] They were of course some of the most fundamental questions in Greek philosophy. But Pliny sweeps them aside in a rhetorical flourish. He did not know or he did not care that the soul as the form of the animal body was central to Aristotle's animal books, the *De Anima* and much of the *Parva Naturalia*, all germane to natural history. It was present life on earth that Pliny was concerned with and he significantly leaves his rhetoric on the vanity of thinking of a future life for a brisk historical account of the first discoveries of the human arts. His point is that since death is final, there can be no divine retribution in an afterlife. He had said, we can recall, that however powerful the ultimate divine being, he could not recall people from death or destroy a past life.

Pliny's denial of human immortality – no shades, spirits or Hades – was very different from the orientation of Christianity, in the first century of which Pliny was living, and which as we shall see came to adopt much Greek philosophy in relation to the soul. Pliny's beliefs about the soul and mortality undoubtedly helped him form his ideas about the physical world in the way he did. If there was divinity, it was in the present world, perhaps it was the world itself. And if the heavens belonged to God, the earth belonged to man. 'Earth', *terra,* was philosophers' talk for one of the elements (which Pliny is dealing with)[151] but for Pliny she was also 'mother', part of nature. Pliny becomes rhetorical: it is mother earth who receives us when we are born, sustains us during life and gives us final shelter in death. It becomes moral rhetoric when Pliny measures man's ungrateful consumption of earth's gifts against his greedy mutilation of the earth itself in the digging of mines and canals. One of the principal crimes of man's ingratitude to the earth, says Pliny, is man's ignorance of her. To redress that ignorance was another reason to write a *Natural History.*

MINERALS, INDUSTRY AND ART

In dealing with metals and minerals especially, Pliny shows two important characteristics of what he thought natural history was. We would not include them in a subject of that name, but as historians we have to listen seriously to what Pliny was saying.

The first – and we have seen many signs of this already – is that his natural history was genuinely historical. This chronological element is mainly apparent when Pliny deals with man's affairs. We have seen how Rome-centred was Pliny's view of man, and what we are dealing with in these books of the *Natural History* is the development of Roman society. This belongs to a history of nature because – to come to the second characteristic – the arts and crafts of man (says Pliny) imitate nature. This is very much part of Pliny's message. Not only did nature provide all things for man but she also taught him the rudiments of craft techniques. This is partly the Stoic denial of the divine origin of the crafts, and Pliny felt justified in spending a great deal of space on the human arts and technologies. For Pliny, giving a history of the arts is to explain their nature; and being a history of a human activity, it is generally Pliny's purpose to demonstrate that it has a culmination (and a new degeneration into luxury) in Roman society.

Let us look briefly at what Pliny has to say on art imitating nature. This is the theme of his substantial sections on painting and sculpture in bronze and marble. He announces his plan at the opening of Book 36, the penultimate: everything he has described so far has been (he says) created for the use of man. But nature has the mountains for herself, to maintain the coherence of the earth and to contain the waters and winds. Yet man mines the metals and minerals, plunders nature's materials, destroys her mountains and with the material obtained, imitates her creativeness. Here again the English language expresses too easily what Pliny is saying, for while it was *natura* who made the mountains for herself, it was *rerum natura* that operated in the plains left when man had removed the mountains, that is, the collective natures of individual things.[152] And as for art imitating nature, when the painter Eupompus said that he followed nature rather than any one of his predecessors, he could mean equally well a universal *natura genetrix* or the expression of the individual nature of a thing.[153] When Pliny finished describing how man's art imitated nature and began the final book of the *Natural History*, it is *rerum naturae* whose majesty is revealed in gems. The same thing may be said about about *iconicae*, portrait statues of three-times winners at the Olympic games[154] and portrait painting, where the *nature* of this or that man (such as king Antigonus) or woman (such as Aristotle's mother)[155] was the nature that the artist was following. Pliny's extensive lists of painters and sculptors is really a history of art imitating nature rather than an examination of the materials (metals, stone and pigments) used in doing so. The story of the copper smith Lysippus, who turned himself into a sculptor as a consequence of overhearing Eupompus' remarks about following nature rather than other artists, has the moral that nature herself in acting as a model, teaches man to imitate her. This is an essential part of the chronological history of art, for it is part of Pliny's Stoic purpose to show that it was not the gods, but nature and man who developed the human arts.

The same reasons lie behind the historical part of Pliny's 'natural-history' description of the metals. This begins with gold, the foremost of the metals. It was foremost because it was the most valuable, and his history of it is partly a history of a means of exchange. We shall see in a later section that Pliny's material was partly the craft knowledge, largely that of agriculture, that had to be transmitted in a semi-literate society for that society to be successful. What we are concerned with here is how people in the cities came to handle a money economy over and above the demands of agricultural production. Pliny knew that in Homer, barter was the method of obtaining necessities, and that some people used ox-hides as a means of exchange; and that in the old laws of Rome fines were specified in terms of cattle.[156] So it is with a strong historical sense that he goes on to describe the introduction of money and the history of the keeping of bullion in Rome. The Romans became aware of the political as well as commercial value of gold when they had to buy peace after the city had been taken by the Gauls in 390 BC.[157] Silver coinage was introduced, according to Pliny, in 269 BC and gold coins half a century later; and a standard was introduced between gold, silver and bronze. The Romans soon learned about devaluation and how to let out money at interest.[158]

It was the way Romans handled their money that gave a value to the products of nature. Pliny routinely gives the price in Rome of raw materials of various grades of quality, and of manufactured materials, together with details of the adulteration often practised on them and tests for detection of such fraud. The prices obtainable in Rome effectively set the norm, and determined how far merchants would go to obtain the raw materials. We have seen above how far this was also determined by Roman military power.

So Pliny was interested in trades and manufactures partly because many of them were based on natural products, expressly nature's gift to man, and partly because art imitated nature. Partly too his sense of morality was served because the use of a natural product as a means of exchange allowed him some easy rhetoric on some people's excessive riches and on most people's degenerate luxury. There was rhetoric available too on the topic of man's mutilation of nature in providing himself with nature's raw materials. In destroying mountains in searching for minerals, said Pliny, man was destroying what nature had marked out for her home territory. He describes how the side of a mountain suspected of containing gold would be undermined so that it collapsed.[159] Part of the operation was to divert mountain streams – by as much as 100 miles, says Pliny – to wash away the debris and extract the gold. Pliny describes how the workmen, taking sightings and marking out the route, worked slung from ropes. The aqueducts they built and the excavations they made must have represented a huge consumption of manpower; it was the waste from such washings, Pliny said, that had extended the coastline of parts of Spain. Even Hannibal, while in Spain, had derived a good supply of silver from a mine that ran a mile and a half into a mountain.[160] For Pliny mines were a renewable resource, for he believed that marble and lead, at least, grew again in abandoned mines and made them fruitful again.[161]

Included in this technology, and entirely proper for natural history in Pliny's sense, is his description of buildings in Rome. This too is very historical and he describes with a mixture of pride and regret the introduction of marble as a luxurious building material. This is a very typical mixture for Pliny: his story is of seven centuries of Roman development, largely by military prowess, culminating in her position as mistress of the world. Yet every victory brought in a new luxury, a new weakening of the Romans' moral fibre. In what would read equally well as a parody of himself Pliny gives equally grand accounts of the aqueducts that brought fresh water to Rome and of the sewers that carried foul water away.

It is worthwhile looking a little closer at this part of Pliny's

Natural History, because it reflects many of Pliny's purposes in writing and characteristics of his techniques of so doing. A chronology of building stone naturally went back to the Egyptians, and Pliny recounts the granite obelisks cut by Rameses II, who ruled at the time of the capture of Troy.[162] But Roman power devoured all, and Pliny proudly reports how the Romans overcame the technical difficulties of shipping obelisks back to Rome. One of them was engraved with the Egyptian interpretation of the nature of things. In Rome itself, the history of building techniques had been comparatively short. The old Building Regulations laid down rules for the mixing of mortar, but despite them rough quarrystone was often laid dry, when the lime (for the mortar) had been stolen. As Pliny observed, this was the reason for the collapse of buildings in Rome, and it gives a picture of a fairly simple domestic architecture.[163] Improvements and style came later and both were Greek. Even bricks were distinguished by their Greek names, and of the three kinds of them, the Romans used only one.[164] The first paved floors, admits Pliny, were a Greek invention and were often painted. They were followed in the time of Sulla by mosaics. The paving of external flat roofs was also Greek.[165] Marble columns also arrived comparatively late in Rome, if we believe Pliny, for the fashion for them grew very much in his own lifetime.[166] It was then, something he could moralise on with confidence, and he uses a telling rhetorical image of masses of luxurious marble destined for a private house being hauled past temples with earthenware pediments. Marble was cut using an iron 'saw' that used a grinding paste of sand: the best came from India, and it gave Pliny another opportunity to complain of extravagance and waste.[167]

But Pliny's morality was not that of a dedicated Stoic. We have seen that he was pround of the Roman achievement, and it softened his complaints about luxury to see that in his day Rome had buildings worthy of a city that ruled the world. To be sure, Rome's power was achieved by military victories, which each introduced a new extravagance, so that pearls and gems became fashionable after the victories of Pompey, gold cloth after those of Lucius Scipio and bronzes and fine paintings after those of Mummius. (It seems to have been partly a question of what foreign artefacts the victor chose to display at his triumph.[168]) But Pliny does not want to condemn the victories nor wholly to blame the Romans for their acquisition of a taste for paintings and sculpture. He is much more concerned with the wholly wasteful extravagance of those who sought to out-display each other on grand occasions. Such a one was Gaius Curio, who, in paying honour to his dead father, found that he had no hope of matching the grossly extravagant display of Marcus Scaurus. Resorting to ingenuity he had built two revolving wooden theatres of great size. At first they faced in opposite directions so that the words of the two sets of actors should not confuse the two audiences. Then the two theatres were turned to face each other and formed a circus in which Curio staged a fight between gladiators. Pliny wails at the image of the Roman people whirling round in a wholly frivolous manner.

> Here we have the nation that has conquered the earth, that has subdued the whole world, that distributes tribes and kingdoms, that dispaches its dictates to foreign peoples, that is heaven's representative, so to speak, among mankind, swaying on a contraption and applauding its own danger![169]

It is through the eyes of one of this race of world leaders that Pliny describes the system of aqueducts that brought water to Rome, as part of his account of building and civil engineering in the imperial city. Perhaps no modern reader needs to have his image of these sharpened by the detail and pride with which Pliny describes them, and would perhaps agree with him that, given the technical mastery, the capital cost and the advertisement of political will, they were unique in the world.[170]

Pliny seems a little puzzled that no other historian had given attention to the construction of Rome's sewers. For him they were as much a cause of celebration of civil engineering as the great public buildings. Part of their attraction was their age and the soundness of their original construction. For seven centuries, he says, the seven rivers that unite in Rome have been contained in a single channel which had been proof to the spate of the rivers, the backflow of the Tiber, the passage of heavy traffic above and the collapse of buildings (built no doubt with too little mortar). He attributes this admirable state of affairs to the soundness of the original construction, under Tarquin Priscus. What he does not say is that while Tarquin exercised considerable political will in doing the job, he does not seem to have spent a great deal of money on it. Perhaps Pliny means us to understand that it was before a money economy came to Rome, but his words suggest that Tarquin simply used his subjects as slaves. Many of the Roman citizens found the labour so excessive that they preferred suicide; but Tarquin crucified their bodies, leaving them to be torn to pieces by animals and birds. Pliny the Roman reports that a Roman sensibility to shame spurred on the remaining citizens to complete the task. Pliny the Stoic remarks that it is an illusion that one would feel shame after death as during life.[171] Pliny the historian says that Tarquin made this *cloaca maxima* big enough for a fully laden hay waggon to drive along. Modern classical scholarship reports that it was cleaned in 33 BC and that Agrippa as aedile inspected it from a boat.[172] The Great Sewer seems to have been something of a tourist attraction, perhaps especially for Greeks, whose architects sometimes forgot to include sewers. Crates of Mallos, the librarian of Alexandria, came to Rome in 168 BC and while visiting the *cloaca*, had the misfortune to slip and break his leg. He whiled away his consequent enforced stay in Rome by giving lectures, which had a considerable impact on the Romans. Even sewers can be cultural resources.

As a representative of a practical people, who were inclined to find fault with the Greeks for their over-subtle philosophy, it must have been disappointing for Pliny to find that most of the sources for extremely practical processes of manufacture were Greek. Although Pliny was fully prepared to learn from artisans – and indeed his constant reference to retail prices probably came from them[173] – yet it is clear that a great deal of his information on the productive aspects of technology came from Greek writings.[174] The term 'metal' itself was derived by Pliny from the Greek for 'one after another' because veins of metals like silver were found close by one another.[175] Antimony was known by the Greek name meaning 'wide eye' because of its use by women to dilate their pupils. Mining terms for the slag drawn from refining silver and the three kinds of 'froth of silver' produced at different stages of the same process, were all Greek.[176] It is important for Pliny to clear up a confusion caused by the different usage by the Greeks and Romans of the terms *minium* and 'cinnebar'. Part of his worry is that doctors were using the wrong, poisonous substance. Another was to avoid the further confusion about what the Greeks called 'Indian cinnebar', that is, the commingled blood of the giant snakes and the elephants, spilled as they crashed in mutal destruction to the ground.[177] It was Greek names by which the medically useful by-products of silver smelting were known – the varieties of *cadmea*. While such an authority as Theophrastus supplied Pliny with many of his Greek terms, when he observes that the best varieties of *cadmea* come from the furnaces of Cyprus[178] almost certainly it shows that he had been talking to those who traded in the substance or used it medically. The refining of copper in Cyprus produced a number of products best known by their Greek names: two kinds of 'shoemakers' black' (what Pliny called *atramentum sutorium*) and two substances that Pliny could only translate as 'bubble' and 'ash'. *Smegma, antispodos,* and *diphryx* are all Greek terms without native Latin counterparts that Pliny notes from metallurgical processes in Greek-speaking lands.[179] Pliny's interest is partly at least in the medical uses of these by-products. Overall the impression that Pliny gives is of the Romans adopting industrial processes, or perhaps in some cases simply their products, from older and more widespread Hellenistic centres. After all, there was the legendary story of the old Greeks fetching *cassiteros* (what Pliny called 'white lead' and probably our tin) in coracles from islands in the Atlantic[180] (perhaps from the Cornish mines).

Like Lucretius and Cicero, Pliny often felt the inadequacy of the Latin language in expressing Greek material. Pliny did not share Lucretius' technical problem of forcing recondite Greek discoveries into verse, but like him saw the need for neologisms[181] to express those discoveries and ideas. He saw that there was no Latin word to express the *symmetria* with which the Greeks expressed aspects of the aesthetics of their statues.[182] He had to borrow the Greek *antipathia* to express the view that rust was somehow 'opposite' to iron.[183] This introduces a major Greek principle that helped to shape Pliny's *Natural History*. 'Now, throughout all these volumes', he says in his last book, 'we have tried to teach about the discord and concord of things, which the Greeks call antipathy and sympathy.'[184] We shall examine sympathies below in relation to medicine, where it is argued that these simple powers of things arise from their *nature*, the nature of a thing that is a major part of Pliny's subject and a dynamic force in the working of his world. Here Pliny is concerned with *adamas*, a term wider than, but including, our 'diamond', on the hardness and strength of which Pliny pours a great deal of admiration. He claims that it cannot be broken on an anvil with the heaviest of iron hammers. He claims that it is not destroyed in fire. The only thing with an antipathy so strong as to destroy it is the fresh and warm blood of a goat.[185] There is a certain symmetry here, namely that the most priceless of natural objects should be anti-pathetic to the vilest of animals (as Pliny calls it) but it is sufficiently bizarre for Pliny in a rather un-Stoic way to rhetorically call it the work of God rather than a reason of nature. Pliny adds that the *adamas* is also antipathetic to the lodestone and hence sympathetic to iron, which it will attract away from a lodestone. The lodestone's sympathy for iron was also bizarre for Pliny, and he had turned to it after discussing the natures of other stones. So different, so much a cause of wonder, was the nature of the lodestone that Pliny felt that something was not quite right: *qua in parte naturae major inprobitas?*[186] It was almost as if the nature-of-the-thing had over-stepped the rationality of nature-in-general, just as the action of the goat's blood had to be referred to a higher cause.

But these were exceptions for Pliny, wonderful *historiae* that lent spice to his account of the physical world. The more usual sympathies that were part of the natural working of the world were conceived partly in human terms. Not only were they like human likes and dislikes, they often had human gender. Pliny held that lodestones were male and female, and that only the former could attract the iron. The distinction was not uncommon, for there were genders of a mineral to be found in silver mines (perhaps compounds of antimony) of which the male was rougher and less desirable; of the gems known as *carbunculi*, of which the male was more brilliant; of those called *sandastros,* where the sparkle of the male was deeper in colour and that of the the female more mellow, properties shared by the genders of the shard, and of lapis lazuli.[187]

NATURAL HISTORY AND THE TRANSMISSION OF KNOWLEDGE

So far we have looked at Pliny from the inside, trying to discover what made him write the *Natural History* in the way he did. Now it is time to look at him from the outside. Leaving aside now Pliny's view of history, what does our view of history tell us about Pliny's work? His earliest sources go back to the beginnings of literacy in Greece, at least in some of the specialist trades he deals with, such as medicine. In many other areas of life Pliny must have been closer to an oral tradition. The men who actually ploughed the soil and sowed the wheat, or cast bronze or made glass, may have supplied some technical details to Pliny but their skill was one acquired only by experience in the company of an already skilled man who was prepared to teach. Necessarily there was a considerable body of oral information being transmitted. Given that one of Pliny's purposes was comprehensiveness, then we must see the context of his *Natural History* as the interplay between oral and literate traditions.

Let us glance at agriculture. It was the basic industry. Men who had been farming successfully since neolithic times necessarily passed on a lot of technical information from generation to generation. Agriculture was the means of subsistence, and when a money economy developed, it was the basis of that. Agriculture was also fundamental to the economics of the Roman Empire, and the context in which we should put Pliny is urbanisation, for literacy is a product of towns. Urban people formed a new class who often wrote but rarely farmed. Pliny as a recorder, close to an oral tradition, reveals some facets of how information was inherited in an oral culture.

The first of these is the format in which the information was presented. It was vitally important to early societies that such information, gathered and proved experientially, should be remembered. There was no need to present it as an argument, to say *why* such a thing should be done. In a non-rationalising society an argument does not make a thing any more true, and in a rationalising (and probably urban) society one argument can always be met with another. What was needed was a format or circumstance that was memorable and induced faith. Indeed faith is not an inappropriate word, for if such undoubtedly significant knowledge was given some sort of religious standing it would be the more memorable. It might have been supposed, as for example in some of the Hippocratic works, that the knowledge had originally been given to man by the gods. It might be appropriate that such knowledge was uttered and transmitted in a hieratic or oracular fashion. Certainly the verbal form in which the knowledge was expressed would have been important and, for example, it is recognised that the structure of verse gives a precision to the memory. Proverbs too are knowledge expressed in a certain format, brief, direct and memorable. Much the same can be said of the aphoristic form. The Hippocratic *Aphorisms* for example, are short pithy statements of a practical nature – about what to do or what will happen – without reasons or arguments and appearing to posses an innate authority distilled from long experience. They are almost certainly preliterate in origin and were written down at an early stage of literacy in Greek medicine.

Pliny's histories of the different crafts often enough give their supposed divine originator, and his text reveals that it was often enough the custom to in some way invoke the god as the craft was practised. Perhaps the most important part of knowledge transmitted in these ways was that which related to time. The farmer had to know when to plant or graft, when his sheep were full grown and how long their pregnancies lasted, when to prune, when to turn the soil and so on. Pliny often uses astronomical phenomena, such as the rising and setting of constellations, to judge the proper moment in the season for an agricultural operation, but it is not always clear whether this includes some belief about astral influences.

Let us take a few examples that seem to show Pliny at the dividing line between a literate and oral culture, and see how far he illustrates the points made above about experiential knowledge, urbanisation and literacy, the role of the gods, aphoristic and other modes of expression and the importance of the seasons. First, of planting: when Pliny gives the weight of different kinds of seeds to be sown per acre he is using knowledge that would have been common to the actual sower and to the head of household who took an interest in the farm. But the kind of soil was also important, and Pliny has rules about sowing more or less seed in poor ground, depending on the species of plant. Here he is at the limits of what a writer on rustic matters might borrow from another, for only experience could determine the right amount. Indeed Pliny here quotes an important proverb of the oral tradition and calls it an oracular utterance: when in doubt, 'do not deny the cornfield its seed'.[188] But when to sow? Pliny begins with the written tradition and reports that Hesiod had one date only, at the setting of the Pleiads. His historical treatment takes him up through Virgil[189] (who used also the autumnal equinox, mid-winter and the setting of Boötes as seasonal indicators for the different species) to those who adopt simple dates, sowing for example emmer wheat on 15 October.[190] Pliny characterises the difference between these authors as paying on the one hand too much, and on the other no attention at all to nature; but, he adds, it is a pointless dispute, for the real issue lies between men who are lettered and know some astronomy and the rustics – *rustici* – who do not. Pliny sides with the former (after all he was lettered and knew *some* astronomy) and thought that the vast task of reducing the rustics' ignorance of celestial matters would show profit in terms of increased crop yields.

Pliny is also firmly in the literate tradition when he gives an account, based on Greek sources, of the different days on which the constellations rise and set in different countries. This is followed by what is probably a glimpse at the season-keeping of the rustics, who would make derisory cuckoo-noises at the man who was pruning his vines late in the season: clearly there was some maxim about having the pruning done before the cuckoo arrives.[191] The practitioner must often have known what to do and when to do it by the sequential association of tasks as well as by aphorisms. There were aphorisms in the literary tradition too. Pliny's own writing style is often terse (he frequently omits the verb) and approaches the aphoristic. Indeed, when he approaches the topic of agriculture he announces that he will be guided largely by 'oracles', *oracula*. He means the pithy and aphoristic rules of farming, but at one end of its range of meanings the word has clear overtones of divine pronouncement or prophecy. At the other, in Pliny's use, it means practical farm wisdom. He justifies calling them oracles by reference to their truth in practice and their time-tested value. 'In no other kind of life', says Pliny, are oracles 'more numerous or more certain.' He is first concerned with literary 'oracles', taken from Cato, maxims for the would-be farmer They lose something of their punch in translation. *Praedium ne cupide emas*, 'In buying a farm do not be too eager'; *operae ne parcas, in agro emendo*, 'Do not be sparing of trouble, least of all in buying land.' Terse language was characteristic of Cato and perhaps natural for prescriptive farming texts. He was once asked (says Pliny) what was the best source of profit on a farm. 'Good pasture', he replied; and when what was second best, answered 'Fairly good pasture'.[192] When Pliny said that it was a true saying that 'the master's face does more good than the back of his head'[193] it was, like these others, an aphorism of the literate, farm-owning class.

Medical knowledge can be thought of in the same way as agricultural knowledge. This too was craft knowledge and there must have been a substantial oral tradition, particularly in surgery, which had to be taught visually and manually. For Pliny medicine does not include surgery and is largely a question of the innate powers of natural objects and their mixtures that are appropriate for various diseases and parts of the body. Such things are easily written down, and it is less likely that Pliny was as close to an oral tradition as he was in the case of agriculture. Another difference is that agricultural knowledge worked in practice. There must always have been a filter of failure, which removed bad husbandry in a competitive market. But it is a very different matter with the thousands of remedies that Pliny poured into the medical books. To modern eyes, some are bizarre and many disgusting. It would need the eye of faith and a huge amount of work to try to work out which, if any, could have been effective. The possibilities for confusion were endless. Many diseases get better of their own accord, and the doctor and patient would be inclined to believe that a cure had been effected by the last remedy given. As Pliny says, how could a mere human mind work out which was the effective ingredient in theriac or mithradatium? And as he also observes, the doctors' success had more to do with their self-advertisment and aristocratic patrons than with cure. There was no acid test, like the failure of a crop, to weed out bad practice. Nor was the law provided with a means of curbing doctors.[194] In other words what was in Pliny's medicine was very much the construct of Roman society.

Pliny's medicine in fact invites an anthropological treatment. Very often his remedies are a kind of specific aphorism, in the form that this or that natural object cures all cases of a certain disease (without explanation). But at other times we can see that the material collected by Pliny falls into various kinds. There are remedies that depend on natural sympathies and antipathies, or upon a quality shared by the object and the disease. There are procedures that carry certain conditions, partly about defilement: for instance it is often said that the object being used must not be allowed to touch the ground, or the person handling it must fulfil certain conditions. Sometimes there are rituals to be observed. There is often transference of disease. Unlike aphorisms, here there are hints of an underlying rationale.

Let us look at some of this in more detail, beginning with disease transference. A simple case is that of a cough that can be cured by spitting into the mouth of the kind of frog that climbs trees and croaks. When the frog is freed, the cough leaves the patient.[195] Likewise complaints of the spleen are to be treated by the application of a fish, which is then returned alive to the sea.[196] The inference is that the disease is transferred to the animal, which then takes it away. A more common form is where the animal with the transferred disease dies, 'killing' the disease also. Pliny reports that domestic animals can be cured of the bots by carrying a wood-pigeon three times around the animal's body. When released, the pigeon dies and the animal is freed from pain.[197] For man, both Melitean puppies and ducks[198] were held to remove pain of the abdomen in dying after being applied to the abdomen. Sometimes the disease can be transferred to an object, which is then thrown away (Pliny's example is chicken bones, for toothache).[199] A more elaborate case is that of pains of the *praecordia*, which for Pliny was a general name for the important organs of the body (the doctors would have said only those around the heart). Pliny reports the opinion that pains here can be transferred to a young puppy, applied to the body. This seemed to carry its own proof, for if the internal organs of the puppy were removed and washed with wine, the diseased condition was seen; then the puppy was buried, to complete the cure.[200]

The concern to avoid defilement of the remedy may have been part of the ritual of the Magi, as indeed may have been the insistence on certain conditions being met, or rituals performed by those who handled it. Pliny often reports on the practices of the Magi, and while he does not always criticise, his language distances him from what he reports. Epileptics, he says, are sometimes treated by the Magi with goat suet, boiled down with an equal weight of bull's gall, stored in the gall bladder without touching the earth (to avoid defilement). This was then taken in water, with the patient standing upright.[201] Another apparently magical remedy (Pliny is not explicit) is the cure of boils by a shrew, killed and hung up so that it does not touch the earth. The ritual was that the shrew was passed three times round the boil, the patient and his attendant spitting the same number of times.[202] A woman in labour is said to be helped by the application of a bitch's placenta which has not been allowed to touch the earth.[203] Characteristic Magi ceremonies were the prevention of epilepsy in babies by feeding them drop by drop and through a golden ring the brain of a she goat, and the use, as an aphrodisiac, of the foam of an ass collected after copulation and kept in a red cloth in a silver vessel.[204] For sciatica the Magi recommended water from a plate that had been broken and mended with iron, upon which an earthworm had been placed and soaked. Then the worm was buried where it had been dug up and, by a combination of ceremony and transference, the disease disappeared.[205] An important part of the Magi's ceremonies was speech. When making an amulet for quartan fevers with a thread tied three times, with three knots, round a caterpillar in a linen bag, the practitioner paused at each knot, reciting the reason for what he was doing. Characteristic conditions put upon such procedures were those involved in making another amulet for quartans. This consisted of four joints of a scorpion's tail, with the sting, wrapped up in a black cloth, and the man who made it and he who applied it and the scorpion itself (which was set free) had to remain out of sight of the patient for three days.[206]

It will be noticed that in some of these cures there is a relationship between the natural object used and the desired outcome (the bitch's placenta for delivery, the foam of the ass as an aphrodisiac). This is part of the generally accepted sympathies of things. Let us remind ourselves that Pliny's natural world as a whole was in some sense alive. Veins of metal grew in its fabric, and replenished themselves when depleted by man. A living world communicated through its parts, and some basic sympathy was universal. On top of this Pliny's special subject of study was the natures-of-things, the source of their particular characteristic expression of life. These natures-of-things had special sympathies and antipathies that were evident in many details of the world, as when Pliny recommends using reed to cut up the *polypus* (perhaps octopus) rather than an iron knife, as the natures of the two disagreed.[207] Likewise the nature of leeches is opposed to that of bugs,[208] and can be used to get rid of them. It seemed natural that the same organ in different animals had special sympathies, which could be used in medicine. Pliny recommends for bladder stones the urine of a wild boar and as food the boar's bladder, smoked and boiled. If the patient was female, the bladder should be that of a wild sow.[209] Heads of snails were used for headache, pains in the liver were treated with the liver of a wild weasel, and for coughing blood the lungs of a vulture were burnt over vine wood, mixed with the blossom of pomegranates, quince and lilies, and taken in wine twice a day. Likewise the spleen of a dog cut from the living animal and eaten was thought to be good for splenic disorders by Pliny, who also reports here the Magi's verbal and physical rituals with the spleen of a sheep.[210]

Also built on the principle of sympathy was the sex-specific qualities of some remedies. Female crabs are to be used for women's diseases and the red mullet to promote menstruation. The female sea-hare brings the danger of miscarriage to women, for which the remedy is a male sea-hare.[211] It was the same principle of sympathy that lay behind the group of remedies that we would call hair-of-the-dog: the bite of a shrew is to be treated ideally by tearing the shrew apart and applying the parts to the bite. This was not always possible, says Pliny, so shrews were kept preserved in oil for this purpose. Vipers' heads were similarly applied to bites from that animal. The major example was the prevention of rabies after a bite from a mad dog. Pliny describes how some ate the head of a dog, while others wore as an amulet a worm from a dead dog and others again applied to the wound the ashes of a dog's head or, finally, the ashes of hair pulled from below the tail of the mad dog itself.[212]

In retailing all this information, Pliny saw himself as taking a leading part in the growth of knowledge taking place in the Roman world. It was his task to bring together information that until then had been separate. Part of it was in the books of the old writers (including the Magi), part in newly exploited regions of the world, opened up by Macedonian and Roman power, and perhaps part from folklore. His object was to present to the Roman people (of his own kind) a rich *materia medica* with which (he hoped) they could be weaned away from their degenerate fascination for Greek doctors.[213] It was not a question simply of going back to the home-spun medicine of the old Romans, because Pliny realised that it had been very limited, at least in comparison to the material he is now able to present. Discussing Roman medicine down to the time of Cato, Pliny implies that for 600 years it consisted largely of the uses of varieties of cabbage.[214] Nor, according to Pliny, was much information to be gathered from the Romans of his own time. This was partly because the only people who lived in the country among the herbs were illiterate rustics – *agrestes litterarumque ignari*[215] – that is, the herbs were not 'known' unless known to the right people, Pliny's class. Pliny did not even know the names of some plants whose medical properties he was aware of.[216] A second reason was that those who did know about herbs refused to share their knowledge (no doubt they were medical practitioners unwilling to disclose a secret stock-in-trade). Indeed even what looks like folklore in Pliny's account seems in fact to have come from books. This is why, despite his reservations about the Greeks and the Magi, he is often full of praise for the old writers, their industry and their admirable openness in passing on what they had discovered (so unlike the Roman practitioners). But then, he argues, the real originator of medicine was nature, who not only generated the plants but took care to teach their uses to men. Only now, for Pliny, was the full extent and wonder of this displayed, when the majesty of Roman power allowed plants from Britain and Ethiopia to be widely known.[217] Pliny returns to the topic of the industry and honesty of the ancients in one of his moral introductions, here to Book 25, in which he deals with mineral remedies. On this subject too, he says, the old Romans were largely ignorant before Cato.[218] Indeed Pliny dates the Roman interest in these things only to Pompeius Lenaeus, a freedman of Pompey. It was Pompey who defeated Mithridates, who according to Pliny was the greatest king of the time, fluent in twenty-two languages and immensely learned in medicine. Pliny's story is that Lenaeus was ordered by Pompey to translate the works of Mithridates, so turning the Romans' interest to medicine.[219]

ANIMALS AND PLANTS

To summarise to this point, Pliny believed that the world itself was in some way divine. This made its productions of greater than passing or practical interest. Man was the centre of attention because providence had made the entire world for his benefit. (The Romans clearly therefore seemed to be following some kind of destiny.) The natural-historical interest in the parts of the world was partly to see what human purpose providence had intended them for, and partly the practical and moral one of seeing if they were being used properly. All natural things had their own characters and powers – they were self-moving and did not share an imposed regularity, and their motions were centred on man. Pliny, unlike the Greeks, was not interested in what caused these powers, but thought that there were more still to be found. There was an order *between* things, partly sympathies and partly because they partook in a common divinity, that is, as parts of a whole. So auguries were possible, but not by special linkages between the gods and the animals commonly linked with them.

It is in accordance with these beliefs that Pliny picks up and uses other people's *historiae.* His accounts of animals and plants are shaped accordingly. In most of them we can find the following elements: (i) the principal characteristics of the plant or animal, given to it by providence for man's use, physical, medical and moral; (ii) sympathies and antipathies that it has for other living things as an expression of the innate powers, its nature-of-the-thing; (iii) its history in relation to man and the arts: how they became known and how they participated in the growth of the human arts; (iv) craft-knowledge and (v) portents associated with it.

Notable among his descriptions of animals are those of man's best friends, the dog and horse. Pliny starts at once with a series of stories of the fidelity of dogs. There are dogs that variously guarded their dead master's body, recognised his murderer, tried to keep his body afloat in the Tiber, and leaped into his funeral pyre. Pliny is combining a number of things here: incidents recorded in the Roman annals, wonderful stories from distant places, the providential attributes of dogs in general and a moral example for man to follow. The physical attribute of the dog most valued by man was its ability to hunt, providence's purpose in making the dog. Pliny has sentimental stories like that of a man carrying his aged dog into the open to allow it to see the coverts and sniff the breeze, and exotic stories from the Alexander-historians of the Indians breeding their dogs from tigers.

He repeats the story of the king of Albania's dogs, sent to Alexander, one of which defeated a lion in battle and even brought down an elephant by making it whirl round and become dizzy.[220]

Pliny's report on dogs then changes its style and we learn about their mode of reproduction, length of gestation and related matters. Where these reports become detailed Pliny has farming-lore: when to breed from the animals, when to expect birth and how to choose the best of the litter. Craft-knowledge of this kind includes medical wisdom, and Pliny advises the reader to mix chicken droppings in the dog's food as a prophylactic against rabies or, if the disease has appeared, to use hellebore. Belief in some kind of sympathetic action is below the surface when Pliny says that a rabid dog is most dangerous to man when the dog-star is visible. Sympathetic action, and Pliny's belief in the growth of the arts, similarly underlies his contention that the only cure for a bite from a rabid dog is the recently discovered remedy of the root of the dog-rose.[221] Thus Pliny's account of the dog includes most of the elements listed above. He ends with the portents that marked the expulsion of Tarquin: a snake that barked and a dog that talked.

Pliny's account of the horse is structured in a similar way. Its use in war gave Pliny, the soldier and writer on javelin-cavalry, the opportunity to employ the craft-knowledge of the soldier, and he tells the reader that experienced horses in the javelin corps sway their bodies to help with difficult movements. His account includes portents in the feats of riderless horses, the imperial nature of Alexander's horse Bucephalus, some details of breeding horses and the traditional story of the *hippomanes*, the love-poison contained in a little structure on the new born foal's forehead. Traditionally the mare bit this off and ate it as soon as the foal was born, and the story shares with a number of others the animal's desire to deprive man of something useful, generally medically.[222]

Dogs and horses had of course always been known to the Romans. When Pliny is discussing stranger animals from distant parts, two more elements can often be found in his accounts, namely how they are captured and when they first appeared in Rome. Even the capturing of animals was for Pliny a human art that developed. Lions used to be taken by pitfalls, says Pliny, but now are captured by the simpler expedient of throwing cloaks over their heads. This was at once transferred to the circus as a trick, no doubt before the lion was set against another. The first fight between several lions had been arranged by Quintus Scaevola (in 95 BC) and the numbers thereafter rapidly escalated. Sulla exhibited a hundred fighting lions, Caesar 400 and Pompey 600. In Pompey's games (of 55 BC) Rome also first saw the *chama,* perhaps a kind of lynx. There, too, was a rhinoceros, although Pliny does not say that this was the first to be seen in Rome.[223] Three years earlier Marcus Scaurus had presented games with a hippopotamus and five crocodiles. The crocodiles are captured, says Pliny, by a race of small people who live on the Nile and who render the animal tractable by inserting a rod between its open jaws. Although at one time the Senate outlawed the bringing of elephants into Italy, the repeal of the enactment in 114 BC opened the floodgates. The import of animals to Rome became big business, with dealers specialising in different species.[224] Pliny records the first tamed tiger and the hundreds of leopards brought in by Scaurus, Pompey and Augustus.

It will be useful to glance at the way in which Pliny tackles the question of bees, for they formed a topic of great interest and utility to moralists as well as philosophers. We saw that Aristotle thought that there was something divine about them and that more observation was needed before an adequate explantion of their behaviour was possible. The problem that there were three kinds of animals in the single category 'bee' had also been a topic for Plato.[225] Pliny's section on bees is huge, but we should hardly expect that he was trying to add empirical observation of the sort that Aristotle wanted, or to solve Plato's philosophical riddle. Instead his account of bees shares with others the topics listed above, with some interesting variations.

In opening his eleventh book with insects, Pliny takes the opportunity to be rhetorical about the tiny size yet great complexity of some of them. It is a natural topic for a rhetor (we shall see that Galen, in the next century, presses home a point about the comparative size of the flea and elephant) and gives a flourish to Pliny's opening. When he wonders in a rhetorical question how nature could locate all the animal's functions in so small a frame, and when he exclaims that nature is nowhere more whole than in her smallest productions, it is *rerum natura,* the 'nature of things' again. Pliny is not really saying that a transcendent nature, having made the elephant, turned her attention to the insect but that the natures of insects and of elephants fully express themselves in both. It is the natures of things that Pliny says he is prepared to believe anything about.[226]

It is in this context that Pliny considers the bee. Despite his early-stated belief that all animals were created for man, it is clear that noisome insects were not. The bee alone was given to man to supply honey, and this is why they are chief among the insects. It is the nature of the bee that is Pliny's topic: how it has shaped the complex bee out of a mere shadow of matter, how it organises bee society in a way that was entirely intelligible to Pliny the soldier, citizen and subject of the emperor, and how it provides honey for man. When the nature-of-the-bee degenerates, it produces wasps and hornets, the bees' enemies.[227]

His account of the bee's society contains hints about where his information came from. When he says that in Italy 'no one bothers about the hives until the beans have flowered', he is retailing an agricultural aphorism of the kind we have met. But most of the technical terms for the parts of the hive and combs are Greek. His three authorites in this section are Greek and the speculation about which plants supply the bee with building materials is mostly Greek speculation about Greek plants. In contrast Pliny's interpretation is Roman. The military metaphor came easily to him, and the hive is a camp, with guards at the gates. The bees are woken at dawn with a bugle call by one of their number, and if the day is fine they set about their tasks. Some bring home flowers, others water. Carrier-bees wait for a suitable wind, like sailors, and if they encounter bad weather they ballast themselves with a pebble (a very common story in antiquity). If night falls bees on manoeuvres camp out, lying on their wings to protect them from the dew. Those at home get on with building, polishing, carrying, and preparation of food for the common mess. Discipline is good, and the idle are punished or even killed. Cleanliness is important, and although bees do not need a *cloaca maxima* their droppings are neatly piled up to make removal efficient.

Pliny does not have the philosophical apparatus to make the acquisition of empirical knowledge of the generation of bees any kind of answer to the problem of why a single 'nature' of beehood (as Plato called it) should have its physical manifestation in the three kinds of bee. He claims to have learned from a Roman landowner who fitted up a transparent hive of horn that bees sit on their eggs to hatch them, but that is all. Instead, his interest characteristically is seized by the various kinds and qualities of honey, from Greece to North Africa and Germany. He believed that honey fell from the sky and was collected by the bees, so naturally enough what part of the sky it fell from, marked by what constellations, was a question closely related to the quality of the honey. How much honey to leave for the bees was an item of farming-lore akin to the proportion of grain to be held back as seed, and Pliny is close again to an oral tradition and rules of procedure. Take too much honey and the bees will perish, as experience shows. The rationale is that to take too much honey is to defraud the bees almost in a contractual sense by going beyond what providence allowed. The rules surrounding the taking of honey included the practical business of smoking the bees, but there were also rules that insisted that the operator should first wash and should not be a menstruating woman.

Other parts of Pliny's account of bees are also typical of his treatment as a whole. Bees are portentous when swarming, generally in a bad significance in the practice of the augurs, but good in some cases, as when they alighted on the lips on of the infant Plato and foretold of his eloquence, and when they swarmed in the camp of Drusus before a famous victory. Pliny also characteristically discusses the illness that bees are heir too and the enemies they face.[228]

Pliny follows the same kinds of topics through his account of plants, although obviously the emphasis is different. Thus while both shrubs and trees were exhibited as trophies in Rome by Pompey, Pliny's account dwells much more on the physical attributes that providence has given to plants for the sake of man. 'For it is for the sake of their timber that Nature has created the rest of the trees', says Pliny (the exceptions including some that were intended for dyeing cloth).[229] For Pliny the most structurally useful tree in this respect was the ash, because it is light and pliant, making good spears and chariots. But besides its physical attributes, the ash had active powers and antipathised with snakes. The wood of the cornel tree was antipathetic to several others, thought Pliny, and he implies that they cannot be worked together.[230]

Pliny seems to have got some of his information from artisans, and when he says of a certain timber that it makes pretty little curly shavings from the plane, it looks as though he had been in workshops too. As we saw with animals and farming often Pliny is recording craft knowledge.[231] It takes on the form of a series of rules which are only partly empirical. Take for example those that governed the felling of trees. Round trees required for turning, for the construction of pillars, should be felled when they bud, for as Pliny says, only then can the bark be fully removed. But timber for beams, where the bark is to be removed by an axe, is to be cut between midwinter and the beginning of the westerly winds. When Pliny further defines the earliest possible times for felling by reference to the setting of certain constellations, he is adopting a common mode of defining the seasons. But the heavenly bodies have a greater role to play in the felling rules than that. Pliny says that it is universally agreed that the best time to fell timber is when the moon is in conjunction with the sun, that is, when the moon is invisible because the sun is not shining on its visible face. He also gives 'enormous importance' to a related rule, that trees should be felled only between the twentieth and thirtieth days of the lunar month. The point behind the rules was to ensure that the timber lasted well when used in construction. Ideally, the conjunction of the sun and moon should occur on the winter solstice, and timber felled then, says Pliny, lasts for ever.[232]

Clearly, such rules had come into craft-lore from traditional views about living things following the waxing and waning of the moon as well as from empirical observation. It was generally believed too that water followed the moon, the most obvious example being the tides. To fell a tree when the moon's influence was at its lowest meant that the timber would be at its driest; and empirical observation *did* show that damp timber rotted quickly. Characteristically Pliny does not add this explanation, perhaps because it approached theory, which he consciously avoided. These felling rules are not simply a collection pulled together by Pliny from *historiae* of distant places, but seem to have been common to his Italian sources, perhaps to the trade of carpenters. Timber for the forum of Augustus was felled when the conjunction of the moon and sun coincided with the rising of the dog-star. When Tiberius wanted larches to rebuild a mock ship in a naval spectacular in Rome, he first specified (no doubt on carpenters' advice) that they should be felled at the *interlunium*, the moon's 'silent' day, when it was in conjunction with the sun.[233]

Characteristically Pliny gives a strong chronological weight to the *historiae* he notes as wonders, like the story of Alexander the Great and the wood that would not rot and about trees of great age. He has a first-time-in-Rome story of big trees used in exhibitions. Pliny's use of history implies that providence's plans are only now coming into effect, for all the arts, including woodwork and dyeing (which we met above), came into being historically, by human ingenuity. Pliny held that mankind first lived on the fruits of trees, such as acorns, and had little use for timber. His account of the Chauci, a people who lack trees and live on islands in flooded plains, eating fish, is intended as an illustration of a primitive stage in human development.[234] *Historiae* selected by others to illustrate an eternal world were put to quite different use by Pliny, as we would expect. We saw above that those who practised grafting (largely on fruit trees) also had a set of rules that must have been the orally transmitted knowledge of husbandmen (but obviously of interest to the literate landowner). For the Stoic in Pliny it is a prime example of what man and nature together can achieve in art – it is literally artificial – and it is very certainly not a technique handed down from the gods.

We can probably see more clearly in the case of plants and animals some of Pliny's purpose in the *Natural History*. He wants Romans to know what is theirs in the natural world. The human history of the arts and of knowledge, he thought, had been through the Greek stage and his job was partly to make Greek knowledge available to the people who now needed it, or to whom it was owed. He accordingly praises those of the ancients,[235] even though Greek, who had made information available to him; and condemns those among the recents (although sometimes Romans) who withhold knowledge. In part this was craft-knowledge (of which we have also seen a medical example). For Pliny a thing was 'known' when it was known to Romans of his own literate class. This is part of the point of giving the dates of when things were seen in Rome for the first time: they become 'known', within the progress of the human arts, as well as demonstrating Roman power.

What Pliny was making known to his peers was partly the regularity of nature. Since providence made all things for man, and man was always man, the things designed for him were constant in their nature. And it was *their* nature, the *rerum naturae* which as we have seen where it is used always indicated the constancy of a thing's attributes or essence. Craft information about calendars and the motions of the heavens, the time for sowing and reaping, which timber to use for what purpose, the rules of felling, pruning and so on were also constants, and progress lay in refining them. This is highlighted by portentous departures from constancy. Pliny notes auguries from fish,[236] from the livers of quadrupeds, from trees and other things.[237] Perhaps fruit appears in the wrong place, or a dead tree comes back to life again. Or a tree might sink into the earth, or change from one kind into another.[238] Most of these are historical examples, drawn from the records of major events in Roman civil and military life, but it is clear that to Pliny part of their significance is that they are departures from the *rerum natura*, the 'nature of the beast', where 'nature' is ordinarily regular.

What Pliny the Roman has found attractive in his Greek sources is the god-free area of natural philosophy. The gods of which it was free were the traditional pantheon, about the adulterous habits of which Pliny was scornful.[239] There remained his less than precise notion of a single supreme deity, or providence or divine world, and he thought that perhaps man might communicate in some way with it by incantation; he was not so sure about charms and sacrifices.[240] We have seen that the elaborate rituals of the Magi offended Pliny, and it was precisely because they did not depend on a regular nature-of-a-thing *or* on a providential divinity, which are Pliny's two main meanings of *natura* (and meanings that we have pursued through this book). Pliny is not being 'rational' in rejecting the 'superstition' of the Magi, in modern terms. Even if we adopt an historically relativist position and argue that rationality is the use of chains of argument (whether to us right or wrong) and that one person's superstition may be another's religion, then Pliny is still less using arguments than piling up examples. What we approve of in Pliny, even when regretting his scientific credulity and apalling misuse of his own language[241] is that he appears, because he adopted so much from the Greeks, to fall into a history of Western thought which we like to derive from the Greeks.

6

ANIMALS AND PARABLES

GREEKS, ROMANS, JEWS AND THE ETERNITY OF THE WORLD

We have seen that both Galen and Strabo knew of Moses as a law-giver to the Hebrews, and they knew also something of the idea of the omnipotence of the Hebrews' god. The Christians came to accept both the god of the Jews and a great deal of Hellenistic philosophy, and their view of nature and the world was formed accordingly. This came to be widespread in the late antique centuries and was important for the Middle Ages. A central question was: Is the world eternal? We have seen that it was for Aristotle, but not for some other Greek philosophers. For the Jews, whose god was above all a creator and controller, it was unthinkable that the world should be eternal. The arguments for and against were partly concerned with the natural changes visibly taking place on earth, and they thus form another arena in which natural history provided material for another enterprise.

A major resource for the later Christians was that produced during the Hellenisation of some of the Jews dispersed in the Diaspora. Many of them went to Alexandria, which became their chief centre. Copious writings by one of them, Philo, have survived.[1] Philo was both 'Judaeus' and 'of Alexandria' and had been trained in both the Jewish and Hellenistic traditions.[2] Philo's principal business was as an exegete of the scriptures. What interests us is how he accommodated the Mosaic account of creation with Hellenistic philosophy. The major difficulty was with the literal meaning of Genesis, where it is said that the work of creation was complete in six days. But a 'day' was the period defined by the sun's passage through the heavens, and the sun and the heavens were themselves products of creation. Another difficulty was that the authority of Aristotle and Theophrastus[3] lay behind the philosophers' claim that the world was eternal.

From Theophrastus himself, who had faced the argument that the world was not eternal, we can learn about the arguments for its recentness. First, the unevenness of land seemed to be evidence of a young world, for it would all be worn away by erosion in infinite time; second, there was evidence of the historical withdrawal of the sea; and third, there were arguments from the dissolution of the parts of the earth and the destruction of kinds of land animals. The islands Rhodes and Delos were said to have emerged from the sea.

The philosophical arguments for the eternal world were, in reply, that parts of it grow and others decay, maintaining a balance. Mountains grow like trees, but due (argued some) to the upward motion of contained fire. As for the sea retreating, what about the instances of the opposite? Atlantis, for example, was surely a good instance of the sea advancing, and was not Sicily once joined to Italy?[4] The history of the crafts does not go back more than a thousand years and it is absurd to say that mankind is no older than that, for man cannot live without the arts: what really happens is that periodical and local catastrophes destroy populations and traditions, so crafts are reinvented or reimported.

Some of these arguments are the vestiges of the old natural philosophers who wanted to deny the actions of the gods in the affairs of men, and were obviously unattractive to Philo with his Hebrew, single and all-powerful God. His philosophical orientation was accordingly towards Plato, whose divine demiurge was also a creator, and whose physical world was therefore not eternal. Philo uses Plato and Genesis to produce a masterly philosophical scripture. He shows that Moses the law-giver is entirely consistent with the Mosaic account of the creation of the world because in essence the Law is *natural* law. It is consistent with the world and the world was put together with this in view. A man who follows the Law is therefore a true citizen of the world. There may be a reflection of Philo's Stoicism in his call to follow nature, and perhaps of the Stoic commonwealth. 'Nature' here is the *physis* of the philosophers, and Philo is utilising philosophy to give strength to his religion when he says that the man who follows nature (and therefore the Law) is following the reasons for which the world was created. Philo held that Moses, philosopher extraordinary, had been instructed by God about the laws of nature (*physis* again).[5]

Philo uses Plato not only because of his agreeable demiurge, but to solve the problem mentioned above, the apparent inconsistency of the literal account in Genesis of the 'days' of creation. He argues that in fact God created everything at once. Before producing anything physical, God created a set of incorporeal ideas, rather like an architect drawing up plans for a city. This incorporeal creation lay in his *logos*, the 'word' that was for Philo both scriptural and Stoic. As incorporeal, it was like Platonic Ideas, the realities of which material things are poor copies. As ideas they are able to be handled by philosophy: they are *intelligible*, to use a technical Philonic term. In contrast, the physical, created world which followed these ideas, was *visible*.[6] Thus Philo has shown that there is no paradox in Genesis, for all the Intelligible ideas were created at once, and sequence and order were attributes of the Visible creation.

But Philo goes further in his use of philosophy to interpret the scriptures. He uses the Stoic device of allegory.[7] That is, while the scriptures had a clear literal reading (like that which threatened problems over the 'days' of creation) it was also possible to read in them the spiritual message or allegory that God had intended.[8] When the literal reading of the scripture gives a physical meaning to terms like 'heaven' and 'earth', the allegorical meaning, Philo asserts, is 'mind' and 'sense perception', which also relate to 'soul' and 'body'. These terms too are open to philosophical handling and allegory is with Philo partly an attempt to put questions to the scripture and receive philosophical answers. His extensive *Allegorical Interpretation* of the second and third books of Genesis does not include the creation of the animals and plants, contained in Book 1; but it was not long before an anonymous Christian author used Philo's techniques on these natural-history subjects. We shall meet him below.

Overall then Philo's enterprise was to use Hellenistic philosophy to explain and extend the meaning of the scriptures. Even the standard education of the time, the Encyclia (literature, logic, rhetoric, mathematics and music), was used in the same way: it was like the Egyptian Gold which as we saw earlier came to be the allegory for the use of pagan learning for religious purposes.[9] Philosophy was an extension of education and could provide deeper meanings. Philosophy was a boon to mankind, says Philo, and it arose from the religious question of the origin of the heavenly bodies.[10] These bodies supply light, the days and seasons, and can foretell the future about animals, crops, weather and earthquakes.[11] The *naturalness* of these 'meteorological' topics is no longer insisted on, as the old philosophers had done in order to lessen fear of them. Indeed, although Philo often uses the term *physis*, there is no real room for nature as a separate principle alongside an omnipotent God, and Philo prefers to say that nature, rather than a craftsman, *artifex*, is an art,[12] that is, God's art. It was for Philo also by God's art that man – visible man – was created last, so that he would astonish all the animals, who would know at once than man was their natural master. This purpose was served too by God having all the animals pass in front of Adam, so that he could name them. To these scriptural sources Philo characteristically adds from philosophy that the reason for man's superiority over the animals is that there is a natural scale of perfection based on the nature of the soul (which in man's case, to return to the scriptures again, is the image of God).

In this chapter, after Philo Judaeus, we are concerned with the early Christian centuries. It was a period in which Greek culture tightened its grip on Roman life. Under Roman political control, the Greeks could not harbour political ambition without being seditious. Perhaps this resulted in their expressing themselves all the more in cultural terms. At all events, when Constantine made Constantinople his Eastern capital in AD 330 and when Theodosius divided the empire in AD 395 into East and West, the processes that made the Eastern Empire entirely Greek were well under way.

It was in these centuries too that the European vernaculars of the Western Empire disappeared and Latin became the common language of the people of the Mediterranean. Formal Latin used for administration and in the Church faced little competition from Greek, which was fashionable in intellectual and social circles. Latin survived through the ultimate collapse of the Western Empire down through the Middle Ages, and provided the slender cultural connection by means of which the developing medieval civilisation sought to claim a paternity in the classical world. The barbarian emperors claimed the title and powers of Caesar while the learned sought out the texts of Greek philosophy.

By the 'late antique' centuries much material on the subjects of natural history had accumulated. Libraries were widespread, and that of Alexandria famous. It was a period of handbooks and encyclopedias. Pliny's *Natural History* was available, but apparently not much used by those who preferred Greek sources. Aristotle's works on animals went through a number of editions after Tyrannion and Andronicus and were extensively used for the preparations of digests and summaries. The *Auscultationes Mirabiles*, attributed to Aristotle, was a much-used source of wonderful stories on natural-history topics. The exploits of Alexander the Great and the marvellous animals and plants were by now legendary. Some persisting accounts of animals and places carried the royal authority of a Ptolemy or Juba. Characteristics of animals, particular events, moral stories and mythical animals were passed from writer to writer, generally being changed in the process, but of great longevity: the oldest of them were certainly a thousand years old by the end of the period and survived at least another thousand.

There was then a huge resource for people who needed stories of nature to illustrate their themes and messages. We have now seen that this is what most people did with the details and structures of natural philosophy and natural history. Whether it was a plea for final causality, a search for the means of living the moral life, an escape from fear or the presentation of a moral, accounts of the natural physical world were used for a particular purpose. The same is true when Christians began to turn to this resource.

AELIAN AND OPPIAN

Accounts of animals and plants could lend force to literature and verse written to entertain, as well as to philosophical argument. Philosophy too was anciently sometimes written in verse and the beauty and intricacy of the metre gave weight to the philosophy as the philosophy gave gravity to the verse. There was little of our modern separation of categories. The poet Oppian illustrates this. He was born in Cilicia, the son of a philosopher who gave him a thorough education. His father's independence of mind prevented him from paying court to Severus (emperor 193–211) when the latter visited Oppian's home town. The philosopher was duly banished to an Adriatic island, and one of Oppian's motives for writing was to rehabilitate his father with the imperial family.[13] No doubt his topic, the hunting and capture of animals, was directed towards imperial tastes in sport (and we can recall how animals from distant places often had a place in a triumph in Rome). (See Plates 21, 22 and 23.) While there is some doubt about which of the Antonines Oppian was addressing, it is generally thought that it was Marcus Aurelius and his son Commodus, Galen's emperors. The poems[14] draw on the rich stock of late antique animal-lore and give further life to the strange and wonderful stories we meet in other authors.

Oppian was thus another Greek to address a Roman emperor,

Plate 21 The Great Hunt: capturing stags alive in a net. From the Piazza Armerina, Sicily.

Plate 22 Animals being led towards a ship waiting to transport them to Italy. From the Piazza Armerina, Sicily.

Plate 23 A major point of interaction between man and the animals was the hunt. This scene of a wild-boar hunt reflects the taste in sport also expressed in Oppian's poem. From the Piazza Armerina, Sicily.

using the matter of natural history in a rather unusual form for a rather special purpose. The case of Aelian is quite different. Claudius Aelianus was born in about 170 in Praeneste, in the hills to the east of Rome. He came from free stock – was *libertus* – and was proud of being Roman.[15] He claimed never to have left Italy or ever to have been on board a ship. Yet in his voluminous work on the natures of animals he does not mention a single Latin author.[16] He wrote, moreover, in Greek, having become 'honey-tongued' in the Attic dialect with a teacher from Caesarea, earning himself the title of sophist for his rhetoric. He enjoyed the patronage of the empress Domna who gathered about her a circle of philosophically inclined figures whose business was done in Greek. It included the Greeks Galen and Oppian.

In other words Aelian shows how fashionable was Greek culture in second- and third-century Rome. Aelian thought that one of the major attractions of his work for his audience was that it was written in Greek, and was not technical in nature. Gone is the Plinian nostalgia for Roman cultural identity; no vestige of the traditional Roman suspicion of Greeks and their philosophy. Indeed, Aelian's cultural hero is Homer, the foundation of Greek learning. His tribute to Homer in quoting him as often as possible is to credit him with a great knowledge of natural history, just as for Strabo Homer had been the father of geography. The tactic gave the dignity of a pedigree to the later writers and reasserted the Greekness of their topics. The learning that their topics represented now resided in material form in the libraries of the big Hellenistic cities, like Alexandria, whose scholars quoted Homer so often that it has been seen as a 'mannerism'.[17] Aelian's chief source indeed seems to have been an Alexandrian, Pamphilius,[18] who excerpted from a number of the old authors. Athenaeus (who also wrote on animals) believed that Aristotle's library had been acquired by Ptolemy and added to the library of Alexandria (but we have seen that this did not include the books Aristotle wrote). Aelian knew of Aristotle, but does not seem to quote the animal books directly, using instead the epitome of Aristophanes of Byzantium,[19] and the *Peri Zoon* based in turn upon it by Alexander of Myndos. Aristophanes was the head of the library in Alexandria, and in abstracting natural-historical details from Aristotle had a taste for the paradoxical, which may have appealed to Aelian, as the following examples suggest. Byzantium, Aristophanes' home, was of course a cultural centre like Alexandria and Pergamon, and the production of written material, a good deal of it in the form of handbooks and encyclopedias, is in contrast to the inactivity of Latin writers. Aelian the collector of ancient snippets looked East, not West. When he wanted a boy-and-dolphin story (Plate 25) to entertain his audience, he took one from Leonidas of Byzantium and derived from Poroselene, not one from the Latin tradition (Pliny has such stories in abundance).

In an ordinary sense we cannot claim that Aelian was a natural historian writing about his subject. Quite apart from the modern category of 'natural history', Aelian was in great contrast to Aristotle, with whom we began, in that Aristotle was collecting observations from nature in an elaborate and deliberate intellectual protocol that had modes of evaluating knowledge and claims about the value of knowledge for its own sake to the philosopher. Yet Aristotle accepted conventional wisdom about animals from non-philosophers and used most of his knowledge to promote his personal conception of final causality. Aelian also accepted conventional wisdom about animals from the non-philosophical side of Greek life: not only the popular wisdom of an Aristophanes or an Aesop, but also that of myths and legends. He draws too from the philosophers but in

263

claiming that his work is attractive because non-technical he is clearly not aligning himself with them. In claiming that it is attractive because written in Greek and based on wide reading, he is not only addressing Hellenised Romans but accepting that his topic is a well-recognised one, to which many authors have contributed, a field in which these features will make his own work better than what has gone before. He says his topic is the surprisingly human and excellent virtues of different animals; we can call it natural history because any educated Roman or Greek of the time who admitted to reading Pliny's *Natural History* would recognise this as being in the same genre and because it was by means of such works that a knowledge of animals was re-formed for the Byzantine East and the Western Middle Ages. ('Knowledge' is used here in the same historical sense: the people of the time knew it and it was therefore knowledge. It does not matter that for us it was wrong.)

AELIAN'S USE OF THE ANIMAL STORIES

Aelian the would-be Greek uses the traditional animal stories in a characteristic way. Just as in non-philosophical Greek wisdom stories about animals could carry a moral, so Aelian seeks an image from them that parallels some other part of Greek culture. The result is mutual reinforcement. When we say that a single swallow does not make a summer, we are drawing on a proverb or conventional wisdom. We also imply that many swallows do make a summer. This seems to have been proverbial too for Aelian, for whom the swallows are happy to come and live with man (they nest in the eaves) and depart when they want. And Aelian adds: as Homer says, greet a guest warmly and speed him on his way when he wants to go.[20] As a literary device, it is effective: Homeric wisdom is united to conventional and both are strengthened; it even distantly implies that Homer knew all about swallows, and certainly reinforces the Greekness of all things. The union of Homeric and natural wisdom is also illustrated in Aelian's story of the hunter who brought up together a young lion, bear and dog. For a long time all went well with these natural enemies, but at length the bear turned upon the dog and killed it. The lion, who had been much attached to the dog, was affronted and killed the bear. As Homer says, moralises Aelian, it is good for a man to leave a son, and nature proves the same.[21]

Something very similar is effected in the case of the hyena. Aelian repeats the account of the hyena changing sex from year to year[22] and cites in parallel the myths in which people were changed by the gods, like Caenis, who was changed by Poseidon into a man, and who changed back after death. Here the parallel is mythical rather than Homeric, but equally Greek and serving equally for mutual reinforcement. For Aelian, then, the *historiae* of nature herself are made to strengthen the Greekness of his adopted culture. Where Aristotle had argued about Purpose and Necessity in the case of the sepia hiding in its cloud of ink, for Aelian it is an image with other connotations: 'It was by veiling Aeneas in such a cloud that Poseidon tricked Achilles.'[23] Aelian's purpose is seen too when he expressly sets out to 'excite astonishment' by relating the *historia* of the copulation of two beautiful young elephants. Elephants traditionally were very discreet about such things, and the circumstance worthy of report in this case was that they did it in the presence of an elder animal. Grossly offended, he began to chastise them, but was prevented by the arrival of hunters, just as Paris was dragged by Menelaus but rescued by Aphrodite.[24]

It was often said that in the mating of vipers the female after copulation bit the head off the male. The offspring when ready for birth, gnawed their way out of the female's uterus, killing her. The tale was ideal for the drawing of morals and it reminded Aelian forcibly of the plots of plays in which the children kill their mother for killing their father.[25] They were Greek plays of course, and Aelian is again setting up a consonance between nature and culture. There is also an air of Greek tragedy about the stories of disasters that befall animals because of some inborn character trait. The purple, the shellfish used for dyeing fabrics, is always caught by reason of its own gluttony.[26] Jackdaws, sociable and inquisitive, are caught by putting down a bowl of oil, in which the bird sees its reflection: thinking it sees a comrade, it attempts to join it.[27] Aelian has numerous accounts of animals that are caught by the hunters exploiting some characteristic of the animals like greed, brotherly love, sexual desire and so on. Thus the parrot-wrasse fish is caught by using a live female as a bait (for Aelian a penalty for lust). But there is a moral about brotherly love too, for the other parrot-wrasses at once try to bite through the fishing line, or pull the captured fish back by his tail.[28] Not only is the parrot-wrasse's downfall, as in Greek tragedy, derived from an inborn fault, but as a fault it is barbarian, not Greek: the parrot-wrasse has many females and luxuriates like barbarians in the pleasures of the bed.[29] Apart from the mullet, which is caught like the parrot-wrasse, other fish are models of continence and are strictly monogamous; in particular to the Etna-fish adultery is unknown. How splendid! cries Aelian, meaning How Greek! Fishing and hunting of course were the point where animal and human natures met most dramatically, and Aelian, addressing perhaps the hunting-class of Graeco-Roman society, and hoping to entertain them as well as to confirm his own Greekness, can most usefully use hunting as part of his strategy.[30]

So here we see Aelian establishing parallels between the natural world and his adopted culture and using nature to support his Greekness. Part of that Greek culture in his time was to bewail the frailties of human nature. This could be done well in moral stories based on animals. This can be illustrated, without leaving the topic of the Greek theatre, by Aelian's theme that in human society playwrights had to contrive elaborate plots to bring out a moral that was quite clear to animals. Animals – particularly the camel and the horse – had no need of the contrivings of the playwright who wrote of Oedipus: Aelian tells the story of the camel's decent reticence when urged by its keeper to mate with its mother. When the keeper succeeded by trickery the enraged and shamed camel killed him and destroyed itself by leaping over a cliff. This was one of a pair of stories, the other of which involved horses (in Aelian of the king of the Scythians) which both jumped over the cliff[31] (since they were a pair, some details seem to have moved from one story to the other).

NATURE AND THE GODS

Aelian was a non-philosophical adoptive Greek. *His* Greek culture included a traditional view of the gods. When we read the philosophers it is a little time before we realise that the behaviour of birds, the insides of animals, the nature of lightning and so on are included in natural histories because information about them was available because it was derived from the practices of divination. The philosophers had no interest in promoting or even referring to divination, but for Aelian divination was another opportunity to connect and mutually reinforce two parts of Greek culture, nature and the gods. It is Zeus whom, like Aristophanes, Aelian calls 'our father', who is in charge.[32] Aelian notes the special connection between Apollo and the ravens, the reason for their use in divination.[33] For the philosophers, the raven's croak was perhaps of little importance as a natural characteristic of the bird, but for Aelian it was evidence of the bird's thirst. The raven was thirsty for the whole summer, and his thirst was a punishment from his master Apollo, who had sent him to fetch water: the raven dallied, waiting for the wheat to ripen so that he could eat it, and was punished in an appropriate way. 'This looks like a fable,' says Aelian, 'but let me repeat it out of reverence for the god.' (Plate 24.) In Aelian's world the gods had direct action on the lives and afterlives of men and animals, the very thing that many philosophers strove to deny. It is the result of the piety of storks as parents that the gods enable them when old to fly to the islands in Ocean, where they become men. Aelian has the story from Alexander of Myndus, and he believes it, at least on paper. Describing the birds of the island of Diomedea, Aelian says they were once Greeks, the companions of Diomedes in the war against Ilium. He does not attribute their being changed to birds to the gods, but he says it explains why the birds become excited when visited by Greeks.[34] He also gives literary credence on divine authority to legendary animals, such as tritons (sea creatures with the form of man down to the waist) which he believes in on the authority of the god Apollo of Didyma.[35] The philosophers argued against the existence of mythical and legendary creatures. Galen argued that the combination of man and fish or man and horse was impossible since the two different structures implied two quite different functions and purposes which were mutually incompatible. Others argued that the man and horse have quite different life-spans and could not coexist in one creature. For Aelian – if he knew of these arguments – this was pedantry. Centaurs may not exist, but they did once; and their modern equivalent is the onocentaur, the front half of which is a man, the rear, an ass.[36] While he accepted the Hydra and chimera as myths, he had no hesitation that the amphisbaena was a snake with a head at each end.[37] We may recall Aristotle on motion, direction, 'front', the senses and the physiological centre of the body, and think of the difference between the philosophical and literary perception of animals.

For Aelian the gods, in addition to the 'nature' of the philosophers, were effective causes of change in the physical world. It is the gods who for example brought about medical cures in the temples, where the patients came to sleep under the guidance of the priests. So commonplace was the practice that Aelian makes it unusual and entertaining by telling the story of a man who took his horse into the temple. It had been wounded in battle and had become blind in one eye; its owner hoped that the gods would take pity – they did – on the horse because it had not brought about its own misfortune

Plate 24 Raven on a Roman tombstone (British Museum). The raven was Apollo's bird, condemned by him to a croaking thirst for his failure to fetch water. The raven was also used in divination. The philosophers were little concerned with the gods or divination. According to Aristotle, Anaxagoras claimed instead that ravens copulated via their mouths. Returning to the traditional theme, Aelian said that thirsty Libyan ravens are intelligent enough to drop stones into a water pot until the water rises far enough for them to drink.

by its own misdeeds (which was so often the case with man).[38] The gods in Aelian's view indeed often used animals directly to change men's lives, both in divination and in medical cures; and animals often had special relationships with the gods (like sea-shells,[39] and the raven and Apollo) and so were sometimes justifiably worshipped.[40] We have already seen that Aelian reported that the gods could change people into animals (which if widely held would have added to the fear of the gods' capriciousness) and Aelian can add weight to traditional stories by repeating it. The battle between the storks (or cranes) and the pigmies had been a *historia* of nature since Homer, and Aelian adds that the cause was the pride of Gerana, the Queen of the Pigmies, who claimed to be more beautiful than the goddesses. They changed her into a stork.[41]

While animals obeyed nature, the source of man's law in Aelian's world, at least in a moral sense, was father Zeus. Man differed from animals, according to Aelian and other late writers, in disobeying the dictates of the law that applied to them. This gave a rich store of examples of how animals behaved so much more morally than man. As Aelian says, men are much more likely than dogs to betray their friends (and so trample on the ordinances of Zeus).[42] He tells the story of a dog who witnessed the murder of its master and faithfully remained by the body until taken into the care of Pyrrhus of Epiris. While Pyrrhus some time later was reviewing his hoplites, the dog recognised the murderers of his master, who duly confessed. Perhaps only elephants were more faithful than dogs: when he was killed at Argos, Pyrrhus' own elephant would not rest until it had rescued his body and brought it back.[43] When Porus, king of the Indians, was wounded in fighting Alexander, his elephant carefully drew out the spears and set him gently to earth.[44] Aelian also upbraids man's faithlessness with moral stories about animals that relate to their own proper recognition of the gods. He is surely referring to the philosophers when he complains that some men wonder whether there are gods and if they take any notice of man.[45] Elephants however are entirely certain that the sun is a deity, and raise their trunks to him at every dawn. It was a better worship than that of Ptolemy Philopater (asserts Aelian) who, having overcome Antiochus, sacrificed his four biggest elephants to the sun, but in vain; and troubled by a dream, he had four bronze elephants made to placate the sun. More pious was Ptolemy Philadelphus, who was given a young elephant, which was brought up in the Greek language (thus proving that elephants could understand more than the Indian language).[46]

PHYSIS AND FRIENDSHIPS

One of the themes of this book has been how the meaning of *physis* changed from Aristotle's nature-of-the-thing to an external principle of growth and life. Aelian's 'nature' is most often not a personalised and creative principle, like that of Galen, and perhaps there was no room in Aelian's traditional pantheon for such a figure. But Aelian was not a philosopher and wanted only to show that nature was wonderful, not in what manner she acted. It was marvellous that *physis* had contrived to bring vipers and moray eels together in sexual embrace[47] (in defiance of the first principle of Aristotle's philosophy of animals). So strange was the turning of colour of the chameleon that *physis* might be thought a sorceress, like Medea and Circe; that these two could kill with a mere touch made them more dangerous than the asp: Aelian characteristically illustrates nature by means of Greek culture and vice versa, and here seems to want to put Nature among the legendary figures.[48]

It was nature as an external principle, if not personalised, that for Aelian governed some at least of the relationships between animals. The belief that large fish need a small one to guide them as they swim is evidence for Aelian either of a collaboration imposed on the two creatures by nature, or of friendship between the two, which resulted in the same behaviour.[49] Aelian of course had a fund of accounts of animal sympathies and antipathies, and many of them gain in the telling. The enmity of snakes for elephants, he says, is the bitterest of all antipathies. The elephant-killing snakes of Ethiopia are 180 feet in length; presumably their behaviour was some variant of the epic snake–elephant story in Pliny. Certainly in India, says Aelian, the snake knows which tree the elephant will come to feed from, and as it draws down its branches so the snake gouges out its eyes before strangling it by winding itself round its neck.[50] Elephants that pass a corpse of one of their fellows killed by some such means throw soil or a branch upon it in some religious ritual and to avoid a curse; a mortally wounded elephant throws dust and grass into the air as if calling to the gods.[51]

Stories of animal antipathies and sympathies that derive from the philosophers, especially Aristotle, were based on rationalisations about their natures, generally that they competed for the same food or preyed upon each other. (Aelian has some of these, like the antipathies of the crows and owls, kite and raven, lions and antelopes, and asp and ichneumon.[52]) But stories from the non-philosophical side of Greek life depended on some other property of vividness or drama to make them memorable and repeatable; and they naturally gained in drama and vividness in the repeating. Perhaps the traditional antipathy between snakes and elephants had something to do with the elephant being 'snake-nosed', but it is the purpose for which the story is repeated that led to the story of 180-foot dragons strangling elephants to death. We can see a natural reason why a footprint of a wolf should be thought to stop a horse, but it is for other reasons that credence should be asked for the story that a wolf's vertebra halts a team of four.[53] The same is true of the natural causes intended in accounts of the birds that antipathise because they eat each other's eggs. Other accounts depend on a natural property of a third party, often plant material: storks put plane leaves on their eggs to keep the bats off, which make them infertile. It is external nature that has given swallows the technique of covering *their* eggs with celery to keep off the cockroaches. These are not regressive departures from science to myth or from philosophy to popular literature, for all animal stories were told with some purpose that was not scientific.

Some of the more interesting stories about the sympathies of animals were those of friendships between animals and mankind. We have seen that it is frequent in late-antique accounts that dolphins often formed attachments with boys, sometimes even refusing to survive them.[54] (Plate 25.) Elephants were capable of falling in love with women and it was notorious that Aristophanes of Byzantium was rivalled in love by an elephant that fell in love with the same flower-girl in the market. It would bring her presents, fondle her breasts and grow angry when she was not there.[55] The snake that fell in love with a woman was also angry when she went away for a while, and thrashed her when she came back.[56] Glauce the harpist excited infatuation in a range of animals; in Aelian it was a dog,[57] elsewhere a goose or a ram.[58] Complete trust existed between the cerastes snake and the Psylli tribe of Libyans, who were immune to its bite: if they suspected one of their women of adultery with an outsider, the test was to drop the child into a box of snakes.[59] There is also a genre of stories that relies on the gratitude and long memory of animals in response to kind treatment by people. Androcles and the lion is an example: he was the slave of a Roman senator and ran away into the Libyan desert and hid in a lion's den. The lion came home with a painful thorn in its foot, which Androcles removed. They lived a consequent peaceful domestic life for three years until Androcles had

Plate 25 Roman water-spout in the form of dolphin and boy. (British Museum.)

the misfortune to be recaptured and sent for punishment to the circus. But his lion was one of the animals expected to destroy him, and overjoyed to see him, it defended him against a leopard.[60] For Androcles at least, it was a happy ending. Of the same kind is the story of the snake who, separated from his boyhood friend by the boy's nervous parents, rescued them when attacked by brigands in the jungle.[61]

DRAGONS AND SIMILAR

The snake that strangled the Indian elephants was a *drakon* in Aelian's Greek, the equivalent of the Latin *draco* and our 'dragon'; often it is the same as 'serpent', and when Solinus tells the elephant-and-snake story *serpentes* are the same as *dracones*.[62] Whether it was 180 feet long, or as others said so wide that grass grew on its back, it was a very wonderful creature. What Aristotle had treated as *historiae*, things worthy of note, have turned into marvels, ever more surprising as a series of authors strove to impress the reader. Among the animal stories that came from the Hellenistic confrontation with India was that of the ants that dug up gold and built it into their nests. In some versions of the story they are 'ant-lions', altogether more formidable, and obliging the natives to retrieve the gold at night. When Aelian came to tell the story, the animal is four-footed like a lion, with white wings and an eagle's beak. So formidable is it that it fears only the elephant and the lion: it is a *grypa*,[63] the ancestor of the medieval griffin.[64] Or at least one of the ancestors: there were griffins celebrated on Etruscan table-ware before Rome became powerful; and traditionally griffins guarded Apollo's gold and fought off the one-eyed race of men who tried to take it (Plates 26, 27 and 28). Of similar pedigree is Aelian's *mantichoras*, the mantichore, said to be as big as a lion, with lions' feet, the face of a man (with three rows of teeth) and the tail of a scorpion. It was able to kill all animals except the elephant.[65]

Along with such traditional accounts Aelian tells of the song sung

Plate 26 An ivory Syrian griffin of the ninth or eighth century BC. (British Museum.)

273

Plate 27 In Greece griffins were traditionally the defenders of Apollo's gold, which the one-eyed Arimaspians tried to steal. On this red-figure jar of *c.* 400 BC such a battle is under way. (British Museum.)

just before death by the swan (its swan-song). It sings, he says, because it has nothing to fear in death. The point of the story could be the Stoic one, that man too should not be frightened of death. But men *were* frightened, and so suffered in comparison to animals. Aelian's usage is characteristic: to tell an animal story, draw a moral and then to find parallels in Greek literature to establish the consonance between culture and nature.[66] The same may be said of a story that served a number of purposes. In Aelian it is attached to the leopard of Mauretania, which had an ingenious method of catching monkeys. It would feign death by lying on its back, inflating its stomach and ceasing to breathe. The monkeys believe it to be dead, approach and even play upon it. Nature has equipped the leopard with the fortitude to withstand this insolence until, when the monkeys are tired, the leopard springs to life and seizes them. Aelian finds a parallel in Homer and derives a mutual moral from his secular scripture and from the attribute that an external nature has given to the animal.[67]

274

Plate 28 Griffins were a popular decorative motif. Like the others (this one is from Apuleia, *c.* 350 BC), these griffins antedate Alexander's campaigns in India, after which stories of Indian gold-digging ants or ant-lions and their enemies seem to have become conflated with older griffin-stories.

Also traditional and enduring are many of the stories Aelian tells of elephants. The white elephant was one of these, and in Aelian's account it is a story of an Indian who found a white calf elephant and brought it up. The local king came to hear of it and desired it, to thwart which the owner took it into the desert. When the king sent an expedition to capture it, the white elephant successfully resisted and defended its master. It is of course a moral story, about the faithfulness of elephants and the opposite in men, who prefer food to friends.[68] In another characteristic story Aelian tells of what amounts to the elephants' graveyard. At the foot of Mount Atlas, he says, are splendid pastures and deep forests, and a spring of abundant pure water. Here nature leads elephants who have grown old. It is of course, nature in an external, transcendent sense, co-operating with the gods of woods and valleys, under whose protection the elephants are. The natives of the place hold the elephants sacred, and

275

do not hunt them; and an expedition by greedy outsiders who wanted ivory was struck and dispersed by disease. Nature, the gods, a moral, all used in Aelian's own way.

PHYSIOLOGUS

Aelian's stories and their kind in late-classical antiquity were very popular. They were also useful. Aelian used them to draw out morals about man's bad behaviour, and to emphasise the superiority of his adopted culture: Homer knew about animals, animals illustrate his wisdom and parallel the actions of the heroes.

It was all very different from the natures-of-animals of Aristotle's natural philosophy. But equally different was the Christian use of animal stories – for these stories were popular and useful to Christians as well. But for them the world was a very different place. Here was no personalised 'nature' of a Pliny or a Galen, or a Stoic source of natural law, no pantheon of an Aristophanes or an Aelian. The Christian God was omnipotent, the direct Creator of all living things. There was no room for a subordinate generative principle,[69] and none for human wonder about how well a creative demiurge had done with intractable matter. This made the natural world a very special place. The Christian was living in God's direct handiwork. It followed that everything in it was instinct with meaning. The sympathies and antipathies, the surprising capabilities of some animals, their interaction with man, could not be wonders without meaning, or random events, or the result of natures or nature. Moreover, God had given, through Moses in the Old Testament, an account of how the world had been created, and which classes of creatures had been made on what day. God's purposes in making the animals and plants could be seen in the sacred page as well as in the accumulated animal-lore of late-classical antiquity.

A Christian writer on animals was in a position not dissimilar to that of Aelian. He had adopted a culture and wanted to express himself in it as a medium. He found that animal stories were useful, and could find a biblical illustration for the stories he used, just as Aelian so often found a Homeric and always a Greek counterpart. Like Aelian, the Christian found that a truth from nature that matched a truth from written authority had a double authority. The Christian writer had a new technique which suited these new circumstances. This was allegory. It was used by the Greek Christian writer Origen, and was a device similar to one whereby Aelian forged links between the natural world and his secular scriptures, Homer. But Origen (and Clement of Alexandria) had seen Philo's use of the technique, and may have taken it from him. For the Christian, God was so important that everything in His Creation signified Him. Parts of Creation become symbolic of God's actions. The natures of animals are no longer their *physis* but allegories of God. Perhaps indeed, thought the Christians, they have been put into the world for that very purpose, to represent aspects of God's creation and remind man of his Creator. If it was assumed (as some Christians did) that the lion was symbolic of the Devil, then it gave added understanding to the biblical statement to this effect if one knew about the nature and actions of lions. This gave the double reinforcement that Aelian sought between Greek literature and the animal stories. It also meant that looking at the natural world (or reading about it) was a religious affair, if not an actual Christian duty.

The use of allegory within Christianity meant that there were two ways of reading the sacred page, as with Philo. The first was the literal reading: the histories of the Old Testament and the actions of the Apostles in the New Testament, for example. But below the literal meaning was the 'spiritual' or allegorical, a deeper level of meaning, in which perhaps the events of the Old Testament presaged and symbolised the events of the New; or in which the parables of the actions of Christ in individual cases became symbolic of the nature of divinity. This was also called the 'moral reading' of the sacred page and is clearly related to the morals inherent in the animal stories of Aesop.

This is illustrated in the text known to us as the *Physiologus*.[70] The title actually refers to a man – it means 'he who talks about nature' – and the text is represented as a series of sayings of Physiologus. It was written in Greek, in the middle of the second century, and so is actually a little earlier than Aelian. It is also earlier than Origen, who quotes it.[71] It draws on the same stock of animal-lore as does Aelian. It became very popular and was soon translated into Latin;[72] during the Middle Ages it was translated into many vernaculars from Icelandic to Syriac and exists in a large number of manuscripts. It was a major source for the medieval bestiary. For a long time the *Physiologus* was attributed to St Epiphanius and although that is now discounted, the traditional details of his life[73] are, shall we say, an allegory of the circumstances that contributed to the *Physiologus*. Epiphanius was born a pauper in a Phoenician city and adopted and educated by Tryphon the Jew. Tryphon taught him the law of Moses, and left him lots of money. But Epiphanius was converted to Christianity by a monastic, entered the monastery and gave his money to the poor. He nevertheless became both famous and a bishop in Cyprus, performed miracles and went to Constantinople. Whether or not he was the author of the *Physiologus,* his life reflects the fact that Christianity derived its monotheism from Judaism (Epiphanius' early education) and that both Christianity and Greek culture (his later) came into the Roman world from the East. The Roman political world is silent in this little biography of Epiphanius, but it provided the means whereby these Eastern doctrines survived in the Latin West.

Let us take a look at how the *Physiologus* handles the animal stories. It is at once clear that, because God is now omnipotent and nature cannot therefore be a separate generative principle, the term 'nature' has a different meaning. It has lost the generalised or transcendent meaning and kept only the meaning of nature-of-a-thing, its essence. But it is not Aristotle's philosophical usage, for an animal may have more than one 'nature'. Thus the lion has 'three natures' which symbolise Christ. Now, lions existed long before Christ, whose temporal nativity was very well known. It seems as though the three natures of the lion were thought somehow to prefigure the coming of Christ, but that the lesson was not available to the old pagans. It is only with the New Testament that the *Physiologus* parables have significance. Its author hit on a clever device: the New Testament was quite recent in his day[74] and he used it, together with the Old Testament of the Hebrews and the stock of animal stories from Greek literature, to put across a new moralism to promote a new religion by means of the Greek device of allegory. These were his resources and he used them, as others used theirs, for his own purposes. The text sometimes gives the appearance of having two sources. The first is 'Physiologus' himself, the speaker about animals and plants, who has scoured the Greek literature for their personalities and properties. Often what he has to say is introduced with some such phrase as 'Physiologus said', generally in the past tense, and what is attributed to him is always the nature of the animal or plant. It is as though a second person has abstracted from Physiologus' discourse and immediately set about *his* business of moralising, ingeniously and in the end triumphantly showing how these natures are entirely consistent with the new world order.[75] He does so directly to the reader in the present tense. There is a good sense in which Physiologus was retailing good information about animals, because it related directly and intelligibly to the new view of God and the world. Nothing mattered about animals unless they illustrated some part of the sacred page – if it did not do this it was not knowledge. What was knowledge was determined by the learned, and the socially powerful, and these were now Christian.

So the nature of the animal was once more its 'essence' as it had been for Aristotle, and although now in a Christian context, it was still *physis* in the Greek and *natura* in the Latin.[76] But as we have seen, unlike Aristotle, Physiologus allows an animal more than one 'nature': some have three and many have two (the second of which is perhaps the origin of our phrase 'second nature'). An animal *can* have three essences if it serves to illustrate three things about God or man in relation to God. While animal stories had been used by many like Pliny to castigate man in general, the *Physiologus* moralist turns to face the audience so to speak and addresses his reader direct (as *tu* in the Latin version): it is *you* that is evil or corrupt, as this story shows.

So what are the three natures of the lion? *Physiologus dixit* that the first is that the lion covers up its footmarks by brushing over them with its tail, so that he cannot be followed by hunters. Aelian too has the story, and it is for him evidence of the sagacity of the lion. But for the moralist in the *Physiologus* it is evidence for much more. The lion symbolises Christ, the spiritual lion of the tribe of Juda, of the root of David, sent by his eternal Father: Christ too covered his tracks (his divinity) from unbelieving Jews. The lion's second nature is that he sleeps with his eyes open and is vigilant; just as in the canticles the betrothed said 'I sleep but my heart is vigilant'; and as the lord sleeps on the cross while his divine nature is always at God's right hand. The lion's third nature is that its cubs are born dead, but after three days of being guarded by the lioness the father comes and blows into their faces, giving them life. The allegory of course is of Christ's resurrection.

In the Latin *Physiologus* there are forty-eight other stories arranged for similar purposes. The biggest of them is perhaps that about the elephant and it illustrates the techniques of the author very clearly. First, he takes elements from the abundant material about elephants current in late antiquity, selecting them for the use he makes of them. We have seen that the elephant was generally regarded as a chaste animal, and Physiologus says that it copulated only to generate offspring. To do so, it took its mate to the East, near Paradise, where there is a tree called mandracora. The female takes a fruit from the tree and entices him with it; she conceives as soon as he eats. When it is time to give birth, the female enters water to the height of her udders and the young is safely delivered and nourished. Meanwhile the male stands on guard against the serpent, its traditional enemy. Should one appear, the elephant kills it, but dies himself.

So even before we have the moral, we see elements of the Old Testament story of Eve's temptation of Adam, together with a serpent who seems to have a biblical role as well as being a figure in an elephant story of which Pliny would have approved. The 'nature' of the elephant is that if it falls, it cannot get up (Physiologus believed like others that the elephant had no joints in its legs). As others had related, the elephant is accordingly captured by the hunters sawing partly through the tree against which it habitually leans in order to sleep. This is the 'nature' of the elephant because it leads to the moral of the story, which now begins to build up in details which may not be older than Physiologus. The fallen elephant (he says) calls for help, and a large comrade comes up, but is unable to assist. The two shout out again, and twelve more elephants appear, but are equally unable to help. Finally a small elephant approaches who is able to put his trunk under the fallen animal and so finally lift him.

The allegory is elaborate and is done by having the elephants 'accept the person' of those they represent. The male and female elephants *personam accipiunt* of Adam and Eve and while they were virtuous did not understand sexuality. But when she ate of the tree, she became pregnant with evils, and left Paradise. The water and the serpent of the story are both biblical; the call for help is that of Adam and Eve to the Lord, the large elephant is the Law, unable to help, the twelve others the prophets. The small elephant is Christ, greater than they but made small, and the only means of salvation.

In this story (it is number 20) Christ is the *sanctus intelligibilis elephans*, the 'holy and intelligible elephant'. But what does 'intelligible' mean in such parables and allegories? It is a word that often appears, for we have an 'intelligible Samaritan' and an 'intelligible mulberry' (story 28). We are reminded at once of Philo Judaeus' use of 'intelligible' to mean the incorporeal ideas of the creation in God's mind before the physical creation began. We are also reminded that Philo's use of allegory was well known to Clement of Alexandria and his pupil Origen. We seem to have close and probably Alexandrian links between Philo, Clement, Origen and Physiologus.

But Physiologus' use of 'intelligible' is rather different. He is not after all concerned with creation, but with 'intelligibility' as the accessibility of the ideas in God's mind (as of course Philo also was). Let us look at a few examples. Story 17 is about the ibis, and Physiologus says that it is in the law the dirtiest of all birds (other authors describe how the ibis purges itself). It is restricted to low-lying marshy places and a diet of dirty little fish. Learn to swim spiritually, says the moralist to the reader, and (unlike the ibis) you may come to the Intelligible and spiritual river and the wisdom of God. Story 19 is an elaborate allegory built upon a dove that lives in a tree in India with soft fruit. The dove's enemy is the *draco*, which fears the shade of the tree but which will eat the dove if it leaves the tree. The tree is God, the shadow Christ; the dragon is the Devil and the Holy Spirit is the Intelligible and spiritual dove. In these stories the Intelligible is the higher truth, because it is in God's mind.

In other stories (for instance 23) 'intelligible' is used of a physical object or event that symbolises a higher truth. Here, a pearl may be found 'intelligibly' between the two shells of an oyster, just as Christ is found between the two Testaments. Christ is the Intelligible pearl, and the intelligibility becomes plain when the symbol (the physical pearl) is connected with its spiritual meaning (Christ) as the story is completed. The Indicus stone (story 26) was used by doctors to cure dropsy. They tied it to the patient for three hours and the disease attached itself to the stone. The cure was effected by then placing the stone with its transferred disease into the sun for an equal length of time. Allegorically, *we* are dropsical, having the waters of the Devil in our hearts; the stone is Christ, who takes up our Intelligible diseases. In another story (32) 'Physiologus spoke of the vulture' which when ready to lay an egg, flies to India for the *eutocium* stone to make the laying easier. In the allegory the reader is pregnant with the evils of the Devil, the physical eutocium is Intelligible and the spiritual stone is Mary and Jesus.

As a final example, story 49 is about a lizard called *eliace*, 'that is, the eel of the sun'. When it grows old and its eyes become dim and it cannot see the sun (a favourite topic of Physiologus) it finds a wall facing east and crawls into a crack so that it may face the rising sun, which cures it. Thus you also, O man, says the moralist, if you have the covering of an old man, take care lest the eyes of your heart are blocked; turn to Christ, the Intelligible sun, who will open the Intelligible eyes of your heart. So here again, as in the example we began with – about the Intelligible elephant – what is 'intelligible' is what is symbolised in the allegory; elsewhere, as we have seen, it is the symbol itself.

It is clear that the use of 'intelligible' in the *Physiologus* is in fact part of the way the allegory was constructed. An 'intelligible' symbol – object or action – was open to Greek philosophy. But what was symbolised was intelligible mostly within the higher spiritual meaning of the scriptures. When Amos said that he was not a prophet but a goatherd plucking the mulberry tree, he was 'accepting the person' of Christ allegorically and so 'mulberry' too became allegorical: it had in fact, a literal or physical meaning and a spiritual meaning, just as Origen and the allegorists found two levels of meaning in the sacred page. Physiologus, the man who spoke about nature, had special knowledge of the physical world and its literal reading, and it was the job of the *Physiologus* moralist to point to the spiritual meaning of the physical world and its plants and animals. As spiritual, it was a higher meaning, not accessible to reason and philosophy, which is precisely why Physiologus is not philosophical. The analogy and symbolism of the allegory are devices to raise the mind to higher truths, leaving reason behind. This is the moralist's *purpose* in retailing animal stories, just as the philosophers and others had had purposes like the avoidance of fear, *ataraxia,* leading the good life or instructing the powerful.

Clearly then, natural knowledge had a place in interpreting the scriptures. The *Physiologus* says so in story 29, observing that the sacred page says nothing without 'intention of intellect' about birds and animals. Discussing the hostility of the panther to the serpent, the moralist says with the Apostle that we are not ignorant of the evil ways of the Devil. His point is that the serpent is allegorically the Devil and the more we know of its ways and how it is opposed the better we can read and understand the sacred page, beginning at the literal, physical level and rising to the spiritual. 'Intention of intellect' is the beginning of this process at the 'intelligible' level.

These features are repeated in many of the stories, most with a long history behind them and a long future in front of them. In that of the ant (story 14) Physiologus and the moralist almost play alternate roles. The moralist begins by taking a text from Proverbs, where Solomon advises the lazy to go to the ants and imitate their ways. The ant has three natures, says Physiologus, supplying details of the ways of the ants. Their first nature is that they march in order, each with a grain in its mouth. The moralist is ready with a quick parable about the foolish virgins. Its second nature, says Physiologus, is when storing the grain to divide it into two to prevent germination. This story of the ant's foresight in keeping the grain useful as food was widespread and Physiologus repeats that it is in this way that the ant avoids starvation. The moralist is elaborate: you (the reader) too will die of hunger unless you divide the spiritual from the carnal when the Word germinates. This is partly the separation of good from evil, but is also again the difference between the spiritual and the literal. The moralist talks of the spiritual law of Paul; about how the letter kills but the spirit vivifies; about the two vivifying things, the two Testaments: the Jews, looking only at the letter (of the Old Testament) are killed by spiritual hunger. We then return to Physiologus for the third nature of the ant, which is to climb the stalks to take the grain at harvest time. But before climbing it smells the grains to discover whether they are wheat or barley, for barley is the food of cattle. Quite so, concludes the moralist; just as the prophet fled from Babylon, that is, a foreign doctrine and foreign glory, the diet of barley, which kills souls.

Other categories of story are used by the moralist according to their natures. We have seen how Aelian and the philosophers treated differently accounts of mythical animals, and it is not part of the moralist's purpose to deny them, for they have a ready message. Sirens (in story 15) are deadly sea-creatures, having a human figure down to the umbilicus and having wings on the other half of its body. The onocentaur is a man in its top half, an ass below. For the moralist such things are parables in themselves, pictures of the duplicity of man's nature. So is the mirmicoleon, which has the face of a lion and the body of an ant: it cannot eat flesh because of the ant-nature of its body, and consequently starves to death (story 33).

Another category of animal story that the *Physiologus* moralist turned to his own uses was that based on sympathies and antipathies. One long-lived tradition of this kind was the antipathy between the deer and the snake. Aelian has a version of it,[77] and it is found in Lucretius, Martial, Pliny and pseudo-Oppian. Pictorial versions have been found on fourth-century silver (in the Mildenhall treasure) and on fifth-century mosaics in Constantinople. Many other stories must have been equally widespread; it is that this one has a historian.[78] In its earlier forms, the story tells of the deer sucking, through his nostrils, the snake out of his hole in the ground, and subsequently killing it. (Plate 29.) In the version told by Physiologus (story 43) the deer is said to blow water into the hole to swill out the snake. This seems to be a new element in the story[79] and was taken up by the Church Fathers as symbolic of baptism and of washing away the effects of the Devil.[80] In the Latin *Physiologus* the snake is *draco*, and 'dragon' or 'serpent' is often the 'intelligible body' that 'assumes the person' of the Devil in allegories. The *Physiologus* moralist explains that the deer's action is like that of Christ in killing the great dragon the Devil with celestial waters. If you have a devil inside you, he says, invoke Christ.

Many of these parables about animals have a new feature. They are about the Devil. Most often perhaps the Devil is represented by the serpent, as we saw in the story of the elephants, or by the related *draco*. Physiologus tells the story (39) of the ichneumon's antipathy to the *draco* (more usually it is the crocodile): the ichneumon covers itself with mud, inflates itself, and kills its enemy. The moralist matches this with Christ accepting an earthly body and killing the intelligible *draco* who sits by the river in Egypt, Pharaoh. At a second allegorical remove, Pharaoh is equated with the Devil. The earlier stories of the crocodile's enemy seem to have given rise to two related accounts, perhaps by passing through different languages.

Plate 29 The traditional antipathy between the deer and the snake is represented in a number of texts and artefacts over a long period. In the classical versions of the story the deer sucked the snake out of its hole with its nostril, and then killed it. In the Christian version, the deer swilled the snake out with water, in an allegory of baptism. Outline drawing restored slightly from a Roman mosaic.

Physiologus tells one after the other. In the second, as we have seen, the crocodile has become a *draco*. In the first it has kept its name but the ichneumon is a *niluus* because it lives in the Nile. The size of a dog, says Physiologus, it leaps, mud-covered, into the open mouth of the crocodile and tears out its viscera. The moral is similar.

The Devil took various forms in Physiologus' stories. We have seen him as a *draco* attacked by the panther, and he was also a whale, the aspidoceleon. So big is it, says Physiologus, that ignorant sailors moor their ships to it thinking it is an island, and make fires to cook their food. But the whale feels the fires and dives, sinking the ships . . . Just as you, O man, says the moralist, will sink to the flames of hell if you tie yourself by faith to the Devil. Here the moralist seems to suggest that the Devil was not only the symbol of everything to be avoided by Christians, but an enemy to Christianity in the sense that there were people who put their faith in him. So often do these parables attack the Devil that there is almost a dualism of God and Devil, something quite new in the world views of the authors we have been examining.[81] The orthodox view in the *Physiologus* was that the Devil was once an archangel. That is, God had originally made him, and so he had an origin in time, but was immortal, without end. He was sempiternal rather than eternal, for it was only God who had no beginning as well as no end. Our moralist even allegorises on a pun: it is the ape who accepts the person of the Devil, for the ape has no tail, as the Devil has no end. It is digusting not to have a tail, and the Devil has no good end.

The Devil was dangerous. He was like the fox, who in Physiologus' story played the trick played by the leopard in Aelian's: hungry, he lies on his back in a hollow, puffing himself and pretending to be dead. Birds descend to eat the body, but are caught and eaten themselves as the fox springs to life. And the Devil is death, says the moralist, and those who wish to communicate with his flesh will die (story 18).

Stories about renewal in one form or another were of course ideal for the purposes of the moralist, reflecting not only Christ's resurrection but the 'new man' one became on joining the Christians. There are the pelicans, who are extremely attached to their young when small. Yet when the young begin to peck the faces of the parents, the latter, driven to distraction, kill them. They are at once overcome by remorse and for three days weep over their bodies. On the third day the mother pecks her own body until the blood flows down over the bodies of her young, which revive (Plate 30). The moralist begins with David, in the Psalms, being as lonely as a pelican, and proceeds through God's destruction of his children (Isaiah) and the blood and water that flowed from the side of Christ on the cross. *Bene arguit Phisiologus de pelicano*, concludes the sixth story. David also spoke of the renewal of the youth of the eagle, which the moralist uses to introduce Physiologus' account of the ageing eagle, with heavy wings and cloudy eyes. When it finds a spring of water, it flies upwards towards the sun, burns its wings and the cloudiness of its eyes, plunges into the water and is renewed. It is the same for you, says the moralist; do you have old clothes? Are the eyes of your heart cloudy? Then seek the lord of the spiritual spring. The phoenix too, which Aelian admired for its ability to work out quicker than the Egyptian priests when its 500 years had passed, was a symbol of resurrection. Physiologus tells us (after the moralist has introduced a text from the New Testament) that the phoenix arrives in Egypt at its appointed time, alights on the pyre constructed by the priests at Heliopolis and ignites it. The priests find a worm in the ashes. On the second day it has turned into a little bird, and on the third it is fully grown. The phoenix accepts the person of Christ, concludes the moralist (stories 8 and 9).

Plate 30 The pelican reviving her young with blood pecked from her breast. A modern doorstop on the steps of the chapel of Corpus Christi College, Cambridge, where the pelican has an appropriate symbolism.

ST BASIL

When the *Physiologus* moralist ended one of the stories with the words 'Justly does Physiologus set up the natures of animals against spiritual things' he is expressing the essence of his allegorical technique. It was a technique exploited too by Origen and has had a place in Christian thinking ever since. But not all the Church Fathers[82] approved wholeheartedly. St Basil[83] did not. He too was interested in animals and plants, because they were God's creation, and he was fully prepared to draw out morals from the traditional stock of stories, but his suspicion of allegory is clear. He saw allegory as a device, almost a trick, designed to persuade the reader. As a formal device, it had rules, which Basil knew other people employed. It was now some two hundred years after the *Physiologus* had used allegory, and even more since the Greeks had formalised it. Basil thought that such people were carried away by the device and were incapable of seeing the literal sense of the Bible. For them, water was not water but 'some other nature'; moreover, such people change the natures of fish and reptiles to suit what is in their allegories. This has been taken as a criticism of Origen, but it would apply equally to the *Physiologus*, where the traditional stories have been at least selected in forms that support allegories and surely were sometimes massaged a little into appropriate shapes.

Basil preferred the literal sense of the Bible. His use of the animal stories was therefore different from that of the moralist of the *Physiologus*. He too was Christian and wanted to draw edifying morals from the natural world. The traditional and mostly pre-Christian animal stories now had to fit another framework, a created world, and serve purposes associated with Basil's literal reading of the sacred page. While the moralist had begun with a 'lesson' from the scriptures that introduced some animal-lore, and ended with an allegory, Basil's task was one of exegesis. His use of the animal stories is in expanding and understanding the account given in Genesis of the creation of the world. The six days of creation provide the structure for his exegesis: he is writing a *Hexaemeron.* It is a literal reading, and Basil comes closer to the old philosophers. The bodies of animals follow the natures of their souls (as Aristotle had said) but as a Christian Basil has to insist on the difference between animal and human souls. It is not simply the addition of rationality and immortality to the human soul that makes the difference, but that animal souls are material: they are blood, which thickens into flesh and ultimately decays into earth.[84] In their actions, too, animals follow the nature of their souls, so that foxes and crabs are crafty and bees industrious.[85]

Basil's literal reading of the Bible seems consistent with a 'physical' reading of the natural world. More than the moralist, he can use fragments of old philosophy in his created world. He even uses 'nature' as a principle at work in the world in a way that had been impossible for the moralist of the *Physiologus*. He means partly the nature of things and partly nature as a generative principle of all things. These were the senses that the Latin term *natura* retained down through the Western Middle Ages, and we can see an example of the genesis of this in the early Latin translation of these sermons of Basil's on creation.[86] It was made by Eustathius Afer in about 440, that is, after the division of the Empire and the sack of Rome, and is one of the few cultural currents from East to West. Basil handles the idea of nature as a generative principle by using the image of a ball that continues to run down hill when pushed: God has set nature in motion and it continues to produce animals according to the original created type. Eustathius uses *rerum naturae*[87] so the nature-of-the-thing is not far away, but when he uses 'laws of nature' in relation to the control of migration of animals it is the exercise of an external controlling principle.[88] Indeed it is nature in this sense that makes many of Basil's morals possible, for he speaks of a 'natural reason' which animals follow in their behaviour and which has lessons for us. He does not mean that animals have reason (we have seen that their souls are of a quite different kind) but an internal law placed in them by God which acts, like reason, for the good of the animal. This is broadly the pursuit of the good and the avoidance of evil, which Aristotle had discussed in philosophical terms. But of course now the Good and Evil are largely moral, and Basil is using an old doctrine for his new purpose. He also has here the old story of the hunting dog at the crossing of the tracks: while for some the dog syllogised, for Basil it is simply using natural reason.

Basil draws out morals too in arguing that we are ignoring our own natural reason in ignoring what is good in God's law: the animals cannot do this and so their behaviour is a lesson for us. His lesson is Trust in God directly. It is the providence of God that the sea-urchin can foretell a coming storm and accordingly weighs itself down with heavy stones. This was a story as well known as that of the halcyon, which laid its eggs in mid-winter but always in the calm that providence provided. If God is providential to sea-urchins and sea birds, then surely more so to you, argues Basil.

Sometimes Basil can draw more than one moral from a story. The distinctly unphilosophical story we met above of the mating of the serpent and the sea-creature – here a lamprey – carries three morals. The first is for women, who are enjoined to obey their husbands, however violent and drunken. The second is for husbands, to be like the serpents going to water, said (for example in the *Physiologus*) first to spit out their venom. The third moral is that this mis-mating, while natural, may be adulterous:[89] avoid adultery.

THE GENEALOGY OF STORIES

While reading Pliny, we were reminded of the oral transmission of practical culture. A complex and important business such as farming must have been transmitted by word of mouth since very ancient times. Folklore and beliefs about animals were similarly transmitted, but while experience constantly tested farming lore, that about animals, plants and minerals changed. There were a number of channels through which the stories of the late-antique natural-history collection came together and were written down. There were the philosophers like Aristotle and Theophrastus. There were moralists like Aesop. There were the three kings of the East and South, Juba, Attalus and the improbable Bogus. They reigned by Roman consent and gave accounts of the natural history of their territories, perhaps in emulation of the stories of strange animals and plants that followed the conquests of Alexander the Great. There were medical men, who used animal, plant and mineral substances in their medicines. There were the Egyptian priests, who had pet crocodiles and gods in the form of animals. Their counterparts in the classical world made divinations from the insides of and the behaviour of animals, and from the appearance of certain plants.

These stories about animals, plants and minerals were very numerous not only because they had many authors, but because they often changed in the telling. Only when they were written down did this stop. By late antiquity there is good reason to suppose that literacy was more widespread. There were royal and private libraries and much of the matter of natural history achieved a durable form, whether it had been fables, folklore or philosophy. The stranger stories were written down and endured as well as the philosophical, and what the Western Middle Ages found in the texts of the ancients was already in parts bizarre. The grotesques that decorate the medieval margins of even Aristotle's physical works and a great deal of, for example, the Hereford *mappa mundi*, are pictorial reconstructions of strange animals described in the words of Pliny. An important access to Pliny's words was provided by the work of Solinus, who took many of his details from Pliny but produced a smaller and more manageable text.

Not much is known about Solinus – no one is certain whether he lived in the first or third Christian century – and we should note only that he was one of the few Latin writers who paralleled the Greek paradoxologists who provided natural-history stories for the Eastern Empire. For Solinus as for Pliny, Rome is the centre of the world, the *caput orbis*. He seems to accept what looks like a Stoic view of the world as animated by a ruling spirit, but does not include himself among the *physici* who deliberate on such matters. He may have believed in the traditional gods (he says that Etna is sacred to Vulcan[90]) and thinks of *natura* as a generalised principle. Solinus has variants of the stories we are familar with: elephants-and-snakes, griffins and the one-eyed Arimaspi, dolphins and boys, dogs that mate with tigers in India, rivers that change the colour of animals, the precious stone that forms from lynx's urine and so on.[91] By repeating it, he added to the credibility of Aristotle's account of the position of the dolphin's mouth (which made it awkward for the dolphin to eat). Other stories are less well known. He reports how the age of dolphins was ascertained by identifying individuals by means of making cuts in their tails.[92]

Many of these snippets of natural history in Solinus and the other authors were of considerable but uncertain age. There is something unsatisfactory about an undated text, and the tidy-minded librarians of Alexandria were ready to attribute, for example, most old Greek medical texts to Hippocrates, and to add bits of physical philosophy to Aristotle. When they were shown not to be by Aristotle most serious scholars preferred to forget about them.[93] But they are of interest if we are looking at how natural-historical details are passed on from one generation to the next. An interesting text in this respect is the *Auscultationes Mirabiles,* 'Wonderful Stories'. It is obviously not an Aristotelian text, but its modern editor finds some peripatetic features,[94] and it has some striking resemblances to what Aristotle has to say on animals. It consists of 178 reports of notable things in the natural world. They are *historiae* worthy of note by the philosopher or dinner-party audience – both Aelian and Athenaeus give their treatise the form of a conversation at dinner (Plate 31). Some of its details are found in other collections – including indeed Aristotle, Aelian and Athenaeus – and it is not easy to tell if Aristotle drew from it or if it is a collection made partly from his works on animals. On the whole it looks more likely that it draws from Aristotle for the entertainment of the reading public. Nevertheless, the Lyceum's research programme, relying on reports from those concerned with

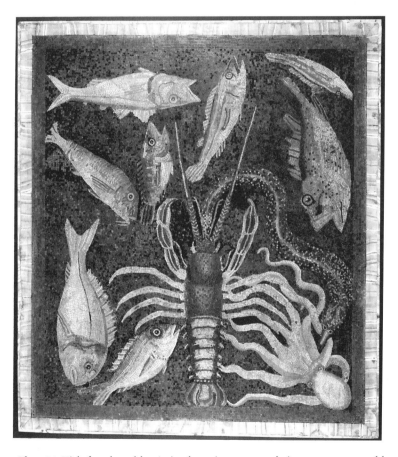

Plate 31 Fish for the table. Animal stories, among their many uses, could provide entertainment for the mind at dinner, while animals themselves entertained the sense of taste. Both Aelian and Athenaeus present their writings in the form of a dinner-party conversation. (From a mosaic in the British Museum.)

animals in distant places, must often have handled documents like this, from which Aristotle drew the details for the *Historia Animalium*. The *Auscultationes* characteristically begins its items with 'Men say . . .' which gives it the air of a report, not of an author seeking to entertain with strange but authoritative tales. There is no argument and the reports, which read like cards from an index, are grouped geographically and loosely by topic (those on minerals coming together for instance).

Thus the first item in the *Auscultationes*[95] is very close to a description in the *Historia Animalium*, which agrees with it in all major points but is slightly longer. It concerns the bolinthos, a large wild ox of Paeonia, said to defend itself from hunters by a forcible ejection of its dung, which flies over 24 feet and is so acrid that it burns the hair off the hunting dogs.[96] Many of the females are said to give birth at the same time, the remainder of the herd forming a circle round them, ready for a common defence of their own particular kind.

The second item in the *Auscultationes* is about camels in Arabia. The young males, it is said, refuse to mate with their mothers, despite the efforts of their keepers. Then follows the story we have met elsewhere of a particular camel induced to mount its mother by the trickery of its keeper, whom he bit to death when he discovered the deception. The story[97] is given also by Aristotle, who does not give its location, Arabia. He puts it with another story of a horse which, in similar circumstances, jumped over a cliff in its shame. This in turn seems to be related to the *Auscultationes'* story of asses in Syria.

Aristotle's account of the cuckoo is also very close to that in the *Auscultationes*. Again he does not locate the story (the *Auscultationes* puts it in Helice) and says the cuckoo lays its eggs in a lark's nest rather than that of a turtle dove or ring dove. And again Aristotle has collected related stories, principally about how the mother bird's own chicks are removed by the cuckoo. Indeed, in this collection of stories the *Historia Animalium* is repetitious, suggesting (as we have seen) that it was a collaborative affair or at least badly edited.[98]

The extra details that Aristotle has in these stories suggest that he was drawing from a source common to the *Auscultationes*, rather than directly from it. His related stories certainly come from elsewhere. But where Aristotle and the *Auscultationes* have two similar stories together in the same order, it looks as if the common source was not distant. The *Auscultationes* says that the plant leopard's bane grows in Armenia and that it is used by hunters to catch leopards. The technique is to anoint an animal victim with the plant and to leave it as bait for the leopard. Having taken the bait the leopard searches for human excrement; the hunters, knowing this, had hung some in a pot suspended from a tree. Attempting to reach it, the leopard becomes exhausted and is caught. Aristotle has the story too, and characteristically does not give the place, Armenia. Nor does he say anything about anointing the victim with leopard's bane. Characteristically too Aristotle adds another story about leopards. When the story turns up again several centuries later in Solinus the leopard has become a panther and the point of the story is that the animal *cures* itself of the poison by eating the excrement.[99] (Plate 32.) Both the *Auscultationes* and the *Historia Animalium* follow this story about the leopard with the story of the bird that flies into the crocodile's mouth to take pieces of meat. The *Auscultationes* specifies Egypt, and the bird involved emerges in English translation as the sandpiper. Aristotle's bird is the trochilus, and a detail he characteristically adds is that the crocodile gives notice to it when about to close its jaws.[100]

Some stories common to the two texts were well known and cause no surprise. That Cretan she-goats (wild goats, says Aristotle) seek dittany to expel arrows was common knowledge to Theophrastus, Aelian, Pliny, Virgil and others. The proverbial 'place where the stag sheds his horns' for somewhere very obscure derived ultimately from the well known story that the stag goes to great pains to hide himself away when losing his horns because he is then helpless. The story varies somewhat. The *Auscultationes* says that the stag also hides because the places where the horns were give him pain, and adds that sometimes ivy is seen growing in the place of the horns. We have seen that Aristotle and Theophrastus were interested in the purposes for which the stag shed its horns and they repeat this story. Again Aristotle does not give the location (Achea, says the *Auscultationes*), nor does he say that the place from which the horns fell was painful. Again, he adds a related story, which here seems to be a fragment or a variant of some original that was once a single story: at Achea a stag was found with ivy growing on its (fully grown) horns. The point is that ivy was the plant of Dionysius and was widely recognised as a portent when seen growing on the stag's horns. Theophrastus says so.[101] Aristotle's discussion of the stag's horns continues with another proverb, that no one has ever seen the animal's left horn, for it keeps it out of sight because it possesses some medicinal quality. The *Auscultationes* matches this with a separate account of how stags (in Epirus) bury their right horn,

Plate 32 The leopard figured large in ancient animal stories. This one, from the Temple of Artemis, Corcyra, was old by Aristotle's time, having been cut in about 580 BC.

which has many uses. It seems to be a version of the same story, and Aristotle was unusual in talking of the *left* horn.[102]

It is a feature of some of the well-known stories that they are concerned with the medical properties of the objects of natural history. Probably these stories gained credence by way of the technical or lay medical literature. It was accepted that the testicles of the beaver were very valuable medically, and that a hunted beaver would bite them off to avoid capture.[103] The urine of the lynx was also useful, and on that account (says the *Auscultationes*) the animal took care to bury it. The same motive lay behind the stag burying its horn, and the lizard devouring its sloughed skin. Aelian too has these last two stories and adds that the skin of the lizard (here a gecko) was used as a cure for epilepsy.[104]

Another well-known story was that tortoises, fond of eating vipers, always finished the meal with marjoram to aid the digestion, Aristotle[105] and the *Auscultationes* have the story almost word for word. (It also occurs in Pliny, Aelian, Plutarch, Philo Judaeus and Nicander, a young contemporary of Galen and a medical man who wrote on medical substances.) Aristotle's account of how pelicans eat mussels is also almost word-for-word similar to that of the *Auscultationes*.[106] All the details of the feeding habits of the wood-pecker in the *Auscultationes* are given also by Aristotle and characteristically Aristotle adds repetitious detail from other sources.[107]

There are a few more minor matters in which there is a parallel between the *Auscultationes* and Aristotle; then we shall briefly look at others who had stories in common with the *Auscultationes*. Aristotle agrees that some mice (in Egypt, not Syrene) are covered with bristles, like hedgehogs, and that real hedgehogs have a north and a south tunnel in their nests to accommodate changes in the wind.[108] Aristotle adds the story of the man who became famous for forecasting the weather by observing the hedgehog's behaviour. For Aristotle the hedgehog story is part of the exposition of the natures of animals, and like all such stories it meant different things to different men. St Basil used it to indicate the providence of God even to small animals. St Ambrose uses the slightly modified story (in which the hedgehog's tunnels are west and north) in a characteristic way. For him it is evidence of the penetration of divine wisdom to all creatures. He does not, as Plutarch does, consider the animals in any sense wise; indeed, it is the very irrationality of their senses that makes their actions so perfect and admirable. How magnificent are thy works, O Lord, cries Ambrose, how much better are such things done by the senses than by rational disputation! When he adds that the testimony of nature is stronger than the argument of doctrine and that nature is the better guide to the truth[109] he is speaking with the voice of the anti-philosophical part of Christianity and is being more Roman than Greek.

We have seen how Aelian treated the story of the viper's mating in his own way. The story turns up too in the *Auscultationes* in its simple form, that is, that the female bites off the head of the male at the end of copulation and that the young are born by bursting through the mother's womb, killing her. The *Physiologus* has the story in an elaborate form. The male viper is said to have the face of a man. The female has a woman's body down to the umbilicus, and then a body of a crocodile. For some related reason the female does not have female genital organs, but male. In mating, the male deposits his semen in the mouth of the female. The male then dies, not because the female bites off his head, but for some reason to do with his sexuality which remains obscure in the Latin *Physiologus* for reasons of delicacy and the difficulties of translating the Greek. The female, having no means of delivering her young, dies when they burst through the uterus. The allegory, says the moralist, is the Pharisees, that generation of vipers whose birth killed their parents. The story has not been modified to fit the allegory but apparently by accretion of details from other stories of animals that copulated through the mouth.

Another text that is related in some way to the *Auscultationes Mirabiles* is that on plants, now known as *De Plantis* or *De Vegetabilibus*. It exists now only in a Latin translation made in the Middle Ages from the Arabic, the Greek having been lost. Most scholars agree that it is not an Aristotelian work but accept that it is peripatetic, that is, in some way related to the Lyceum and its work. Certainly it has features that we associate with the collaborative work of the Aristotelians. There are discussions about how the ancients were wrong. There are references to other works in the physical series, which is what we would expect to find in a book promised by Aristotle on plants. But there is no final causality, which Aristotle would have seen so clearly in a category of living and self-generating things like plants. Instead, the mechanisms of change *De Plantis* discusses are concerned with material structure, like density and rarity.

These mechanisms of change are what we meet in Theophrastus, in place of Aristotle's coming-to-be, and there are other Theophrastean features of the text. For example the second book of the *Historia Plantarum* begins with the propagation of plants, spontaneous, or from seeds, roots, cuttings and so on. *De Plantis* contains a very similar discussion, including the belief we met above that plants (mostly fruit trees) grown from seed degenerated in comparison to those grown from cuttings. Where both texts discuss the improvement of pomegranates when manured with pig's dung and water, and the improvement of almonds made by driving pegs into the trunks of the trees, the agreement is very close.

There is also a close agreement between Theophrastus' *Historia Plantarum* and *De Plantis* on the question of what a 'part' of a plant is, and it might be, as has been suggested,[110] that the pseudo-Aristotelian texts have been derived in part from Theophrastus. But there are also similarities between these two texts and a third, the *Auscultationes Mirabiles.* We have seen that this was in some way connected to the Lyceum's programme and this link with Theophrastus is more evidence. Theophrastus says that some 'parts' may in fact naturally be lost, like the horns shed by deer (which we met in his discussion of finality) and the feathers lost by birds 'in holes' (presumably hibernating). The same pair of examples appears in the *Auscultationes* but it is difficult to say whether one text draws from the other or from a common source. *De Plantis* also has the story of the deer's horn, and matches the other story with a discussion of fur being lost from animals in holes, not feathers from birds. Again, it is difficult to establish priority of texts. Where the pseudo-Aristotelian texts have more detail than the Aristotelian or Theophrastean, they cannot wholly have been drawn from them. Thus when the *Auscultationes* discusses the 'mad' vine, it is that variety that Theophrastus talked about which produced both green and black grapes. But it says, which Theophrastus does not, that it comes from Libya.[111] In a similar way there are related elements in the discussions about sexuality in plants given by both Theophrastus and *De Plantis.*[112]

STORIES AND PEOPLE

Let us take two final examples of stories that changed with the interests and purposes of the teller.

The image of a bird engaged in the apparently hazardous business of securing a meal from the open jaws of a crocodile is one comparatively well known to modern viewers of nature films, but we can see why it was an *historia* worthy of report in the Graeco-

Roman ancient world. We have seen how this story was told by some as an example of 'sympathy' between different animals. As a story of a natural marvel, it gained by the addition (as we have seen) of the crocodile warning the bird when it was about to close its mouth. With Plutarch, whose purpose was to demonstrate that animals are intelligent, the story was an excellent device to illustrate rational communication between animals when another element was added to it, that the bird in turn warns the crocodile of the approach of its traditional enemy, the ichneumon.[113]

Where the purpose of the story was to entertain by its strangeness, then the stranger the better. We met in the Alexander-literature the story of the hunting dog that would only deign to tackle a lion. Aelian gives the story twice, first in a fairly unembellished form, admiring the steadfast nature of the dog that would not let go of its antagonist even if its leg was cut off. Later he gives a stranger form, namely that the Indian dog has a tiger for a father, and sometimes too a grandfather. In front of Alexander its keepers released a boar, a bear and a stag. Only when they released a lion did the dog attack.[114] So unrelenting was its bite that it ignored the pain of its tail being removed. Not only did it likewise suffer the loss of a leg but without releasing the lion it unflinchingly lost a second and a third. Its tormentors finally cut its body from its head.[115]

Ants and bees have always to man provided a striking image of industry. One of the reasons is that both animals, like man, live in a community and that the bees moreover had a ruler, workers and idlers. They also presumably followed laws and interacted with each other in an ordered way. We saw that the Christians moralised and allegorised about ants, for religious purposes. We have also seen that the bee in particular provided for Aristotle not only an example of what was divine in animals but also an example of the limits of observational knowledge. Aristotle nevertheless here also made claims for the superiority of observational over rational knowledge, claims lauded by historians and philosophers of science. But then Aristotle was a philosopher and his business was to evaluate the different kinds of knowledge. His own personal claim to knowledge, and one which shaped so many of the *libri naturales*, was that it rested on purpose and that purpose could only be approached by adequate description. His statement about bees reflects this personal message.

The bee was also puzzling to Aristotle because there were in one hive different *kinds* of bee, with different purposes and different shapes. By the rules of his own philosophy they should therefore have had different natures, yet they clearly lived for the common good. Other writers without Aristotle's natural philosophy did not share his scruples. Writers whose message was entertainment and moral edification naturally selected from the the the old accounts of bees aspects that suited their purpose, which was essentially to comment on human life. Aelian identifies the drones as the lazy kind of bee, hiding among the combs and stealing the honey when the other bees are asleep at night. They are generally caught and Aelian says that on the first occasion they are beaten and on the second, killed.[116] Aelian adds an obvious moral. He also says that bees are sometimes deserted by their king, but that they go and fetch him back (presumably this is lore about swarming from beekeepers). They do so because they like him, for he is gentle and without a sting. A king is anyway necessary to a society, says Aelian, and the king of the bees behaves in a way that the philosophers recognise as being that of both a citizen and a king. Aelian means that to have a king whose actions are not unlimited is both natural and rational.[117] The moral is that it is only man who has *tyrants*. Aelian's human example is Dionysius of Syracuse, who made the young women of the town dance naked in pursuit of doves in the story we have already met. (Aelian the adopted Greek does not tell a Roman and equally suitable story from among those about the Tarquin tyrants.)

It is possible to suggest some generalisations about these plant and animal stories. Clearly there was a common stock of them in the later antique world and the various authors borrowed freely from each other. The volume of them, clear in the large works of Aelian and Athenaeus, is evidence of the ready availability of libraries to those who lived in the major cities, and evidence too of how libraries and literacy had grown since Aristotle's time some 500 years before. The change is striking. Aristotle's library, reputedly the first in Europe, was a working collection devoted in his lifetime to a philosophical programme with a large empirical component. Royal libraries in contrast were much more catholic and much larger and their librarians not necessarily philosophers. They could select from a wide range of material and add to the growing market for handbooks and anthologies.

PARADOXOGRAPHERS

The librarian of the greatest royal library, that of Alexandria, under Ptolemy Philadelphos, was Callimachus of Cyrene, who was one of the first to contribute to the genre of marvel-literature, which clearly found a market with the Greek reading public. (The Romans professed to find the Greek authors fanciful and Greek readers gullible,[118] but Pliny catered to the same market among the Romans.) One of the few marvel writers whose work has survived is the Greek Antigonus, who illustrates quite nicely how such stories were gathered together and made avaible for later collectors of oddities and wonders, like those we are now discussing. Antigonus, who flourished in the first half of the second century BC, drew extensively from Callimachus and thus benefited indirectly from the collections in the Library. He also had in front of him the animal books of Aristotle, which he used even more. He abstracted from Aristotle (and Theophrastus) many of the facts that Aristotle had set out to secure from others and which derived from Macedonian expansion. Such empirical findings now became literature, as we may also say in relation to Antigonus' other major source, the historians. He is inclined to be suspicious of the stories handed down from Ctesias, the early Greek explorer who worked for the Persians, but he uses with apparent confidence Megasthenes, Theopompus and Timaeus, the author of the *Siculan Histories.*[119]

Writers of collections of 'paradoxes' did not limit themselves to the earlier philosophers and drew even from legend. One of them, whose name we do not know,[120] included changes introduced into the countryside by the exploits of the gods, like Apollo's affair with Daphne; and he noted particular trees which were once virgins pursued by Boreas, the north wind (touch the trees, he says, and the wind rises angrily). Phlegon, writing *On Wonders*, made use mostly of human marvels, only some of them physical. Phlegon had no philosophical objection to strange beasts and reported on a hippo-centaur sent from Egypt as a gift for Caesar; it died from the change of air. He is most notable for a little collection of wonders from the earth, in our terms fossils, which most ancient writers give little account of. Phlegon's context is earthquakes, which had been of interest to the natural philosophers and which lent themselves readily to the purposes of the paradoxologists and historians. Theopompus had collected many details in his *Book of Earthquakes*[121] and had given an account of large bones found after an earhquake at the Bosphorus. Phlegon adds similar stories from Rhodes and Sicily. In some cases at least the bones were taken to be human, and their marvel was their great size, such as the ribs 11 cubits long reported from the cave of Diana in Dalmatia. Phlegon also cites the *Description of the Earth* by Eumachus, the historian of Hannibal, on large bones revealed at Carthage.

When Phlegon tells the story of cities vanishing by reason of earthquakes, he takes it from Apollonius 'grammaticus'. This may be Apollonius of Pergamum, also cited by Pliny, and it is possible that both or either of these is the Apollonius whose collection of marvels also survives, at least in part.[122] This Apollonius used Antigonus' collection, or a source common to them both, extensively. Both have a story of scorpions that are dangerous to the locals but not to visitors; they have the tradition that represented the length of Britain as 40,000 stadia (Strabo said it was 50,000) and that there was a British fruit without a kernel; they describe wood that behaves like a magnet; and they both have Aristotle's account of the tortoise continuing alive after the removal of its heart. In general Apollonius keeps closer to the philosophers than does Phlegon. Aristotle's *Problems* naturally provided a fund of 'things without answers' or paradoxes, and Apollonius uses it a number of times, noting that Aristotle 'tries to find causes'. Apollonius also often cites Theophrastus, for example on the effects of hellebore on the body, scorpions, seedless fruit and, from a work now lost, on the medical effects of music. On the same topic he cites Aristoxenus 'musicus', that is, a pupil of Aristotle, who also wrote on physical philosophy. Apollonius is rather precise on the titles of works he refers to, and distinguishes, as many did not, between Aristotle's two works on animals and Theophrastus' two on plants. We wonder then, what Aristotle's *On Drunkenness* was like and what Theophrastus meant by the *Divine Impetus*.

The paradox-mongers also relied on the historians and travel-story men, and tell us more about them. We have met Ctesias, whose *Things Persian* is used by Apollonius (the unusually soft and luxurious wool of a camel). But we have not yet been introduced to Phylarcus, from whose *Histories* Apollonius takes an account of a medically useful root from India. Nor have we met Dalion, from whose *Things Ethiopian* comes a story that we also have not encountered before. It tells of the wild *crocotta*, which creeps up to houses and listens to conversations. If a boy's name should be mentioned, the *crocotta* returns after nightfall, calls out the name and seizes the boy who comes out in response.[123] The same collection of paradoxes includes stories of the type with which we are now familar, including the barbarity of people far from the Greek centre of things. The reader is told that the Dardanes, an Illyrican tribe, wash three times only during their lives, after birth, at marriage and at death.

We see too that the stories change from one author to another. For example the dung-throwing ox-like bolinthos of Aristotle and the *Auscultationes Mirabiles* is a monotus in Antigonus (and becomes bonnacon in the Middle Ages).[124] (Plate 33.) Sometimes this suggests oral transmission and an imperfect recollection of a story once listened to and then re-told. The works of Aelian and Athenaeus[125] were both presented as if they were oral performances at a meal, which no doubt reflected actual practice at fashionable salons.[126] Thus stories about animals and plants would be circulated partly by conversation, as well as becoming part of the written literature, and Aelian sometimes gives the impression that he has been asking about for stories and repeats some that may well have gained or lost in the telling before becoming fixed in form in his text.[127]

But while such changes in stories repeated partly orally may have been owing to imperfect recollection, there is a more important reason. Stories are told for a purpose. The moralist, the allegorist, the philosopher, the after-dinner story-teller, the medical man, the Christian: all selected stories that fitted their purposes. Like Athenaeus' or Aelian's dinner-guests they would have had a wealth of stories at their disposal and would remember best what struck a

Plate 33 The bonnacon, the medieval descendant of Antigonus' monotus and Aristotle's bolinthos. From the thirteenth-century Mappa Mundi in Hereford Cathedral.

chord with their interests and beliefs. These interests and beliefs and the purpose of retelling a story were primary and the story secondary, a method of making a point. To return to a point made at the beginning of this book, it was not so much that the stories had a life of their own or were transmitted down the ages by some innate principle of motion, but rather that they formed a resource that could be used by people who came afterwards.

A final word on transmission. It is a striking fact that it was some of the simplest and everyday things, like animals and plants, that did not survive the passage from one culture to another. When Pliny was discussing fish often he did not know what his Greek sources were writing about. Many Greek names of fish did not have accepted counterparts in Latin, and when Pliny invents one, it is often enough unintelligible to us. The same thing is apparent when Strabo is trying to give an account of the fish in the Nile and when he discusses Libyan vegetables. What a Libyan or an Indian might have had for dinner every day might be wholly unknown to a Macedonian or Roman. Simple nouns do not themselves carry meaning, which is carried by the context, such as the attributes of the thing designated. Recognition comes when we see enough of these attributes to match something in our own experience. (Sometimes the recognition does not come at all, and then the animal is defined by the story, like the phoenix.) In direct contrast to the case of simple things, complex philosophies or religions have the appearance of crossing cultural boundaries with comparative ease. But they are not 'transmitted' for again we recognise only what we know. Remember the Macedonians interviewing the Indians. They asked Greek questions formed by Greek culture and knew what the answers would look like. They took it to be obvious that they were talking to philosophers and sophists. They knew the truths of the world and were in practice seeking how far the Indians knew them too. It is not surprising that they constructed an 'Indian philosophy' in Greek terms to take home to Greek audiences. Even if the Indians had only possessed a fragmentary philosophy of the natural and the divine, systematic Greek questions would lead to answers that would naturally be constructed systematically. As Strabo said, the gods of the Ethiopians were black, and if animals could say what their gods were like, they would be in the form of animals. Historical discontinuity across time and cultures is shown by ignorance about ordinary things like fish and vegetables, while the apparent continuity of complex things like philosophies and religions is due to their reconstruction.

NOTES

INTRODUCTION

1 See C. W. Fornara, *The Nature of History in Ancient Greece and Rome*, Berkeley, 1983, p.15.
2 ibid., p.169.
3 See ibid., for the ancient kinds of historical writing.
4 W. Jaeger, *Aristotle. Fundamentals of the History of his Development*, Oxford, 1962, often calls Aristotle scientific in this way.
5 Fornara, *Nature of History*, p.197 argues that history became 'scientific' in the eighteenth and nineteenth centuries.
6 See T. A. Dorey (ed.), *Latin Historians*, London, 1966, especially E. Badian, 'The early historians', pp.1–38.
7 James S. Romm, *The Edges of the Earth in Ancient Thought*, Princeton, 1992, p.84.
8 ibid., p.86.
9 Herodotus II.35 especially; see for example the translation by David Grene, *Herodotus. The History*, Chicago, 1987.
10 Herodotus II.74.
11 Herodotus II.18–20.
12 Herodotus' account of the crocodile begins at II.68 and incorporates many of the features of later stories, including the bird that eats from its mouth (which opens to the west); the Egyptians who hold it sacred and those that eat it; how to cover its eyes with mud when capturing it. Herodotus was shown paintings of the phoenix and accepted that it returns every 500 years, but is sceptical about other parts of the story.
13 Romm, *Edges of the Earth*, ch. 2.
14 It is so called by D'Arcy Thompson. See Chapter 1 below. Aristotle as a natural historian is Aristotle who is looking at the *historiae* of the natures of things.
15 See Chapter 4 below.

1 ARISTOTLE AND THE NATURES OF THINGS

1 By Hellenistic times philosophers often shared a common life in institutions and the 'professor had gradually come to be a social type like the farmer or soldier'. L. Edelstein, *The Idea of Progress in Classical Antiquity*, Baltimore, 1967, p.152.

2 A collection of accounts of animals from the literature of ancient Greece is presented by Norman Douglas, *Birds and Beasts of the Greek Anthology*, London, 1928.

3 Strepsiades: 'Yes, yes, by Apollo! I suffer, I get colic, then the stew sets up a-growling like thunder and finally bursts forth with a terrific noise. At first 'tis but a little gurgling *pappax, pappax!* then it increases, *papapappax!* and when I seek relief, why 'tis thunder indeed, *papapappax! pappax! papapappax!!!* just like the clouds.' The analogy is natural: they still say in Herefordshire that perry 'goes round and round like thunder and out like lightning'.

4 On atheism and naturalism see W. K. C. Guthrie, *The Sophists*, Cambridge, 1971, pp.228ff. In a parallel to the case of Aristophanes and Socrates, Euripides attacked Anaxagoras for reducing the all-seeing Helios in his heavenly chariot to a lump of hot matter.

5 Aristophanes, *The Eleven Comedies*, The Tudor Publishing Company, n.p., n.d, based on an anonymous translation published by the Athenian Society, London, 1912: two vols in one; vol. 1, pp.295–307. As Guthrie, *The Sophists*, p.228, says of the attack on the gods, 'Athenian officialdom was nervous and touchy about it. The cult of the gods was integral to the life of the state and a powerful cohesive force.' The gods were defended and philosophical beliefs about the heavens were attacked by the introduction of new laws in the fifth century. See also R. Olson, *Science Deified and Science Defied. The Historical Significance of Science in Western Culture*, Berkeley, 1982, pp.78–86.

6 Aristotle, *Meteorologica*, 357a.

7 ibid., 356b.

8 See W. H. Stahl, *Martianus Capella and the Seven Liberal Arts*, 2 vols, New York, 1971; vol. 1.

9 Ernest Barker, *The Politics of Aristotle*, Oxford, 1958, p.xiii.

10 Plato's *Laws* were finished after his death by members of the Academy.

11 Barker, *Politics*, p.xx.

12 These are among the opening words of the *De Partibus Animalium* (639a).

13 Barker, *Politics*, p.xi.

14 See also Harold Cherniss, *Aristotle's Criticism of Presocratic Philosophy*, New York, 1983.

15 The doctrine of 'becoming' – *physis* becoming actual from a potency – is said to be Ionian. Aristotle uses it in the *Poetics* in the case of tragedy and for the development of the polis in the *Politics*.

16 See G. E. R. Lloyd, *Aristotle: the Growth and Structure of his Thought*, Cambridge, 1968, p.100. Maybe, too, Aristotle (whose father was a doctor) was familiar with the case histories of Hippocrates. Books 4 to 6 of the *Politics* have a 'biological' air – the constitutions. See Barker,

Politics, p.xi. Like animals, the polis had a 'nature' that could be usefully compared to others; it had also the four causes. See Aristotle, *The Athenian Constitution*, trans. P. J. Rhodes, London, 1984, Introduction, pp.9, 17. Rhodes argues against direct authorship of this text by Aristotle, and claims that Aristotle's students were sent out to collect constitutions as others were sent to collect animals and plants.

17 It is a vexed question whether Aristotle's most valued kind of knowledge, that which was 'demonstrable' philosophically, is to be found in the natural works. See for example Robert Bolton, 'Definition and scientific method in Aristotle's *Posterior Analytics* and *Generation of Animals*', in Allan Gotthelf and James G. Lennox (eds), *Philosophical Issues in Aristotle's Biology*, Cambridge, 1987, pp.120–166.

18 We could argue that Aristotle was the first historian of 'the sciences' as the term is used in this volume. The collection of material continued under Theophrastus.

19 Werner Jaeger, *Aristotle. Fundamentals of the History of his Development*, 2nd edn (1948), Oxford, 1962, p.335.

20 ibid., p.335: the 'first considerable collection of books we know of on European soil'.

21 Barker, *Politics*, pp.xxix, xxxii.

22 There was also a shrine to Apollo. See Barker, *Politics*, p.xxxii.

23 W. Charlton, *Aristotle's Physics*, Oxford, 1970, p. 51.

24 Anthony Preus, *Science and Philosophy in Aristotle's Biological Works*, Hildesheim/New York, 1975, p.184; see especially ch. 4 (p.183ff.). Preus is surely correct; but not all scholars agree. See Scott Atran, *Cognitive Foundations of Natural History. Towards an Anthropology of Science*, Cambridge, 1993, p.86, who argues that Aristotle's use of *physis* as an internal principle of motion *is* 'nature' in general, p.86. He also (p.104) thinks that Aristotle's range of natural kinds is the same size as most 'folkbiology' and of the same kind.

25 See Preus, *Science and Philosophy*, p.183.

26 Edelstein, *Idea of Progress*, p.45.

27 See the very useful chapter by G. E. R. Lloyd, 'The invention of nature' in his *Methods and Problems in Greek Science*, Cambridge, 1991.

28 See W. K. C. Guthrie, *The Greeks and their Gods*, London, 1950, p.38. *Zeus Kataibates* was the Zeus who descended in the lightning and thunderbolts, and sacrifices were made to him in houses to avoid a strike.

29 The example is given by Lloyd, *Methods and Problems*, p.420.

30 Zeus was often thought of as being the sky. See Guthrie, *The Greeks*, p.38.

31 But the material necessity of the animal books does not square with that of the *Metaphysics*. This makes a problem for the more philosophically inclined commentators, a problem explored by Preus, *Science and Philosophy*. Preus also argues (p.188) that cyclical processes have some sort of simple necessity in Aristotle.

32 Aristotle also gives them the name 'nature' so that all things have a 'material nature' and a 'formal nature'. This doctrine is at its most basic in the simple mixtures and more elaborate in the case of living things. See also Joseph Owens, C. Ss. R., 'The Aristotelian argument for the

material principle of things', in *Naturphilosophie bei Aristoteles und Theophrast*, Heidelberg, 1969, pp.193–209.

33 *Historia physice* is the Greek term translated as 'natural history'; see *De Incessu Animalium*, 704b, note 5 in the Oxford translation. '*Historia Animalium*' is close to the Greek: *zoon istoriai*. See *The Works of Aristotle*, ed. J. A. Smith and W. D. Ross, Oxford, 1965, vol. V.

34 See J. Kung, 'Aristotle's "De Motu Animalium" and the separability of the sciences', *Journal of the History of Philosophy*, 20, (1982) 65–76.

35 *Meteorologica*, 338a; *De Motu Animalium*, 698a.

36 See W. Charlton, trans. and ed., *Aristotle's Physics, Books I and II*, Oxford, 1970.

37 I have not striven for consistency in using either English versions of the original Greek title of Aristotle's *libri naturales* or the Latin versions, made traditional in the West by their centuries of use in the universities.

38 *De Caelo*, 272a, 274a, 311a.

39 See the introduction by W. K. C. Guthrie to the Loeb *Aristotle*, vol. 6: *On the Heavens*, Cambridge, Mass. and London, 1986, p.xvi.

40 *De Caelo*, 284b.

41 Much Aristotle scholarship since Jaeger has been concerned to plot the growth and development of Aristotle's thought in a chronological way, and generally as a move away from the opinions of the Academy. It should be emphasised that no such attempt is made here, and that we are concerned with Aristotle's exposition, not his development.

42 *De Caelo*, 279b.

43 ibid., 294b.

44 *De Caelo*, the beginning of Book 3. The atomists also claimed that matter – atoms – was what was unchanged. On the whole topic see David Furley, *The Greek Cosmologists*, 2 vols, Cambridge, 1987; vol. 1, chs 12 and 13.

45 *De Caelo*, 310a.

46 Aristotle also asked: If the atomists said it was the void in light substances that made them light, why did the void not rise on its own without its atoms?

47 *De Caelo*, 311a.

48 ibid., 301a.

49 ibid., 276a, 279a.

50 *De Generatione et Corruptione*, 315b, 318a, 320b, 329a, 323a, 331a, 336a, 336b, 337a.

51 *Meteorologica*, 338a.

52 ibid. 339a.

53 ibid. 339a, 390a.

54 ibid. 334b.

55 ibid. 338b.

56 ibid. 339a.

57 ibid. 340a.

58 ibid. 339a.

59 ibid. 339b.

60 ibid. 338b.

61 ibid. 341b.

62 ibid. 344b.
63 ibid. 342b.
64 ibid. 347a.
65 ibid. 352b.
66 ibid. 349a.
67 See 352b.
68 Jaeger, *Fundamentals*, p.331.
69 *Meteorologica*, 352a.
70 ibid. 351b.
71 ibid. 351a.
72 ibid. 351a.
73 See also 353a.
74 ibid. 352a.
75 ibid. 253a.
76 ibid. 339b.
77 ibid. 353a.
78 ibid. 354b, 356a.
79 ibid. 362a.
80 ibid. 361a.
81 On Greek agriculture see Signe Isager and Jens Erik Skydsgaard, *Ancient Greek Agriculture. An Introduction*, London and New York, 1992, esp. ch. 11.
82 *Meteorologica*, 365a.
83 ibid. 366b.
84 ibid. 368a.
85 ibid. 369b.
86 ibid. 366b.
87 ibid. 365a.
88 ibid. 369a.
89 ibid. 369b.
90 ibid. 390a.
91 ibid. 378a.
92 ibid. 380a.
93 ibid. 381a.
94 ibid. 382a.
95 ibid. 382b.
96 ibid. 385a.
97 ibid. 385a.
98 ibid. 386a.
99 ibid. 385b.
100 ibid. 388a.
101 ibid. 385a, 389a.
102 ibid. 389b.
103 The study of Aristotle's 'development' was a field prompted by Jaeger's attempt to show that Aristotle gradually abandoned Platonic positions, and there was a tendency to see the works on animals as coming late in Aristotle's life. But it is argued by Thompson and Lee that the animal books are comparatively early. See H. D. P. Lee, 'Place names and the date of Aristotle's biological works', *Proceedings of the Cambridge*

Philological Society, 179 (1964), 7–9. Lee concludes that most of Aristotle's work was done near Mitylene. See also D. M. Balme, 'Aristotle and the beginnings of zoology', *Journal of the Society for the Bibliography of Natural History*, 5, 4 (1970), 272–283.

104 *Meteorologica*, 390b; *De Sensu et Sensato*, 436b; *De Respiratione*, 480b.

105 *De Anima*, 402a.

106 ibid. 403b, 404a.

107 That is, up to 412a.

108 For example, Anaxagoras. At 404b he discusses the elementary soul of Empedocles and Plato's *Timaeus*. He discusses the old principle of like-perceives-like and those who distinguish soul from mind. 405a: it was commonly accepted that soul must be a natural first principle (Thales, Diogenes) and immortal (Alcmaeon). 405b: Hippocrates was 'superficial' in claiming that the soul was water because semen is watery. Others like Critias say soul is blood. So, concludes Aristotle, all make the soul from their first physical principles, generally elements.

109 *De Anima*, 412a.

110 ibid. 402b.

111 ibid. 403a.

112 The position of *De Anima* in the teaching curriculum of the Lyceum is difficult to discover. The text could derive from early discussions about human rationality and physical life which largely directed the nature of his enquiries into the interesting features of animals. Or, as a principle of animal life, it might be partly informed by the analysis of what animals were. This doubt is reflected in the references to other works that Aristotle makes in *De Anima*. He seems to refer back to the *Physics* at 406a, which would locate it after the beginning of the enquiry into nature. It ends on the topic of the senses (435a) which might indicate that they were intended to follow directly. Certainly the smaller works on the faculties of the animated animal (and therefore of the soul) as a whole rather than in particular all refer back to it (*De Memoria et Reminiscentia*, 449b; *De Somniis*, 459a; *De Respiratione*, 474b; *De Sensu et Sensato*, 436a,b) and it ends (435a) on the topic of the senses, but it is not clear that Aristotle intended to go to these topics when discussing the soul. Likewise *De Motu Animalium* seems to take the existence of this treatise for granted (698a and 700b).

113 *De Anima*, 408b.

114 ibid. 406a ff.

115 ibid. 407a.

116 ibid. 406b.

117 ibid. 433b.

118 To put the question of the location of *De Anima* in the teaching of the Lyceum another way, when Aristotle came to discuss animals there is little firm evidence that he intended it to follow either the work on the soul or that on the homogeneous parts of nature (that is, up to the *Meteorologica*). But once the curriculum of the Lyceum had started on animals, there is again a great deal of cross-reference. Early in the programme must have been the texts on anatomy, or dissections (referred back to in *De Respiratione*, 478a,b). Its natural partner, the

Historia Animalium, is indeed anticipated by the text on meteorology (339a) and more substantially referred back to by the works on the generation and motion of animals (715a and 714b) and those on youth and age and on respiration (469a, 477a, 478a,b). So again the works later in the curriculum refer back to the earlier more confidently than vice versa, just as we might expect of a teacher who knew where he was going but did not know whether he could complete the course.

119 'Both studies have their attractions. Though we grasp only a little of the former, yet because the information is valuable we gain more pleasure than from anything around us just as a small and random glimpse of those we love pleases us more than seeing many other things large and in detail. But the latter, because the information about them is better and more plentiful, take the advantage in knowledge.' See the translation by D. M. Balme, *Aristotle's De Partibus Animalium I and De Generatione Animalium I*, Oxford, 1972: 644b. Aristotle would have seen animals being cut up not only by butchers, but no doubt also by those concerned with auspices. In the *Historia Animalium* 559b he mentions the unnatural and portentous eggs of a cock, and at 507a he records that it was regarded as supernatural that the liver and spleen were occasionally found transferred in position in quadrupeds.

120 Aristotle's Ionian father was a physician, and according to Barker, *Politics*, p.xi, practised dissection.

121 Diogenes Laertius lists eight books of Aristotle's *Dissections* and one book of extracts from it. See James G. Lennox, 'Divide and explain: the *Posterior Analytics* in practice', in Gotthelf and Lennox, *Philosophical Issues*, pp.90–119; p.97, note 5.

122 *Historia Animalium* (hereafter HA), 594b.

123 HA 497b.

124 HA 513a.

125 HA 511b.

126 Aristotle said that the heart in blooded animals varied from having one cavity (in the smallest) to two (in those of medium size) and three (in the largest). Thompson suggests that a traditional or mystical view had influenced Aristotle (see his notes to *Historia Animalium* 496a and 513a in the Oxford translation). Compare Ogle on *De Somno et Vigilia*, 458a (in the same series). I have offered a tentative solution in my *The History of the Heart. Thoracic Physiology from Ancient to Modern Times*, Aberdeen, 1979. See also A. Platt, 'Aristotle on the heart', in C. Singer, *Studies in the History and Method of Science*, 2 vols, Oxford, 1921, vol. 1. A general view of the subject is offered by C. R. S. Harris, *The Heart and the Vascular System in Ancient Greek Medicine*, Oxford, 1973.

127 HA 496a, 510b.

128 HA 583b.

129 *Generation of Animals* (hereafter GA), 779a.

130 HA 503b; HA 531b.

131 HA 561a; HA 565b.

132 HA 497a, HA 565a, GA 719a respectively.

133 HA 566a, HA 509b, *Parts of Animals* (hereafter PA) 689a, HA 550a, HA 525a.

134 HA 550a, HA 510a. The geometrical diagrams in the works on meteorology and memory also help the reader to visualise Aristotle's meaning.

135 PA 674b, PA 680a.

136 GA 746a.

137 PA 684b. At HA 530a Aristotle refers the reader to the text on dissections for differences between crabs, and, at HA 529b, for the structure of the limpet.

138 PA 650a.

139 PA 666a.

140 *Parva Naturalia* 456b, 474b, 478b (dissection to reveal relation of heart and gills in fish).

141 GA 740a. PA 668b also refers to the *Treatise on Dissections* for the relations of the major vessels.

142 PA 666a.

143 GA 740a.

144 HA 538b and 545a.

145 HA 547b 16 and 28.

146 HA 518b and 519a.

147 HA 603b, referring to the rest of Book VIII.

148 HA 608b.

149 HA 534b, 620b.

150 HA 627b.

151 HA 499a.

152 HA 489a.

153 HA 491a.

154 HA 489a.

155 HA 490a.

156 HA 609a.

157 HA 609b.

158 HA 608b.

159 HA 612a.

160 PA 663a.

161 HA 608b.

162 See Thompson's note to HA 609a in the Oxford translation.

163 HA 609b.

164 HA 610b.

165 HA 609b.

166 HA 588a.

167 HA 610b.

168 HA 611a.

169 HA 611a.

170 HA 612a.

171 HA 612a.

172 HA 612b.

173 HA 616b.

174 See Thompson's note at the beginning of Book 9. Physiognomy was a search for the expression of traits of soul as the nature-of-the-person.

175 591b. See Thompson's note at HA 591b and at PA 696b; at HA 492a Aristotle knows the dolphin well enough to frame the generalisation that it was the only viviparous mammal to lack ears.

176 D. M. Balme, 'Aristotle's biology was not essentialist', in Gotthelf and Lennox, *Philosophical Issues*, pp.291–312; 299.

177 HA 597a.

178 HA 597a and 598a.

179 HA 605b.

180 HA 606a.

181 HA 606b. Thompson suggests that a jerboa is meant.

182 PA 639a.

183 PA 639a–b.

184 PA 642a.

185 This link between the *Physics* (220a) and the *Parts of Animals* (639b) leads Lee, 'Place names', to argue that the two works were written close together in time.

186 PA 640a.

187 PA 640a.

188 PA 640b.

189 Much of the discussion about Aristotles 'zoology' has centred on what he meant by terms like *eidos* and *genos*. The discussion has been informed by the modern taxonomic scheme in which smaller groups are clustered into larger, like species into genera. This has obvious attractions for those concerned with Aristotle's dialectic, but to the present account, relying on the individuality of the natures, discussion of hierarchies and subdivision is not Aristotelian. For a sophisticated analysis, see Lloyd, *Methods and Problems*, pp.372–397: 'Aristotle's zoology and his metaphysics: the status questions. A critical review of some recent theories'.

190 It seems more likely that a subclass 'four-footed' was subdivided in this way.

191 PA 642b.

192 PA 643b.

193 PA 669a.

194 PA 697b.

195 PA 697b.

196 PA 689b.

197 See Preus (1975) p.204; G. E. R. Lloyd, 'The development of Aristotle's theory of the classification of animals', in his *Methods and Problems in Greek Science*, Cambridge, 1991, and more especially his *Science, Folklore and Ideology. Studies in the Life Sciences in Ancient Greece*, Cambridge, 1983, p.44.

198 Cf. 657a.

199 See Aristotle's discussion at the beginning of Book 1.

200 PA 695b.

201 PA 657a.

202 PA 660b.

203 PA 686b.
204 GA 731b.
205 GA 732b.
206 GA 718b, 733b. Aristotle ignores the amphibia.
207 GA 732a, 758b.
208 GA 759a. Aristotle is not always clear whether the *scolex* always grows up to be an adult, especially where it is the product of spontaneously generated adults (see 721a and compare Book 3). Aristotle says these insects arise from putrefying matter: fleas, flies and cantharides. Gnats do not arise from other gnats nor do they copulate. Of those that do copulate Aristotle says that observations are not complete enough to make distinction into classes possible. He is clearly at the limit of his information (and he says it is not known whether insects emit semen) and does not want to promote any great scheme. At 758b he says that all insects produce a *scolex* and those that are spontaneously generated also appear first as a *scolex*.
209 GA 718b.
210 For example at GA 718b.
211 GA 770b.
212 See also the discussion by Preus, *Science and Philosophy*, pp.200–206.
213 GA 770a.
214 PA 644b.
215 PA 645a.
216 PA 645a.
217 PA 646a.
218 GA 722b.
219 Only recently has interest been given again to Aristotle's works on animals. Morsink observes that the only full-length commentary on Aristotle's *Generation of Animals* is that of Michael of Ephesus in the sixth century. But most of the modern interest is from philosophers and there has been little direct historical work. See Johannes Morsink, *Aristotle on the Generation of Animals. A Philosophical Study*, Washington, 1982.
220 GA 731b.
221 Moreover, if they did not resemble the parts from which they had come, there could be no objection to saying that in fact they came from a single part of the body, as Aristotle believed.
222 GA 723a.
223 GA 723b.
224 GA 723b.
225 PA 681a and see HA 588b.
226 GA 715a.
227 GA 715a.
228 GA 715b. Yet at 732b Aristotle does allow that some insects can arise spontaneously and yet have sexual differentiation and the ability to mate and produce a *scolex*.
229 On spontaneous generation see James Lennox, 'Teleology, chance and Aristotle's theory of spontaneous generation', *Journal of the History*

of Philosophy, *XX*, 3 (1982), 219–238, who is worried about what happened to the final cause, but does not give a final answer.

230 It should be added that Aristotle often expresses a belief that matter is only matter *of something*. This means that the material nature is wholly subordinated to the formal nature.

231 HA 546b.

232 HA 547b.

233 HA 547b.

234 HA 548a.

235 HA 548a.

236 HA 551a.

237 HA 762b.

238 We can recall that the use of air was the ultimate difference between the animals on Aristotle's scale of nature.

239 GA 760b.

240 HA 760a.

241 GA 761b.

242 GA 760a.

243 The topic of the identity of 'bee' – beehood – had been raised in the Academy and is expressed in Plato's *Meno* in a dialectical way. Socrates says to Meno 'If I asked you what a bee really is, and you answered that there are many kinds of bees, what would you answer me if I asked you then: "Do you say there are many kinds of bees, differing from each other in being bees more or less? Or do they differ in some other respect, for example in size, beauty and so forth?"' Quoted by Atran (1993) p.81. Aristotle's originality lay in calling for more empirical knowledge to solve a recognised problem.

244 GA 766a.

245 GA 736a.

246 GA 736b.

247 GA 741a.

248 GA 736b.

249 GA 740a.

250 GA 735a.

251 GA 741a.

252 GA 764a.

253 See also GA 769a.

254 GA 767b.

255 Aristotle thinks of the mother and father as opposites and that the process of development must go to one or the other. So characteristics of the father, although not essentially male in themselves, will be naturally found in his sons. But maleness can be separated from the individual, so that a boy will resemble his mother.

256 GA 741b.

257 GA 743b.

258 Aristotle believed the brain occupied only the front part of the skull.

259 PA 677b.

260 PA 678a.

261 PA 679a.

262 PA 672a–b, 658b.
263 GA 740a.
264 GA 744b.
265 GA 744b.
266 GA 744b.
267 PA 650b.
268 PA 650b, 651b.
269 PA 655a.
270 PA 658a.
271 PA 685b.
272 PA 659a.
273 PA 659a.
274 PA 662a, 660a, 661b respectively.
275 PA 693a.
276 PA 687a.
277 PA 661b. No animal with sharp interlocking teeth has tusks, because the former are defensive and that is all it needs.
278 PA 663a.
279 PA 663b.
280 This could be supported from the case of birds, in the generation of which earthy matter can flow up to the beak, or down to the feet for talons and spurs, but never both together. (This is necessary in a rather material way, but also intended for the animal's advantage.) See PA 694b. The doe does not have horns, yet still has no top front teeth. Aristotle says the reason is that deer are naturally horned animals but that the doe nevertheless does not have them because they are disadvantageous. The male does have them because he is strong enough to carry them.
281 GA 778a.
282 GA 778b.
283 GA 715a.
284 GA 779b.
285 GA 684a.
286 GA 716a. Males and females are essentially different, with a *logos* that Platt says is the definition and final cause. The different organs simply express this.
287 GA 715a–b.
288 *De Motu Animalium* (DMA) 701a.
289 DMA 698a.
290 DMA 699a–b.
291 DMA 702b.
292 DMA 700b.
293 DMA 703a.
294 But it does not use the nerves, of which Aristotle was ignorant, or the muscles, which he did not see as sources of motion.
295 Compare PA 674a, where Aristotle refers forward to the works on generation and nutrition as anticipating the purpose of the parts he is presently describing.
296 Most modern editions follow Bekker.

297 At PA 690b and 692b Aristotle refers back to *De Incessu Animalium* as prior to PA in sequence of exposition; and at 689b the intended sequence is also clear: HA and *Dissections*, PA, GA. See also PA 692b, 695a.

298 *De Incessu Animalium* 704b.

299 ibid., 705a.

300 PA 665a. See also Lloyd, *Methods and Problems*, pp.27–48, 'Right and left in Greek philosophy'.

301 *De Incessu Animalium* 707a.

302 PA 652b, 656a.

303 PA 655b; cf. 647a.

304 PA 681b.

305 PA 684b. Compare *De Incessu Animalium* 703b, where Aristotle has a diagram relating to motions about a centre.

306 GA 758a.

307 GA 743a. Aristotle refers to diagrams of the blood vessels hung on the walls.

GA 750b. *Historia Animalium* is often used as a reference text, where more information is to be had. So it is not simply programmatically prior but is to be used in conjunction with GA. At 753b Aristotle refers back to HA for more details, but they are not there. Perhaps drawings were meant: the vascular arrangements of the foetus, and its membranes. At 761a Aristotle says that differences between wasps, hornets and bees are to be found mainly in HA and its drawings. At 763b the reader is referred to HA for the insides of ascidians.

308 GA 736b.

309 See L. P. Gerson, *God and Greek Philosophy. Studies in the Early History of Natural Theology*, London, 1990, ch. 3, p.82.

310 Much to the exasperation of modern philosophical commentators, for whom it is a problem. See Gerson, *God and Greek Philosophy*, p. 119.

311 *De Caelo* 283b (Book 2).

312 *De Caelo* 294a.

2 THEOPHRASTUS, PLANTS AND ELEPHANTS

1 Details of his life are largely drawn from Diogenes Laertius. See *Theophrastus of Eresus. Sources for his Life, Writings, Thought and Influence*, ed. and trans. W. W. Fortenbaugh, P. M. Huby, R. W. Sharples and D. Gutas, 2 vols, Leiden, New York, Cologne, 1992.

2 It is circumstances of this kind that make the philosophies of men like this a Greek enterprise. It would be easy to imagine societies in which the Republic would be a subversive text.

3 On the question of intellectual freedom, see K. J. Dover, 'The freedom of the intellectual in Greek society', *Talanta*, 7 (1975), 24–54. Broadly the Athenians expected pupils to be like their teachers; the difficulty was that some parts of philosophy encouraged variety rather than conformity. Often, too, 'intellectual' teachers were foreign and hence with suspect loyalty and accountability. The Athenians were sensitive to

atttacks on their Eleusinian mysteries and most condemnations were for impiety.

4 Theophrastus like other peripatetics was interested in history and politics. See W. W. Fortenbaugh, *Theophrastus of Eresus. On his Life and Work*, New Brunswick/Oxford, 1985 (Rutgers University Studies in Classical Humanities, vol. 2): A. J. Podlecki, 'Theophrastus on history and politics', pp.231–249. The Peripatetics continued to take an interest in empirical history. For example Dicaearchus of Messene dealt with myth, prehistory and early history of Egypt, and the constitution of Sparta. Demetrius of Phaleron was Theophrastus' pupil and wrote on constitution of Athens, laws and politics. Theophrastus' works were listed by Diogenes and include an *On Kingship*, and others that relate directly to laws, politics, legislators, history, constitutions and ethics. Diogenes gives a very long list of titles and estimated that Theophrastus wrote over 100,000 lines.

5 *Parts of Animals* (hereafter PA), 653a refers to a future treatise on the principles of disease. PA 650b shows that Aristotle wrote or intended to write a separate treatise on nutrition, which is also referred to in the future in *De Anima* 416b.

6 PA 676a refers to a piece in the *Problems* on the formation of rennet in many-stomached animals, but it is not in our collection. *De Juventute et Senectute* 470a (control of a fire by banking) refers back to *Problems*, but the topic is not in our version. *Generation of Animals* 747b (the mixture of bronze and tin) refers to a topic in Aristotle's *Problems* but which is not in our version. (*De Somno et Vigilia* 456a also refers to the *Problems*.)

7 PA 653a.

8 PA 679b.

9 *Meteorologica* 341a.

10 *Generation of Animals* 753b.

11 See Platt's fourth note to *Generation of Animals* 753b in the Oxford translation.

12 *Generation of Animals* 757b.

13 *Meteorologica*, 361; note also *Meteorologica* 343a where Aristotle refutes a notion (about comets) as though it had previously been listed for refutation; it had not.

14 *Meteorologica* 339a.

15 *Generation of Animals* 726a. There is another paragraph of this kind, certainly somewhat strange, at 726b (on seminal fluids and stucco).

16 A. Laks, G. W. Most and E. Rudolph, 'Four notes on Theophrastus' metaphysics', in W. Fortenbaugh and R. W. Sharples (eds), *Theophrastean Studies on Natural Science, Physics and Metaphysics, Ethics, Religion and Rhetoric*, New Brunswick and Oxford, 1988, pp.224–256.

17 Theophrastus calls his questions 'beginnings', and calls for more work in the metaphysics, both of which might suggest that it had an early place in his writings.

18 Fortenbaugh *et al.*, *Theophrastus*, p.21; Theophrastus implies that the habit of making revisions was coming to an end.

19 As suggested by the editors of the Loeb edition: Benedict Einarson and George K. K. Link (trans.) *Theophrastus de Causis Plantarum*, 3 vols, London and Cambridge, Mass., 1976; vol. 1, p.xi.

20 Theophrastus took over the Lyceum when Aristotle died in 322, and since his pupil Demetrius of Phalerum (under Cassander) was in control of Athens, Theophrastus was allowed to buy property for the school.

21 Theophrastus as the pupil of Aristotle continued to work on similar topics. Both wrote on kingship, politics and laws. Theophrastus' *Nomoi* is extant: it is comparative treatment of laws with a philosophical look at the theory behind them and was intended to be of use to prospective legislators.

22 PA 689a; *History of Animals* (hereafter HA) 489a.

23 *Generation of Animals* 727a.

24 PA 676b.

25 At PA 664b only the description is given (again).

26 On causality and motion see also Joseph B. Skemp, 'The *Metaphysics* of Theophrastus in relation to the doctrine of κίνησις in Plato's later dialogues', in *Naturphilosophie bei Aristoteles und Theophrast*, Heidelberg, 1969, pp.217–223.

27 See John Vallance's 'Theophrastus and the study of the intractable: scientific method in *de lapidibus* and *de igne*', in Fortenbaugh and Sharples, *Theophrastean Studies*, pp.25–40.

28 Vallance (ibid.) argues that in not looking for Aristotle's causes, Theophrastus was in effect opening up fields like mineralogy, where empirical description looks more appropriate than theories of causes.

29 V. Coutant (ed. and trans.), *Theophrastus De Igne. A Post-Aristotelian View of the Nature of Fire*, Assen, 1971.

30 V. Coutant and V. Eichenlaub (eds and trans.), *Theophrastus de ventibus*, Notre Dame, Ind., 1975.

31 *De Ventibus* xl.

32 ibid. x.

33 ibid. xi.

34 Perhaps large harbour towns had manuals of navigation with wind-lore, and one scholar thinks there was a weather station near Troy. Greece entered a cool wet period about 500 BC, warmed up again about 100 BC. But the climate in Theophrastus' time was not greatly different from now and his wind-lore is in line with modern observations. It suggests collected observations over a substantial number of years. But foreign winds are badly described. *De Ventibus* xviii, xxiv, xxxiv.

35 Antiperistasis was an explanation of projectile motion in which air displaced by the moving object was said to move to its rear and contribute to its forward motion. *Horror vacui* was nature's attempt to prevent the formation of a vacuum (which Aristotle said could not exist).

36 *De Sensu et Sensato*, 441a.

37 See note 3 to 441a in the Oxford translation.

38 But it is sometimes regarded as a separate work. See G. Wöhrle, 'The structure and function of Theophrastus' treatise *de odoribus*' 3–13 in Fortenbaugh and Sharples, *Theophrastean Studies*, esp. p.5 where it is

clear that there is little final causality; but Wöhrle does not want to allow this as a conscious rejection of Aristotelian teleology.

39 George Malcom Stratton, *Theophrastus and the Greek Physiological Psychology before Aristotle*, Amsterdam, 1964.

40 e.g. *Causes of Plants* (hereafter CP) VI. 3.4.

41 *De Lapidibus* was written in or shortly after 315–314 BC: D. E. Eichholz (trans. and ed.), *Theophrastus De Lapidibus*, Oxford, 1965, p.1 (i.e. seven or eight years after Aristotle died).

42 See Eichholz, *Theophrastus*, p.5.

43 Sir Arthur Hort (ed. and trans.), *Theophrastus. Enquiry into Plants and Minor Works on Odours and Weather Signs*, 2 vols, Cambridge, Mass. and London (Loeb), 1990 and 1980, Introduction, p.xxiii.

44 *De Lapidibus* p.6.

45 *De Lapidibus* p.79.

46 e.g. *History of Plants* (hereafter HP), 1.2.3; A. Gotthelf, 'Historiae I: plantarum et animalium', in Fortenbaugh and Sharples, *Theophrastean Studies*, pp.100–135; 124.

47 HP 5 3.1.

48 HP, Introduction, p.xxv. In contrast Theophrastus' *Characters* is a highly polished piece of writing.

49 HP xxiii.

50 See the beginning of HP Book 1.

51 HP I. 1.4.

52 HP I. 1.11.

53 HP I. 1.11.

54 HP I.1.6.

55 For example HP I. 9.3 to I. 10.9.

56 See esp. HP I.10.6.

57 HP III.5.6: Theophrastus' mode of presentation here is to choose topics – speed of growth, length of roots, seasons of budding – and to illustrate them with a few examples.

58 See also the editor of the Loeb text: Sir Arthur Hort, *Theophrastus. Enquiry into Plants*.

59 As Gotthelf says (*Historiae I: plantarum et animalium*), it is about generation.

60 CP II. 11.7.

61 See Part 2 of Theophrastus' text on the senses: Stratton, *Theophrastus and the Greek Physiological Psychology*, p.119.

62 ibid. p.111.

63 CP I. 16.3, I. 19.5.

64 See also CP I. 21.2.

65 CP I. 3.2.

66 CP I. 9.1.

67 CP I. 9.2; I. 18.4.

68 CP I. 15.3; I. 18.4.

69 CP I. 16.1.

70 CP I. 16.1.

71 CP I. 16.13.

72 CP III. 1.2. In connection with this the Loeb editors see, where others perhaps might not, a material efficient and final cause.
73 CP II. 15.5.
74 See esp. CP III. 2.1.
75 CP II. 16. 2; CP V. 3.6.
76 See the beginning of Book 4 of *Causes of Plants*.
77 CP V. 7.2.
78 CP II.11.2.
79 CP V. 3.6.
80 HP II.3.3. Here too Theophrastus reports without scepticism on the change from bergamot mint to mint, and wheat to darnel.
81 CP V. 7.1.
82 CP II. 16.6.
83 CP III. 7.7.
84 CP III. 8.4.
85 CP IV. 11.5.
86 CP II. 13.5.
87 See also CP III. 10.8.
88 CP II. 18.1.
89 CP II. 18.4.
90 CP II. 18.2.
91 CP II. 17.9: HA 547b.
92 CP II. 18.1.
93 In our version of HA, 553a, 759a, 564a.
94 CP I. 20.2.
95 M. van Raalte, 'The idea of the cosmos as an organic whole in Theophrastus' metaphysics', in W. Fortenbaugh and R. W. Sharples (eds), *Theophrastean Studies on Natural Science, Physics and Metaphysics, Ethics, Religion and Rhetoric*, New Brunswick and Oxford, 1988, pp.189–215, 193.
96 Vallance, '*Theophrastus and the study of the intractable*'.
97 Raalte, 'Idea of the cosmos', pp.195–196.
98 See Vallance, op. cit.
99 The suggestion is Vallance's (p.31).
100 Pliny, *Natural History* II. 75.
101 Pliny, *Natural History* VI. 21. Other vast distances, particularly between towns, including the new ones founded by Alexander, were listed by Baeton and Diognetus, his surveyors.
102 ibid. VI. 26.
103 Strabo, XVI.4.10.
104 *Natural History* VIII. 17: translation modified from Rackham. Another form of the story is given by Barker (p.xviii): he asserts that Alexander gave 800 talents from his oriental victories for Aristotle's researches and that Callisthenes (the historian and philosopher who went with Alexander) sent specimens back for Aristotle. H. Rackam (trans.), *Pliny. Natural History*, Cambridge, Mass. and London (Loeb), 10 vols, 1967–1971; E. Barker, *The Politics of Aristotle*, Oxford, 1958.
105 But Jaeger insists that the information in the *Historia Animalium* 'presupposes' the experiences of the march into India. See Chapter 1,

above. Werner Jaeger, *Aristotle. Fundamentals of the History of his Development*, trans. Richard Robinson, 2nd edn, Oxford, 1962.

106 The work known in the Latin tradition as *De Mundo*, 'On the World', attributed to Aristotle, is an invention of this kind and is addressed to Alexander. It belongs to the late Hellenistic world of summaries, introductions and handbooks which flourished in particular in the early Roman Empire. It is not a peripatetic examination of causes, or a Stoic or Epicurean search for *ataraxia*, but a theologising description of the natural world, especially its meteorology, with a view to explaining the remoteness and impassivity of God. Aristotle, *On Sophistical Refutations, On Coming-to-be and Passing-away, On the Cosmos*, the latter trans. D. J. Furley, Harvard and London (Loeb), 1955, p.330. The accounts of the rainbow and lightning are probably derived from Posidonius and were the common property of Stoics. See Seneca in Chapter 4, below.

107 HA 596a.

108 On elephants in antiquity and the question of small North African elephants, see H. H. Scullard, *The Elephant in the Greek and Roman World*, London, 1974.

109 HA 630b; 488a.

110 HA 571b.

111 HA 610a.

112 HA 605a.

113 HA 506b, 507a.

114 HA 501b. Aristotle says that the tusks of female elephants point down.

115 HA 500b, 509b, 497b, 517a.

116 HA 546b, 540a.

117 HA 630b.

118 HA 540a.

119 PA 658b. It is notable that in HA the elephant is said not to be a river-animal, while in PA Aristotle bases his reasoned account of the animal on the fact that it is.

120 PA 659a.

121 PA 663a.

122 *Generation of Animals* 777b.

123 PA 688b.

124 HA 630b.

125 HA 596a.

126 HA 571b.

127 HA 540a.

128 HA 578a.

129 HA 546b.

130 HA 604a.

131 HA 499a.

132 Jaeger, *Aristotle. Fundamentals*, p.330.

133 It has been suggested that the Egyptian Atum, the all-containing one and the world-mound arising from water, was suggested by mounds revealed as the flooded Nile receded. See R. T. Rundle Clark, *Myth and Symbol in Ancient Egypt*, London, 1959, p.38.

134 Pliny, *Natural History* V.10.
135 V. Rose (ed.), *Aristoteles Pseudoepigraphus*, Leipzig, 1863; *De Inundationi Nili* is pp.633–643. This text was used by the thirteenth-century teachers of the new university in teaching the whole range of Aristotle natural books. Jaeger (*Fundamentals*, p.331) thinks that the work is genuinely Aristotelian, and Clagett thinks that the extant work is a fragment of a bigger Aristotelian text. Marshall Clagget, *Greek Science in Antiquity*, London, 1957, p.47.
136 There are other texts besides that on the flooding of the Nile that were attributed to Aristotle, perhaps in Alexandria. That on physiognomy is taken as a development of Aristotle's doctrine that the body is an expression of the soul. This tract also begins with a list of earlier opinions for refutation; and is little more than a list of what signs of the body lead to knowledge of the soul, character or 'nature' of the animal or man. It is included in the sixth volume of the Oxford translation: Sir David Ross (ed.), *The Works of Aristotle*, vol. 6, (*Opuscula*), Oxford, 1967. The text on colours is based on the four elements that Aristotle and others recognised. The pure colours of the elements are said to be changed by mixture, combustion and dissolution. (*De Coloribus* is included in the *Opuscula*.) In a not dissimilar way the text *On Indivisible Lines* is based on Aristotle's discussion of the 'similar' parts and their indefinite divisibility. Do all parts have parts? Would one ultimately reach the Indivisible, the atom? (*De Lineis Insecabilibus* is also included in the *Opuscula*.)
137 They were included in the 'new corpus' of Aristotelian *libri naturales* that was in use from perhaps the 1270s in the universities.
138 This is how the scholastics saw it: see Bartholomew of Bruges in Rose, *Aristoteles Pseudoepigraphus*, pp.640–643.
139 Arrian, *The Campaigns of Alexander*, trans. A. de Sélincourt (introduction and notes by J. R. Hamilton), London, 1971, pp.301–302. The Roman expedition of Nero (or Seneca) to find the source of the Nile was also made possible by imperial power. See Chapter 4 below.
140 The two stories are suspiciously close and perhaps the earlier has been borrowed to fit Alexander. That the *Inundation of the Nile* does not attribute the story to Alexander perhaps argues for an Aristotelian date of composition.
141 See Chapter 4 below; also Pliny, *Natural History* V. 10.

3 GEOGRAPHY AND NATURAL HISTORY

1 This series of anatomical drawings are known to historians of medicine as the 'five-figure series'.
2 See O. A. W. Dilke, *Greek and Roman Maps*, London, 1985. There are a few medieval maps of the world, like that in Hereford Cathedral. They are based on ancient sources, however, and that in Hereford contains in visual form many of the stories from natural history that appear in the present volume.

3 Strabo refers to it at the beginning of Book II. Anaximander is said to have made the first map: Strabo I.1.11.

4 Strabo V.2.7.

5 Dilke, *Greek and Roman Maps*, pp.41, 65.

6 Characteristically, Greek estimates of the size of the earth and the extent of continents were made mathematically on astronomical observations; the Romans simply added up the number of miles on the milestone on imperial routes.

7 Strabo II.5.10.

8 ibid. II.5.16.

9 Crates of Mallos may have been the source of Strabo's assertion that a globe should be 10 feet in diameter, for he said the same and was one of Strabo's preferred authors. Dilke, *Greek and Roman Maps*, p.36.

10 Werner Jaeger, *Aristotle. Fundamentals of the History of his Development*, Oxford, 1962, p.335.

11 Strabo XIII.1.54.

12 See Luciano Canfora, *The Vanished Library*, London, 1991, p.28.

13 Strabo XIII.1.54.

14 Strabo XIV.1.37. See also XIII.1.54. Strabo reports for example that Smyrna had a library and a Homerium, a quadrangular portico with a wooden statue to Homer and a shrine to the basic element of Greek education.

15 Strabo XIII.1.54.

16 At *Natural History* XIII.1.34 it is Attalus I who is Pliny's authority (on a particularly big pine tree). Pliny's *Attalus rex* should not be confused with the Stoic Attalus, who taught Seneca and made a special study of practices of divination from lightning.

17 See W. H. Stahl, *Roman Science. Origins, Development and Influence to the later Middle Ages*, Madison, 1962, p.42.

18 Pliny, *Natural History* V. 1. Pliny quotes him here on the euphorbia growing on Mt Atlas. The Athenians made a statue of Juba and the Aethiopians thought he was a god.

19 Pliny, *Natural History* VI. 24.

20 On the library at Alexandria and its fate see Canfora, *Vanished Library*.

21 ibid. p.20.

22 Strabo XVII.1.8.

23 ibid. VI.1.2.

24 M. van Raalte, 'The idea of the cosmos as an organic whole in Theophrastus' metaphysics', in W. Fortenbaugh and R. W. Sharples (eds), *Theophrastean Studies on Natural Science, Physics and Metaphysics, Ethics, Religion and Rhetoric*, New Brunswick and Oxford, 1988, pp.189–215; 206.

25 Many of Strabo's sources, for example Eratosthenes, I.3.3, had pointed out that much more information had become available after Alexander's campaigns. The first great Parthian monarch was Mithradates I in the second century BC, and in the first century BC the Romans, having replaced the Seleucids, came up against the Parthians with indifferent success.

26 This 'expanded world' was a west–east swathe of Europe and Asia from

Britain to the Indus. It was bounded to the south by desert and did not extend north of the Black and Caspian Seas, where the winter temperatures were extreme. The northern limit of the Roman Empire was in fact quite close to the northern limit of beechwoods. Neither could stand lakes and coastal seas that froze in the winter.

27 H. L. Jones and J. R. S. Sterrett, *The Geography of Strabo*, 8 vols, Cambridge, Mass. (Loeb), 1917–1932, vol. 1 (reprinted 1989), Introduction, p. xviii. At II.3.8 Strabo says that Poseidonius imitates Aristotle's search for causes too much, just what Strabo's 'school', the Stoics, avoids.

28 Strabo XVII.1.36.

29 ibid. I.3.4. Shells of oysters, scallops and mussels, together with salt marshes and jets of salt water (together with fragments of ships) were to be found in the neighbourhood of the Temple of Ammon.

30 Strabo here follows Eratosthenes and Strato: I.3.4.

31 Strabo I.3.5.

32 ibid. I.2.8 and cf. X.3.23.

33 ibid. II.5.2.

34 P. W. Wallace, *Strabo's Description of Boiotia. A Commentary*, Heidelberg, 1979, p.2.

35 See also Germaine Aujac, *Strabon et la science de son temps*, Paris, 1966, p.16.

36 H. E. Tozer, *Selections from Strabo*, Oxford, 1893, p.28.

37 Strabo I.1.11.

38 We saw in Chapter 1 above that Aristotle, even when arguing for the philosophical certainty gained from dissection, praised the dignity of knowledge of the stars. Traditionally, too, the heavens were the abode of the gods and 'divine' in another way, as Strabo implies in his definition of philosophy.

39 Strabo I.1.15; see also I.1.1–3.

40 Posidonius had a reputation in the Roman world equal to that of Aristotle in the Greek. He was very important in the development of Stoicism. But because very little of his work survives, we cannot safely reconstruct what his enterprise was, and he can only be mentioned in passing.

41 See also the introduction to Jones and Sterret, *Geography of Strabo*, vol. 1, pp.xxv, xxix.

42 Strabo I.1.14.

43 ibid. I.1.21.

44 ibid. I.1.18.

45 ibid. I.1.17.

46 ibid. I.1.15–17.

47 ibid. II.5.17.

48 The point is made by Lloyd that Plato's purposes in the Academy included producing 'statesmen-philosophers, men who could and would influence the course of events in their cities and in the Greek world at large'. G. E. R. Lloyd, 'The social background of early Greek philosophy and science', in his *Methods and Problems in Greek Science*, Cambridge, 1991, pp.121–140; 138.

49 Strabo I.1.15.
50 ibid. XVI.1.6.
51 Strabo XVII.1.3; XVII.1.5. Again, at XVII.1.46 the priests of Thebes are said to have been philosophers and astronomers, and this is why the people calculate the year by the sun rather than the moon, as above. All such wisdom they say is derived from Hermes: contrast the insistence by the Greek philosophers that the arts are human inventions.
52 Strabo XVII.1.28.
53 They are said to have learned a little of the heaven-lore of astronomy, in particular how to calculate fractions for the leap year. They had 12 months each of 30 days, and added 5 days at the end of the year and another day every 4 years. The process of learning astronomy from the Egyptians was still going on in Strabo's day, the Greeks having been ignorant of so much, he says.
54 Strabo IV.4.4.
55 ibid. XI.9.3.
56 See Chapter 5, below. The three oriental kings or wise men of the Christian story are traditionally Magi, guided by astrological principles, and the story reflects Western perceptions of the comparatively new Parthian power.
57 Strabo XV.1.39.
58 Strabo XV.1.68, where the Indian 'philosophers' are compared to the Magi in Persia in giving advice to the kings.
59 Strabo XV.1.58. The view arose from Megasthenes, and although Strabo has some reservations about it, it is only that the vine, as an indication of Dionysian practices, was not unique to the mountains, where the Dionysian philosophers were said to reside.
60 Strabo XV.1.59.
61 ibid. XV.1.63.
62 ibid. XV.1.66.
63 Calanus accompanied Alexander for some time and finally demonstrated his self-control by burning himself to death on a pyre.
64 Strabo I.2.15.
65 ibid. I.4.9.
66 ibid. VII.3.5; VII.3.11.
67 ibid. XIV.5.4.
68 ibid. X.3.7.
69 ibid. X.3.9.
70 ibid. X.3.10.
71 ibid. X.3.20.
72 ibid. X.3.32.
73 See the Introduction, p.xxv, of the first volume of the Loeb translation. The argument goes back beyond Tozer, *Selections from Strabo*, p.28, who is surely right to conclude that it must be Romans to whom Strabo is addressing such a practical book.
74 Stahl, *Roman Science*, p.47.
75 Strabo III.4.19.
76 On Roman views of the Greeks see also A. Wardman, *Rome's Debt to Greece*, London, 1976. The main Roman complaints about the Greeks

related to their idleness, duplicity, impractical behaviour and *levitas*, 'fickleness': see p.7. To this list N. Petrochilos, *Roman Attitudes to the Greeks*, Athens, 1974, adds the Greeks' apparent lack of masculinity and love of luxury.

77   Strabo V.3.8.
78   ibid. V.3.2–3.
79   ibid. V.3.7.
80   ibid. V.4.4 and V.4.7.
81   ibid. VI.1.2.
82   ibid. VI.1.12.
83   ibid. I.2.1.
84   ibid. VI.4.8.
85   ibid. VI.4.1.
86   ibid. XVII.3.25.
87   ibid. I.2.3.
88   ibid. I.2.22.
89   ibid. I.2.22.
90   ibid. I.2.29.
91   ibid. I.2.13.
92   ibid. I.2.21.
93   I.1.8. Strabo is largely basing his opinion on Homer. See also II.2.5, where Strabo says the length of the habitable world is about 70,000 stadia and its north–south latitude about 30,000.
94   Strabo I.1.20.
95   ibid. I.1.23.
96   ibid. II.5.14.
97   ibid. I.4.1.
98   ibid. II.5.8.
99   ibid. IV.5.2.
100 ibid. III.4.18. The Greek word for the animal is *mus* which can mean either mouse or rat.
101 ibid. I.2.1.
102 ibid. I.3.21.
103 On Roman views of barbarians, see A. N. Sherwin-White, *Racial Prejudice in Imperial Rome*, Cambridge, 1967, which deals first with Strabo and the northern barbarians.
104 Strabo I.3.16–18.
105 ibid. I.3.20.
106 ibid. XV.1.56. Megasthenes also reported on other men with their feet facing back to front and others with dogs' heads or a single eye.
107 ibid. IV.5.4.
108 ibid. II.1.9.
109 ibid. II.1.6.
110 ibid. II.5.12.
111 ibid. III.3.8.
112 ibid. III.4.16.
113 The olive in particular needs warm weather and was found only in the southern portions of the west–east Roman-Hellenistic empire.
114 Strabo XI.10.1. See also II.1.14.

115   ibid. XVII.3.4.
116   ibid. IV.5.2.
117   ibid. XII.3.18.
118   ibid. VII.5.7.
119   ibid. III.4.16.
120   ibid. III.4.18.
121   ibid. XI.5.3.
122   ibid. XI.5.1.
123   ibid. XIII.1.25.
124   ibid. VI.1.6.
125   ibid. VI.2.9.
126   ibid. V.4.8.
127   See also Strabo VI.2.3 and XIII.4.11.
128   ibid. VI. 1.13.
129   ibid. XIII.4.14.
130   ibid. XV.1.23. Strabo attributes to Aristotle the notion that the water of the Nile requires less heat to make it boil.
131   ibid. XV.1.25.
132   ibid. XVII.1.38.
133   The story is also found in Aristotle, *Historia Animalium* 612a and in Pliny, Plutarch, Nicander, Aelian, Antigonus and Strabo.
134   Strabo XVII.1.44.
135   ibid. III.2.8.
136   ibid. XV.1.30.
137   ibid. XV.1.44.
138   ibid. XI.2.19.
139   ibid. XVII.3.11.
140   ibid. XI.11.5.
141   ibid. III.5.11.
142   See item 93, where copper mines are said to have been refilled with iron.
143   Strabo V.2.6, VII.5.8.
144   ibid. XV.1.9. Nevertheless, at XI.11.1 Strabo makes strong claims about the influence of the Greeks in India before Alexander and about their general military prowess.
145   Strabo XI.1.2.
146   ibid. XV.2.13.
147   ibid. XV.1.20.
148   ibid. XV.1.21. Compare Theophrastus. It is said to have been a banyan tree.
149   ibid. XV.1.28.
150   ibid. XV.1.24.
151   ibid. XV.1.18.
152   ibid. XI.7.3.
153   ibid. XV.1. 28.
154   ibid. XV.1.13.
155   ibid. XV.1.20.
156   Perhaps it was sugar cane, too, that was sent home to his wife by Bogus, king of the Mauritanians, in North Africa. He was warring against the Western Ethiopians and Strabo claims – we might call it a bogus story

- that the 'reed' contained a gallon and a half of liquid between each joint; Bogus is also said to have also sent asparagus of the same size.

157 Strabo XVII.3.4.
158 ibid. XVII.2.5. The fact that the dolphin is an air-breathing 'fish', important for Aristotle, had little bearing on the purposes of Strabo's geography. See also XVII.2.4, where the modern reader has to be satisfied with transliterations from the Greek for the names of fish indigenous to the Nile.
159 ibid. XV.1.45.
160 ibid. XV.1.37.
161 ibid. XVII.2.1.
162 ibid. XVII.1.5.
163 ibid. I.1.20.
164 The text attributed to Aristotle was included in the natural philosophy of the early universities.
165 Strabo XVII.3.4.
166 ibid. XVII.3.4.
167 ibid. XVI.2.35–36.
168 ibid. XVI.2.37.

4 GREECE AND ROME

1 W. H. Stahl, *Roman Science. Origins, Development, and Influence to the Later Middle Ages*, Madison, 1962, p.45.
2 For Epicurus in general see also Benjamin Farrington, *The Faith of Epicurus*, London, 1969.
3 Strict Aristotelians would of course also have depended on natural knowledge, and they were also present in Rome. 'Peripatetics' – those from the Lyceum – in contrast often abandoned Aristotelian causality and even adopted forms of atomism.
4 Epicurus lived 341–270 BC; see Lucretius, *De Rerum Natura*, with trans. by W. H. D. Rouse and ed. by M. Ferguson Smith, Cambridge, Mass. and London (Loeb), 1975, p.xxviii (hereafter DRN).
5 St Jerome, at the end of the fourth century, says that Lucretius was driven mad by a love potion and committed suicide. There is a dispute among the historians and Rouse, the Loeb editor, has a preference for the story being a Christian fabrication, DRN p.xxii, and it is certainly more evidence of a Christian disapproval of some pagan authors, which militated against the survival of their works. The poem was unknown in the West for most of the Middle Ages. A manuscript was found in a monastery in 1418. Since then, two ninth-century manuscripts have been discovered and two fragments from a similar period. Three complete manuscripts is a stark contrast to the hundreds of copies of works of which the church did not disapprove.
6 The lack of a creator in atomistic accounts of the world would also have been disliked in Christian centuries when the only reality was a God who had created out of nothing and could equally totally destroy matter. It was an Epicurean principle to avoid pain and enjoy pleasure,

sometimes enduring a small pain for a greater pleasure: DRN p.xxxix. This must have looked self-indulgent to Christians.

7 DRN p.xxxix.
8 Because of the paucity of the manuscript evidence, it cannot be certain that this was the title given to the poem by Lucretius himself. See Diskin Clay, *Lucretius and Epicurus*, Ithaca and London, 1983, p.82.
9 DRN 3.323: *Haec igitur natura . . . .*
10 DRN 3.349: *coniunctam quoque naturam . . . .*
11 DRN 5.93.
12 DRN 2.721.
13 DRN 1.598.
14 DRN 1.586; 2.302; 5.310; 5.924; 6.907: *naturae.*
15 DRN 3.931.
16 Boethius of course also used allegory in an effective way, and in all the points listed here, Lucretius is followed by Alain of Lille in the twelfth century (but it is very unlikely that Alain knew of Lucretius).
17 DRN 2.1117.
18 Clay (1983) pp.83, 87–88.
19 DRN 2.598.
20 The eunuch-priests were called corybantes, who used wild frenzied dancing and loud music.
21 DRN p.xliv.
22 The 'study of nature' with which to dispel gloom and fear of divine action is *naturae species ratioque.* DRN 1.148.
23 DRN 5.772.
24 DRN 5.826.
25 DRN 5.862.
26 The trees and corn are never confused in their parts and always follow the law of nature – *foedere naturae.* The same phrase is used at 5.310 to show that all man-made things and even mountains crumble away in time and cannot resist nature's laws.
27 DRN 5.878.
28 DRN 1.187, 199; 5.901; 6.66.
29 DRN 6.109.
30 DRN 5.196.
31 DRN 1.175,187.
32 DRN 5.1105.
33 DRN 5.1194.
34 DRN 6.96.
35 Also DRN 6.330.
36 DRN 6.269.
37 *fulmen*: DRN 6.295.
38 DRN 6.80. Compare Pliny, *Natural History* 2.143 (see Chapter 5 below).
39 DRN 6.379 and note.
40 DRN 6.423–537.
41 DRN 6.577 and notes.
42 DRN 6.639 and note c: Spartacus and his followers camped in the crater in 73 BC.

43 DRN 6.680. That wind is air in motion was not obvious in the ancient world, and we have seen that Aristotle denied it.

44 DRN 6.705.

45 DRN 6.712.

46 DRN 6.738.

47 DRN 6.760: *naturali ratione.*

48 Ernest Barker (ed. and trans.), *The Politics of Aristotle*, Oxford, 1958, p.xlviii.

49 *Politics* 1252b. Aristotle had begun the whole work by saying that constitutions aim at some good, and this is the Good we have seen in the physical works. Here he says nature is the end or perfection of the polis. It is also the final cause of the polis. Man is by nature an animal intended to live in a polis. The polis is prior to the family and the family to the individual. There is no conflict that art is used in constructing the polis, for this is merely a means to allow man's nature to be perfected. See Barker's edn., pp.1–2.

50 Barker, *Politics*, p.365.

51 ibid. p.369.

52 See H. F. Jolowicz, *Historical Introduction to the Study of Roman Law*, Cambridge, 1939, pp.103–105: the Aristotelian discussion above had an influence on Roman law.

53 Cicero identifies *ius naturale* with *ius gentium.*

54 F. R. Cowell, *Cicero and the Roman Republic*, Harmondsworth, 1965, quotes (pp.354–355) a surviving passage from an otherwise lost *Commonwealth* or *Republic* to the effect that true law is right reason, conformable to nature, pervading all things, constant and eternal. The state or people cannot alter it, and it applies to all people, every age, to Rome as to Athens.

55 Gaius opens his *Institutes* with a theoretical distinction between the civil law of a particular state and the *ius gentium*, which arises from natural reason common to all men. Jolowicz, *Historical Introduction*, says that this is rather Aristotelian, and certainly it is a nature-of-man opinion. See F. de Zulueta (trans.), *The Institutes of Gaius*, 2 vols, Oxford, 1953, vol. 1, p.2: 'quod vero naturalis ratio inter omnes homines, id apud omnes populos peraeque custoditur vocaturque ius gentium.'

56 *Institutes of Gaius*, vol. 2, p.82. Gaius also has a little on the natural law of acquisition. *Alluvio* (vol. 1. p.77) is when land is acquired by reason of a river depositing silt. If a man puts up a building or plants a tree on your land, the building or tree becomes yours by natural law (but you have to pay his original expenses if you want to have it). What is captured from an enemy belongs by natural law to the captor. So on the whole in Gaius natural law is natural either by natural reason or by the natures of things. It is also natural reason that a child of a slave made pregnant by a Roman citizen should be free if the mother was made free before it was born. In contrast the children of a free woman and a slave are slaves by a particular Roman *lex*. They are free by *ius gentium* elsewhere. See vol. 1, p.29.

57 Cicero, *De Natura Deorum. Academica*, trans. H. Rackham, Cambridge, Mass. and London (Loeb), 1979, II.V; II.XI; II.XVIII. (Hereafter ND.)

58 Zeno, Posidonius, Cleanthes: ND Book II *passim* and II.XXIII.
59 *vim quandam sine ratione cientem motus in corporibus necessarios.* ND II.XXXII.
60 *omnium quae sint naturam esse corpora et inane.* ND II.XXXII.
61 At ND II.XLIX Balbus says that many of his examples are drawn from Aristotle.
62 ND I.XV.
63 ND II.LXI.
64 ND II.LXIV.
65 ND II.III.
66 ND II.V.
67 On Seneca's career, see M. T. Griffin, *Seneca. A Philosopher in Politics*, Oxford, 1976.
68 Aristotle is said to have written an *On Kingship* to Alexander. It has not survived. See Werner Jaeger, *Aristotle. Fundamentals of the History of his Development*, Oxford, 1962, p.259.
69 A. A. Long, *Hellenistic Philosophy*, 2nd edn, London, 1986, p.113.
70 Seneca, *Letters from a Stoic. Epistulae Morales ad Lucilium*, trans. R. Campbell, London, 1969, p.64.
71 *Letters*, pp.85,104. In the *Quaestiones Naturales* Seneca quotes thirty Greek sources and only a single Latin. Villy Sørensen, *Seneca the Humanist at the Court of Nero*, Edinburgh and Chicago, 1984, p.229.
72 *Letters*, p.97.
73 ibid. pp.99,204.
74 ibid. p.98.
75 ibid. p.16.
76 *L Annaei Senecae Naturalium Quaestionum libri viii*, ed. A. Gercke, Stuttgart (Teubner) 1970, p.97. The work is referred to as QN hereafter.
77 *Letters*, p.190.
78 ibid. p.207.
79 ibid. pp.46, 56, 107.
80 ibid. pp.72, 104.
81 ibid. pp.72, 53, 59, 65.
82 ibid. pp.118–121.
83 ibid. p.124.
84 See for example Long, *Hellenistic Philosophy*, ch. 4.
85 See for example Gercke, QN p.1.
86 *Letters*, pp.122, 123.
87 QN p.2: *quis auctor aut custos, quid sit deus . . ..*
88 *Letters*, p.124; QN p.1ff.
89 *Letters*, pp. 160, 161. In the *Natural Questions* (ch. 7) he mourns the passing of philosophy as a whole: the Old and New Academies have gone and there are no more Pyrrhonists or Pythagoreans. Also vanished is even the new Roman sect of the Sextii, father and son, who taught a vigorous combination of Pythagoreanism and Stoicism in Seneca's youth.
90 QN 1, 4.
91 i.e. superficial simulcra.
92 QN 1, 16.

93 QN 2,1.
94 QN in Clarke's trans.: J. A. Clarke, *Physical Science in the time of Nero*, London, 1910, p.60.
95 Pliny, about a dozen years later, has the same story, no doubt from a common source (see Chapter 5 below).
96 QN, Clarke's trans., p.78.
97 ibid. p.81.
98 *Letters*, p.154.
99 Caecina too made such a study; both were reported on also by Pliny (see Chapter 5 below).
100 QN II, 35, 36.
101 QN, Clarke's trans., p.103.
102 Pliny, *Natural History* XXXVI 7.
103 ibid. XXXV 36; XXXVII 11.
104 ibid. XXXV 33, 36.
105 QN, Clarke's trans., p.126.
106 ibid. p.74.
107 ibid. p.250ff.
108 ibid. p.150.
109 Seneca had an historical feeling for the gradual introduction of human vices, and as a lawyer saw the history of legal codes as ever more detailed attempts to contain the problem. *Letters* p.163.
110 QN, Clarke's trans., pp.143–53.
111 ibid. p.156: it is the Senecan moral story at the end of Book 3.
112 ibid. p.171.
113 *Letters*. See Campbell's introduction and p.6.
114 However, Griffin, *Seneca*, p.43 thinks that Seneca's account of the Nile does not necessarily come from personal observation.
115 QN, Clarke's trans., pp.231ff.
116 ibid. p.171.
117 ibid. p.225.
118 ibid. pp.231, 240, 251.
119 Vol. 12 of *Plutarch's Moralia*, trans. H. Cherniss and W. Helmbold, Cambridge, Mass. and London (Loeb), 1968, p. 325. The Pythagoreans were kind to animals as a model for civil behaviour (see also pp.353–354).
120 For Plutarch's view of history and the morality expressed in his *Lives*, see Philip A. Stadter, *Plutarch and the Historical Tradition*, London, 1992.
121 Autobulus, the huntsman in Plutarch's dialogue, quotes from 'the philosophers' who say animals have reason in as far as they have purpose, preparation, memory, emotions, care for young, resentment and gratitude: *Moralia*, Loeb edn, vol. 12, pp. 347, 361.
122 *Moralia*, Loeb edn, vol. 12, p.339.
123 ibid. p.501.
124 ibid. p.517.
125 ibid. p.523.
126 ibid. p.318.
127 ibid. p.409.
128 ibid. p.377.

129 ibid. pp.441, 443.
130 ibid. p.357.
131 ibid. p.445.
132 Loeb edn, p.413. The priestly Egyptian crocodile that ignored the presence of a Ptolemy, argued Autobulus, was foretelling his death.
133 Abraham Terian, *Philonis Alexandini de Animalibus. The Armenian Text with an Introduction, Translation and Commentary*, Chico, 1981.
134 Terian, *Philonis Alexandini de Animalibus*, pp.86, 87.
135 His version of the story includes details not always found, like the pain felt by the animal at the place where the antlers were (the wound attracts flies, says Alexander) and the proverb about the obscurity of the place where the antlers fell. Terian, *Philonis Alexandini de Animalibus*, p.82.
136 Caesar Germanicus (who died in 19 AD): Terian, *Philonis Alexandini de Animalibus*, p.79.
137 Terian, *Philonis Alexandini de Animalibus*, p.97.
138 ibid. p.87.
139 W. T. Costello, *The Scholastic Curriculum at Early Seventeenth-Century Cambridge*, Cambridge, Mass., 1958, p.25.
140 The Stoic Chrysippus had said the same of the pig.
141 Terian, *Philonis Alexandini de Animalibus*, p.44.
142 See Peter H. Niebyl, 'The non-naturals', *Bulletin of the History of Medicine*, 45 (1971), 486–492.
143 A. J. Brock (ed. and trans.), *Galen on the Natural Faculties*, London and New York (Loeb), 1916.
144 See Brock's note, p.2 of the Loeb edn.
145 Indeed, up to p.13 of the Loeb edn Galen gives a fair summary of Aristotle's doctrine of natural change, and states that his own notion of 'faculty' (as in 'natural faculties') is to be identified with Aristotle's notion of the causes of natural change, but limited to the living body. So we are here justified in concluding that for Galen as for Aristotle *physis* is the nature-of-a-thing.
146 See also Brock's introduction to *On the Natural Faculties*, Loeb edn, p.26.
147 The point is important for this present series of books, which is partly designed to provide historians of later periods with an idea of what there was in ancient views about the physical world that made resources available for later formulations. Doctrines like 'nature does nothing in vain' imply an autonomous creating principle that has little justification in Aristotle but which meant a lot – to take one example – to Harvey in the Latin-English tradition of *natura*.
148 *On the Natural Faculties*, p.56.
149 See Brock's introduction, p.xxix.
150 *On the Natural Faculties*, p.43.
151 ibid. p.43.
152 ibid. p.47.
153 ibid. p.143.
154 One of Galen's purposes seems to be to actually extend what Aristotle had written because, Galen argued, Aristotle did not know all the actions of the parts and so could not tell what all the uses were. See

M. T. May (ed. and trans.), *Galen on the Usefulness of the Parts of the Body*, 2 vols, Ithaca, New York, 1968, p.10. (Hereafter *De Usu Partium*.)

155 *De Usu Partium*, p.729.
156 ibid. p.189.
157 ibid. pp.725, 731.
158 ibid. p.730. The argument from design is also to be found in Cicero's *De Natura Deorum. De Usu Partium*, p.10.
159 *De Usu Partium*, p.725.
160 ibid. p.611.
161 ibid. p.107.
162 The sophists also mocked Hippocrates, Galen's hero, for saying the physician should do what nature does in a crisis: the sophists did not believe that a crisis was the work of nature. *De Usu Partium*, p.733.
163 *De Usu Partium*, p.67.
164 ibid. p.202.
165 Probably too Galen's demiurgic nature owes something to the 'creative reason' of the Stoics. See Long, *Hellenistic Philosophy*, p.112, where the similarity between Stoic creative reason and the Platonic demiurge is emphasised.
166 R. Walzer, *Galen on Jews and Christians*, Oxford, 1949, p.9. Galen's views on Jews are those of educated Greeks. Josephus wrote in Rome for a Greek-speaking public while Philo of Alexandria was unknown outside Jewish circles in that city. Philo's work survived owing to Clement and Origen; perhaps meeting antagonism, later Jews did not continue to assimilate Hellenism.
167 Waltzer (1949) p.11.
168 ibid. p.13.
169 *De Usu Partium* was written between 169 and 176. Some nearby Christian dates are: Justin Martyr d. 166; Tertullian *fl.* before 218; Clement d. 216; Origen d. 254; Lactantius before 300.
170 *De Usu Partium*, p.532.
171 ibid. p.278.
172 ibid. pp.85, 252.
173 ibid. p.358.
174 ibid. p.620.

5 THE *NATURAL HISTORY* OF PLINY

1 See the useful study by Mary Beagon, *Roman Nature. The Thought of Pliny the Elder*, Oxford, 1992, p.5.
2 See also Nicholas Phillies Howe, 'In defense of the encyclopedic mode: on Pliny's *Preface to the Natural History*', *Latomus*, *44* (1985), 561–576.
3 For the Roman's practical attitude towards philosophy see also Beagon, *Roman Nature* pp.12, 13.
4 Book I of the *Natural History* (hereafter NH) is taken up with listing his sources; these are the opening words of Book II. H. Rackham, W. H. S. Jones and D. E. Eicholz (trans.), *Pliny. Natural History*, Cambridge, Mass. and London (Loeb), 10 vols, 1967–1971.

5 See also Martin P. Nilsson, 'The new conception of the universe in late Greek paganism', *Eranus Rudbergianos*, *44* (1946), 20–27. Pliny of course took much from the Greeks, including the changes that occurred in cosmological thinking as a result of a perceived expansion of the world. See also J.-P. Dumont, 'L'idée de Dieu chez Pline', *Helmantica*, *37* (1986), 219–237; and E. V. Arnold, *Roman Stoicism*, London, 1911.

6 *idemque rerum naturae opus et rerum ipsa natura*. NH II.1.

7 *si haec infinitas naturae omnium artifici possit adsignari*, ... NH I.1. Of course, this could equally well read 'if this infinity of the nature of all things can be assigned to a creator, ...' which would support the interpretation of 'nature' as set out above.

8 NH II.5.

9 NH II.4.

10 NH II.5(20): *inridendum agere curam rerum humanarum illud quicquid est summum.*

11 NH II.5(30): *Verum in his deos agere curam rerum humanarum credi ex usu vitae est, poenasque maleficiis aliquando seras, occupata deo in tanta mole . . . .*

12 NH II.5(26): *proximo illi genitum.* The translation is that of Rackham, in the Loeb edition: vol. 1 (1967), p.187.

13 NH II.5.

14 Rackham's translation makes Pliny identify God and nature. Some justification for this might be found later, NH XXVII.2 where Pliny apparently identifies as a single thing Chance, God and the mother and mistress of all things. There is however some question about the status of this sentence.

15 NH VII.1.

16 NH VIII.42.

17 At NH XXII. 14, for example, Pliny uses *divinitas* precisely as he elsewhere uses *natura* (here in providing seasonal plant remedies for animals). 'Nature' is implied by *parens illa ac divina rerum artifex* (and it is nature who a few lines later is said to produce all her work perfectly). NH XXII.56. *Sacra illa parens* of NH XXIV.1 is clearly nature.

18 NH II.3. These seeds were particularly prolific in the sea, which contained forms of life parallel to all those on earth, and many more: NH IX.1.

19 Temples were dedicated to *Venus Genetrix*: NH VII.38.

20 NH II.13. 'Ecliptic' is my translation; Rackham has 'zodiac'.

21 Mars and the rest follow such *leges*: NH II.14.

22 NH II.45. Pliny is showing that in following laws, the winds are natural. This is essentially what Seneca argued, but Pliny does not stress the 'do not fear the gods' argument.

23 NH XXII.56.

24 NH XI.1. Compare Galen on the structure of the flea and the elephant. See E. T. May (ed. and trans.), *Galen on the Usefulness of the Parts of the Body*, 2 vols, Ithaca, 1968; vol. 2, p.724: Book 17, Galen's 'epode'.

25 *rerum natura nusquam magis quam in minimis tota sit.* NH XI.1.

26 For example NH X.91.

27 NH VII.2, *ludibria*.

28 NH IX.52, XXI.1.
29 The story of the enormous snakes ultimately derives from Greek ventures into India. Strabo has at second hand accounts of snakes up to 140 cubits in length (see Chapter 3 above).
30 NH VIII.11,12.
31 NH VIII.35.
32 NH VIII.33.
33 On Pliny and animals in general, see L. Bodson, 'Aspects of Pliny's zoology', in R. French and F. Greenaway (eds), *Science in the Early Roman Empire: Pliny the Elder, his Sources and Influence*, London, 1986, pp.98–110.
34 NH IX.7.
35 NH XVI.23. Very often Pliny has some form of words which mean that natural objects were 'born for' a certain human purpose. Unless nature is directly indicated in these words, these examples have not been used here.
36 NH XXVI.21.
37 NH VII.1.
38 Another example is at NH XI.77, where *providens natura* has provided all the principal internal organs of animals with a protective membranous sheath.
39 NH XVI.46.
40 The opening of Book XXII.
41 NH II.55.
42 *mores*: NH XI.4.
43 NH XXI.1.
44 NH XXI.17, 40.
45 NH XVII.24.
46 NH XVII.9, 10, 23.
47 NH XI.28.
48 NH XVI.65.
49 NH XVI.93.
50 NH XVII.12.
51 NH XVI.67, 83; XIX.26, 44.
52 NH VIII.19; X.24.
53 NH X.95.
54 NH XVI.24.
55 NH IX.15.
56 See J. Reynolds, 'The elder Pliny and his times' in French and Greenaway, *Science in the Early Roman Empire*, pp.1–10; p.8. In Rome a wealthy and important figure would act as Patron to a number of Clients. He would meet them at his meals, protect and promote them. In return they would offer any specialist service they might have and would, by their number, enhance the Patron's status. No legal prosecution was possible between Patron and Client.
57 NH II.5.
58 NH XXVII.1.
59 NH X.70.
60 NH Preface, 16.

61 NH III.20.
62 On the Romans' attitude to the races they had conquered, see A. N. Sherwin White, *Racial Prejudice in Imperial Rome*, Cambridge, 1967.
63 NH III.5. The translation is Rackham's.
64 NH VI.31.
65 NH VI.35.
66 NH XII.8.
67 NH VII.25, 26.
68 NH XI.109.
69 NH V.1. The commander was Suetonius Paulinus, the father of the biographer.
70 NH VI.35.
71 NH XII.31. Juba was Pliny's main source for the troglodytes of the Red Sea. See J. Desanges, 'Les sources de Pline dans sa description de la troglodytique et de l'Ethiopie', *Helmantica*, 37 (1986), 277–292.
72 NH VI.20.
73 NH VI.24.
74 NH XI.32.
75 NH XII.40.
76 NH XIV.6.
77 NH XII.41.
78 See J. Innes Miller, *The Spice Trade of the Roman Empire, 29 BC to AD 641*, Oxford, 1969.
79 NH XIII.4.
80 NH VI.31.
81 NH XIII.21.
82 NH, the preface to Book VII.
83 NH XVI.1.
84 NH V.12. At NH VII.55 he thinks the Assyrians had always had writing, and gives a little history of the importing of the Phoenician alphabet into Greece.
85 NH XIII.27.
86 NH VII.56–58.
87 NH V.60.
88 Pliny came from Gaul. On the morality of his class see Reynolds, 'The elder Pliny', p.1.
89 NH XVIII.2 and 3 where Pliny derives Cicero from *cicer*, chick-pea.
90 NH XVIII.4.
91 NH XVIII.28.
92 NH XIV.1.
93 NH XV.20.
94 NH XIX.19–37.
95 NH VIII.6.
96 NH VIII.10.
97 See the convenient account in D. R. Kelley (ed.), *Versions of History from Antiquity to the Enlightenment*, New Haven, 1991, p.35.
98 *Capti celerrime mitificantur hordei suco*. NH VIII.7.
99 Pliny discusses elephants in the first thirteen chapters of *Natural History*; this is VIII.2. *Mirum*, says Pliny about the climbing elephants,

et adversis quidem funibus subire, sed maxime regredi, utique pronis.
Somewhere behind Pliny's terse words is a Roman circus spectacular
involving some arrangement of ropes; but we can only translate
directly.

100 See Elizabeth Rawson, *Intellectual Life in the Late Roman Republic*,
Baltimore, 1985, esp. p.285 where the poverty of Roman philosophy,
particularly of *physica*, is clear. It is argued by P. Grimal, 'Pline et les
philosophes', *Helmantica*, 37 (1986), 239–249, that Pliny shows signs
of having adopted facets of an Empedoclean philosophy.

101 NH II.1, 20.

102 NH XV.5.

103 NH XVIII.34.

104 The telling of tall stories from distant lands was seen by the Romans
as a characteristic vice of the Greeks. See A. Wardman, *Rome's Debt
to Greece*, London, 1976, p.9. But Pliny perforce has to use them.

105 NH II.13.

106 NH IX.20.

107 NH VII.1.

108 NH IV.10.

109 These figures are taken from Book I of *Natural History* where Pliny
names his sources. I refer only to authors whom Pliny uses more than
once. These figures can only be approximate because Pliny's docu-
mentation is far from modern standards, both here and in the text.
Many of his authors he must have met at second hand through
handbooks and compilations.

110 NH VIII.17: *summo in omni doctrina viro . . .* The only exception is
that he is surprised that Aristotle gives so much credence to physiognomy: XI.112.

111 NH II.23, II.60. He also cites Aristotle for the belief that some winds
arise from the earth's being curved: NH XVIII.77.

112 NH IX.6.

113 IX.78.

114 NH VII.2.

115 NH VII.29.

116 At NH VIII.10 Pliny has it from Aristotle that elephants gestate for
two years and bear only one infant at a time. Similarly, NH VIII.43:
hyenas do not change sex; ravens do not mate or lay eggs via the beak;
X.84: the amazing fertility of mice. At the other end of their life-span
Pliny thinks it worthy of abstracting from Aristotle the fact that
animals die only when the tide is ebbing: NH II.101.

117 NH IV.12; VII.56.

118 See NH XXIV.158ff. Pliny also attributes to Democritus the story of
a boy's pet snake, which his parents threw out in disgust, but which
saved them all when attacked by brigands.

119 NH XXIX.1; as Jones says, he either forgot or did not know of
Scribonius Largus. (W. H. S. Jones, Loeb edition.)

120 NH XXIX.5(11): *ingeniorum Graeciae flatu impellimur.*

121 NH XXIX 8(27).

122 NH XXIX.7: *et quod bonum sit illorum litteras inspicere, non per-
discere . . . .*

123 Some help through Pliny's work here is offered by J. Stannard, 'Herbal medecine [*sic*] and herbal magic in Pliny's time', *Helmantica*, *37* (1986), 95–106.

124 There is a text called *Medicina Plinii* that was compiled in the fourth century. See my chapter, 'Pliny and Renaissance medicine', in French and Greenaway, *Science in the Early Roman Empire*.

125 NH XXX.1: *Magicas vanitates . . ..*

126 NH XXX.2(8).

127 NH XXX.1.

128 NH XXX.4.

129 NH XXX.4. Pliny rejoices that Nero, as emperor, discovered the frauds of the Magi. NH XXX.6.

130 NH XXX.28. (Jones's translation, Loeb edition.)

131 NH XXX.17. In Christian literature the Magi were identified with the Three Wise Men. Pliny's account is surely a major resource of the later western idea of 'magic' as a mixing of strange things, together with an incantation.

132 NH XXXVII.73.

133 NH XXXVI.34.

134 NH XXXVII.56.

135 NH XXXVII.37, 40.

136 NH XXXVII.13, 37, 54, 60.

137 See J. Reynolds, 'The elder Pliny and his times', in French and Greenaway, *Science in the Early Roman Empire*, pp.1–10; p.7. Pliny gives the details at NH XXXIV.16 and XXXVI.27.

138 See also Beagon, *Roman Nature*, pp.3, 8. Mucianus was instrumental in bringing the Flavians to power and was Vespasian's general. Vespasian also may have been a Patron of Pliny.

139 The traditional curriculum became seven again when Martianus Capella removed the subjects added by Varro. See W. H. Stahl, *Martianus Capella and the Seven Liberal Arts*, 2 vols, New York, 1971; vol.1, p.202.

140 This is argued by O. Pedersen, 'Some astronomical topics in Pliny', in French and Greenaway, *Science in the Early Roman Empire*, pp. 162–196; 163.

141 NH XVIII.4.

142 NH II.3.

143 NH II.65.

144 See also Beagon, *Roman Nature*, pp.10–12, 18–20.

145 This point is made by Pedersen, 'Some astronomical topics in Pliny', pp.162–196; 163.

146 ibid., p.175.

147 NH II.65.

148 NH II.4.

149 NH XVI.39.

150 NH VII.55.

151 NH II.63.

152 NH XXXVI.1.

153 NH XXXIV.19.
154 NH XXXIV.9.
155 NH XXXV.36.
156 NH XXXIII.3.
157 NH XXXIII.5.
158 NH XXXIII.13, 14.
159 NH XXXIII.21.
160 NH XXXIII.31.
161 NH XXXIV.49; XXXVI.24. So productive were the lead mines of Britain that Rome imposed a limit on what could be taken.
162 NH XXXVI.14.
163 NH XXXVI.55.
164 NH XXXV.49.
165 NH XXXVI.32–34.
166 NH XXXVI.12.
167 NH XXXVI.2, 9.
168 NH XXXVII.6.
169 NH XXXVI.24.
170 NH XXXVI.24.
171 NH XXXVI.24.
172 XXXVI.24 For Pliny's view of Agrippa, see M. A. T. Burns, 'Pliny's ideal Roman', *Classical Journal*, 59, 1 (1963) 253–258.
173 e.g. NH XXXIII.26.
174 See the beginning of Book XXXV.
175 On metals in general, see J. F. Healy, 'Pliny on mineralogy and metals', in French and Greenaway, *Science in the Early Roman Empire*, pp.111–146.
176 NH XXXIII.31, 34, 35.
177 NH XXXIII.38.
178 NH XXXIV.22.
179 NH XXXIV.31–36. It is characteristic of Pliny that he is concerned with the retail end of the market in natural products that have been brought long distances or are the end result of manufacturing processes. Often he gives the prices and grade of quality. On mineral products see F. Greenaway, 'Chemical tests in Pliny' in French and Greenaway, *Science in the Early Roman Empire*, pp.147–161.
180 NH XXXIV.37.
181 *De Rerum Natura* 1.136.
182 NH XXXIV.19.
183 NH XXXIV.43.
184 NH XXXVII.15.
185 NH XXXVII.15.
186 NH XXXVI.26.
187 NH XXXVI.25; XXXIII.33; XXXVII.25; XXXVII.28; XXXVII.39.
188 NH XVIII.55: *huc pertinet oraculum illud magno opere custodiendum.*
189 Despite the fact that Virgil was also a Roman, Pliny is often antagonistic to him. See Richard T. Bruère, 'Pliny the Elder and Virgil', *Classical Philology*, 51 (1956) 228–246.
190 NH XVIII.56.

191 NH XVIII.66.
192 NH XVIII.6.
193 NH XVIII.6.
194 See V. Nutton, 'The perils of patriotism: Pliny and Roman medicine', in French and Greenaway, *Science in the Early Roman Empire*, pp.30–58.
195 NH XXXII.29.
196 NH XXXII.32.
197 NH XXX.50.
198 NH XX.14 and 20 respectively.
199 NH XXX.8.
200 Pliny gives the remedy twice: NH XXX.14 and 20.
201 NH XXVIII.63.
202 NH XXX.34.
203 NH XXX.44.
204 NH XXVIII.78,80.
205 NH XXX.18.
206 NH XXX.30.
207 NH XXXII.42.
208 NH XXXII.42.
209 NH XXVIII.60.
210 NH XXIX.36; XXX.16; XXX.17.
211 NH XXXII.46(134); XXXII.16; XXXII.3.
212 NH XXIX.27; XXIX.21; XXIX.32.
213 On the question of whether he knew the writings of the Greek, Dioscorides, see J. André, 'Pline l'ancient botaniste', *Revue des Etudes Latines*, *33* (1955), 297–318. See also John Scarborough, 'Pharmacy in Pliny's *Natural History*: some observations on substances and sources', in French and Greenaway, *Science in the Early Roman Empire*, pp.59–95. Scarborough counts over 900 pharmaceutical substances in the *Natural History*, compared to less than 600 remedies in Dioscorides and fewer than 550 plants mentioned by Theophrastus.
214 NH XX.33.
215 NH XXV.6.
216 On Pliny's treatment of plants in general, see A. G. Morton, 'Pliny on plants: his place in the history of botany', in French and Greenaway, *Science in the Early Roman Empire*, pp.86–96.
217 NH XVII.1, 2.
218 NH XXV.1–3.
219 NH XXV.3.
220 NH VIII.61.
221 NH VIII.63. Pliny thus seems to have believed that something in the structure of the word related to the nature of the thing it represented. In this case the remedy was 'discovered' from an oracle.
222 NH VIII.66.
223 NH VIII.28, 29.
224 See in general, J. M. C. Toynbee, *Animals in Roman Art and Life*, London, 1973. It is argued by R. Auguet, *Cruelty and Civilization: The Roman Games*, London, 1972, p.107, that the games' appetite for

animals caused the extinction of a 'degenerate' kind of North African elephant. On the existence of a small variety of elephant and the ancient belief that Indian elephants were bigger than African, see H. H. Scullard, *The Elephant in the Greek and Roman World*, London, 1974, p.60.

225 See Scott Atran, *Cognitive Foundations of Natural History*, Cambridge, 1993, p.81.

226 NH XI.1–21.

227 NH XI.19: *impugnat eas naturae eiusdem degeneres vespae atque crabrones.*

228 Pliny's account of bees occupies NH XI.4 to 23.

229 NH XVI.24: *Materiae enim causa reliquas arbores natura genuit.* The trees for dyeing are at NH XVI.30.

230 NH XVI.83.

231 But of course much of his information was literary, as well. See P. Chevallier, 'Le bois, l'arbre et la forêt chez Pline', *Helmantica, 37* (1986), 147–172. Juba again figures among Pliny's sources.

232 NH XVI.74.

233 NH XVI.74.

234 The Chauci lived in an area of Germany where Pliny had been a cavalry commander. See J. Stannard, 'Pliny and Roman botany', *Isis, 56* (1965), 420–425.

235 NH XXVII.1–2; XXVI.6.

236 NH XXXII.8: it is a good omen if the fish take their food eagerly.

237 NH IX.22. The augury worked by symbolism: when during the Sicilian war Augustus was walking on a beach, a fish leapt from the sea before his feet. The priests took it to be a sign that Sextus Pompeius, who was being successful in sea-battles, was favoured by Neptune, but that control of the sea would pass to Augustus. See NH XI.73 for the liver in divination (it is absent or double in the sacrificial animal).

238 NH XVII.38.

239 NH II.5. It was argued earlier in this book that some of the content and boundaries of natural philosophy were determined by the areas of activity of some gods of the pantheon. It is therefore of interest to see why Pliny rejects the traditional gods. It is because they now appear parochial, childish fancies of equal standing to those of nations who have animals for gods. The expanded Roman world made such things relative, and Pliny puts in their place that 'mortal to help mortal is god'. He has not forgotten his earlier statements about the nature of god, but is preparing to argue that on this basis Vespasian is a god. Yet it is clear from Pliny that people in his day were still frightened of the gods, especially the lightning-throwing Zeus.

240 NH XVII.48; XXVIII.4.

241 I use 'scientific' here advisedly because to see science in Pliny is an error that parallels that of seeing him use his written language badly. Both are the views of modern scholars who think that they know what Pliny should have been doing; the latter view is encapsulated in the opinion of J. Wight Duff, expressed some sixty years ago: '"Nowhere" thundered Duff, in tones that evoke a vanished age of English imperial education,

"Nowhere is Pliny more exasperating than in his maltreatment of the ablative case".' I quote Vivian Nutton, 'The perils of patriotism: Pliny and Roman Medicine', in French and Greenaway, *Science in the Early Roman Empire*, pp.30–58; 46.

6 ANIMALS AND PARABLES

1 F. H. Colson and G. H. Whitaker (trans.), *Philo*, 10 vols, London and New York (Loeb), vol. 1, 1929. (hereafter *Philo*). For Philo on Genesis see also F. E. Robbins, *The Hexaemeral Literature. A Study of the Greek and Latin Commentaries on Genesis*, Chicago, 1918.

2 There is no evidence that he knew of Christ or Christians. Nor is it clear that he knew the Hebrew old testament. Nahum N. Glatzer, *The Essential Philo*, New York, 1971, preface, p.vii. See David T. Runia, *Exegesis and Philosophy. Studies on Philo of Alexandria*, Aldershot, 1990, item I, 'Philo, Alexandrian and Jew'.

3 See *Theophrastus of Eresus. Sources for his Life, Writings, Thought and Influence*, ed. and trans. W. W. Fortenbaugh, P. M. Huby, R. W. Sharples and D. Gutas, 2 vols, Leiden, New York, Cologne, 1992; vol. 1, p.343.

4 ibid. vol. 1, p.352.

5 Colson and Whitaker, *Philo*, vol. 1, p.9.

6 See also Runia, *Exegesis*, item III, 'Polis and megalopolis: Philo and the founding of Alexandria', p.399.

7 Glatzer, *The Essential Philo*, preface.

8 See also Runia, *Exegesis*, item II, 'How to read Philo'.

9 *Philo*, p.xvi.

10 ibid. pp.39–43.

11 ibid. p.45.

12 ibid. p.53.

13 See A. W. Mair (ed. and trans.), *Oppian Colluthus Tryphiodorus*, London and New York (Loeb), 1928, Introduction.

14 There are two poems attributed to Oppian, *Halieutica* and *Cynegetica*, of which the latter may in fact have been written by a Syrian imitator.

15 A. F. Scholfield, *Aelian on the Characteristics of Animals*, 3 vols, London and Cambridge, Mass. (Loeb), 1958–1959, introduction p.xi (hereafter *Aelian*).

16 *Aelian*: Introduction, p.xiii.

17 ibid. p.xv.

18 ibid. p.xvi.

19 Aristophanes of Byzantium died in 180 BC. His summary of the *Historia Animalium* provided extracts for Sopatros of Apameia in the fourth century AD and similar usages preserved the animal books in Byzantium through the Western Middle Ages. *Aelian*: introduction, p.xxix.

20 *Aelian* I,52.

21 ibid. IV.45.

22 ibid. I.25.

23 ibid. I.34.

24 The story, probably from Juba, opens Book X.

25 *Aelian* I.24.
26 ibid. VII.34.
27 ibid. IV.30.
28 ibid. I.2; I.4.
29 ibid. I.13; I.14.
30 See, e.g., I.55.
31 *Aelian* III.47.
32 ibid. III.47.
33 ibid. I.48.
34 *Aelian* I.1; at IV.42 he gives an account of women who have changed into birds. The story of the Diomedean birds is also told by Solinus: C. Julius Solinus, *Collectanea Rerum Memorabilium*, ed. Th. Mommsen, Berlin, 1958, p.42.
35 *Aelian* XIII.21.
36 ibid. XVI.9.
37 ibid. IX.23.
38 *Aelian* XI.31. He refers to the medical cures effected by sleeping in the temples also at IX.33.
39 *Aelian* XIV.28.
40 ibid. XI.32–35; XII.1–5.
41 *Aelian* XV.29. We are also told, III.26, that hoopoes were once men; they surround their nest with human excrement, but Aelian does not say why.
42 *Aelian* VII.10.
43 ibid. VII.41.
44 ibid. VII.37.
45 ibid. VII.32.
46 ibid. XI.25.
47 ibid. I.50.
48 ibid. I.54, II.14.
49 ibid. II.13.
50 ibid. II.21, VI.21.
51 ibid. V.49.
52 ibid. III.9; V.48.
53 ibid. I.36.
54 It is at II.5 that Aelian gives the story from Leonidas of Byzantium of the boy and dolphin from Poroselene. Here the boy does not ride the dolphin, which brought fish for the boy and his parents. At VI.15 Aelian has the story of the boy that rode on a dolphin at Iassos; it accidentally killed him and committed suicide in remorse. Something similar happened at Puteoli.
55 *Aelian* VII.32.
56 ibid. VI.17: with the help of the gods.
57 ibid. I.6.
58 ibid. V.29.
59 ibid. I.57.
60 ibid. VII.48.
61 ibid. VI.63.
62 Solinus, *Collectanea*, p.112.
63 IV.27. Aelian has the more usual ant-story at III.4.

64 In Herodotus the human race associated with the griffin – here a bird – is that of the northern one-eyed Arimaspians. See James S. Romm, *The Edges of the Earth in Ancient Thought*, Princeton, 1992, p.69.

65 *Aelian* IV.20.

66 ibid. V.34.

67 ibid. V.54.

68 ibid. III.46.

69 True generation – viz. *ex nihilo* – was, according to Aristotle (*De Generatione et Corruptione*, 302a) impossible, as it would involve a void, that is, the empty place in which the generand appeared. Aristotle allowed that one kind of matter could turn into another, like fire from air. Certainly an actual body could be generated from a potential, but there was no pre-existent magnitude as a basis for generation. The potential body, concludes Aristotle, must already be some other body in actuality.

70 The basic treatment is *Physiologus*, ed. F. Sbordone, Milan, 1936, which gives the Greek text.

71 *Sancti Patris Nostri Epiphanii, Episcopi Constantiae Cypri, ad Physiologum*, ed. Consalus Ponce de Leon, Antwerp, 1588, p.3. Ponce (p.7) says that Origen cites Physiologus in homily 17 on Genesis. F.J. Carmody, 'Physiologus Latinus Versio Y', *University of California Publications in Classical Philology*, 12, 7 (1941), 95–134; p.97 says that Physiologus was used by Justin Martyr (died 166), Origen (about 255), and Tertullian (230).

72 See Carmody, 'Physiologus'.

73 Epiphanius is in the *incipit* of the Greek given by Ponce, and in the *incipit* of the text given by Dimitris Kaimakis, *Der Physiologus nach der ersten Redaktion*, Meisenheim am Glan, 1974.

74 Sbordone (1936) p.xii.

75 Ponce in the *ad lectorem* treats Physiologus as simply a collector of the items of natural history. See also Carmody, 'Physiologus', p.103.

76 *Natura* is generally used to translate *physis*. Sbordone, *Physiologus*, p.1, *tres naturas* of the lion in Latin (Carmody, 'Physiologus', p. 103) are *treis physeis* in the Greek. *Prima natura est* is *prote autou physis estin*. At p.5 and p.103 *Secunda natura* is *Deutera physis*, etc.

77 *Aelian* II.9.

78 R. Ettinghausen, 'The "snake-eating stag" in the East', in K. Weitzmann (ed.), *Late Classical and Mediaeval Studies in Honor of Albert Mathias Friend, Jr.*, Princeton, 1955, pp.272–286.

79 ibid. p.273.

80 The story got into Arabic, perhaps by way of the Syriac *Physiologus*.

81 By the time of St Augustine, the dualism of the Manichees was well known and Augustine himself was for a time tempted by their creed.

82 For the Greek Fathers see also D. S. Wallace-Hadrill, *The Greek Patristic View of Nature*, Manchester, 1968; and Robbins, *The Hexaemeral Literature*; for Basil, see p.42; Gregory of Nyssa and Theophilus of Antioch are also dealt with.

83 For Basil, see H. Wace and P. Schaff (eds), *A Select Library of Nicene and Post-Nicene Fathers of the Christian Church*, 2nd series, vol. 8: *St*

Basil: *Letters and Select Works*, Oxford and New York, 1895. The Hexaemeron begins at p.51; the laws of allegory are discussed at p.101.

84 ibid. p.95.

85 The crab is said to throw a stone between the valves of the shell of the oyster to stop it closing (ibid. p.91) while the bees (p.97) naturally provide a big moral about hard work.

86 E. A. de Mendieta and S. Y. Rudberg, *Eustathius. Ancienne Version Latine des Neuf Homélies sur l'Hexaéméron de Basile de Césarée*, Berlin, 1958 *(Texte und Untersuchungen zur Geschichte der altchristlichem Literatur).*

87 *Eustathius*, p.15.

88 ibid. pp.93, 94: *lex naturae.*

89 *adulterium naturae*: *Eustathius*, p.96.

90 *Vulcano Aetna sacer est*: Solinus, *Collectanea*, p.49.

91 ibid. pp.40, 79, 84, 86, 112.

92 ibid. p. 78: it is an *experimentum*, he says, that proves that dolphins can live for thirty years. The story is akin to that which claimed that Alexander the Great put silver bands round the necks of stags so that they could be identified later. Solinus (p.95) repeats the story and says that the stags were still alive a hundred years later.

93 For example the texts on plants and on the flooding of the Nile were dropped from the medieval curriculum when they were no longer considered Aristotelian. Most modern commentators look at Aristotle for philosophical interest and consequently find that the spurious works lack complexity *and* the name of Aristotle.

94 See the preface by W. D. Ross in the Oxford translation: W. D. Ross (ed.), *The Works of Aristotle*, vol. 6, Oxford, 1913: the text starts at 830a.

95 830a.

96 *Historia Animalium* (HA) 638a, which has details of colour not in the *Auscultationes*. The story is given also by Aelian, for whom the name of the bull is monops. See *Aelian* VII.3.

97 *Auscultationes*, 830b, HA 630b.

98 HA 563b, 618a.

99 Solinus, *Collectanea*, p.91. *Leopardus* and *panthera* in Latin are taken from the Greek; *pardus* is 'male panther'.

100 HA 612a; *Auscultationes* 831a.

101 *De Causis Plantarum* II 17; HA 611b.

102 *Auscultationes* 835b; HA 611a.

103 A late appearance of the story is in Solinus, *Collectanea*, p.81.

104 *Aelian* III.17.

105 HA 612a.

106 HA 614b.

107 HA 614b.

108 *Auscultationes* 832b; HA 581b. It will be evident in these notes how the stories that Aristotle has in common with the *Auscultationes* are grouped together over a fairly small range of the *Historia Animalium*.

109 *Melior enim magistra veritatis natura est.* Carolus Schenkl (ed.), *Sancti Ambrosii Opera pars prima*, Prague, 1896, p.217. (Vol. 32 of the series

Corpus Scriptorum Ecclesiasticorum Latinorum.)

110 See *De Plantis* 1.3 in Ross, *Works of Aristotle*, vol. 6, note 5, 818a.

111 *Auscultationes*, 161.

112 *Historia Plantarum* (HP) I.12.5. In wild plants what is most noticeable is their separation into sexes. *De Plantis* I.7 (821b) seems to make cultivated plants female, wild, male (but this would be an easy misreading of having sex differentiation in both wild and cultivated). See also HP III.7.8 where he says that this kind of distinction is of the same kind that distinguishes wild from cultivated, which is the point developed in *De Plantis*.

113 H. Cherniss and W. C. Helmbold, (trans. and ed.), *Plutarch's Moralia*, vol. 12, London and Cambridge, Mass. (Loeb), 1968, p.499.

114 Plutarch (p.389 of the 1968 Loeb edn) has the story in this form.

115 *Aelian* IV.19, VIII.1. A variant of the story appears in Solinus, *Collectanea*, p.83, where it is the king of Albania who sends the dogs to Alexander.

116 *Aelian* 1.19.

117 Aelian has a large moral excursus on the nature of bees, V.10–13.

118 See A. Wardman, *Rome's Debt to Greece*, London, 1976, p.7, and N. Petrochilos, *Roman Attitudes to the Greeks*, Athens, 1974.

119 See Antigonus Carystius, *Historiarum Mirabilium Collectanea*, ed. Johannes Meursius, Leiden, 1619.

120 Two paradoxographers are known only by the name of the location of the manuscript in which their works appear, in the Vatican and in Florence. They are included by Giannini. This is the Vatican collection. *Paradoxographorum Graecorum Reliquiae*, ed. Alexander Giannini, Milan, n.d., *c*.1956.

121 It is quoted by Phlegon, *De Mirabilibus*, in Giannini, *Paradoxographorum*, pp.169–219. Phlegon calls the author Theopompus Sinopensis.

122 Giannini, *Paradoxographorum*, p.121.

123 The same anonymous paradoxologist (Vatican) who collected Dalion's story also cited Agesias (on Thracian pigs) who is known to classical scholars as the Platonist who was prevented from lecturing by one of the Ptolemies because so convincingly did he teach on the immortality of the soul that a proportion of his audience committed suicide.

124 For example on the Hereford *mappa mundi*.

125 *Athenaeus. The Deipnosophists*, trans. C. B. Gulick, London and New York (Loeb), 7 vols, 1927–1941. Athenaeus lived in Rome at the end of the second and beginning of the third century AD and the work was probably finished shortly after 228. Like others of his time, although in Rome, he wrote in Greek, and his enormous library was presumably also mostly Greek. (He claimed that it was bigger than that of Aristotle and Theophrastus: I.3.) Pliny, the Roman, is never mentioned; the Greek-writing Galen and Plutarch are speakers in the symposium. The *Deipnosophists* is essentially an entertainment based on cooking and eating and although it gives many of the plant and animal stories, like the boy and doplphin (XIII.606), we cannot give it full attention here.

126 Book II opens with Aelian postponing a full recital for some later time when it will be pleasanter for him and more convenient for his hearers.

127 XIV.28. Two stories have 'reached' him in their circulation, as if he had been asking about for stories (rather than reading). Telling a short tale in the middle of a lengthy history is giving the hearer a rest and sweetening the narrative, he says.

INDEX